Teaching the New English

Published in association with the English Subject Centre
Director: **Ben Knights**

Teaching the New English is an innovative series concerned with the teaching of the English degree in universities in the UK and elsewhere. The series addresses new and developing areas of the curriculum as well as more traditional areas that are reforming in new contexts. Although the Series is grounded in intellectual and theoretical concepts of the curriculum, it is concerned with the practicalities of classroom teaching. The volumes will be invaluable for new and more experienced teachers alike.

Titles include:

Gail Ashton and Louise Sylvester (*editors*)
TEACHING CHAUCER

Charles Butler (*editor*)
TEACHING CHILDREN'S FICTION

Michael Hanrahan and Deborah L. Madsen (*editors*)
TEACHING, TECHNOLOGY, TEXTUALITY
Approaches to New Media

Andrew Hiscock and Lisa Hopkins (*editors*)
TEACHING SHAKESPEARE AND EARLY MODERN DRAMATISTS

Anna Powell and Andrew Smith (*editors*)
TEACHING THE GOTHIC

Forthcoming titles:

Gina Wisker (*editor*)
TEACHING AFRICAN-AMERICAN WOMEN'S WRITING

Teaching the New English
Series Standing Order ISBN 1–4039–4441–5 Hardback 1–4039–4442–3 Paperback
(*outside North America only*)

You can receive future titles in this series as they are published by placing a standing order. Please contact your bookseller or, in case of difficulty, write to us at the address below with your name and address, the title of the series and the ISBN quoted above.

Customer Services Department, Macmillan Distribution Ltd, Houndmills, Basingstoke, Hampshire RG21 6XS, England

Also by Andrew Hiscock

THE USES OF THIS WORLD: Thinking Space in Shakespeare, Marlowe, Cary and Jonson

MIGHTY EUROPE: Writing an Early Modern Continent (*editor*)

DANGEROUS DIVERSITY: the Changing Faces of Wales from the Renaissance to the Present Day (*co-editor with Katie Gramich*)

AUTHORITY AND DESIRE: Crises of Interpretation in Shakespeare and Racine

2008 YEARBOOK OF ENGLISH STUDIES: Tudor Literature (*editor*)

CONTINUUM HANDBOOK TO SHAKESPEARE STUDIES (*co-editor with Stephen Longstaffe*)

Also by Lisa Hopkins

BEGINNING SHAKESPEARE

CHRISTOPHER MARLOWE: an Author Chronology

CHRISTOPHER MARLOWE: a Literary Life

THE FEMALE HERO IN ENGLISH RENAISSANCE TRAGEDY

GODDESSES AND QUEENS: the Iconography of Elizabeth I (*co-editor with Annaliese Connolly*)

SHAKESPEARE ON THE EDGE: Border-crossing in the Tragedies and the *Henriad*

Teaching Shakespeare and Early Modern Dramatists

Edited by

Andrew Hiscock
Reader in English, University of Wales Bangor

and

Lisa Hopkins
Professor of English, Sheffield Hallam University

First published in 2007 by
PALGRAVE MACMILLAN
Houndmills, Basingstoke, Hampshire RG21 6XS and
175 Fifth Avenue, New York, N.Y. 10010
Companies and representatives throughout the world.

PALGRAVE MACMILLAN is the global academic imprint of the Palgrave Macmillan division of St. Martin's Press, LLC and of Palgrave Macmillan Ltd. Macmillan® is a registered trademark in the United States, United Kingdom and other countries. Palgrave is a registered trademark in the European Union and other countries.

ISBN-13: 978–1–4039–9475–2 hardback
ISBN-10: 1–4039–9475–7 hardback
ISBN-13: 978–1–4039–9476–9 paperback
ISBN-10: 1–4039–9476–5 paperback

This book is printed on paper suitable for recycling and made from fully managed and sustained forest sources. Logging, pulping and manufacturing processes are expected to conform to the environmental regulations of the country of origin.

A catalogue record for this book is available from the British Library.

A catalog record for this book is available from the Library of Congress.

10 9 8 7 6 5 4 3 2 1
16 15 14 13 12 11 10 09 08 07

Printed and bound in Great Britain by
Antony Rowe Ltd, Chippenham and Eastbourne

For Bronwen and Huw Hiscock and Sam Hopkins

Contents

Acknowledgements

The editors wish to thank everyone who has been involved in bringing this project to fruition, most especially Linda Jones, research administrator at University of Wales Bangor, and Christine Ranft, the volume's copy editor. Without their invaluable input, this would not have been possible. The editors would also like to thank Paula Kennedy at Palgrave Macmillan for her steadfast support for the project. Lisa Hopkins is grateful, as always, to Chris and Sam, and Andrew Hiscock, to Siân, Bronwen and Huw.

Andrew Hiscock
Lisa Hopkins
April 2007

Series Preface

One of many exciting achievements of the early years of the English Subject Centre was the agreement with Palgrave Macmillan to initiate the series "Teaching the News English." The intention of the then Director, Professor Philip Martin, was to create a series of short and accessible books which would take widely-taught curriculum fields (or, as in the case of learning technologies, approaches to the whole curriculum) and articulate the connections between scholarly knowledge and the demands of teaching.

Since its inception, "English" has been committed to what we now know by the portmanteau phrase "learning and teaching." Yet, by and large, university teachers of English—in Britain at all events—find it hard to make their tacit pedagogic knowledge conscious, or to raise it to a level where it might be critiqued, shared, or developed. In the experience of the English Subject Centre, colleagues find it relatively easy to talk about curriculum and resources, but far harder to talk about the success or failure of seminars, how to vary forms of assessment, or to make imaginative use of Virtual Learning Environments. Too often this reticence means falling back on received assumptions about student learning, about teaching, or about forms of assessment. At the same time, colleagues are often suspicious of the insights and methods arising from generic educational research. The challenge for the English group of disciplines is therefore to articulate ways in which our own subject knowledge and ways of talking might themselves refresh debates about pedagogy. The implicit invitation of this series is to take fields of knowledge and survey them through a pedagogic lens. Research and scholarship, and teaching and learning are part of the same process, not two separate domains.

"Teachers," people used to say, "are born not made." There may, after all, be some tenuous truth in this: there may be generosities of spirit (or, alternatively, drives for didactic control) laid down in earliest childhood. But why should we assume that even "born" teachers (or novelists, or nurses, or veterinary surgeons) do not need to learn the skills of their trade? Amateurishness about teaching has far more to do with university claims to status, than with evidence about how people learn. There is a craft to shaping and promoting learning. This series of books is dedicated to the development of the craft of teaching within English Studies.

Ben Knights
Teaching the New English *Series Editor*
Director, English Subject Centre
Higher Education Academy

The English Subject Centre

Founded in 2000, the English Subject Centre (which is based at Royal Holloway, University of London) is part of the subject network of the Higher Education Academy. Its purpose is to develop learning and teaching across the English disciplines in UK Higher Education. To this end it engages in research and publication (web and print), hosts events and conferences, sponsors projects, and engages in day-to-day dialogue with its subject communities.

http://www.english.heacademy.ac.uk

Notes on the Contributors

Rick Bowers is Professor of English at the University of Alberta. His recent publications, on Marlowe, Middleton, medieval drama, Sir John Harington, Roger Crab, and James VI, appear in such journals as *Notes and Queries, Renaissance and Reformation, Early Modern Literary Studies, The Seventeenth Century,* and *English Studies in Canada.*

Susan Bruce is Senior Lecturer at Keele University. She is the editor of *Three Early Modern Utopias* (1999), *Shakespeare: King Lear* (1997), and *Fiction and Economy* (2007) as well as the author of articles on various subjects from More to Harper Lee, published in academic and more popular fora. With colleagues in English and in Education departments, she is currently embarking on a project entitled *The Production of University English*, generously funded by the English Subject Centre.

Alizon Brunning is Senior Lecturer in English Literature and Creative Writing at the University of Central Lancashire. She has had several articles and book chapters published in her main research area, Jacobean City Comedy. She is currently researching the relationship between host, parasite, and hospitality in early modern drama.

Richard Dutton is Humanities Distinguished Professor of English at Ohio State University. He has published widely on early modern drama, especially on questions of censorship and authorship. He has edited *Volpone* for the forthcoming Cambridge Ben Jonson and is completing a monograph on *Volpone* and the Gunpowder Plot.

Andrew Hiscock is Reader in English at the University of Wales Bangor. He has published on authors and texts across the early modern period and his most recent monograph is *The Uses of this World: Thinking Space in Shakespeare, Marlowe, Cary and Jonson* (2004). He is currently researching into textual discussions of memory in the period 1520–1620.

Lisa Hopkins is Professor of English at Sheffield Hallam University and co-editor of *Shakespeare*, the journal of the British Shakespeare Association. She has published books on Marlowe, Shakespeare, and Ford, and on the representation of queens in Renaissance drama.

Carol A. Morley was born in Leeds. After degrees at the University of Cambridge and the Shakespeare Institute, she has combined a freelance career in theatre with teaching and academic editing. She is author of *The*

Plays and Poems of William Heminge (2005) and is now a Lecturer at Rose Bruford College, Kent.

Helen Ostovich is Professor of English at McMaster University. She has recently edited *The Magnetic Lady* for the Cambridge Works of Ben Jonson, *The Late Lancashire Witches* for the Richard Brome Electronic Editions, and *All's Well that Ends Well* for Internet Shakespeare Editions. She is a general editor of Revels Plays and of the Queen's Men Editions.

Karen Raber is Associate Professor of English at the University of Mississippi. She is author of *Dramatic Difference: Gender, Class and Genre in the Early Modern Closet Drama* (2001), co-editor with Ivo Kamps of *William Shakespeare, Measure for Measure: Texts and Contexts* (2004), and co-editor with Treva J. Tucker of *The Culture of the Horse: Status, Discipline and Identity in the Early Modern World* (2005) as well as a number of articles on early modern women writers, ecocriticism and horse culture.

David Ruiter is Associate Professor of English, Director of the Literature Program, and the Liberal Arts Fellow for the Center for Effective Teaching and Learning at the University of Texas at El Paso. Ruiter has published the book *Shakespeare's Festive History* (2003), and regularly gives presentations on the effective teaching of Shakespeare at high school, community college, and university levels.

Matthew Steggle is Senior Lecturer in English at Sheffield Hallam University. His publications include *Richard Brome: Place and Politics on the Caroline Stage* (2004), and *Laughing and Weeping in Early Modern Theatres* (2007). He is completing a project on self-guided learning exercises for EEBO, funded by the English Subject Centre.

Adrian Streete is Lecturer in English at Queen's University, Belfast. His research interests focus on early modern literature, religion, and theory and he is co-editor of *Refiguring Mimesis: Representation in Early Modern Literature* (2005) and has published articles in journals such as *Literature and Theology* and *Literature and History*.

Ceri Sullivan is Reader in the School of English, University of Wales Bangor. She specializes in early modern rhetoric, and in mercantile and devotional texts.

Rowland Wymer is Head of English, Communication, Film and Media at Anglia Ruskin University, Cambridge. His publications include *Suicide and Despair in the Jacobean Drama* (1986), *Webster and Ford* (1995), and *Derek Jarman* (2005), as well as a number of co-edited collections of essays, including *Neo-Historicism* (2000) and *The Accession of James I: Historical and Cultural Consequences* (2006).

Introduction

Andrew Hiscock and Lisa Hopkins

> Thou that do'st rail at me for seeing a play,
> How wouldst thou have me spend my idle hours?
> (Richard Perkins 'To My Loving Friend and
> Fellow, Thomas Heywood' (1607–8))[1]

Many university courses devoted to early modern drama often begin by emphasizing the lack of status which theatrical performance enjoyed in the Elizabethan and Jacobean periods compared to poetic composition, for example, or the sermon. In this context, Philip Sidney in *A Defence of Poetry* (probably composed late 1570s–early 1580s), was clearly not unrepresentative in his glum conclusions about play-making in the final decades of the sixteenth century:

> Our tragedies and comedies (not with cause cried out against), observing rules neither of honest civility nor skilful poetry—excepting *Gorboduc* (again, I say, of those that I have seen), which notwithstanding as it is full of stately speeches and well-sounding phrases, climbing to the height of Seneca's style, and as full of notable morality, which it doth most delightfully teach, and so obtain the very end of poesy, yet in truth it is very defectuous in the circumstances, which grieveth me, because it might not remain as an exact model of all tragedies.[2]

However, Sidney's intervention (like a number of others) does demonstrate that criticism of early modern drama began in the period itself and he touches upon two themes which recur with surprising regularity in contemporary discussions of the genre: comparison with the work of classical playwrights; and the moral functions of dramatic texts. Interestingly, in the Caroline period when Jonson drew up a "Scriptorum Catalogus" (in his commonplace book *Timber or Discoveries* of contemporary "wits" to rival those of Rome), he included no dramatists at all—though had he been alive, Sidney for one might have drawn some comfort from the discussion: "as it is fit to read the best authors to youth first, so let them be of the openest and clearest. As Livy before Sallust, Sidney before Donne: and beware of letting them taste Gower, or Chaucer at first . . ."[3]

In the dedicatory material to *The right Excellent and famous Historye of Promos and Cassandra* (1578), George Whetstone had been eager to emphasize that in comedy "by the reward of the good, the good are encouraged in well doing, and with the scourge of the lewd, the lewd are feared from evil attempts . . . And to these ends Menander, Plautus, and Terence, themselves many years since entombed, by their comedies in honour live at this day."[4] By the next century, Thomas Heywood was able to wax lyrical about "our domestic histories" on the stage in his *Apology for Actors* (1607–8): "So bewitching a thing is lively and well-spirited action that it hath power to new-mould the hearts of the spectators and fashion them to the shape of any noble and notable attempt . . . To . . . look back into Greece. The sages and princes of Grecia . . . trained up their youthful nobility to be actors, debarring the base mechanics so worthy employment."[5] And by the beginning of the Caroline period, Philip Massinger in his tragedy *The Roman Actor* (1629) had one of the characters (who plays an actor) condemn those critics of the theatre who

> . . . grudge us
> That with delight join profit, and endeavour
> To build their minds up fair, and on the stage
> Decipher to the life what honours wait
> On good and glorious actions, and the shame
> The treads upon the heels of vice . . .
>
>   1.i.19–25

There are examples from the period of criticism of individual texts and dramatists in the prefatory material to published plays. These are, given the context, mostly celebratory such as Donne's Latin verses in the quarto of *Volpone*, Beaumont's and Fletcher's verses on Jonson's *Catiline*, for example, or Jonson's poem "To the memory of my beloved, the author Mr. William Shakespeare" appearing at the beginning of Shakespeare's *First Folio* (1623). Here, Shakespeare is hailed as the "Soul of the Age" but Jonson also deplored his fellow dramatist's departures from the classical unities of time, place and action which had been codified in Aristotle's *Poetics*. In this tract, the Greek philosopher had promoted the influential idea that a play should have only one setting and one plot, and that all the events should take place within twenty-four hours: such notions would prompt Jonson in his lyric "Ode to Himself" to dismiss one of Shakespeare's plays, *Pericles*, as a "mouldy tale." Elsewhere, John Webster, in his preface to *The White Devil*, also gave a fascinating survey of his distinguished contemporaries whom he praised for various features of their style:

For mine own part I have ever truly cherished my good opinion of other men's worthy labours, especially of that full and heightened style of

Master Chapman; the laboured and understanding works of Master Jonson; the no less worthy composures of the both worthily excellent Master Beaumont, and Master Fletcher; and lastly (without wrong last to be named) the right happy and copious industry of Master Shakespeare, Master Dekker, and Master Heywood . . . [6]

Margaret Cavendish, was clearly indebted to Shakespeare's dramatic narratives in the plotting of her own plays which were published in the Restoration. However, in "Letter 123" from her collection *Sociable Letters* (1664) she composed one of the very earliest assessments of an early modern dramatist to survive from the period: "*Shakspear* did not want Wit, to Express to the Life all Sorts of Persons . . . Who would not think he had been such a man as his Sir *John Falstaff*? . . . one would think that he had been Metamorphosed from a Man to a Woman, for who could Describe *Cleopatra* Better than he hath done . . . ?"[7]

Nevertheless, the growing appetite for literary criticism and discussion of Aristotelian precepts in seventeenth-century France gradually made its appearance across the Channel in the second half of the century. Amongst the dramatists from the previous generation, the names of Shakespeare, Jonson, Beaumont, and Fletcher recur with the greatest frequency when the genre is considered at all. In his prologue to *The Tempest* (1667), Dryden celebrated "Shakespeare, *who (taught by none) did first impart / To* Fletcher *wit, to laboring* Jonson *art.*" More famously in his *Essay of Dramatic Poesie* (1668) Dryden had the flaws and virtues of the earlier generation's output surveyed by a group of critics. The gallophile Lisideius argues that since the early decades of the century "we have been so long together bad *Englishmen*, that we had not leisure to be good Poets; *Beaumont, Fletcher*, and *Johnson* . . . were onely capable of bringing us to that degree of perfection which we have," meaning the world of neo-classical aesthetics. Whilst Lisideius argues that "There is no Theatre in the world so absurd as the *English* Tragi-comedie," Neander celebrates the expert handling of intrigue in Beaumont and Fletcher's *The Maid's Tragedy*, and Jonson's *The Alchemist* and *Epicoene*.[8] However, in general, the cause of early modern English drama in the shape of Shakespeare, Beaumont, Fletcher, and Jonson is championed by a more patriotic Eugenius. In the later "Essay of the Dramatic Poetry of the Last Age" (1672) Dryden was much more strident in his promotion of neo-classical precepts and took particular exception to the "copiousness" of the Elizabethans and Jacobeans—and earned himself much criticism as a consequence. Moreover, in 1691 Gerard Langbaine condemned a play like *'Tis Pity She's a Whore* as immoral on the grounds that it was too sympathetic to its sinning characters.

In the following century, as will become apparent in the more detailed discussions in the chapters which follow, much valuable criticism of Shakespeare in particular was conducted in the prefatory material and annotations to new editions of the plays, like those of Pope and Johnson. Elsewhere in

letters and journal articles of the period there is evidence of a growing awareness of the larger corpus of plays by Shakespeare and others. In a piece for
the periodical *The Champion* (1 March 1739–40), for example, Henry Fielding
submitted:

> I remember about 12 Years ago, upon the Success of a *new* Play of
> *Shakespear's*, said to have been found somewhere by Some-body, the Craft
> set themselves to searching, and soon after I heard that several more Plays
> of *Shakespear, Beaumont* and *Fletcher*, and *Ben Johnson* were *found*, and the
> Town to be *entertain'd* with them; but the Players, for I know not what
> Reason, discouraging this Practice, it hath since ceased.[9]

(A generation later, Wordsworth would rehearse a similar but more virulent
line of argument in the preface to the *Lyrical Ballads*: "The invaluable works
of our elder writers . . . the works of Shakespeare and Milton, are driven into
neglect by frantic novels, sickly and stupid German Tragedies, and deluges of
idle and extravagant stories in verse."[10]) In a slightly later piece from 1 July
1740, Fielding clearly felt keenly the chronological and cultural distance of
the early modern period from his own, confessing "Many Characters in antient
Plays (particularly in *Shakespear*) which were drawn from the Life, lose half
their Beauty to us who are unacquainted with their Originals. Sir *John Falstaff*
and his whole Gang must have given much more Entertainment to the
Spectators of Queen *Elizabeth's* Days, than to a modern Audience."[11]
A more sustained and substantial period of criticism of early modern
drama got under way in the closing decades of the century when the transgressive energies visible in so much of the work of the earlier generation of
dramatists developed new appeal. There was a growing number of essays
being printed which particularly resisted "neo-classical" criticism of
Shakespeare and focused upon the powerful impressions made by his most
memorable characters: for example, Elizabeth Montagu's *An Essay on the
Writings and Genius of Shakespeare, compared with the Greek and French
Dramatic Poets* (1769), Elizabeth Griffith's *The Morality of Shakespeare's Drama
Illustrated* (1775), Maurice Morgann's *An Essay on the Dramatic Character of
Sir John Falstaff* (1777) and Walter Whiter's *A Specimen of a Commentary on
Shakespeare* (1794). Furthermore, whereas Thomas Dabbs has proposed that
Marlowe as we now understand him is essentially a product of the nineteenth
century,[12] in fact the first serious critical engagement with Marlowe came
slightly earlier, with the publication of Thomas Warton's *History of English
Poetry* in instalments between 1774 and 1781.
Some of the most distinctive Shakespearean criticism of the period was
articulated by Coleridge in his notes and lectures, Charles Lamb (*Specimens of
Dramatic Poets who lived about the time of Shakespeare* [1808] and "On the
tragedies of Shakespeare" [1811]) and Hazlitt in his *Characters of Shakespeare's
Plays* (1817). Lamb in particular argued that the plays realize their greatest

potential before a reader rather than a theatre audience, but all of these critics hailed Shakespeare's pre-eminent "genius" and his peerless gift for characterization and for generating empathy for his creations. Whilst from the 1820s onwards the works of Shakespeare gained an ever increasing following of devotees on the European continent and beyond, the celebration of his "natural" and "instinctive" intelligence meant that dramatists adhering to quite different aesthetic aims, like Jonson, were often neglected. An exception is Marlowe, whose alleged atheism made him attractive to the climate of intellectual exploration which followed the French Revolution: in 1796 Goethe planned a work on the Hero and Leander story and in 1808 Lamb's *Specimens of English Dramatic Poets* praised the death scene of Edward II. More generally, Scott's *The Ancient British Drama* (1810), which included such plays as *Edward II* and *The Jew of Malta*, brought Renaissance plays to an audience outside the libraries of the great stately homes in which copies of the original quartos were preserved. It was followed in 1814 by C. W. Dilke's *Old English Plays* and in 1816 by a new edition of Dodsley's *Old Plays*. In 1818 Edmund Kean revived *The Jew of Malta*, apparently the first time that a Marlowe play had been seen on the stage since the seventeenth century, and in the same year Goethe recorded his admiration for *Doctor Faustus*. In 1819 J. P. Collier began to produce a series of articles "On the Early English Dramatists" for the *Edinburgh Magazine*, and in 1820 came William Hazlitt's Lectures *Chiefly on the Dramatic Literature of the Age of Elizabeth*. Hurst and Robinson's *Old English Drama* was added to the field in 1825, and in 1826 the first collected edition of Marlowe heralded a growing vogue for editions of plays by Renaissance dramatists.

It is a similar story for another early modern playwright, John Ford, who challenged orthodoxy and who "suddenly rose to a high reputation in 1808."[13] Whereas interest in Ford both before and after this period tended to centre on *'Tis Pity She's a Whore*, many Romantic writers responded most passionately to other plays, most particularly *The Broken Heart* and *Perkin Warbeck*. New editions were produced, first that of Weber (1811), which was immediately savaged by Gifford in *The Quarterly Review*, and then, most notably, that of Gifford himself (1827), which found its way into important libraries like that of Sir Walter Scott at Abbotsford and triggered critical responses from, amongst others, Swinburne, Hazlitt, and Havelock Ellis. Most especially, Ford and his works seem to have been of intense concern to two unconventional women connected respectively with Shelley and with Byron: Mary Shelley and Lady Caroline Lamb, of whom the first used Ford as a source for her novel *The Fortunes of Perkin Warbeck* and the second gave her heroines the same names as Ford's.

In the Victorian period, the growing cult of "bardolatry" (as it was later termed by Shaw) and the renewed respect for conventionality meant that other early modern dramatists often gained attention only as Shakespeare's contemporaries rather than as writers in their own right. Thomas Carlyle, for example, turned his attention to the pre-eminent genius of a poetic "hero" Shakespeare in *On Heroes, Hero-Worship and The Heroic in History* (1840):

> Of this Shakespeare of ours, perhaps the opinion one sometimes hears a little idolatrously expressed is, in fact, the right one; I think the best judgement not of this country only, but of Europe at large, is slowly pointing to the conclusion, That Shakspeare is the chief of all Poets hitherto; the greatest intellect who, in our recorded world, has left record of himself in the way of Literature.[14]

Continuing in this vein in "The Study of Poetry" (which introduced T. H. Ward's collection *The English Poets* [1880]), Matthew Arnold later affirmed that for his "present purpose" he did not need to "dwell on our Elizabethan poetry, or on the continuation and close of this poetry in Milton. We all of us profess to be agreed in the estimate of this poetry; we all of us recognize it as great poetry, our greatest, and Shakespeare and Milton as our poetical classics."[15] Nevertheless, in 1844 Leigh Hunt's *Imagination and Fancy* gave some evidence that early modern playwrights were at last coming into their own and this was confirmed when several of them received entries in the late nineteenth-century's great information-gathering project, *The Dictionary of National Biography*, while William Poel's Elizabethan Stage Society was also allowing many of the plays to be seen for the first time. However, even by 1870 the position of the early modern dramatists was still far from "fixed" and the influential critic and academic Edward Dowden was arguing in the *Fortnightly Review* that:

> The study of Shakespeare and his contemporaries is the study of one family consisting of many members, all of whom have the same life-blood in their veins . . . Yet there can be little doubt that [Shakespeare] was in a considerable degree the master of the inferior and younger artists who surrounded him. It is the independence of Ben Jonson's work and its thorough originality, rather than comparative greatness or beauty of poetical achievement, which have given him a kind of acknowledged right to the second place amongst the Elizabethan dramatists . . . But Ford, and Webster, and Massinger, and Beaumont and Fletcher and the rest (who were content, like Shakespeare, to write "plays", and did not aspire to "works") are really followers of the greatest of all dramatic writers, and very different handiwork they would probably have turned out had they wrought in their craft without the teaching of his practice and example . . . [Marlowe was] the one man who, if he had lived longer and accomplished the work which lay clear before him, might have stood even *beside* Shakespeare, as supreme in a different province of dramatic art.[16]

The family metaphor here may alert us to the importance of Shakespeare in particular to the growing debate about Charles Darwin's theory of evolution. Henry Maudsley's impressively-titled Darwinian essay *Heredity, Variation and Genius, with an essay on Shakespeare: "Testimonied in his own bringingsforth" and address on Medicine: Present and Prospective* (1908), for instance, first speculates on Shakespeare's own heredity:

> he, like every other mortal, proceeded by rigorous laws of descent and development from an ancestral line of beings and testified to his stock; was what he was, they being what they were, and could not have been otherwise. That it was not a poor stock, but pregnant with native vigour, is proved by the splendid fruit which it bore when, by a happy conspiracy of circumstances, a slip of it lighted on very favourable conditions of growth, albeit after that supreme effort the exhausted stock drooped and died.[17]

Maudsley then goes on to turn Shakespeare into a poster boy for Social Darwinism and the value of having to struggle and compete for scarce resources:

> It is not credible that Shakespeare any more than hundreds of like-born persons of equal natural capacity who have lived and died in nameless obscurity, clean forgotten as though they had never been born, would have ever been the great poet he was had he not been forced to leave his native town to seek sustenance elsewhere and been thus luckily thrown into circumstances admirably suited to develop his native talents.[18]

At the same time, however, Shakespeare also provided reassurance for those troubled by the implications of the non-human ancestry posited by Darwinian theory. The image of Hamlet in particular became an increasingly familiar one in counter-evolutionary discourse, with Daniel Wilson in *Caliban: the Missing Link* (1873) arguing of Shakespeare that

> To him of all men the distinction between man and his lower fellow-creatures seemed clear and ineffaceable. Hamlet, in his deprecatory self-torturings does indeed ask himself the question:-
> "What is a man,
> If his chief good and market of his time
> Be but to sleep and feed? a beast, no more."
> But it is only that he may the more clearly infer that man is no such mere animal, but, on the contrary, is the sole living creature endowed with "god-like reason."[19]

Shakespeare's usefulness to both sides of this debate was not the least of the many factors keeping him firmly in the public eye throughout the nineteenth century. Whereas, for example, in *A Study of Shakespeare* (1880) Swinburne unveiled an Olympian figure creating superlative dramatic narratives, in various individual studies (collected at the end of his life as *The Age of Shakespeare* [1908]) he also opened the frame of discussion to encompass a good number of his contemporaries. Most of Swinburne's criticism is rather general and effusive: he lauds the "majestic and exquisite excellence of various lines and passages" in Marlowe, but finds his plays in general to lack unity of purpose and texture. If Webster is but a "limb" of Shakespeare, he is certainly the "right arm" for his ability to match the Bard in creating worlds of tragic savagery. More unexpectedly, Marston emerges as an "independent and remarkable poet" and *The Revenger's Tragedy* means that Tourneur (who was then thought to have written it) is offered "the indisputable title to a seat in the upper house of poets."[20] In the same period, Oscar Wilde commented on early modern drama and most especially Shakespeare in a range of different places. In an 1886 book review, for example, he insisted that Jonson's "art has too much effort about it, too much definite intention. His style lacks the charm of chance"; nevertheless, he finds "Jonson's characters are true to nature."[21] Given his more general commitment to aestheticism rather than didacticism in art, it comes as no surprise that in an 1890 letter to the editor of the *Scots Observer* he stressed "Iago may be morally horrible and Imogen stainlessly pure. Shakespeare, as Keats said, has as much delight in creating the one as he had in creating the other."[22] George Bernard Shaw offered an even more thorough, if equally disparate, assessment of Shakespeare throughout the prefaces to his own plays. Profoundly irritated by his society's unquestioning and singular veneration of the Bard, Shaw proceeds regularly in his prefaces to inform his readers (quite casually, but authoritatively) of the vices and virtues of their preferred dramatist, as in the case of the preface to *Man and Superman* (1901–3):

> This is what is the matter with Hamlet all through: he has no will except in his bursts of temper. Foolish Bardolaters make a virtue of this after their fashion: they declare that the play is the tragedy of irresolution; but all Shakespear's projections of the deepest humanity he knew have the same defect: their characters and manners are lifelike; but their actions are forced on them from without, and the external force is grotesquely inappropriate except when it is quite conventional, as in the case of Henry V.[23]

In general, in the early twentieth century the critical emphasis was all too often upon the "decadence" (a favourite term) of most of the early modern playwrights rather than their merits. However, A. C. Bradley's landmark study *Shakespearean Tragedy* (1904), with its painstaking analyses and emphases upon character motivation, the heroic and tragic *anagnorisis*, has been widely seen as inaugurating the modern age in the criticism of early modern drama. Bradley only took into account *Hamlet, Othello, Macbeth*, and

King Lear in his study but, in raising a greater awareness of early modern dramatists rather than just Shakespeare for a whole generation, T. S. Eliot was also clearly an enormously strategic figure at the beginning of the twentieth century. In the inter-war years his critical essays ranged ambitiously across the generation of Elizabethan and Jacobean figures and if his assessments appear in retrospect rather peremptory, they were enormously influential upon subsequent generations of scholars and students alike. Apart from studies of figures like Marlowe ("Marlowe's rhetoric consists in a pretty simple huffe-snuffe bombast"), Jonson ("damned by the praise that quenches all desire to read the book . . . afflicted by the imputation of the virtues which excite the least pleasure") and Ford ("['*Tis Pity She's a Whore*] may be called 'meaningless', and in so far as we may be justified in disliking its horrors, we are justified by its lack of meaning"), Eliot alerted a more general readership to consider neglected texts such as *A Yorkshire Tragedy, A Woman Killed With Kindness* and *Arden of Feversham* in order to assess fully the achievement of the drama of the period and thus made a significant contribution to the scholarship of early modern literature.[24]

One group which was clearly influenced by the critical lead given by Eliot was the group of Cambridge critics led by F. R. Leavis whose work found a voice in their journal *Scrutiny* from the 1930s to the 1950s. Despite L. C. Knights's emphasis upon the social and economic environment of playmaking in works such as *Drama and Society in the Age of Jonson* (1937), the figures associated with this group were most likely to approach early modern plays as "dramatic poems," attending most particularly to verbal textures (and often themes of moral and ethical import) rather than issues of character or theatrical performance. Amongst early modern dramatists, Shakespeare once again claimed the lion's share of critical attention with this group and this was also the case amongst another generation of critics emerging on both sides of the Atlantic associated with the label *The New Criticism*. From the 1930s onwards in North America, figures such as Allen Tate, Cleanth Brooks and Robert Penn Warren urged their readers to practise a formalist, rather than historicized, form of criticism which concentrated on questions of genre, figurative language, rhetorical strategy, and semantic crises of interpretation. A similar emphasis in Britain upon rigorous engagement with the "words on the page" had been taken up by the Cambridge academic I. A. Richards in works such as *Practical Criticism* (1929) and would be developed in a most sophisticated fashion by one of his students, William Empson, most famously in *Seven Types of Ambiguity* (1930).

Nevertheless, this proved not to be the only narrative of criticism on early modern drama in the inter-war years. Turning away from the concern with plays as "dramatic poems" in such studies as *The Wheel of Fire* (1930), *The Imperial Theme* (1931) and *The Crown of Life* (1947), G. Wilson Knight argued for Shakespeare's plays being considered in their entirety in order to comprehend fully their symbolic discourses of transcendence. Theatre figures such as the producer Harley Granville-Barker were publishing discussions of individual Shakespeare plays in terms of "audience" and "actor" engagement with these texts. Moreover, H. B. Charlton despaired of the current fashion for viewing early modern plays as "poems" in *Shakespearian Comedy* (1938), and most famously in publications such as *What Happens in Hamlet* (1935), John Dover Wilson pursued a Bradleyan mode of analysis, attempting to "resolve" the *minutiae* of questions of plot and character motivation with such enthusiasm that it not infrequently led him into the realm of speculation. Meanwhile, moving the focus away from Shakespeare alone, critics such as M. C. Bradbrook in *Elizabethan Stage Conditions* (1932) and Una Ellis Fermor in *The Jacobean Drama* (1936), for example, insisted upon the strategic importance of analysing theatrical environments, questions of authorship and textual transmission.

During the Second World War and the years which followed there was in many ways a notable continuity in the ways critics approached early modern drama. E. M. W. Tillyard's study *The Elizabethan World Picture* (1943), with its reassuring affirmation of a body of cosmological and political thinking apparently widely in evidence in the early modern period, inevitably appealed to readers having recently endured the trauma of conflict. However, Derek Traversi, who was originally associated closely with Leavis's *Scrutiny* group, argued in *Shakespeare from Richard II to Henry V* (1957) that historicization was detracting attention away from an appreciation of the artistic achievement of the plays. More compellingly in *Angel With Horns* (1961), A. P. Rossiter showed himself willing to take up the gauntlet laid down by Tillyard by problematizing the latter's highly selective study. Rossiter was particularly influential in stressing the ambiguities of early modern genre development and the intellectual points of conflict in the works themselves. He became one of the most notable voices to question Tillyard's appetite for fixity and, indeed, for world-pictures *per se*. In *Shakespeare's Festive Comedy* (1959) C. L. Barber explored in his analyses of dramatic narrative the rituals, cere-monies, and festivities associated with Elizabethan church and civic calen-dars, and thus added more energy to the historicizing impulse in early modern literary studies during the period. Building on the widely acclaimed achievement of *The Anatomy of Criticism* (1957), in the 1960s Northrop Frye continued to excite enthusiasm for a more anthropological approach to literary criticism, taking up the case of Shakespearean drama in *A Natural Perspective* (1965) and *Fools of Time* (1967). Spurred on by interests in the development of genre across chronological and geographical divides, Frye argued that early modern dramatic texts such as Shakespeare's should be firmly embedded in cultural narratives involving analogies with folklore and ritual as well as texts from quite different cultural traditions.

Certainly during this period audiences and critics were being asked with increasing regularity to widen their lens upon early modern drama. This was apparent in the growing number of annotated editions of individual texts in this period and the appearance of more ambitious anthologies for the student and general reader. In 1961, for instance, Oxford University Press published a collection of essays, edited by R. J. Kaufmann, on Marlowe, Lyly, Marston, Chapman, Jonson, Middleton, Webster, Beaumont and Fletcher, Massinger and Ford under the general title *Elizabethan Drama: Modern Essays in Criticism*, and William A. Armstrong's *Elizabethan History Plays* appeared in 1965. Elsewhere, the emphasis was upon biography but, more importantly, upon the *oeuvre* of the dramatist rather than just one or two acknowledged "masterpieces": this was certainly the case for A. L. Rowse's *Christopher Marlowe: His Life and Works* (1964) and J. B. Steane's *Marlowe: a Critical Study* (1964), both published to mark the quatercentenary of Marlowe's birth. Indeed, in a study such as *The Jonsonian Masque* (1965), Stephen Orgel alerted students and scholars alike to the importance of not equating early modern drama simply with the activities of the London playhouses. The question of authorship and the early modern dramatist was probed in studies such as Anne Righter's *Shakespeare and the Idea of the Play* (1963) and, acknowledging the enormous contributions of works by archival theatre historians such as E. K. Chambers's *The Elizabethan Stage* (1923), a number of studies began to concentrate once again upon theatrical performance, source material and textual practices: examples here include J. M. Nosworthy's *Shakespeare's Occasional Plays: Their Origin and Transmission* (1965) and Geoffrey Bullough's *Narrative and Dramatic Sources of Shakespeare* (1957–64).

Eldred Jones's *Othello's Countrymen: the African in English Renaissance Drama* (1965) was one of the earliest studies to begin to consider the question of cultural discourse which (in the shape of race, class, sexuality, and gender) would come to dominate studies of early modern drama in the later decades of the century and into the twenty-first. Alternatively, with a much more Eurocentric emphasis, Jan Kott's *Shakespeare Our Contemporary* (1964) produced a thoroughly modern Shakespeare, conversant with post-war existential enquiries and forecasting the experience of terror in Cold-War Europe. With the 1970s and 1980s the narrative of this critical field becomes infinitely more complex as a whole range of movements (feminist, Marxist, new historicist, cultural materialist, psycho-analytical, reader-reception, post-colonial, performance, queer theory . . .) began to concentrate their attentions on early modern drama, amongst a host of other quarry, and diversified and enriched the number of dramatists, texts, and cultural discourses which needed to be taken into account in order to appreciate fully the complexity of the subject. From those decades onwards, issues of textual transmission and practices of modern critical editing also began to occupy scholarly discussion more and more as school and university curricula around the world wished to broaden study of the discipline in new and innovative ways. Whilst some preliminary reading for criticism on early modern drama from the modern period is given in the bibliography below, readers will be guided through significant landmarks in the rich multifariousness of criticism on this subject in the more specialized chapters which follow.

Notes

1. Brian Vickers (ed.), *English Renaissance Literary Criticism* (Oxford: Clarendon Press, 1999), p. 477.
2. Sir Philip Sidney, *A Defence of Poetry*, ed. J. A. Van Dorsten (Oxford: Oxford University Press, 1978 reprint), p. 65.
3. Ben Jonson, *Ben Jonson*, vol. 8, ed. C. H. Herford, Percy and Evelyn Simpson (Oxford: Clarendon Press, 1947), p. 618.
4. Brian Vickers (ed.), *English Renaissance Literary Criticism* (Oxford: Clarendon Press, 1999), p. 173.
5. *English Renaissance Literary Criticism*, pp. 487, 488.
6. John Webster, *The White Devil*, ed. John Russell Brown (Manchester: Manchester University Press, 1996), Preface.
7. Margaret Cavendish, *Sociable Letters*, ed. James Fitzmaurice (Toronto: Broadview Editions, 2004), p. 177.
8. John Dryden, *The Works of John Dryden. Vol. 17: Prose 1668–1691*, ed. Samuel Holt Monk et al. (Berkeley: University of California Press, 1971), pp. 33, 35, 49.
9. Henry Fielding, *Henry Fielding. Contributions to The Champion and Related Writing*, ed. W. B. Coley (Oxford: Clarendon Press, 2003), p. 213.
10. William Wordsworth, *The Prose Works of William Wordsworth*, ed. W. J. B. Owen and Jane Worthington Smyser (Oxford: Clarendon Press, 1974), p. 128.
11. Fielding, *Contributions to The Champion and Related Writing*, p. 395.
12. Thomas Dabbs, *Reforming Marlowe: the Nineteenth-Century Canonization of a Renaissance Dramatist* (Lewisburg: Bucknell University Press, 1991).
13. John Ford, *The Broken Heart*, ed. T. J. B. Spencer (Manchester: Manchester University Press, 1980), introduction, p. 26.
14. Thomas Carlyle, *On Heroes, Hero-Worship and the Heroic in History* (London: Chapman and Hall, 1840), pp. 95–6.
15. Matthew Arnold, *Matthew Arnold's Essays in Criticism*, ed. G. K. Chesterton (London: Dent, 1964 reprint), p. 250.
16. Edward Dowden, "Christopher Marlowe," *Fortnightly Review* 7 (1870): 69–81, pp. 69, 70.
17. Henry Maudsley, M.D., *Heredity, Variation and Genius, with an essay on Shakespeare: "Testimonied in his own bringingsforth" and address on Medicine: Present and Prospective* (London: John Bale, 1908), pp. 111–12.
18. Maudsley, *Heredity, Variation and Genius*, pp. 62–3.
19. Daniel Wilson, *Caliban: the Missing Link* (London: Macmillan, 1873), p. 188.
20. Algernon Charles Swinburne, *The Complete Works of Algernon Charles Swinburne*, Prose Works: Vol. 1, ed. Sir Edmund Gosse and Thomas James Wise, pp. 271, 281, 353, 468.
21. Oscar Wilde, *The Artist as Critic. Critical Writings of Oscar Wilde*, ed. Richard Ellmann (London: W. H. Allen, 1970), pp. 34, 35.
22. Wilde, p. 248.
23. Bernard Shaw, *The Complete Prefaces of Bernard Shaw* (London: Paul Hamlyn, 1965), pp. 162–3.
24. T. S. Eliot, *Selected Essays* (London: Faber and Faber, 1972 reprint), pp. 119, 147, 196.

Suggested further reading

Belsey, Catherine. *The Subject of Tragedy*. London: Methuen, 1985.
Bergeron, David M. *Practising Renaissance Scholarship: Plays and Pageants, Patrons and Politics*. Pittsburgh: Duquesne University Press, 2000.

Braunmuller, A. R., and Hattaway, Michael (eds). *The Cambridge Companion to English Renaissance Drama*. Cambridge: Cambridge University Press, 1990.

Callaghan, Dympna. *Shakespeare without Women: Representing Gender and Race on the Renaissance Stage*. London: Routledge, 2000.

DiGangi, Mario. *The Homoerotics of Early Modern Drama*. Cambridge: Cambridge University Press, 1997.

Dollimore, Jonathan. *Radical Tragedy: Religion, Ideology and Power in the Drama of Shakespeare and His Contemporaries*. Basingstoke: Palgrave Macmillan, 2004.

——, and Sinfield, Alan (eds). *Political Shakespeare*. Manchester: Manchester University Press, 1985.

Floyd-Wilson, Mary. *English Ethnicity and Race in Early Modern Drama*. Cambridge: Cambridge University Press, 2003.

Gurr, Andrew. *Playgoing in Shakespeare's London*. Cambridge: Cambridge University Press, 1987.

Hall, Kim F. *Things of Darkness: Economies of Race and Gender in Early Modern England*. Ithaca: Cornell University Press, 1995.

Johnson, Nora. *The Actor as Playwright in Early Modern Drama*. Cambridge: Cambridge University Press, 2003.

Kerrigan, John. *Revenge Tragedy*. Oxford: Clarendon Press, 1997.

Leinwand, Theodore B. *Theatre, Finance and Society in Early Modern England*. Cambridge: Cambridge University Press, 1999.

Lopez, Jeremy. *Theatrical Convention and Audience Response in Early Modern Drama*. Cambridge: Cambridge University Press, 2003.

McAlindon, Tom. *English Renaissance Tragedy*. Basingstoke: Macmillan–now Palgrave Macmillan, 1988.

Maus, Katharine Eisaman. *Inwardness and Theater in the English Renaissance*. Chicago. University of Chicago Press, 1995.

Mousley, Andy. *Renaissance Drama and Contemporary Literary Theory*. New York: St. Martin's Press–now Palgrave Macmillan, 2000.

Mullaney, Steven. *The Place of the Stage: License, Play, and Power in Renaissance England*. Ann Arbor: University of Michigan Press, 1995.

Neill, Michael. *Putting History to the Question: Power, Politics, and Society in English Renaissance Drama*. New York: Columbia University Press, 2000.

Newman, Karen. *Fashioning Femininity and English Renaissance Drama*. Chicago: University of Chicago Press, 1991.

Rose, Mary Beth. *The Expense of Spirit: Love and Sexuality in English Renaissance Drama*. Ithaca: Cornell University Press, 1988.

Waith, Eugene M. *Patterns and Perspectives in English Renaissance Drama*. Newark: University of Delaware Press, 1988.

Wall, Wendy. *Staging Domesticity: Household Work and English Identity in Early Modern Drama*. Cambridge: Cambridge University Press, 2002.

Zimmerman, Susan. *Erotic Politics: Desire on the Renaissance Stage*. London: Routledge, 1992.

For more information/resources on teaching English (both print and web-based) please go to the following link on the English Subject Centre web site:

http://www.english.heacademy.ac.uk/explore/resources/scholarship/publication.php

1
Early Modern Theatre History

Helen Ostovich

Chronology of early theatres in London

1567   The Red Lion in Stepney, the first known purpose-built playhouse, erected by John Brayne, brother-in-law of James Burbage (see the Theatre below). It had a huge stage of 30 by 40 feet, at a height of 5 feet above floor level, with a trap door, galleries, and an upper space 20 feet or more above the stage, probably for ascents and descents. It seems not to have housed acting companies after its first year.[1]

1575   Paul's, a small private theatre established by Sebastian Westcott within St Paul's Cathedral precincts as a venue for choir-boys to perform, ostensibly to improve their voices and stage presence for their principal employment in the cathedral choir; but Paul's Boys became very popular performers of plays by major playwrights. Audience capacity: 500.

1576   The Theatre, at Shoreditch, London, built by James Burbage and John Brayne, and used by Leicester's Men, Admiral's Men, and Chamberlain's Men among others. Burbage had a 21-year lease which expired in 1597 with his death, and owing to exorbitant fees demanded for a new lease, Burbage's sons had the Theatre dismantled, and its timbers moved to Bankside, Southwark, for the construction of the Globe in 1597–98.

1576   First Blackfriars, built within former thirteenth-century Dominican monastery buildings by Richard Farrant, Master of the boy choristers called the Children of the Chapel Royal, who performed there until it was closed 1584. Burbage bought the space in 1596 as a winter home for the Lord Chamberlain's Men, but subsequent legal entanglements prevented the company from using the space except for rental income until 1608. (See Second Blackfriars below.)

1577   The Curtain, in Curtain Close, Finsbury Fields, Shoreditch, built by Henry Lanman, manager until 1592. Among the companies who performed here was the Lord Chamberlain's Men, later the King's Men (Shakespeare's company). The theatre remained open until 1622.

1577–80   Newington Butts, Southwark, about one mile from Bankside in a field originally used for archery practice, was an early purpose-built theatre in the amphitheatre style. Little is known about this theatre, except that Philip Henslowe remodelled it in 1592, and later the Admiral's Men played there three days a week.

1587   The Rose, built by owner/theatre-manager Philip Henslowe in 1587. His diary is a rich source of information about the daily expenses and activities of early playhouses, as well as their dimensions. The stage at the Rose was approximately 15 by 32 feet. The Rose, the first playhouse on the Bankside in Southwark, became the home of the Admiral's Men, whose leading actor was Edward Alleyn.

1595   The Swan, Bankside, built by Francis Langley. This theatre was considered a model playing space, subsequently imitated by the Globe. Audience capacity: 3000.

1599   The Globe, Bankside, built by Peter Smith, carpenter, and Burbage's sons, Cuthbert and Richard, specifically for Chamberlain's Men. The first Globe burned down in 1613, and was rebuilt in 1614. Audience capacity: possibly well over 3000.

1600   The Fortune, Golding Lane, Finsbury, was built by Philip Henslowe and Edward Alleyn, when the Rose began losing money because of the popularity of the Globe. Henslowe hired the Globe's builder to imitate some of the Globe's features, but had the Fortune built on a rectangular plan, instead of the Globe's octagonal shape.

1604   The Red Bull, in Upper Street, Clerkenwell, was built by Aaron Holland, and for several years housed Queen Anne's Men, formerly known as Worcester's. This theatre became associated with low-brow plays of violence, and seems to have incited brawls and misbehaviour in its audiences, members of which were taken to court on various charges.

1606   Whitefriars, built in the refectory of a former monastery between the western wall of London and the Inns of Court. The theatre was used successively by children's companies, but, plagued by scandal, notably in Ben Jonson's *Epicoene* (1609), the playhouse closed by about 1613.

1608   Second Blackfriars, owned and rebuilt by the King's Men, and used as a winter performance venue until 1642. This playhouse was perhaps the most "modern" in London: it had artificial lights, traps, and mechanical devices to enhance performance.

Audience capacity: about 700, and some spectators were allowed to sit on the stage.

1613   The Hope was built by Philip Henslowe as a multi-purpose entertainment space, in which bear-baiting (in the pit) was to alternate with theatrical playing (on a movable stage over the pit). Jonson's *Bartholomew Fair*, which played here in 1614, comments on its stench; after 1616, the Hope was used solely for bear-baiting and related sports.

1616   The Cockpit, originally built for cock-fighting in 1609, became the first theatre located in Drury Lane when it was converted into a playhouse by Christopher Beeston. It burned down in 1617 during a riot, and was rebuilt in 1618, renamed the Phoenix, because it rose from the ashes.

1619   Banqueting House, on Whitehall across from the Horse Guards, was designed by Inigo Jones for James I's royal receptions, ceremonies, and the performance of masques.

1623   The Fortune is rebuilt, after burning down in 1621.

1629   Salisbury Court Theatre, a private playhouse built by Richard Gunnell and William Blagrove, near Whitehall. Although soldiers destroyed it in 1649, it was one of the first theatres to reopen after the Restoration. William Beeston restored it in 1660, and Samuel Pepys records seeing a play there in 1661.

Critical overview

Recent theatre historians have enriched our understanding of early theatrical life by clarifying conditions of space for actors and for audiences, based on research into public and private records of the period. Travelling players, the records show, had been touring most of England regularly during the late medieval and Tudor periods, and between tours returning to their patron's principal residence, or following him to court for holiday seasons or other significant occasions. The REED (Records of Early English Drama) *Patrons and Performances Web Site*[2] is a good place to start looking at the interactive maps identifying specific playing spaces, distances between towns, number of performances at each venue, and information on patrons of companies. The REED volumes themselves offer minute details on entertainment in England and Wales from the medieval period to the closing of the theatres in 1642.[3] Touring continued to be a lucrative and essential part of the playing companies' careers even after the establishment of purpose-built theatres in London. No one knows precisely how many companies existed, and reshufflings and amalgamations of companies were frequent; only eighteen companies have been tracked with certainty so far.[4] Professional players were nevertheless a welcome addition to local entertainment provided by amateurs in parish plays, civic entertainments, and school and university performances.

Before 1567, companies performed mostly indoors in available large local venues, such as guildhalls, parish or common halls, inns, castle great halls, and other private residences. And indoor playing spaces continued to be preferred, as they are now, despite the success of amphitheatres like the Globe. Often temporary indoor stages were built for the players, sometimes using barrels and boards, sometimes constructing a more sophisticated platform. But the chief point to keep in mind is that theatre, professional and amateur, flourished before the Elizabethan period, even though permanent theatres had not yet been built. The Boar's Head Inn, for example, offered space for players from at least 1557. Throughout their long history, both Oxford and Cambridge stored stages and other theatrical properties for occasional but regular use, as did the Inns of Court in London, where the yearly revels always included plays and masques. Stagings in college halls were often elaborate, including galleries, platforms, staircases, and multi-levelled stage houses; such properties were "pre-fab," made to be dismantled and stored for re-use.[5] Certain schools, especially choir-schools but also Eton where playwright Ulpian Fulwell was headmaster, had plays performed as part of the curriculum. After 1567, the boom in theatrical building made London the primary site of the playhouse business: see the detailed descriptions on the web site for *Shakespeare's London*, which lists many of the playing spaces and gives short histories of the venues, the owners, and the companies.[6] Touring, however, continued to be a lucrative part of a playing company's professional life.

Because theatre is a collaborative medium, in which playwright, actors, playhouse, set, costume, and audiences all participate, the contexts of playing are a vital consideration in the understanding of early theatre. We know more about conditions at the Globe and the Blackfriars than about other theatres, partly because their playwrights embedded comments about those sites in the plays. *Henry V*'s Chorus, for example, urges the audience to share imaginatively in the theatrical experience within the Globe's "wooden O" (Prologue, 13) during regular appearances that put the king's final victory over France into perspective.[7] Jonson's *Every Man Out of His Humour* (first performed in 1599) has built-in privileged spectators who comment frequently on the amenities of the Globe. *Hamlet* uses the Globe's "discovery-space" to locate eavesdroppers, particularly Polonius, murdered behind the arras that covered it. A fund of theatrical information generally, Hamlet offers an affectionate and respectful welcome to the travelling players, including a special word to the boy-actor, and listens enthusiastically to a favourite speech by the first player, despite Polonius's grumpy comment, "This is too long" (II.ii.489). In the *Mousetrap* scene, Hamlet urges the actors to perform what is written, not to improvise, to over-gesticulate, or fail to moderate their voices, to the detriment of the play. He also reveals the dumbshow to the offstage audience. The presence "in state" (their thrones on a dais) of the king and queen means that their own "performance" in reaction to the play's material is also under scrutiny by courtiers and specifically by Hamlet and

Horatio. Tying the whole experience together is Hamlet's critical commentary accompanying the action, prompting Ophelia's remark, "You are as good as a chorus, my lord" (III.ii.230).

Beaumont's *The Knight of the Burning Pestle* has an even stronger level of self-conscious theatricality as it takes place literally in the Blackfriars theatre. Performed by the Children of Blackfriars, this play demonstrates the different demands that audiences put on a play by interlacing the intended performance of a city comedy, *The London Merchant*, with other kinds of performances paid for and inserted by a naive merchant and his wife. These two characters are stagesitters and their apprentice improvises additional material, much to the annoyance, frustration, and subsequent amusement of the professional players and the rest of the more sophisticated audience. This density of collaboration represents theatrical pleasure as both a conscious stimulation of the senses and wit, and an involuntary response to conflicts and events that propel both actors and audiences into the effective interaction that constitutes— ideally—a play in performance. But, for some in early modern London, that shared experience was an immoral seduction similar to the gaming-houses and brothels that shared neighbourhoods or even the same space with theatres (the Cockpit and the Hope are cases in point). Indeed, Jonson's *The Alchemist* similarly conflates audiences who come to the Blackfriars playhouse with customers who come to a Blackfriars brothel.

Topicality was another significant feature of early theatre, a way of exploring issues in a time without newspapers. The most pointedly political theatre was staged at London's law school, the Inns of Court. Even though these performances were not "public" in the same way as those at the Theatre or the Globe, or "private" (meaning restricted to those who could pay a substantial entrance fee), like those at Paul's or Blackfriars, they did reach their own specialist audience of lawyers, judges, diplomats, and courtiers, often including the monarch. One important staging at the Inner Temple was the first English tragedy, *Gorboduc*, in January 1562. A courtier's report of the event survives, including his comments on the effective dumbshows that begin each act, and on the play's topicality in arguing the case for Elizabeth to marry and provide an heir for the throne—this was indeed daring, given the queen's presence in the audience.[8] The use of plays to influence audiences ideologically is part of the argument about the creation in 1583 of the Queen's Men, an elite troupe of players who performed in England, Scotland, Ireland, and Europe as possible intelligence-gatherers and promoters of Protestant politics.[9] Among the many reasons for players to travel, the primary motive was profit, certainly not the need to get away from plague in London. If a troupe were suspected of carrying plague, the actors would not be allowed to enter the town or to play in the area, for fear of infection. As Alan Somerset points out, "If a city or borough did not hold out the promise of profit it would be avoided in favour of greener pastures" and, generally speaking, a city that welcomed players in one year was very likely to go on welcoming them in subsequent years. Indeed, Siobhan Keenan adds, "if there was a deliberate reduction in civic patronage of theatre . . . (and not simply a decline in players' visits) it is likely that it was prompted by socio-economic and political factors as much as moral or ideological objections to theatre."[10] On the positive side, a touring company spread information through the provinces, and brought back news to the patron. It increased the patron's prestige beyond his local base, and kept distant communities from feeling left out. Sally-Beth MacLean argues that these touring companies were media through which patrons could articulate, demonstrate, buttress, and magnify their political and social power; reciprocally, towns could curry favour with powerful patrons by rewarding the players well.[11] A London-based company could similarly enhance the status of its patron, if the topicality of the plays did not create a backlash, as happened to the Blackfriars Boys when they became Children of the Queen's Revels: scandals over three plays—Daniel's *Philotas*, Chapman, Jonson, and Marston's *Eastward Ho!*, and Day's *The Isle of Gulls*—made Queen Anne withdraw her patronage.

Another aspect of early modern theatre in current criticism investigates the erotics and titillation of the audience, especially but not exclusively by boys who play women's parts. Although many scholars have recognized a homosexual dynamic in this fascination (to name a few: Alan Bray, Steve Brown, Jonathan Goldberg, Stephen Greenblatt, Laura Levine, Stephen Orgel, and Bruce Smith) arguably, women were just as titillated as men when they watched and fantasized about the boys' androgyny.[12] Why did boys play women's parts in England at a time when female actors performed in Europe? The answers to this question are various and unconvincing, but the fact remains that until the closing of the theatres in 1642, the average adult company of actors consisted of 11 or 12 men and 3 or 4 boys. All-boy companies were wildly popular between 1576 and about 1610, after which the fashion for boys waned, possibly because the last of the trained companies of boys grew up. This single-gender factor should not be foreign to modern students, given the popularity of all-male or all-female casts now. To what extent did boys capture effectively the women they performed? Apparently, although some puritans questioned the male monopoly on female roles as a lascivious convention seducing the audience by its immoral mimicry of the feminine, not enough people objected in principle to the all-male English stage, since the test of a performance is the audience's belief in what the stage projects. When Jonson wrote his outrageous stage direction describing Wittipol's making love to Mistress Fitzdottrel, "*He grows more familiar in his courtship, plays with her paps, kisseth her hands, etc.*" (II.vi.70 sd),[13] no record suggests that the audience rejected the "paps" as impossible; so too for Shakespeare's ageless Cleopatra, or Webster's heavily pregnant Duchess of Malfi, or any other portrayal of a female character as having a body like any woman's. But English women did fill roles in performance, if not as actors on the professional stage, then certainly in parish, court, and household drama and masques.[14] Mary Wroth's *Love's Victory* (1621) was probably performed by family and friends in a private Sidney residence, possibly Penshurst; Wroth's aunt, Mary Sidney, had translated a French play by Robert Garnier as *The Tragedie of Antonie* (1595) for performance under those conditions, and the Cavendish sisters, Elizabeth Brackley and Jane Cavendish, wrote *The Concealed Fancies* (*c*.1645) for home entertainment as well.[15] The distinction here is again between public and private, and female-actors in the domestic local sphere were accepted, but any attempt to transfer into the public sphere would have caused an uproar, even at court where ladies participated only silently in masques. When Queen Henrietta Maria performed spoken dialogue in plays with her ladies, as she had done in France, she was severely criticized.

Pedagogic strategies

When I teach a survey of early drama, from medieval cycle plays to the eighteenth century, or a Shakespeare course, I begin by disseminating as much information as possible on the collaborative nature of theatre—managers, company shareholders, playwrights, designers, dancers, musicians, puppeteers, acrobats, and even animal-trainers whose talents all contribute to the magic of theatre. I also point out that, under travelling conditions, actors would not have access to a playhouse, and therefore students should look at university great halls, tennis courts, and large taverns to figure out how those spaces might be converted to playing spaces.

- This information is best conveyed graphically: that is, project overheads illustrating early modern theatres (like the now-suspect Johannes de Witt sketch of the Swan) showing the stage, the stage doors (were there two or three doors?), pillars (if there are any), discovery space (if it exists), galleries, location of the trap, the tiring-house. Have students pace off, for example, the smallish 14-foot square space used for performances in the Great Chamber at Richmond, and then add more students to pace off the additional feet to show spaces in great halls or parish halls, and work out how much of that space actors might use. For example, the Leicester Guildhall's great hall was 62 by 20: if the actors performed on 20 by 20 feet of space, how many spectators would fit into the remaining space? Given the generally smaller dimensions of people in 1600, calculating "bums on seats" should not be generous; Gurr calculates about 18 by 18 inches per person. Somerset points out that in Bristol, on more than one occasion, "the great press of spectators damaged parts of the Guildhall there, suggest[ing] that audiences sometimes packed themselves in."[16]
- How much space would actors have to move in? Select fourteen students to move around in a prospective space, such as the 20 by 20 suggested above, perhaps improvising a battle scene, and see what it looks like, from

the perspective of the rest of the students, squeezed as tightly as possible into the remaining space of the classroom as audience. Dimensions of great halls can vary by 10 to 50 feet in length or width. What does that tell us about the flexibility of touring actors who must reconfigure that room into performance space and audience space?[17] Is doubling a tactic for dealing with space? Even if not on tour, actors expected to be invited to court occasionally for a royal performance. Space is something they had to be able to deal with rapidly.

- How did London audiences get to a theatre? I talk about urban and sub-urban conditions: taking a boat to Bankside, or walking across London Bridge; the reputations and populations of various neighbourhoods that had theatres: Blackfriars (what is a liberty?); Bankside; Shoreditch, Smithfield; the locations of inns that supported performance like the Bell Savage, or the Cross Keys, and other gathering spots, like Paul's Cross, the New Exchange, and the distracting spread of new shops and lodgings along the Strand. Detailed maps of early modern London, like Hollar's "Long View of London from Bankside" and others that show the winding of the Thames west toward the Inns of Court, Westminster, and Whitehall, and east toward Greenwich; and the marking of houses, streets, and guilds in the city, so that students can locate Cheapside, the two counters, the location of the Tower or gates in the London Wall, and the various stairs down to the Thames—all of this information brings the old city to life and demonstrates early modern urban squeeze and sprawl in a vivid and accessible way. The hubbub of London life helps to illustrate or defend the habit of multiple layers of character and plot, and even the mix of genres, in the plays of the period.

- Early modern London was the place where, if you did not want to live there (and too many people did, despite repeated edicts ordering people back to their country estates or parishes), you certainly wanted to visit. Brief readings—for example, from Greene's cony-catching tales about con-men in St Paul's Cathedral, Dekker's *The Gull's Hornbook* (especially the chapter about attending the theatre), and the diary of John Manningham, a law-student, who comments on street life and attractions such as public speakers, hangings, or the witticisms of his fellow-students—can convey the early modern vernacular in stories, jests, pranks, sermons, accounts of criminal activity, and other noteworthy events. Such material familiarizes students with early modern life through shock or laughter, a good way to learn.

These aspects of early modern life are—like plays in performance—essentially ephemeral. What helps us retain or capture the medium is the emphasis on performance and visual signs of meaning in costume and gesture, aural signifiers in tone and pacing of dialogue, the aside, the soliloquy, the switch between verse and prose. All of these features, for example, arise in *The*

Taming of the Shrew, usually the first play on my Shakespeare course. Even though we have the play-text, much of the meaning is submerged because it is stripped of its collaborators who bring it to life. I point out to my students that the playbook in the early modern period was literally a piece of *ephemera*, used eventually for purposes more practical than theatrical; I find the irreverence reduces their fear of old plays and lets them see scripts instead.

- All of my students for the past twelve years have been required to perform a scene with a group, treating it both as a collaborative assignment and as the basis for an independent research essay that includes aspects of theatre and production history. One exercise I usually practise with them in the first month of class is how to read the verse aloud and appreciate the ephemera of voice, poetic/musical rhythms, and intonation. For about an hour we scan lines, take turns reading them, sometimes repeating the same line with different speakers, changing emphasis or tone each time. And we discuss the implications of each reading, whether for the specific scene or the whole play. The exercise—especially finding the caesura, and projecting the last word of the line—is a good way to get the groups started on their rehearsals. It makes them, in addition, pay attention to the artistic placement of words in a poetic line: why is this word first, or that word on the stress of the third foot, or at the end? This exercise is fun, even with a class of eighty students.

My teaching tricks are not particularly difficult or critically complex, but they do inculcate certain principles of early modern theatre. After the introductory class (about two hours) and the voice class, I discuss theatre history as it pertains to specific plays on the course and the problems they present. *The Spanish Tragedy*, for example, arguably the most popular play of the entire period, is superb for discussing the upper stage, the location of the frame-characters during the action, the logistics of stage-death by hanging, or of apparently biting out one's tongue. When is it feasible to use stage blood, and how can the actor keep his costume clean? Did early modern actors use stage-weapons? Hamlet certainly expected Laertes to have a cap on the point of his rapier in the last scene of Act 5, but the records of Norwich tell us that when a spectator sneaked into a Queen's Men performance in the yard of the Red Lion Inn and then refused to pay, three actors, stage-rapiers in hand, pursued him out of the inn and down the street, where the altercation ended in the death of the illicit play-goer.[18] This incident is a lesson in control over what might be the most important space of all: the gate by which the audience enters the theatre. But the "gatherers" who gather in the fees might, according to Gurr, prove unreliable, as in his story of gatherers who "seem to scratch their heads where they itch not, and drop shillings and half-crown pieces in at their collars"![19]

Acknowledgements

I am grateful to the Social Sciences and Humanities Research Council of Canada for funding the research assistant, Andrew Griffin, who helped me review material for this essay. Many thanks to both!

Notes

1. Christopher Phillpotts, "Red Lion Theatre, Whitechapel, Documentary Research Report," 1E0418-C1E00–00004, commissioned by MoLAS on behalf of Cross London Rail Links Limited (London: Museum of London Archeology Service and Crossrail, August, 2004), p. 6. [Online as 14-page pdf file] <http://billdocuments. crossrail.co.uk> Cited 20 October 2005. This research report detailing the exact location and dimensions of the theatre further substantiates Paul Whitfield White's observations about the general acceptance of the Red Lion as the first known theatre in "Playing Companies and the Drama of the 1580s: a New Direction for Elizabethan Theatre History?", *Shakespeare Studies* 28 (2000): 266.
2. REED's *Patrons and Performances Web Site* <http://link.library.utoronto.ca/reed/> is co-developed by Sally-Beth MacLean (University of Toronto) and Alan Somerset (University of Western Ontario) (University of Toronto, 2003–5).
3. *Records of Early English Drama* volumes, organized by area, are available in libraries, or online at the *Internet Archive* (www.archive.org/) in pdf pages.
4. See Andrew Gurr, *The Shakespearean Stage, 1574–1642* (Cambridge: Cambridge University Press, 1980), chapter 2, for a good start.
5. Alan Nelson, *Early Cambridge Theatres* (Cambridge: Cambridge University Press, 1994), chapter 4.
6. *Shakespeare's London* is part of the web site created by Linda Alchin, *William Shakespeare info* <http://www.william-shakespeare.info/elizabethan-theatre-locations.htm>, 2005. Cited 20 October 2005. The site includes the complete works online.
7. All Shakespeare citations are from the Oxford World's Classics series of individual editions: *Henry V*, ed. Gary Taylor (Oxford: Oxford University Press, 1982), and *Hamlet*, ed. G. R. Hibbard (1994).
8. See Norman Jones and Paul Whitfield White, "*Gorboduc* and Royal Marriage Politics: an Elizabethan Playgoer's Report of the Premiere Performance," *English Literary Renaissance* 26, 1 (1996): 3–17; and Jessica Winton, "Expanding the Political Nation: *Gorboduc* at the Inns of Court and the Succession Revisited," *Early Theatre* 8, 1 (2005): 11–34. For an historical perspective on the queen's marriage as seen by the Inns of Court, see Marie Axton, *The Queen's Two Bodies: Drama and the Elizabethan Succession* (London: Royal Historical Society, 1977).
9. Scott McMillin and Sally-Beth MacLean, *The Queen's Men and their Plays* (Cambridge: Cambridge University Press, 1998), chapters 2 and 3.
10. Alan Somerset, "'How Chances it they Travel?': Provincial Touring, Playing Places and the King's Men," *Shakespeare Survey* 47 (1992): 51; and Siobhan Keenan, "Patronage, Puritanism and Playing: Travelling Players in Elizabethan and Stuart Maldon, Essex," *Theatre Notebook* 58, 2 (2004): 64.
11. Sally-Beth MacLean, "Tracking Leicester's Men: the Patronage of a Performance Troupe," in *Shakespeare and Theatrical Patronage in Early Modern England,*

ed. Paul Whitfield White and Suzanne R. Westfall (Cambridge: Cambridge University Press, 2002), pp. 246–71, esp. pp. 250–7.

12. Richmond Barbour, "'When I Acted Young Antinous': Boy Actors and the Erotics of Jonsonian Theatre," *PMLA* 100 (October 1995): 1006–22, esp. p. 1117.

13. Ben Jonson, *The Devil is an Ass*, ed. Peter Happé, Revels Plays (Manchester: Manchester University Press, 1996).

14. For the most recent extensive study, see Pamela Allen Brown and Peter Parolin (eds), *Women Players in England, 1500–1660: Beyond the All-Male Stage*, Studies in Performance and Early Modern Drama (Aldershot, Hampshire and Burlington VT: Ashgate, 2005).

15. All three plays are in *Renaissance Drama by Women: Texts and Documents*, ed. S. P. Cerasano and Marion Wynne-Davies (London: Routledge, 1996); for performance information see pp. 15, 93 and 127. For the Cavendish play, see also Lisa Hopkins, "Play Houses: Drama at Bolsover and Welbeck," *Early Theatre* 2 (1999): 25–44.

16. Somerset, "'How Chances it they Travel?': Provincial Touring, Playing Places and the King's Men," p. 59.

17. See McMillin and MacLean, chapter 3, esp. 67–83, which includes photographs of various spaces, including the Leicester Guildhall and Hardwick Hall spaces.

18. McMillin and MacLean, pp. 42–3; and Somerset, p. 55.

19. Gurr, *The Shakespearean Stage, 1574–1642*, p. 69.

Selective guide to further reading and resources

Cox, John D., and Kastan, David Scott (eds). *A New History of Early English Drama*. New York: Columbia University Press, 1997.

Dutton, Richard. *Mastering the Revels: the Regulation and Censorship of English Renaissance Drama*. Iowa City: University of Iowa Press, 1991.

Gurr, Andrew, and Ichikawa, Mariko. *Staging in Shakespeare's Theatres*. Oxford: Oxford University Press, 2000.

Ingram, William. *The Business of Playing: the Beginnings of the Adult Professional Theater in Elizabethan London*. Ithaca: Cornell University Press, 1992.

King, T. J. *Casting Shakespeare's Plays: London Actors and Their Roles, 1590–1642*. Cambridge: Cambridge University Press, 1992.

Knutson, Roslyn. *The Repertory of Shakespeare's Company: 1594–1613*. Fayetteville: University of Arkansas Press, 1991.

———. *Playing Companies and Commerce in Shakespeare's Time*. Cambridge: Cambridge University Press, 2001.

Milling, Jane, and Thomson, Peter (eds). *The Cambridge History of British Theatre: Volume 1: Origins to 1660*. Cambridge: Cambridge University Press, 2004.

Shapiro, Michael. *Gender in Play on the Shakespearean Stage: Boy Heroines and Female Pages*. Ann Arbor: University of Michigan Press, 1994.

Westfall, Suzanne. "'Go sound the ocean, and cast your nets': Surfing the Net for Early Modern Theatre." *Early Theatre* 5, 2 (2002): 87–132.

Worthen, W. B. *Shakespeare and the Authority of Performance*. Cambridge: Cambridge University Press, 1998.

Internet sites

Britannica On-line. *Shakespeare and the Globe, Then and Now.* Encyclopedia Britannica, 2005 <http://search.eb.com/shakespeare/index2.html>

Gray, Terry A. *Shakespeare and the Internet* <http://shakespeare.palomar.edu/> 1995–2005

Leed, Drea. *The Elizabethan Costuming Page* <http://costume.dm.net/> 1997–2000

Secara, Maggie P. *Life in Elizabethan England: a Compendium of Common Knowledge, 1558–1603* 8th Edition <http://renaissance.dm.net/compendium/index.html> Summer 2005

2
Kyd and Revenge Tragedy

Adrian Streete

Chronology and context

Thomas Kyd was born in London in 1558, the same year that Elizabeth I ascended to the throne of England. Though firm biographical facts about Kyd are hard to come by, there is a reasonable degree of scholarly consensus about the bare outlines of his life.[1] His father, Francis, was a scrivener, a copier or drafter of important documents. There seems little reason to doubt Arthur Freeman's suggestion that the young Kyd grew up "in a lively commercial quarter of London, in a comfortable middle-class household, and in the company of a younger sister, a brother and a servant or two."[2] Nevertheless, this should not be taken to imply that the Kyd family's social standing was one of straightforward bourgeois solidity. In fact, the social status of scriveners in early modern England was a mixed one.

Though they were undoubtedly a crucial profession in terms of servicing the early modern state, scriveners also attracted a fair amount of opprobrium throughout the sixteenth and seventeenth centuries. As James R. Siemon notes, they were attacked because they had access to prior knowledge of the financial dealings of all sections of society, for acting as loan brokers and financial intermediaries, "as well as more generally for vulgar aspiration to distinction and high art"[3] through their mastery of calligraphy. Whether Kyd experienced either directly or indirectly the hostility that Francis Kyd's profession attracted must remain a matter of biographical speculation. But what can be said is that like his contemporaries or near-contemporaries Greene, Lyly, Marlowe, Nashe, and Peele, Thomas Kyd was part of a generation of writers that emerged from that highly mobile social grouping referred to by L. C. Knights as "the 'new men' of commerce and industry."[4] It is perhaps then no coincidence that such a socially mobile group was quick to recognize the newly established London commercial theatre as a potential route to economic as well as social advancement.

In 1565 at the age of seven, Kyd began to attend the Merchant Taylors' School. Others who were schooled here included the writers Edmund Spenser and Thomas Lodge, as well as the future Jacobean bishop Lancelot Andrewes.[5] The headmaster of the School was the famous humanist and scholar Richard Mulcaster, author of two well-known books of Elizabethan pedagogy, *Positions* (1581) and *The First Part of the Elementary* (1582). Though ostensibly set up for reasons of charity and a humanist-inspired belief in the social efficacy of the *studia humanitatis* that included Latin and Greek, it seems that not everyone was convinced by the broad social aims of the Merchant Schools. Indeed, as Mulcaster himself wrote: "They will give a scholer some petie poore exhibition to seeme to be religious, and under the sclender veale of counterfeit liberalitie, hide the spoil of the ransacked povertie."[6] Whether or not Mulcaster's comment parallels Kyd's own experience, it is noticeable that unlike all the other contemporaries mentioned (but, interestingly, like the younger Shakespeare) Kyd did not go on to either of the universities. There is no direct evidence that Kyd followed in his father's trade.[7] Still, it is worth noting that more than most other dramas of the period, *The Spanish Tragedy* is a play in which the business of reading and writing are emphasized almost obsessively.[8] The letters that save Alexandro from burning at the stake; Bel-imperia's letter written in blood to Hieronimo; the empty box that should contain Pedringano's pardon; Hieronimo's play written in "unknowne languages" (IV.i.172);[9] the pen-knife that Hieronimo kills himself with: these examples (and others) evince the extent to which various forms of textuality are significantly implicated and problematized in the social world of the play.

The first probable mark that Kyd makes on London's literary scene is in the years around 1585 when he is recorded as writing plays (now lost) for the stage: he also served for a brief time in the household of an unidentified nobleman, possibly Ferdinando Stanley, Lord Strange.[10] In the Armada year, 1588, an edition of Torquato Tasso's *The Householders Philosophie* translated by a "TK" was published and a few years later, in 1591, Kyd is recorded as lodging with the dramatist and poet Christopher Marlowe. Between those dates, it seems likely that *The Spanish Tragedy* was first written and performed on the London stage, though the first surviving edition is generally accepted to date from 1592.[11] What can be in no doubt is the sheer popularity of the play with the theatre-going public.[12] It was one of the most regularly performed dramas of the day and in 1602 the impresario Philip Henslowe paid Ben Jonson for certain additions[13] to Kyd's original that, along with the publication of a constant stream of editions, ensured the continuing popularity of the play well into the seventeenth century. *The Spanish Tragedy* was endlessly referred to, parodied and reworked, and many names and phrases from the drama quickly attained proverbial status amongst playwrights and playgoers.

As the reference to Jonson's 1602 additions implies, Kyd did not live long enough to savour the continued popular success of his play. In 1593, Kyd and Marlowe's lodgings were searched on the order of the Privy Council who were looking for evidence connecting either or both of the writers to a sharp rise in racial tensions across the city.[14] What they apparently found instead were certain heterodox theological papers concerning the divinity of Christ. It seems that the content of these papers was enough to put both men under suspicion and Kyd was arrested and tortured on the order of the Privy Council. Not long after this, Kyd wrote a letter to a member of the council, Sir John Puckering, protesting that there "were founde some fragments of a disputation toching that opinion affirmed by Marlowe to be his, and shuffled with some of myne (vnknown to me) by some occasion of our wrytinge in one chamber twoe yeares synce."[15] In one of those strange quirks of history, the dramatist who explores so brilliantly the exigencies of early modern textual culture in *The Spanish Tragedy* finds himself fatally compromised by those very exigencies. Kyd outlived his roommate by barely a year. He was buried in London in August 1594 at the age of 36.

The various "afterlives"[16] of the play, from Jonson's additions to T. S. Eliot's references to its central figure Hieronimo in *The Waste Land* (1922), indicate that the peculiar force and resonance of Kyd's text might go beyond a simple recognition of its traditional place as the progenitor of the early modern tragic lexis. In terms of pedagogy, like many other of the plays examined in this book, *The Spanish Tragedy*'s canonical status extends well beyond the purview of a narrowly defined "early modern" syllabus, a fact that can provide a useful point of departure for the teacher of early modern drama. That said, the play's potential status and function within a periodized or thematically-based syllabus devoted to, say, "early modern drama," "early modern litera-ture" or "revenge tragedy," will be my prime focus. While it is certainly necessary to be aware from the outset of *The Spanish Tragedy*'s canonical exemplarity, it is also important to recognize its "present" critical status as a play that might enable teachers and students to ask theoretically engaged questions about issues such as politics, language, intertextuality, subjectivity, religion or gender. To that end, one of the central purposes of this chapter will be to chart the various developments in the play's critical reception, and then to draw upon recent scholarly work on the play in order to examine how this might inform general and directed discussion in the classroom.

Critical overview

The Spanish Tragedy is a play whose critical fortunes have been indelibly marked by its historical position as the English theatre's first popular revenge tragedy. Such a position has not always been helpful for the play's critical reputation. For many years, much scholarship on *The Spanish Tragedy* was marked by what one critic has recently called "a patronizing tone."[17] Kyd's play, and the genre of revenge tragedy that it initiated, was often seen as standing at the head of a bloodthirsty, unsophisticated and faintly embar-rassing dramatic sub-genre. If the play was studied, then it was largely in terms of a kind of historicized antiquarianism.[18] Critics would duly note

Kyd's important use of various classical antecedents (noticeably Virgil and Seneca) and then go on to observe how the dramatic figures, plot devices, objects, and themes within *The Spanish Tragedy* provided what we would now call intertextual points of reference and departure for numerous other writers of the period. Before the advent and impact of structuralist and post-structuralist theory on literary studies in the 1960s and 1970s, the majority of this earlier scholarship on *The Spanish Tragedy* tended to conform to an old historicist paradigm whereby early modern drama was largely seen as "reflecting" a pre-existing and largely static moral background. Such an approach is well summed up in M. C. Bradbrook's general assertion about drama in *Themes and Conventions of Elizabethan Tragedy* (1935): "The audience was prepared to see the whole play related to a moral precept."[19] Any play is merely the conduit through which this precept is disseminated to what is presumed to be a largely passive audience.

In relation to Kyd, one especially important manifestation of this approach was the work of T. S. Eliot, and in particular his essay "Seneca in Elizabethan Translation." Though now somewhat dated, Eliot's essay has remained a seminal piece for those scholars interested in the reception and impact of classical literature in early modern literature.[20] The essay was first published in 1927 as the Introduction to an original spelling edition of the first Elizabethan translations of Seneca.[21] While drawing on the almost contemporaneous research of F. L. Lucas in his *Seneca and Elizabethan Tragedy* (1922),[22] Eliot's rationale is perhaps more explicitly stated than Lucas's. In the essay, Eliot examines the historical, literary and moral influence of Seneca in order to determine "the sanguinary character of much Elizabethan drama," thereby aiming to uncover, much like M. C. Bradbrook, "the temper of the epoch."[23] Nevertheless, his general aesthetic distaste for "the horrible and revolting"[24] in Elizabethan drama is also extended to a similarly disparaging comment on the general merits of *The Spanish Tragedy* and its author: "if Senecan Kyd had such a vogue, that was surely the path to facile success for any hard-working and underpaid writer."[25] Though he is marginally more charitable towards him elsewhere in the essay, here Eliot sees Kyd as little more than an opportunistic hack whose work was mainly of interest because it offered others a way to make easy money. Seen in this way, the play becomes in the words of Robert N. Watson "Famous as a kind of prop-room for later Renaissance tragedy,"[26] but little else. This is a judgement that Eliot's essay, for all its penetrating insight, amply bears out.

However, since the pioneering work of Lily B. Campbell and Fredson Bowers in the 1930s and 1940s,[27] both *The Spanish Tragedy* and the genre of revenge tragedy that it initiates have, in the main, been accorded a much more serious and measured historical and critical appraisal than allowed by Eliot and others. When Bowers published *Elizabethan Revenge Tragedy 1587–1642* in 1940, he was concerned to place debates about the form and legitimacy of revenge within the framework of early modern state power: "In spite of the fact that justice was the sole prerogative of the Elizabethan state, with any encroachment on its newly won privilege liable to severe punishment, the spirit of revenge had scarcely declined in Elizabethan times: its form was merely different."[28] In particular, the early modern state looked to draw a distinction between unregulated "private" revenge and the right of the state to assume responsibility for the punishment of wrongs. This distinction, argues Bowers, led to the structural tension that underpins revenge tragedy: "The right to punish their own wrongs was clear to many Elizabethans, who did not approve the interpretation of premeditated malice put by the law upon their revenges."[29] Caught between the imperatives of vengeance and those of the state, the individual was forced to negotiate his own personal dilemma.

Though such work was crucial for scholarship on *The Spanish Tragedy*, it was still underpinned by certain old historicist assumptions about the relationship between literary production, culture, and subjectivity.[30] Understanding the shift away from these attitudes is inextricably linked to the critical re-evaluation that *The Spanish Tragedy* has undergone since the 1970s. In his book *The Tragedy of State* (1971), J. W. Lever offers a critique of these old historicist assumptions by decentring the "individual" and placing him/her within complex political and social matrices, which Lever argued it was the business of early modern drama to actively interrogate:

> I do not see the Jacobean revenge play as so-called "pure theatre" where the spectators are meant to peel off their rational minds, their political and social preoccupations, for a vicarious sauna-bath in the collective unconscious. Nor, at the other extreme, would I regard these plays as exemplary warnings on the evils of taking the law into one's own hands. What Bowers fails to allow for is that in Jacobean tragedy it is not primarily the conduct of the individual, but of the society which assails him, that stands condemned.[31]

Here Lever anticipates the emergence in the late 1970s and 1980s of cultural materialism, an explicitly political form of critique concerned with the mutual imbrications of literary production, culture, and subjectivity, as well as certain versions of new historicism interested in the relationship between state power and the subject.[32] Whether maintaining in the case of cultural materialism that "culture does not (cannot) transcend the material forces and relations of production,"[33] or emphasizing "a reciprocal concern with the historicity of texts and the textuality of history"[34] that characterizes new historicism, both critical schools initiated a broader re-evaluation of early modern drama that enables a play like *The Spanish Tragedy* to be seen not simply as a slightly distasteful literary exemplar "reflecting" fixed moral categories, but as a complex political and social document implicated in a range of disparate and contesting contemporary discourses.

It is interesting to note that, in general, new historicists have been more directly concerned with *The Spanish Tragedy* than have cultural materialists.[35] Drawing on Michel Foucault's work on the connections between state punishment and the subject, new historicism found fertile ground in Kyd's play for exploring this relationship.[36] For example, in his essay "Tragedies naturally performed: Kyd's Representation of Violence" published in 1991, James Shapiro offers a Foucauldian-inspired account of the inter-relations between Elizabethan execution practice and representation. Focusing on the execution of Pedringano, he finds that: "The lines separating official and theatrical violence are blurred, as Kyd's play insistently seeks out representational no-man's-land, testing the boundaries between the prerogatives of the state and those of the theatre."[37] Similarly in her essay "The Theatre and the Scaffold: Death as Spectacle in *The Spanish Tragedy*" (1992), Molly Easo Smith suggests that the success of the play is due to the "ingenious transference of the spectacle of public execution with all its ambiguities from the socio-political to the cultural worlds."[38] While both of these essays arguably demonstrate a tendency in some new historicist critique to collapse all forms of social experience into a politically neutral "poetics of culture," they do show how Kyd's play is deeply implicated in early modern debates about the practice, form and abuse of state power. To this end, perhaps the most politically sophisticated analysis of *The Spanish Tragedy* is Frank Whigham's 1996 work on the "fantasies of power and control"[39] operating in the play. Though densely written, it reveals much about the play's engagement with early modern political configurations.

Another aspect of *The Spanish Tragedy* that has been the source of a number of interesting studies relates the play to the context of early modern European politics, noticeably England's problematic religio-political relationship with Spain.[40] In the words of Huston Diehl: "It is surely significant that Kyd sets his play in Roman Catholic Spain, a country that in the 1580s not only attempted to invade England but sought as well to return it to the Roman Church."[41] Diehl reads the play primarily in terms of theological debates surrounding the signifying function of the Eucharist. Frank Ardolino's work, on the other hand, is interested in the play's use of biblical apocalypticism. For example, in a 1990 essay he reads *The Spanish Tragedy*'s numerous references to the book of Revelation in terms of an apocalyptic conflict between England and Spain. As he notes: "*The Spanish Tragedy* is a providential tragicomedy, a *comedia apocalyptica*, presenting the tragedy of Babylon-Spain's fall and the comedy of Protestant England's defeat of the Antichrist."[42] More recently (2001), Eric Griffin has sought to build upon and revise Ardolino's research by seeing the play in terms of a pan-European debate that seeks to project the idea of "Empire" "well beyond the boundaries of both the text itself and the individual 'nations' the play labors to represent."[43] Amongst other things, he points out that Hieronimo "bears a name so sacred—literally *hieros nym*, the sacred name [that it] demands exegetical attention,"[44] and that the Hebrew and Latin typology of Bel-imperia's name, associating her first with the idolatress Bel in Isaiah and second with the Latin term for "empire," suggests that she can be figuratively and thematically read as "the beautiful 'Idol of Empire'."[45]

In two well-received books published in 1994 and 1997 respectively, both Robert N. Watson and Michael Neill offer somewhat less "localized" readings of *The Spanish Tragedy*. This is perhaps unsurprising, given that the topic of both scholars' investigation is early modern attitudes towards death. Nonetheless, both offer rich analyses of the play's engagement with what Watson terms the "struggle between morality and personal identity."[46] Watson sees the play's tragic action in terms of an endlessly repeated cycle of murder, revenge and mourning, writing that:

> Hieronimo's final revenge allows the audience to participate in powerful action on behalf of the deceased; it also reminds the audience that such actions must be performed on the level of fantasy, whether by viewing a play like *The Spanish Tragedy*, or by performing some other metonymous act, some other act of substitution, upon one's own psychic stage.[47]

Drawing attention to the terrifying final line of the play where Revenge promises, "Ile there begin their endless Tragedie,"[48] Watson notes that the play dramatizes the way in which certain psychological compulsions stand as fantasmatic substitutes for a subjective plenitude that can never be fully obtained. Michael Neill, on the other hand, is less drawn towards psychological/psychoanalytic readings of early modern death. Commenting on Revenge's promise quoted above, Neill writes:

> there is something sinister in the vision of an afterworld which is to consist of endless re-enactments of the drama of retribution we have just seen enacted: it is as though Kyd were picking up the hint of infinite regression in *The Spanish Tragedy*'s Chinese-box design, to create another version of *Doctor Faustus*' horror of no-end.[49]

In this account, the *structural* refusal of a conventional narrative ending has a greater imperative than any subjective response to that refusal. To this end, it might be useful to draw attention to John Kerrigan's 1996 account of early modern revenge, which seems to stand somewhere between Watson and Neill's readings. As Kerrigan observes: "Revenge cannot bring back what has been lost. Only memory, with all its limitations, can do that."[50]

Pedagogic strategies

There is barely an early modern play that does not at some level deal with the idea of revenge.[51] It is therefore critical that any curriculum concerned with revenge tragedy should consider the structural and generic parameters that Kyd negotiates with in *The Spanish Tragedy*, and which he and other dramatists then innovate upon. To that end, for the first seminar on the undergraduate course that I teach on "Renaissance Revenge Tragedy," students are asked to read Seneca's *Thyestes* in tandem with *The Spanish Tragedy*. Beginning the course with this kind of contextual reading enables students to see from the outset the degree to which Kyd's play is involved in a very self-conscious negotiation with its Senecan model. For example, *Thyestes* opens with a "framing" discussion between the Ghost of Tantalus and a Fury.[52] We also have a Chorus who plays an active part in the drama. Kyd's opening scene reworks this model, however, in significant ways. Here, we are presented with the Ghost of Don Andrea and Revenge personified, who interestingly concludes the scene thus: "Heere sit we downe to see the misterie, / And serve for *Chorus* in this Tragedie" (I.i.90–1). This comparison could be used as a point of departure to discuss the relationship between Tantalus and the Fury, and Don Andrea and Revenge. Are Kyd's figures essentially dispassionate stoics, or does their choric status imply a degree of operative agency in the play's action? How might Kyd's "framing" device have been staged in the early modern theatre? And how might students stage it now? These questions might also be modified in relation to later revenge tragedies such as *Hamlet*, *The Atheist's Tragedy* or *The White Devil* where the ghosts appear to play a more "active" part in the play's world.

The Senecan "frame" might alternatively be broached by examining Don Andrea's description of a Senecan/Virgilian underworld: "my soule descended straight / To passe the flowing streame of *Acheron*" (I.i.18–19). What are we to make of a Ghost who was (presumably) in life a Christian describing the afterlife in these terms? C. L. Barber's assertion that "Kyd is dramatizing not a Senecan world but a good world becoming Senecan"[53] might be a useful starting point for exploring the ideological function that classical discourse serves both here and elsewhere in the play. It could also enable students to consider possible tensions between early modern Christian monotheistic culture and its use of pagan/polytheistic models. A related theme raised throughout *Thyestes* and transmuted into *The Spanish Tragedy* is the relationship between ritual, sacrifice, and tragedy. Students might compare the way in which violence is only reported in *Thyestes* but acted out in *The Spanish Tragedy*—what does this imply? Discussion may also focus on ritual space and ritual objects. In one passage in *Thyestes*, Atreus describes the golden ram of "mystic origin" and explains that "The owner of the ram is king."[54] However, Thyestes stole this "sacred beast" and this caused the "mutual enmity" between the brothers. Atreus achieves his vengeance by taking Thyestes' children to "an ancient grove, / The sanctuary of the royal house,"[55] sacrificing them and tricking his brother into eating them. Though the parallels with Shakespeare's *Titus Andronicus* are well known, there are also parallels in relation to *The Spanish Tragedy*. For example, Hieronimo's speech when he discovers Horatio's body in the arbour ("O, earth why didst thou not in time devoure, / The vile prophaner of this sacred bower" II.v.26–7); the handkerchief spotted with Horatio's blood that becomes almost a fetish-like object for Hieronimo ("Seest thou this hand-kercher besmerd with blood, / It shall not from me till I take revenge" II.iv.105–6); the way he reveals his dead son's body at the end of the play[56] ("See heere my shew, looke on this spectacle" IV.iv.93); or his murder of Castille's children ("Why hast thou butchered both my children thus?" IV.iv.170) can all lead to interesting discussions about the ritual origins of tragedy.[57] What, for example, is the difference between sacrifice and revenge? How might religion, broadly conceived, fit into the equation?

Nevertheless, there is of course much more to *The Spanish Tragedy* than comparisons with Seneca. One such aspect, already touched upon in the discussion of critical material, is the complex relationships between the state, the subject, and law. The obvious starting point in *The Spanish Tragedy* is Hieronimo's great speech in Act three, scene fourteen:

> *Vindicta mihi.*
> I, heaven will be reveng'd of every ill,
> Nor will they suffer murder unrepaide:
> Then stay, *Hieronimo*, attend their will,
> For mortall men may not appoint a time.
> > *Per scelus semper tutum est scleribus iter.*
> Strike, and strike home, where wrong is offered thee,
> For evils unto ils conductors be,
> And death's the worst of resolution:
> For he that thinkes his life with patience to contend
> To quiet life shall easily ende.
> > (III.xiv.1–11)

In this amalgam of biblical injunction and Senecan tags, Hieronimo sets out a series of structural problems that will be continuously debated by early modern dramatists up to the civil war. Is revenge a matter of divine or personal vengeance? Who stands for the law? Who offers justice to those responsible for dispensing or representing justice? What if the ultimate secular authority is unjust? Each of these questions is addressed in Shakespeare's two revenge tragedies, *Titus Andronicus* and *Hamlet*. Teachers of early modern drama will be well aware of the connections here, particularly in each play's explorations of revenge, suicide, and madness. But Hieronimo's debate also informs a range of other less obvious early modern dramas. For example, Beaumont and Fletcher's *The Maid's Tragedy* offers a good comparison here with *The Spanish Tragedy*. In this play, we get a number of possible answers to Hieronimo's problem. To start with, when Amintor finds out that his new bride Evadne has a lover, he swears revenge. But when the lover is revealed to be the King, his attitude changes:

> O thou hast named a word that wipes away
> All thoughts revengeful. In that sacred name,
> The King, there lies a terror; what frail man
> Dares lift his hand against it? Let the gods
> Speak to him when they please, till when let us
> Suffer, and wait.
>
> (II.1.286–91)[58]

Amintor rejects the possibility broached in the second half of Hieronimo's speech, opting instead for a metaphysical mystification of kingly power. Significantly it is in fact Evadne who represents the play's radical answer to the problem of revenge: she ends up killing the King herself. In a scene beginning with echoes of *Hamlet* III.iii and filled with dark eroticism, Evadne decides: "My vengeance / Shall take him waking, and then lay before him / The number of his wrongs and punishments" (V.i.29–31). Such examples may lead to a discussion of the ways in which later drama both eroticizes and genders questions of revenge. This could begin with discussion of Isabella's desire for revenge in *The Spanish Tragedy* that eventually drives her mad ("whither shall I runne / To finde them out, that murdered my sonne?" III.ix.23–4). Or it could look at how Bel-imperia uses her sex in order to manoeuvre a political position for herself ("But how can love finde harbour in my brest, / Till I revenge the death of my beloved. / Yes, second love shall further my revenge" I.iv.64–6). Three plays that could offer good comparisons are Marston's "revenge-comedy" *The Dutch Courtesan*, Barksted and Machin's (after Marston) *The Insatiate Countess* or Middleton and Rowley's *The Changeling*. Such comparisons may encourage students to consider more generally other ways in which later writers borrow from, alter or indeed improve upon Kyd's model.

Bel-imperia's relationship with her brother Lorenzo and his friend (and her suitor) Balthazar provides a starting point for considering the ways in which masculine and feminine power is structured in *The Spanish Tragedy* and in early modern drama. Both Lorenzo and Balthazar despise Horatio's relationship with Bel-imperia because they see him as a social upstart ("Although his life were ambitious proud,/ Yet he is highest now he is dead" II.v.61–2). Yet it is significant that Lorenzo's Machiavellian manipulation of his sister throughout provides a number of later dramatists with a model that is taken up, copied, and reworked. For example, in his play *The Duchess of Malfi*, John Webster refigures the Lorenzo–Balthazar–Bel-imperia triad, with the Duchess and her two brothers, the Cardinal, and the sexually pathological Ferdinand. Not only does the Duchess choose a social inferior,

Antonio, as a lover, but like Bel-imperia her assertion of sexual agency causes her to be physically removed from the court by her brothers. Perhaps the most useful comparison is the discussion between Lorenzo, Balthazar, and Bel-imperia in Act Three, scene ten in *The Spanish Tragedy*, and the exchange between the Duchess and Ferdinand in Act Three, scene two of *The Duchess of Malfi*. In what ways does each scene demonstrate male anxieties about the expression and regulation of female sexual desire? Is it possible for a female to assert a degree of subjective agency within these structures, or is this agency only ever conditional? This could potentially extend into a more general consideration of female death and revenge tragedy, perhaps using Isabella's suicide (IV.ii) or Bel-imperia's suicide (IV.iv) as starting points. Is the recently revived critical category of "female tragic hero" apposite in these cases and others?[59] If so, then in what ways might this shift our generic conception of revenge tragedy? Using Kyd's play as a starting point, obvious dramas for discussion could include Webster's *The White Devil* and *The Duchess of Malfi*, Middleton and Rowley's *The Changeling*, Middleton's *The Maiden's Tragedy* and *Women Beware Women* and Ford's *'Tis Pity She's a Whore*.

As I have shown, even if *The Spanish Tragedy* did not stand at the head of the early modern revenge tragedy genre it would still demand our pedagogic attention as a rhetorically sophisticated, politically engaged, and dramaturgically important play. More than this, it continues to inspire a range of historically and theoretically important criticism that can be brought fruitfully to bear in the classroom. The challenge is making that connection between the text and the best critical work. As teachers of early modern drama, we are aware of the extent to which students will often need help in "translating" early modern drama, especially non-Shakespearean texts. Perhaps one place to start is with contemporary film's saturation in images of violence and punishment. Certainly, we must be careful not to collapse early modern culture into post-modern culture. However, as Stevie Simpkin points out:

> Both plays and films are preoccupied with the disjunction between what should be and what is in a fallen (or degenerate) world. In a society over-familiar with corruption, and certainly for a public which has already supped its fill on horrors, perhaps the visions of excess that the two popular genres offer to their respective audiences constitute a logical next step. It is here that we may draw parallels between contemporary society and the early modern world, as we puzzle over the extreme violence of revenge tragedy and the increasingly graphic, recurrent and protracted violence in contemporary cinema.[60]

Though Simpkin perhaps over stresses the decadent, world-weary similarities between early modern and post-modern takes on violence, he does enable us to see that the politics of violent representation always speak to historically specific contingencies. In other words, just as dramatists like Kyd rewrote the violent structures of their Senecan models in order to explore early modern tensions and faultlines, so post-modern cinema rewrites the politics of violence for a twenty-first century audience. By asking students to think theoretically about their own culture's political and mimetic obsessions with violence, it may then be less of a leap for them to ask similarly theoretically engaged questions about the structures of violence operative in early modern culture.

Notes

I am grateful to my colleague Caroline Sumpter for helpful comments on this chapter.

1. In what follows, I draw upon Arthur Freeman, *Thomas Kyd: Facts and Problems* (Oxford: Clarendon Press, 1967) as well as the "Chronology" in Emma Smith's edition of the play. Thomas Kyd, *The Spanish Tragedie* with Anonymous, *The First Part of Jeronimo*, ed. Emma Smith (London: Penguin, 1998), pp. viii–ix.
2. Freeman, *Thomas Kyd*, p. 5.
3. James R. Siemon, "Sporting Kyd," *English Literary Renaissance* 24, 3 (1994): 573.
4. L. C. Knights, *Drama and Society in the Age of Jonson* (Harmondsworth: Penguin, 1962), p. 19.
5. *English Renaissance Literary Criticism*, ed. Brian Vickers (Oxford: Clarendon Press, 1999), p. 175.
6. Cited in Richard Halpern, *The Poetics of Primitive Accumulation: English Renaissance Culture and the Genealogy of Capital* (Ithaca and London: Cornell University Press, 1991), p. 23.
7. Siemon has drawn attention to "the calligraphic mastery of Thomas Kyd's surviving signature and the precise handwriting over that signature," which may suggest that Kyd was at least taught calligraphy by his father. Op. cit., p. 572.
8. This point has been made before. For a good summary, see Michael Neill, *Issues of Death: Mortality and Identity in English Renaissance Tragedy* (Oxford: Clarendon Press, 1998), p. 211. See also Carla Mazzio, "Staging the Vernacular: Language and Nation in Thomas Kyd's *The Spanish Tragedy*," *SEL* 38, 2 (1998): 207–32.
9. All references are to Emma Smith's original spelling edition of the play, op. cit.
10. "Introduction," Thomas Kyd, *The Spanish Tragedy*, ed. J. R. Mulryne, The New Mermaids (London: Ernest Benn, 1970), pp. xiii–xiv.
11. Kyd may also have been responsible for the posthumously published 1594 play *Cornelia*, translated from Robert Garnier's *Cornélie*.
12. Emma Smith notes that *The Spanish Tragedy* was "the third most popular play of the period," op. cit., p. viii.
13. See Lukas Erne, "Enter the Ghost of Andrea: Recovering Thomas Kyd's Two-Part Play," *ELR* 30, 3 (2000): 339–72. In this essay, Erne advances a complex argument about the difficult textual history of the play, arguing that *The Spanish Tragedy* should be seen as a sequel to an earlier play, *Don Horatio*, which now only exists in corrupt form.
14. For more on the relationship between Kyd and Marlowe and their possible implication in the racial "libels" posted against the Dutch and French communities in London, see Charles Nicholl, *The Reckoning: the Murder of Christopher Marlowe* (London: Vintage, 2002), pp. 346–73.
15. Cited in Jeffrey Masten, "Playwrighting: Authorship and Collaboration," in *A New History of Early English Drama*, ed. John D. Cox and David Scott Kastan (New York: Columbia University Press, 1997), p. 360.

16. I take the term from Emma Smith's edition of the play where she concludes with a section examining "Hieronimo's Afterlives." Op. cit., pp. 133–59.

17. Smith, "Introduction" to *The Spanish Tragedie*, p. xv.

18. Though still a useful book, a good example of the type of criticism I am referring to can be found in F. L. Lucas's *Seneca and Elizabethan Tragedy* (Cambridge: Cambridge University Press, 1922).

19. M. C. Bradbrook, *Themes and Conventions of Elizabethan Tragedy*, 2nd edn. (Cambridge: Cambridge University Press, 1980), p. 70.

20. The best modern account is Robert S. Miola, *Shakespeare and Classical Tragedy: the Influence of Seneca* (Clarendon Press: Oxford, 1992).

21. *Seneca His Tenne Tragedies Translated into English Edited by Thomas Norton Anno 1581*, with an Introduction by T. S. Eliot, 2 vols (London: Constable, 1927).

22. Lucas, *Seneca and Elizabethan Tragedy*.

23. T. S. Eliot, "Seneca in Elizabethan Translation," in T. S. Eliot, *Essays on Elizabethan Drama* (New York: Harcourt, Brace, 1956), p. 27.

24. Eliot, "Seneca," p. 21.

25. Eliot, "Seneca," p. 20.

26. Robert N. Watson, *The Rest is Silence: Death as Annihilation in the English Renaissance* (Berkeley and London: University of California Press, 1994), p. 56.

27. See Lily B. Campbell, "Theories of Revenge in Renaissance England," *Modern Philology* 28 (1931): 281–96 and Fredson Bowers, *Elizabethan Revenge Tragedy 1587–1642* (Princeton: Princeton University Press, 1940).

28. Bowers, *Elizabethan Revenge Tragedy*, p. 8.

29. Bowers, *Elizabethan Revenge Tragedy*, p. 10.

30. Other important critical work on the play that broadly falls under this "old histori-cist" aegis includes S. F. Johnson, "*The Spanish Tragedy*, or Babylon Revisited," in *Essays on Shakespeare and Elizabethan Drama in Honor of Hardin Craig*, ed. Richard Hosley (Columbia: University of Missouri Press, 1962), pp. 23–36; G. K. Hunter, "Ironies of Justice in *The Spanish Tragedy*," *Renaissance Drama* 8 (1965): 89–104; Scott McMillin, "The Book of Seneca in *The Spanish Tragedy*," *SEL* 14, 2 (1974): 201–8; Scott McMillin, "The Figure of Silence in *The Spanish Tragedy*," *ELH* 39, 1 (1972): 27–48.

31. J. W. Lever, *The Tragedy of State: a Study of Jacobean Drama*, Introduction by Jonathan Dollimore (London and New York: Methuen, 1987), p. 12.

32. See Kiernan Ryan, *New Historicism and Cultural Materialism: a Reader* (London and New York: Arnold, 1996). I do not examine Eugene Hill's "Senecan and Vergilian Perspectives in *The Spanish Tragedy*," *ELR* 15, 2 (1985): 143–65 or Steven Justice's "Spain, Tragedy, and *The Spanish Tragedy*," *SEL* 25 (1985): 271–88 here, though both are important essays.

33. Jonathan Dollimore and Alan Sinfield, "Forward," *Political Shakespeares: Essays in Cultural Materialism*, 2nd edn. (Manchester: Manchester University Press, 1994), p. viii.

34. Louis Montrose, "Professing the Renaissance: the Poetics and Politics of Culture," in *Literary Theory: an Anthology*, ed. Julie Rivkin and Michael Ryan (Oxford: Blackwell, 2000), p. 781.

35. Catherine Belsey deals with the play in *The Subject of Tragedy: Identity and Difference in Renaissance Drama* (London: Methuen, 1985) but neither Jonathan Dollimore nor Alan Sinfield have written at length on it. Similarly, Kyd's play is not one of those that Franco Moretti examines in detail in *Signs Taken for Wonders: Essays in the Sociology of Literary Forms*, trans. Susan Fischer, David Forgacs, and

David Miller (London and New York: Verso, 1988). See Katharine Eisaman Maus, *Inwardness and Theater in the English Renaissance* (Chicago and London: University of Chicago Press, 1995), pp. 55–71 for an account of the play's interest in inwardness that build on cultural materialist and new historicist accounts.

36. For a cultural materialist account of early modern execution, albeit one that focuses on Shakespeare's *Titus Andronicus*, see Francis Barker, *The Culture of Violence: Essays on Tragedy and History* (Manchester: Manchester University Press, 1993), pp. 143–206.

37. James Shapiro, "Tragedies naturally performed: Kyd's Representation of Violence," in *Staging the Renaissance: Representations of Elizabethan and Jacobean Drama*, ed. David Scott Kastan and Peter Stallybrass (New York and London: Routledge, 1991), p. 100.

38. Molly Easo Smith, "The Theatre and the Scaffold: Death as Spectacle in *The Spanish Tragedy*," in *Revenge Tragedy*, New Casebooks, ed. Stevie Simpkin (Basingstoke: Palgrave–now Palgrave Macmillan, 2001), p. 83.

39. Frank Whigham, *Seizures of the Will in Early Modern English Drama* (Cambridge: Cambridge University Press, 1996), p. 22.

40. See J. R. Mulryne, "Nationality and Language in Thomas Kyd's *The Spanish Tragedy*," in *Langues et Nations au Temps de la Renaissance*, ed. M. T. Jones-Davis (Paris: Klincksieck, 1991), pp. 67–91.

41. Huston Diehl, *Staging Reform, Reforming the Stage: Protestantism and Popular Theater in Early Modern England* (Ithaca and London: Cornell University Press, 1997), p. 112.

42. Frank Ardolino, "Now I Shall See the Fall of Babylon: *The Spanish Tragedy* as Protestant Apocalypse," *Shakespeare Yearbook* 1 (1990), p. 99. See also Johnson, "*The Spanish Tragedy*, or Babylon Revisited."

43. Eric Griffin, "Ethos, Empire, and the Valiant Acts of Thomas Kyd's Tragedy of 'the Spains'," *ELR* 31, 2 (2001), p. 194.

44. Griffin, "Ethos," p. 222.

45. Griffin, "Ethos," p. 208.

46. Watson, *The Rest is Silence*, p. 64.

47. Watson, *The Rest is Silence*, p. 65.

48. IV.v.48.

49. Neill, *Issues of Death*, p. 212.

50. John Kerrigan, *Revenge Tragedy: Aeschylus to Armageddon* (Oxford: Clarendon Press, 2000), p. 188.

51. At the end of the first introductory meeting of my "Renaissance Revenge Tragedy" class I get the students to read and then discuss Francis Bacon's short essay "Of Revenge." Bacon's celebrated paradox "Revenge is a kind of wild justice" is a good starting point for enabling students to think about the structural and political problems of vengeance in early modern society. Francis Bacon, Of Revenge," in *The English Works of Francis Bacon: Vol. I, The Essays and The New Atlantis*, ed. Sidney Lee (London: Methuen, 1905), p. 9.

52. Seneca, *Four Tragedies and Octavia*, trans. E. F. Watling (Harmondsworth: Penguin, 1972), pp. 45–52.

53. C. L. Barber, *Creating Elizabethan Tragedy: the Theater of Marlowe and Kyd*, ed. Richard P. Wheeler (Chicago and London: University of Chicago Press, 1988), p. 143.

54. Seneca, *Four Tragedies*, p. 55.

55. Seneca, *Four Tragedies*, p. 74.

56. This "showing" of the corpse is of course central in many revenge tragedies, not least Middleton's *The Revenger's Tragedy* and Chettle's *Hoffman*.

57. The work of C. L. Barber, René Girard, and Naomi Conn Liebler is the best known in this regard.
58. All references to *The Maid's Tragedy*, in *Four Jacobean Sex Tragedies*, ed. Martin Wiggins (Oxford: Oxford University Press, 1998).
59. See *The Female Tragic Hero in English Renaissance Drama*, ed. Naomi Conn Liebler (Basingstoke and New York: Palgrave–now Palgrave Macmillan, 2002); and Lisa Hopkins, *The Female Hero in English Renaissance Tragedy* (Basingstoke and New York: Palgrave–now Palgrave Macmillan, 2002).
60. Stevie Simpkin, "Introduction," in *Revenge Tragedy*, p. 19.

Selective guide to further reading

Editions

Readily available and scholarly editions of *The Spanish Tragedy* are:

Kyd, Thomas. *The Spanish Tragedy*. Ed. David Bevington. Manchester: Manchester University Press, 1996.

———. *The Spanish Tragedy*, in *Four Revenge Tragedies*. Ed. Katharine Eisaman Maus. Oxford: Oxford University Press, 1995.

———. *The Spanish Tragedy*. Ed. J. R. Mulryne. The New Mermaids. London: Ernest Benn, 1970.

———. *The Spanish Tragedie* with Anonymous, *The First Part of Jeronimo*. Ed. Emma Smith. London: Penguin, 1998. This is the edition that I have quoted from in this chapter. As well as a fine Introduction and appendices it also contains the anonymous *The First Part of Jeronimo* as well as the seventeenth century ballad "The Spanish Tragedy."

Additional reading

NB: This list comprises material not referred to in the endnotes.

Callaghan, Dympna. *Women and Gender in Renaissance Tragedy*. London and New York: Harvester Wheatsheaf, 1989.

Dollimore, Jonathan. *Radical Tragedy: Religion, Ideology and Power in the Drama of Shakespeare and his Contemporaries*. 2nd edn. London and New York: Harvester Wheatsheaf, 1989.

———. *Death, Desire and Loss in Western Culture*. London: Penguin, 1998.

Drakakis, John, and Liebler, Naomi Conn. *Tragedy*. Harlow: Longman, 1998.

Eagleton, Terry. *Sweet Violence: the Idea of the Tragic*. Oxford: Blackwell, 2003.

Girard, René. *Violence and the Sacred*. Trans. Patrick Gregory. London and New York: Continuum, 2005.

Green, André. *The Tragic Effect: the Oedipus Complex in Tragedy*. Trans. Alan Sheridan. Cambridge and London: Cambridge University Press, 1979.

Greenblatt, Stephen. *Renaissance Self-Fashioning: From More to Shakespeare*. Chicago and London: University of Chicago Press, 1980.

Loomba, Ania. *Gender, Race, Renaissance Drama*. Manchester: Manchester University Press, 1989.

Rozett, Martha T. *The Doctrine of Election and the Emergence of Elizabethan Tragedy*. Princeton: Princeton University Press, 1984.

Sawday, Jonathan. *The Body Emblazoned: Dissection and the Human Body in Renaissance Culture*. London and New York: Routledge, 1996.

Sinfield, Alan. *Literature in Protestant England 1560–1660*. London and Canberra: Croom Helm, 1983.

———. *Faultlines: Cultural Materialism and the Politics of Dissident Reading*. Oxford: Clarendon Press, 1992.

Stallybrass, Peter, and White, Allon. *The Politics and Poetics of Transgression*. London: Methuen, 1986.

Weimann, Robert. *Authority and Representation in Early Modern Discourse*. Ed. David Hillman. Baltimore and London: Johns Hopkins University Press, 1996.

3
Marlowe
Lisa Hopkins

Chronology

Christopher Marlowe was christened at St George's Church, Canterbury, on 26 February 1564. Elizabethan customs for the baptism of babies would suggest that he was no more than a few days old at the time. He was the second child and first son of John Marlowe, a relatively recent immigrant to busy commercial Canterbury from the quieter Kent town of Ospringe, and of John's wife Katherine, who was originally from Dover. This was also the year that William Shakespeare was born (he was christened at the Holy Trinity Church, Stratford-upon-Avon, on 26 April 1564), but although Marlowe and Shakespeare were to grow up as unquestionably the two greatest dramatists of the time, and despite persistent speculation that they collaborated on the *Henry VI* plays, there is no actual proof that they ever met each other. Nevertheless, their works were undoubtedly in dialogue.

For much of Marlowe's early life, little is known. Not until December 1578 does Marlowe's life begin to take concrete shape, for in that month he was enrolled as a scholar at the King's School, Canterbury. Since fourteen was unusually late for an Elizabethan boy to start attending grammar school, there seems to be some irregularity here, and the likeliest explanation is that Marlowe was in some way promising enough to have been allowed to deviate from the usual system. He did not stay at the King's School long, because by December 1580 he had arrived as a scholar at Corpus Christi College, Cambridge, to study divinity. He was the beneficiary of a scholarship set up by Archbishop Matthew Parker, of which the terms were that on graduation he would take Holy Orders. This means that at this stage of his life Marlowe must either have believed in God or must have been prepared all along to break the terms of his scholarship and to act a part.

Marlowe's time at Cambridge passed, as far as is known, without either incident or any particular academic distinction until some time in the early summer of 1587, when the Privy Council wrote to the Cambridge authorities ordering them to stop making difficulties in the matter of conferring

Marlowe's degree, because "he had done Her Majesty good service, & deserved to be rewarded for his faithful dealing."[1] Two things seem to be relatively clear here. The first is that the authorities were reluctant to allow Marlowe to proceed to the degree because he had been away somewhere, hence presumably failing to fulfil the university's strict residence requirements. The draft wording of the Privy Council's minute (which is all that survives) says that "it was reported that Christopher Morley was determined to have gone beyond the sea to Reames and there to remain."[2] But what does this mean—that Marlowe had never in fact gone to "Reames" (i.e., in the French city of Rheims) at all? Or that he had gone there but had not intended to stay?

Fortunately, there is not much doubt about what Marlowe would have been doing in Rheims if he had in fact gone there, and that gives us a pretty good clue to what this was all about. Since 1578, Rheims had been the home of the seminary to which English Catholics could go in secret to train for the priesthood, which they were forbidden to do in Protestant England. An atmosphere of paranoia about Catholic plots had prevailed in England after the Pope had excommunicated Elizabeth I in 1570 and thus effectively given Catholics a licence to kill her. In such a climate, to go to Rheims was a treasonable act. Presumably the implication of the Privy Council's letter is that it had been erroneously rumoured that Marlowe was one of these young men.

Since we have the Privy Council's word for it that this was not in fact the case, two possibilities remain open: firstly, that the entire Rheims story was a total red herring and that Marlowe had actually been somewhere else entirely; secondly, that Marlowe had in fact been to Rheims, but for completely the opposite purpose to that rumoured—not because he himself was a Catholic, but because he was spying on Catholics. This is what has generally been accepted by Marlowe scholars as the more likely possibility.

After his degree had duly been awarded, Marlowe left Cambridge and reappeared almost immediately in London, where his play *Tamburlaine the Great* became an overnight success, to be followed in quick succession by *Tamburlaine the Great*, Part Two, *Doctor Faustus*, *The Jew of Malta*, *The Massacre at Paris*, and *Edward II*. Most of our knowledge of Marlowe for the six remaining years of his life derives from his periodic legal difficulties: he was arrested on 18 September 1589 for his part in the killing of Thomas Bradley by his friend Thomas Watson; on 26 January 1592 for coining in Flushing; on 15 September 1592 for fighting in the streets of Canterbury with a tailor; and on 9 May 1592 he was bound over in the sum of £20 to keep the peace towards a constable and a beadle, and to appear at the General Sessions in October. On 30 May 1593, he was fatally stabbed at Deptford, for reasons which remain unclear.

The single most startling thing about Marlowe to his contemporaries, and the thing on which they most often commented, was his alleged atheism. (He also seems to have been a homosexual and to have smoked—or at least praised—tobacco, two other things which would have shocked contemporaries.) The

Baines Note, which was handed to the authorities either immediately before or immediately after Marlowe's death, links Marlowe's atheism directly to the mathematician and philosopher Thomas Hariot's observation "That the Indians, and many authors of antiquity, have assuredly written of above 16 thousand years agone, whereas Adam is proved to have lived within six thousand years." Hariot, whom Marlowe knew, went to America with the Grenville expedition in 1585, and his *A Brief and True Report of the new-found Land of Virginia* appeared in 1588. It is a commonplace that Columbus's discovery of America had rocked Renaissance Europe, not least because it called into question the authority of the Bible, which failed to mention America. Marlowe, who was fascinated by geography, would have been interested in this New World not just for its own sake but also because its discovery prompted the rush to colonize it, and colonization is something looked at in a number of Marlowe's plays. Moreover, Sir Walter Ralegh, the principal impetus behind English voyages to America, is one of the shadowy figures who may well have had some connection with Marlowe's death.

Critical overview

The earliest criticism of Marlowe tended to focus on two things: the relationship of his works to his own apparently transgressive lifestyle, and / or their relationship to those of Shakespeare, often with a view to proving that Marlowe was inferior. At its best, the first could be an exhilarating approach. In *Christopher Marlowe: the Overreacher* (1961), Harry Levin made his plays sound as challenging and provocative as their author:

> His protagonist is never Everyman, but always *l'uomo singulare*, the exceptional man who becomes king because he is a hero, not hero because he is a king; the private individual who remains captain of his fate, at least until his ambition overleaps itself; the overreacher whose tragedy is more of an action than a passion, rather an assertion of man's will than an acceptance of God's.[3]

This does, however, come at the cost of making all Marlowe's plays sound like the same play, while the title clearly suggests that Marlowe's hero is in fact Marlowe himself, an approach which Lawrence Danson has neatly summed up as assuming "that the Scythian shepherd is really only the Cantabrigian Marlowe in fancy-dress."[4] Tying Marlowe to his life could also be directly negative, as when in *The Dramatist and the Received Idea: Studies in the Plays of Marlowe and Shakespeare* (1968), Wilbur Sanders, having dismissed "The serious limitations of Marlowe's conceptions of the human," suggested that

> It was known before the age of psychoanalysis that misanthropy was the uneasy bedfellow of self-contempt and guilt, and I am making no revolutionary proposal if I suggest that there is a strange congruency in

the fates of Edward, the dabbler in sodomy, and of Faustus, the religious sceptic, which might be accounted for as a neurotic desire for symbolic punishment and expiation.[5]

More recent criticism has tried to break away from these positions and read Marlowe's plays neither as crude manifestations of his psyche nor as sub-Shakespearean, but on their own terms as products of their cultural moment. Thus Emily Bartels finds an exciting, transgressive playwright whose "central characters include a Scythian barbarian, a black magician, a Machiavellian Maltese Jew, a homosexual king, and an African queen,"[6] while Sara Munson Deats speaks non-judgementally of "the discordant rebels thronging Marlowe's plays, challenging all conventional rubrics of sex, gender, and desire" and declares that "although I use the conventional terms 'feminine' and 'masculine' to discuss traditional gender stereotyping, I am implicitly placing these terms under erasure, employing these arbitrary designations in a historically accepted although not necessarily ontologically valid sense."[7]

In *The Cambridge Companion to Christopher Marlowe* (the first instance of a Companion devoted to Marlowe, but not necessarily the last), Patrick Cheney's "Introduction: Marlowe in the twenty-first century" presents its subject as the most urgent and contemporary of dramatists. Cheney argues that "Marlowe deserves to be placed at the forefront of any conversation about the rise of English republicanism, simply because he is the first Englishman to translate Lucan's counter-imperial epic"[8] (which is also, he might have added, the only classical epic not to use "machinery"—that is, direct intervention by the gods—and so lends itself to an atheist interpretation). Cheney also points to the originality of "Marlowe's centralized staging of two cultural topics now absorbing the world, the fate of Jews and the role of Islam," and suggests that indeed "Marlowe himself seems to have been fascinated by the idea of firstness."[9] Later in the same volume, Garrett Sullivan relates Marlowe to the intersection of geography and literature, in which much exciting work is currently being done, and suggests that "in his tragedies, and especially in *Tamburlaine*, Marlowe stages the collision between geographies new and old,"[10] while Kate Chedgzoy offers a way of approaching even what is possibly the least accessible of all Marlowe's plays when she argues that "*The Massacre at Paris* vividly illustrates the ways in which the relationships of elite men and women are caught up in the dynamics of power and social order."[11] Elsewhere, Leah Marcus declares that "many literary scholars have watched the unfolding of recent events in Afghanistan and Iraq with Marlowe on their minds,"[12] and suggests that after 9/11 Marlowe has come to the forefront as the playwright of the present.

There has also been much recent work on Marlowe's life, beginning with Charles Nicholl's magisterial *The Reckoning* and subsequently including the recent biographies by Constance Kuriyama and David Riggs as well as Roy Kendall's examination of the intertwining careers of Marlowe and his nemesis Richard Baines. In most of these works, though, the focus is very much on the life as distinct from the works rather than the life as a way to read the works. Marlowe and his plays have broken free from each other, and each faces an exciting future on their own.

Pedagogic strategies

Now that we have this new, more exciting Marlowe, then, how are we to teach him? There seem to me to be three main issues: teaching Marlowe alongside other playwrights (most obviously Shakespeare); ways of teaching more than just the "usual suspects" of *Doctor Faustus* and very occasionally *Tamburlaine the Great* or *Edward II*; and ways of making Marlowe accessible to students. In each case, my aim is to seek ways of enabling students to engage with the plays and formulate informed personal responses to them.

For the first, there are some very productive possible pairings of the two men's plays. Perhaps the most obvious of these is the pairing of *The Jew of Malta* with *The Merchant of Venice*, since both have Jewish heroes in Mediterranean settings whose daughters fall in love with Christians, and both, too, are generically uncertain. Slightly less obvious but certainly no less interesting is another possible pairing of *Edward II* with *Richard II*, two tragedies of kings of England to whom suspicions of homosexuality accrue. Finally, a perhaps even less obvious but certainly equally suggestive pairing is of *Doctor Faustus* with *Hamlet*. There are two particular points of interest here. In the first place, both plays have heroes educated at Wittenberg, and this allows for discussion of the impact of Luther and the Reformation in ways which can make the issues seem real and urgent rather than merely dry (see also the final section on *Doctor Faustus* and theology). Secondly, both these plays deploy the idea of the *translatio imperii*. This is something which is difficult for students to come to terms with because it is so remote from anything they likely to have encountered previously, but it is crucial to the understanding of Renaissance literature. In essence, the story of the *translatio imperii* (literally "the translation of empire") tells of the transfer of the cultural authority of ancient Troy first to Rome and then ultimately to England. It is transmitted through the descendants of Aeneas, who escaped the destruction of Troy and was told by the gods to found a new city. Initially, he settled in Carthage with Queen Dido, but on the orders of the gods he moved on, upon which the deserted Dido killed herself. Aeneas duly founded Rome, but two generations later his great-grandson Brutus had to leave the city after involuntarily killing his father, and came to a deserted island which he named Britain, after himself. This is, then, our story, and though there was scepticism in the Renaissance about its actual truth value, it continued to be held in great affection. Moreover, it was politically a very useful tool for dramatists, since their treatment of this story could reflect either support or indictment of the Tudor and Stuart rulers who claimed descent from Brutus through his supposed descendant King Arthur.

In *Hamlet*, this story is directly reflected on when Hamlet asks the Player King to repeat a part of "Aeneas' tale to Dido." Its presence is less obvious in *Doctor Faustus*, which is indeed not set in England at all, but the ultimate object of desire for Faustus is Helen, who was the cause of the Trojan War, and he himself proposes to be a new Paris and to sack Wittenberg. The question, then, would be: given that the presence of the *translatio imperii* story in plays often allows them to glance ironically at current politics and rulers, what might *Hamlet* and *Doctor Faustus* be saying in this respect?

There are also other, even less obvious possible pairings of Marlowe and Shakespeare plays, and these too can be fruitful, not least in that they offer a way of teaching some of the lesser-known Marlowe plays. Two other plays which address the idea of the *translatio imperii*, for instance, are *Dido, Queen of Carthage* and *The Tempest*, both of which are so heavily indebted to Virgil that they can almost be put side by side for comparison as translations or at least adaptations of the *Aeneid*. (Again, there is scope for a glance at contemporary politics here, since Dido's other name of Elissa is so close to "Eliza," by which Queen Elizabeth was often known.) Particularly useful questions for consideration here might be how Prospero compares with Aeneas or how Dido compares with Miranda, as well as the wider one of what both seem to have to say about England's view of itself as possessing an imperial destiny. *Dido, Queen of Carthage* can also be profitably compared with *Antony and Cleopatra*, since both focus on an African queen who is first wooed and then deserted by an adventurer intent on a Roman destiny. Finally, *Tamburlaine* and *Henry V* offer a very interesting pairing. Besieging Harfleur, Henry threatens that if its citizens continue to resist, he will treat them in exactly the same way that Tamburlaine would have done, allowing his men to burn, pillage, and rape. Do we really believe that he would in fact have carried out this threat? If we do, do we think better or worse of him for it? Does an emergent nation need a leader with the strength and ruthlessness of Tamburlaine, or does history, as the increasingly fashionable writings of Tacitus suggested, have ironies of its own which mean that ultimately the power of chance can always outweigh the doings of an individual?

It is not only with Shakespeare, however, that Marlowe can profitably be juxtaposed. As has often been pointed out, *Doctor Faustus* forms a very interesting pairing with Ford's *'Tis Pity She's a Whore*. Giovanni's Faustian rhetoric can help alert us to the fact that Giovanni wishes not just to love his sister, but also to acquire forbidden knowledge: "to know" often carried the overtones of "to know carnally," and Giovanni makes the link explicit when he explores the interior of his sister's body and removes her heart. The connections between knowledge, power, and the exotic are also something that can be usefully explored in connection with *Doctor Faustus*. What, ultimately, does Faustus want? Even the little-studied *Massacre at Paris*, which Wilbur Sanders dismissed with "how did Marlowe come to write this nasty piece of jingoistic bombast?" and condemned for "the terrible thinness of both drama and poetry,"[13] might start to look more accessible and more interesting alongside Chapman's *Bussy d'Ambois* and *The Revenge of Bussy d'Ambois*, which also treat of French history and recur to *Massacre*'s motif of the Guise's anger at his cuckolding.

It is not only other texts which can illuminate Marlowe's, though, but also contexts. I would suggest as particularly fruitful here the close chronological correspondence between *Doctor Faustus*, with its fantasies of American silver and recollections of "Indian Moors," and Hariot's *A briefe and true report of the new found land of Virginia*; the similarities between Marlowe's Edward II and James VI of Scotland; the ways in which Dido's status as unmarried queen desirous of a husband might recall both Elizabeth I and Mary, Queen of Scots; and the parallels between Tamburlaine's conquests and those which Elizabethans such as Sir Walter Ralegh were attempting in Ireland. My own specific choices for contextual material to be introduced to seminars (in the form of handouts which are physically given out and also made available via a Blackboard site) are as follows:

Tamburlaine the Great (taught over two weeks as separate plays)

i)   A chronology of the life of Timur the Lame, taken from Lisa Hopkins, *Christopher Marlowe: an Author Chronology* (Palgrave, pp. 10–12). It is my experience that students tend to know little about Timur, and may indeed even have assumed that he was entirely fictional; moreover, mapping out his life clearly shows that by the end of the first play, Marlowe had taken his hero to within two years of his death, and explains why he had to seek elsewhere for material to fill Part Two.

ii) Spenser on the Irish and the Scythians from *A View of the Present State of Ireland*.

iii) A chronology of Marlowe's own life, showing the Armada, and Philip Gawdy's description of the accident which occurred during the staging of *2 Tamburlaine*, and including the text of the Dutch Church Libel.

iv) An illustration from Abraham Ortelius's map of Asia in *Theatrum Orbis Terrarum*.

Questions to consider might include:

- To what extent does Tamburlaine conform to Spenser's ideas about Scythians? Are the Elizabethan campaigns in Ireland of any relevance to *Tamburlaine the Great*?
- How accurate is Marlowe's geography?
- Is Tamburlaine distinctively a creature of 1587?
- What has Marlowe kept in of the historical Timur, and what has he left out? What might have prompted these choices? Is there any incident or aspect which would have been particularly easy or difficult to stage in the Elizabethan theatre?

The Jew of Malta

i)   An excerpt from Machiavelli.

ii) A brief account of the history of the Knights of Malta and a chronology of the principal events of the 1565 Siege of Malta, including the fact that the Archbishop of Canterbury ordered prayers to be said in English churches.

iii) Passages from the Bible alluded to in the play, including the story of Barabbas.

iv) An account of Richard Baines's alleged plot to poison the well at Rheims.

Questions to consider might include:

- Why might Marlowe have chosen Malta as a setting?
- Does his play challenge or endorse contemporary views of Jews?

Doctor Faustus

i)   An excerpt from Thomas Hariot's *A briefe and true report of the new found land of Virginia.*

ii) The text of the Baines Note.

iii) A chronology of key dates in the textual history of the play.

Questions to consider might include:

- To what extent is the context of the New World relevant to this play?
- How does *Doctor Faustus* square with the idea of an atheist Marlowe?
- Does either version of the play seem more reliable to you?

Dido, Queen of Carthage

i)   An excerpt from Virgil describing Aeneas's first landfall in Africa.

ii) An excerpt from Lydgate illustrating the alternative history of Aeneas as a traitor.

iii) A panegyric poem addressing Elizabeth I as Eliza.

iv) A chronology of the events surrounding the Babington plot and the death of Mary, Queen of Scots.

v) Hakluyt's "Epistle Dedicatory to Sir Walter Ralegh" (1587).

Questions to consider might include:

- Is Aeneas hero or villain?
- Is the portrait of Dido satirical or sympathetic?
- What does this play say about queens?
- What does it say about the *translatio imperii*?
- What does it say about English aspirations to empire?

Edward II

i)   Holinshed's description of the king's murder.
ii) A chronology of events surrounding the relationship of James VI of Scotland and Esmé Stuart, Earl of Lennox.
iii) Comparative information on the Admiral's Men and the Earl of Pembroke's Men.

Questions to consider might include:

- Are *Edward II* and its hero qualitatively different from Marlowe's other plays and heroes?
- Elizabethan history plays are often perceived as political, and being as much about the present as the past. Is this true of *Edward II*?
- How sympathetically does Marlowe view same-sex love?

A Massacre at Paris

i)   The Collier Leaf.
ii) A chronology of English involvement in the affairs of Henri IV.
iii) A contemporary account of the St Bartholomew's Day Massacre.

Questions to consider might include:

- Can we make sense of this play?
- Is this a lost episode of *Blackadder*, or serious political commentary—or could it be both?

Doctor Faustus and theology

However much we may diversify into the rest of the Marlowe canon, *Doctor Faustus* will probably always lie at its heart. This play, which has been well termed the spiritual autobiography of an age, combines the formal features of the mediaeval morality play with the sense of spiritual doubt which will become perhaps the keynote of early modernity, and encapsulates arguably better than any other play of the period the sense of cultural indebtedness to Greece and Rome. It is also a play with a surprisingly simple premise and plot to which students are easily able to relate. Ironically, though, for all its strength and power, it is also a play that is unusually difficult to deal with in the classroom, not only because of the need to choose which of the two texts to teach but because an informed engagement with *Doctor Faustus* requires a grasp of the complexities of Renaissance theology. One way to grapple with both these issues is to focus on the crucial moment at which the Good Angel says, in the A-Text, that it is "Never too late, if Faustus can repent," and in the B-Text "Never too late, if Faustus will repent,"[14] for while the second of these leaves the door open for the possibility of human agency affecting individual salvation, the first takes the Calvinist line that the individual cannot choose to repent.

Notes

1. *Acts of the Privy Council*, VI, 29 June 1587.
2. *Acts of the Privy Council*, VI, 29 June 1587.
3. Harry Levin, *Christopher Marlowe: the Overreacher* (London: Faber and Faber, 1961), p. 43.
4. Danson, "Christopher Marlowe: the Questioner," p. 11.
5. Wilbur Sanders, *The Dramatist and the Received Idea: Studies in the Plays of Marlowe and Shakespeare* (Cambridge: Cambridge University Press, 1968), pp. 129, 140.
6. Emily C. Bartels, *Spectacles of Strangeness: Imperialism, Alienation, and Marlowe* (Philadelphia: University of Pennsylvania Press, 1993), p. 3.
7. Sara Munson Deats, *Sex, Gender, and Desire in the Plays of Christopher Marlowe* (Newark: University of Delaware Press, 1997), pp. 13, 15.
8. Patrick Cheney, "Introduction: Marlowe in the twenty-first century," in *The Cambridge Companion to Christopher Marlowe*, ed. Patrick Cheney, pp. 1–23 (Cambridge: Cambridge University Press, 2004), p. 15.
9. Cheney, "Introduction," p. 17.
10. Garrett A. Sullivan, Jr, "Geography and Identity in Marlowe," in *The Cambridge Companion to Christopher Marlowe*, pp. 231–44, p. 232.
11. Kate Chedgzoy, "Marlowe's men and women: gender and sexuality," in *The Cambridge Companion to Christopher Marlowe*, pp. 245–61, p. 246.
12. Leah Marcus, "Marlowe *in tempore belli*," in *War and Words: Horror and Heroism in the Literature of Warfare*, ed. Sara Munson Deats, Lagretta Tallent Lenker, and Merry G. Perry, pp. 295–316 (Lanham: Lexington Books), p. 295.
13. Sanders, *The Dramatist and the Received Idea*, pp. 22–3.
14. Christopher Marlowe, *Doctor Faustus*, ed. David Bevington and Eric Rasmussen (Manchester: Manchester University Press, 1993), A-Text II.iii.79, B-Text II.iii.80.

Selective guide to further reading and resources

Bartels, Emily C. *Spectacles of Strangeness: Imperialism, Alienation, and Marlowe.* Philadelphia: University of Pennsylvania Press, 1993.

Cheney, Patrick. *Marlowe's Counterfeit Profession.* Toronto: University of Toronto Press, 1997.

———. (ed.). *The Cambridge Companion to Christopher Marlowe.* Cambridge: Cambridge University Press, 2004.

Deats, Sara M. *Sex, Gender, and Desire in the Plays of Christopher Marlowe.* Newark: University of Delaware Press, 1997.

DiGangi, Mario. *The Homoerotics of Early Modern Drama.* Cambridge: Cambridge University Press, 1997.

Hiscock, Andrew. *The Uses of This World: Thinking Space in Shakespeare, Marlowe, Cary and Jonson.* Cardiff: University of Wales Press, 2004.

Hopkins, Lisa. *Christopher Marlowe: a Literary Life.* Basingstoke: Palgrave–now Palgrave Macmillan, 2000.

Kuriyama, Constance B. *Christopher Marlowe: a Renaissance Life*. Ithaca: Cornell University Press, 2002.

Marcus, Leah. *Unediting the Renaissance: Shakespeare, Marlowe, Milton*. London: Routledge, 1996.

————. "Marlowe *in tempore belli*," in *War and Words: Horror and Heroism in the Literature of Warfare*, ed. Sara Munson Deats, Lagretta Tallent Lenker, and Merry G. Perry, pp. 295–316. Lanham: Lexington Books, 2004.

Nicholl, Charles. *The Reckoning*. London: Jonathan Cape, 1992.

Riggs, David. *The World of Christopher Marlowe*. London: Faber and Faber, 2004.

Spenser, Edmund. *A View of the State of Ireland*, ed. Andrew Hadfield and Willy Maley. Oxford: Blackwell, 1997.

Web resources

The Baines Note is available at
  <http://www.wwnorton.com/college/english/nael/16century/topic%5F1/baines.htm>

The Complete Works are available at the Perseus Project's site:
  <http://www.perseus.tufts.edu/Texts/Marlowe.html>

Thomas Hariot's *A briefe and true report of the new found land of Virginia* (1588)
  Online: <http://www.people.virginia.edu/~msk5d/hariot/1588/1588titl.html>

Holinshed on the death of Edward II is available at
  <http://www.routledge.com/textbooks/0415187346/companiontext/pdf/edwardII1.pdf>

Anniina Jokinen's excellent Luminarium site on Marlowe is at
  <http://www.luminarium.org/renlit/marlowe.htm>

The Literary Encylopedia's Marlowe entry is accessible from
  <http://www.litencyc.com/>

An illustrated account of the Siege of Malta with particular reference to Marlowe can be found in Lisa Hopkins, "'Malta of Gold': Marlowe, *The Jew of Malta*, and the Siege of 1565," *(Re)Soundings* 1, 2 (June 1997).
  <http://www.millersv.edu/~resound/*vol1iss2/topframe.html>

A good introduction to the question of the two texts of *Doctor Faustus* is Andrew Duxfield, "Modern Problems in Editing and the Two Texts of Marlowe's *Doctor Faustus*," *Literature Compass*, <http://www.literature-compass.com/section.asp?section=2>

Freely accessibly articles in refereed electronic journals include Lisa Hopkins, "'And shall I die, and this unconquered': Marlowe's inverse colonialism," *Early Modern Literary Studies* 2, 2 (August, 1996):
  <http://www.shu.ac.uk/emls/02-2/hopkmarl. html>, and Dennis Kay, "Marlowe, *Edward II*, and the Cult of Elizabeth," *Early Modern Literary Studies* 3, 2 (September 1997): <http://www.shu.ac.uk/emls/03-2/ kaymarl.html>; David Webb, " 'Pageants Truly Played': Self-dramatization and natural character in *The Jew of Malta*," *Renaissance Forum* 5, 1 (2000):
  <http://www.hull.ac.uk/renforum/v5no1/webb.htm>

William Perkins's chart on salvation can be found at
  <http://members.aol.com/Graceordained/predchrt.html>; see also
  <http://www.apuritansmind.com/WilliamPerkins/PerkinsGoldenChainChart.htm>

Health warning

Alongside the many scholarly websites devoted to Marlowe and Renaissance drama there are some less reliable ones. One good guide is the URL: anything with an .edu or an ac.uk suffix, denoting American and British universities respectively, ought to be safe. However, beware of anything which seeks to persuade you that Marlowe was Shakespeare—there is no evidence worth the name for this theory.

4

Shakespeare: the Tragedies

Andrew Hiscock

Chronology

1564	Born Stratford-upon-Avon, Warwickshire to John Shakespeare and Mary Arden. Baptized 26 April.
1567	First purpose-built playhouse in Britain since Roman times constructed in north-east London—entitled *The Red Lion*.
1582	Married Anne Hathaway.
1583	Birth of daughter, Susanna.
1585	Birth of twins, Hamnet and Judith.
late 1580s	Arrival in London. Possible associations with companies of Lord Strange's Men and the Earl of Pembroke's Men until 1594.
1590–94	*Henry VI* plays, *The Two Gentlemen of Verona*, *Richard III*, *The Comedy of Errors*, *Titus Andronicus*, *The Taming of the Shrew*, *Love's Labours Lost*, part revisions of *Sir Thomas More*.
1592	Scorned in Robert Greene's *A Groats-worth of Wit* as an "upstart crow" who "is in his own conceit the only Shake-scene in a country."
1593	*Venus and Adonis*.
1594	*The Rape of Lucrece*.
1595	Named in accounts of the Treasurer of the Royal Chamber as member of Lord Chamberlain's Men for court performances in previous year.
1595–99	*Richard II*, *Romeo and Juliet*, *Midsummer Night's Dream*, *King John*, *The Merchant of Venice*, *Henry IV* plays, *The Merry Wives of Windsor*, *Much Ado About Nothing*, *Henry V*, *Julius Caesar*, *As You Like It*.
1596	Death of son Hamnet.
1597	Purchases New Place in Stratford.
1598	Francis Meres refers to "mellifluous and honey-tongued Shakespeare" in *Palladis Tamia*. Acted in Jonson's *Every Man in His Humor*.

1599	Lord Chamberlain's Men move to Globe on the South Bank. Capitalizing on Shakespeare's reputation, London publisher William Jaggard brings out the poetry collection *The Passionate Pilgrim* with Shakespeare's name attached to it—only five poems are verifiably by Shakespeare.
1600–6	"The Phoenix and the Turtle," *Twelfth Night, Hamlet, Troilus and Cressida, Measure for Measure, Othello, All's Well That Ends Well, King Lear, Macbeth, Antony and Cleopatra.*
1603	Lord Chamberlain's Men become The King's Men.
1604	Shakespeare and other principal members of the company recorded as Grooms of the Royal Chamber in accounts of Master of the Wardrobe.
1607–13	*Coriolanus, Timon of Athens, Pericles, Sonnets* and "A Lover's Complaint," *Cymbeline, The Winter's Tale, The Tempest.* With John Fletcher: *Cardenio, All is True or Henry VIII, The Two Noble Kinsmen.*
1608	The King's Men sign a 21-year lease for the use of indoor Blackfriars theatre.
1613	Purchase of a house in Blackfriars area. Globe Theatre burns down during a performance of *Henry VIII*. Ceases writing plays for the King's Men.
1616	Died.
1623	Publication of 1st Folio. Death of Anne Shakespeare (née Hathaway).

Critical overview

Any account of the history of scholarship on Shakespearean tragedies must necessarily be highly selective as they have served down the centuries as one of the most popular textual spaces in which to conduct critical thinking—and indeed to carve out one's name as a critic. Nonetheless, I have endeavoured within the periodizations of "1590–1790," "1790–1900" and "1900 to the Present Day" to offer a concise discussion of some of the major critical contributions to this field which complements the outline given in the above chronology and the bibliography at the end of this chapter.

1590–1790

During Shakespeare's own lifetime there is evidence of a growing recognition of his talents as a tragic dramatist. Whilst Greene had dismissed him in general terms as an "upstart crow," the normally irascible Gabriel Harvey acknowledged that *Hamlet* and *The Rape of Lucrece* were pleasing "the wiser sort" of Elizabethan. In his commonplace book *Palladis Tamia* (1598), Francis Meres insisted that "as *Plautus* and *Seneca* are accounted best for Comedy and Tragedy among the Latins so Shakespeare among the English is the most excellent in both kinds for the stage"—highlighting (*faute de mieux* in 1598) *Titus Andronicus* and *Romeo and Juliet* for praise. This emphasis upon Shakespeare's place amongst the classical masters would resurface notably in Ben Jonson's dedicatory elegy in the 1623 Folio: ". . . Leave thee alone, for the comparison / Of all, that insolent Greece, or haughty Rome." In his commonplace book *Timber, or Discoveries* and in his recorded conversations with Drummond of Hawthornden Jonson was nevertheless rather more sparing in his praise. He observed, for example, with reference to *Julius Caesar*, that "Many times [Shakespeare] fell into those things, could not escape laughter: As when hee said in the person of *Caesar . . . Caesar did never wrong, but with just cause*: and such like; which were ridiculous. But hee redeemed his vices, with his vertues."[1]

Whilst Meres had grouped history plays under the heading of tragedy, when the 1623 Folio was published the history play was dignified with its own category whereas *Timon of Athens* and *Cymbeline* were included in the roll call of tragedies. *Troilus and Cressida* was sandwiched (unannounced in the preliminary "Catalogue" page) between the last history and the first tragedy in the volume. In the Restoration the taste for Shakespearean tragedy continued undimmed and plays like *Othello* enjoyed particular popularity. Nonetheless, much attention was devoted by critics and playwrights alike to the structural and thematic "irregularities" of the plays. Such concerns were pondered at length in Dryden's *Essay of Dramatic Poesie* (1668), for example, and earned Shakespeare biting criticism in Thomas Rymer's *A Short View of Tragedy* (1692). One remedy presented itself to contemporaries in the shape of rewriting the plays in accordance with neo-classical principles so that they observed the "unities" and did not violate the *bienséances*. With this aim in mind, Dryden's *All for Love* (1677) reshaped *Antony and Cleopatra*, Edward Ravenscroft offered a more "regular" *Titus Andronicus, Or the Rape of Lavinia* (1687), but most famously perhaps Nahum Tate's *The History of King Lear* (1681) concluded with Edgar's marriage to Cordelia and Lear exiting with the prospect of the "nursery" of retirement that he had been seeking for five acts.

Many of the most strategic interventions in the criticism of the tragedies in the eighteenth century came in the form of prefatory material to new editions of Shakespeare. Nicholas Rowe's edition (1709–10) sought to turn attention away from a faulty neo-classicist playwright to one who was nourished under "the mere light of nature." Rowe was also one of the first scholars to point up the enormous cross-fertilization of genres in Shakespeare's works and thus to problematize further issues of dramatic taxonomy. Alexander Pope's 1725 edition of Shakespeare continued to exonerate him of any suspicion of impropriety of diction or plotting and reserved particular praise for his matchless characterization. Samuel Johnson's annotated edition appeared in 1765 and his sensitive and deeply reflective discussions remain some of the richest sources of early criticism on the tragedies. Although he affirms that "in tragedy [Shakespeare's] performance seems constantly to be worse, as his labour is more," he hailed his drama's achievement as a whole and dismissed the neo-classical objections of earlier critics: "There is no reason why a mind thus wandering in extasy should count the clock, or why an hour should not be a century in that calenture of the brain that can make the stage a field."[2] However, he did confess that "I was many years ago so shocked by Cordelia's death, that I know not whether I ever endured to read again the last scenes of the play till I undertook to revise them as an editor."[3] In his comments upon individual plays Johnson is suitably impressed by "the fiery openness of Othello, magnanimous, artless, and credulous," but with reference to the development of the "universally celebrated" Brutus–Cassius relationship in *Julius Caesar* he had "never been strongly agitated in perusing it, and [thought] it somewhat cold and unaffecting." *Macbeth* was found to have "solemnity, grandeur, and variety" of action, but "perhaps overstocked with personages." However, most intriguingly, Jonson revealed an eye for Molièresque comic structures, affirming "the tragedy of *Coriolanus* [to be] one of the most amusing of our authour's performances."[4]

Interestingly, whilst Milton's status as a European writer of note was established by this period, Shakespeare still had considerable ground to cover to gain widespread appreciation. In this context, Voltaire's experience is significant as one of the earliest instances of an eminent European intellectual recording his responses to Shakespearean drama. During his stay in England in the 1720s he had attended performances of some of the plays. He acknowledged in his essays the enormous fertility of Shakespeare's mind but became increasingly disconcerted by his "barbaric" and "vulgar" disregard for dramatic propriety. As a consequence, the plays resemble the curate's egg—being only good in parts. Voltaire came round increasingly to the conclusion that Shakespeare had lived in an intellectual climate with little or no understanding of aesthetic taste. Nonetheless, more unreserved and indeed enthusiastic praise would be forthcoming in the new century from figures such as Pushkin, Goethe, Victor Hugo, and Schlegel, hailing what they considered to be the incomparable "genius" of the English dramatist for representing the emotional and intellectual life of the human mind.

1790–1900

Productions of Shakespeare's tragedies attracted increasing attention and often served as showcases for the acting talents of the most eminent actors of the age throughout the eighteenth and nineteenth centuries. However, the growing emphases on virtuouso performances by leading actors, extravagant acting styles and appetites for visual grandeur in the theatres often led critics from Charles Lamb to Henry James to question the viability of staging Shakespearean drama in a satisfactory manner for contemporary audiences. As Keats's "On sitting down to read *King Lear* once again" indicates, some of the most notable recorded experiences of the tragedies for many writers and critics in this period were frequently as readers rather than spectators. In

"On the tragedies of Shakespeare . . ." (1811) Lamb remained unconvinced about their performability for it was only the reader, it seems, who could ponder the intricacies of the inner lives of Shakespeare's heroes which were the texts' dominant interests. This focus on sympathetic enquiry into the crisis-ridden mind of the protagonist was also shared by De Quincy in his essay "On the Knocking at the Gate in *Macbeth*" (1823). However, Coleridge is distinctive for the time and energy he devoted to Shakespeare (and especially the tragedies) in his notes and lectures in this period. Apart from challenging the neo-classical criticisms of earlier generations, he was most attentive to the persuasiveness of Shakespeare's "instinctive" powers of characterization (the "motiveless malignity" of Iago, Lear's "feeble selfishness, self-supportless and leaning for all pleasure on another's breast") which stimulate thorough reader engagement. However, he also emphasized the moral and intellectual enquiries at work in the dramas: "*Hamlet* was the play, or rather Hamlet himself was the character in the intuition and exposition of which I first made my turn for philosophical criticism . . ."[5] Like many of his contemporaries, William Hazlitt in *Characters of Shakespear's Plays* (1817) did not envisage the plays primarily in terms of theatrical performance but as the work of a superior intelligence ("the great distinction of Shakespeare's genius was its virtually including the genius of all the great men of his age")[6] and he is frequently found to concentrate upon the ways in which the reader is drawn to enter imaginatively the consciousness of Shakespeare's characters: "(Hamlet's thoughts) are as real as our own thoughts. Their reality is in the reader's mind. It is *we* who are Hamlet."[7]

In the Victorian age, the cult of the Bard (or "bardolatry" as it would later be reviled by Shaw) grew in increasing strength, focusing upon a celebration of his life and times. He emerged as a fount of all wisdom for figures such as Thomas Carlyle, Alfred Tennyson, and Matthew Arnold and many critical endeavours focused in this period upon the deciphering the mysteries of his biography and linking these investigations to the "evolution" of the dramatist's career. The spawning of a host of Shakespeare societies brought with it an appetite for encyclopaedic annotation and freer access to his work: the result was a proliferation of concordances, bibliographies, and dictionaries in addition to scholarly editions of the plays from the 1860s onwards in the shape of the Cambridge Shakespeare and the Clarendon Shakespeare series, for example. Edward Dowden's enormously popular *Shakspere: a Critical Study of His Mind and Art* (1875) stands out as one of the period's most enduring contributions: this was a celebratory study which mapped out the plays in terms of the dramatist's maturing career and "mind." As far as the tragedies were concerned, the bard was seen by Dowden to take his reader forward into daunting areas of philosophical enigma and spiritual interrogation: "Tragedy as conceived by Shakespeare is concerned with the ruin or the restoration of the soul, and of the life of men. In other words its subject is the struggle of good and evil in the world . . . There are certain problems which

Shakespeare at once pronounces insoluble. He does not, like Milton, propose to give an account of the origin of evil."[8]

1900 to the present day

Professor of Poetry at Oxford University in the early years of the twentieth century, A. C. Bradley had a series of his lectures published in 1904 as *Shakespearean Tragedy*. This landmark study remains in print and whatever the level of criticism it has provoked in the responses of subsequent generations of scholars, it has remained one of the most commented upon studies in this field. Approaching Shakespeare's "pure" tragedies of *Macbeth*, *King Lear*, *Othello* and *Hamlet* as if they resembled George Eliot's novels more than texts for theatrical performance, Bradley locates the heart of their critical interest in conflicts of character (rather than plot) and encourages his readers forward into the worlds of tragedy, inviting us to articulate our engagement both in terms of sympathy and judgement. Interestingly, it was only in the later decades of the century that scholars would be willing to widen their enquiries into Shakespearean tragedy substantially beyond Bradley's chosen texts to anything like the multifarious grouping proposed in the First Folio. The dominant pattern in Shakespeare scholarship in general has been characterized by the resistance of individuals and critical schools to prevailing schemes of received thinking about the works—and Bradley is no exception to this rule. Rather than assenting to the previous century's veneration of the Bard as a "natural" genius who had almost supernatural access to all human knowledge and as a philosopher who forces upon us all manner of enigmatic meditations, Bradley was keen to observe how the texts were carefully and strategically shaped to engage the reader in intelligent investigation. Well-versed in Hegelian modes of analysis, he probed with detailed analysis (and speculation, on occasions) the ways in which the dramatization of the protagonists' cycles of experience encouraged readers to explore larger ethical dilemmas.

Ernest Jones's *Hamlet and Oedipus* (1910) underwent numerous revisions by him during the first half of the twentieth century but it has remained popular as the first notable analysis of a Shakespearean tragedy using the resources of Freudian thinking. Training attention upon the prince as a psychologically coherent entity, Jones prosecutes a central thesis that the hero's crisis is centred on the fact that Claudius's actions fulfil his own Oedipal ambitions to destroy his father. The lead given by Jones in psychoanalytical criticism of a Shakespearean tragedy would be taken up enthusiastically by many critics in the last quarter of the century. T. S. Eliot's most celebrated encounter in print with Shakespearean tragedy was his essay on *Hamlet* in which he found the unwieldy text could not be resolved into a satisfying unity of purpose and direction because the audience was forced too often to ponder the fault-lines in the dramatic narrative, most importantly the sketchiness of Gertrude's characterization. In his other considerations of the tragedies he is notable in wishing to position them not in terms of character but in terms of the intellectual climate in which they were produced. In such works as *Othello: an Historical and Comparative Study* (1915), *Hamlet: an Historical and Comparative Study* (1919), *Art and Artifice in Shakespeare* (1933), E. E. Stoll took into account questions of genre and staging and argued, like Levin Schücking (*Character Problems in Shakespeare's Plays* [1917, trans. 1922] and *The Meaning of Hamlet* [1937]), that character should be considered firmly in the context of the acting conventions and the appetites for theatrical effect of the time.

However, it was only in the 1930s that the scholarly analysis of Shakespeare's tragedies began to depart in any real sense from an obsession with character. Critics like John Dover Wilson (most famously in his *What Happens in Hamlet* [1935]) maintained an emphasis upon the *minutiae* of character analysis; and from 1927 onwards, for example, the theatre producer Harley Granville-Barker was publishing his prefaces to Shakespeare's plays in different formats, arguing that "we have still much to learn about Shakespeare the playwright . . . scholars . . . have been apt to divorce their Shakespeare from the theatre altogether."[9] He maintained an enthusiasm for character analysis allied with a particular sensitivity to staging: "Let the actor [of Brutus] be wary . . . let him see that he does not compete with Cassius [in this scene]."[10] Nonetheless, elsewhere a need was being articulated for a rather different approach. Caroline Spurgeon's *Shakespeare's Imagery and What It Tells Us* (1935), for example, brought together earlier studies in which she had traced underlying patterns and clusters in figurative language in selected texts (disease imagery in *Hamlet*, for example) and how these had an impact on our experience of the play's evocations of setting and mood changes. (Later critics such as Wolfgang Clemen in *The Development of Shakespeare's Imagery* [1951] were clearly indebted to Spurgeon's important scholarship but he chose to stress that a study of the play's figurative language should act as a stepping stone into a consideration of the play as a whole rather than dismantling it into strata of verbal textures.) With works such as *The Wheel of Fire* (1930), *The Imperial Theme* (1931) and *The Crown of Life* (1947), G. Wilson Knight also concentrated upon the "larger pattern" of the plays and was to have a tangible influence upon the ways in which Shakespeare's tragedies, amongst others, were appreciated by post-war audiences. Paying particular attention to symbolic and mystical resonances in the texts, Wilson Knight pursued a largely unhistoricized but often very energetic analysis of the texts in terms of moral allegory, spiritual cycles of sacrifice, damnation and redemption, and themes of human transcendence—this often led him into the realm of viewing the plays as mystical visions and/or "mood" pieces, as in the case of his discussion of the "Othello music." One of his most lasting legacies for succeeding critics was the problematizing of the heroic with his promotion of Hamlet as a "dark and dangerous force," the "free-hearted" Antony with his "thriftless pleasures," and the "eroticism" of

Rome in *Julius Caesar*, for example.[11] Another was his important contribution in focusing critical interest upon hitherto neglected plays such as *Coriolanus*, *Troilus and Cressida* and *Timon of Athens*.

At the beginning of the 1930s, the Cambridge critics such as F. R. Leavis, Q. D. Leavis, L. C. Knights, D. A. Traversi, and others, who were closely involved with *Scrutiny*, were also resisting the character-based criticism synonymous with the Bradley era—famously, as one of the opening salvos, Knights published in 1933 his pamphlet "How Many Children Had Lady Macbeth?" Turning to the plays now as "dramatic poems," these critics pursued a rather nostalgic mode of textual analysis which concentrated not on authorial intention or character motivation but upon "organic" thematic development and figurative language which fed the "larger" expression of human emotion and "felt" experience. An active socialist, Knights was distinctive for impressing upon his readers the economic and social environment of playmaking in the early modern period, but elsewhere in the group the critical emphasis was frequently upon the verbal textures of the plays. Eager to return attention to the theatricality of Shakespeare's texts and the developing tradition of early modern drama, critics such as M. C. Bradbrook in *Themes and Conventions of Elizabethan Tragedy* (1935) and William Farnham in *The Medieval Heritage of Elizabethan Tragedy* (1936) expressed a marked resistance to viewing the plays as "dramatic poems." (A similar emphasis would be in evidence in a number of post-war studies such as Herbert Joseph Muller's *The Spirit of Tragedy* [1956] and M. R. Margeson's *The Origins of English Tragedy* [1967].) In *Shakespeare's Tragic Heroes: Slaves of Passion* (1930), Lily Bess Campbell made an ambitious attempt to historicize the tragedies by exploring early modern genre expectations in moral, didactic, and political terms. She furnished her readers with insights into the early modern schemes of thinking in the areas of cosmology, psychology, theology, medical theory, and classical influence and only then turned to studies of the plays themselves: ". . . if *Hamlet* is read against a background of contemporary philosophy, it will come to life as a study of passion."[12]

The "New Criticism," which aimed to counteract critical emphases on biographical narrative, historical contextualization, and philological study, came to dominate textual analysis in schools and universities in the English-speaking world in the post-war period until the mid-1970s. This approach had began to become established before the war and was particularly associated with figures such as Cleanth Brooks, John Crowe Ransom, and Robert Penn Warren; and in Britain I. A. Richards did much to further an analogous programme of close reading which sought to pay attention solely to the form, structure, rhetorical strategies, and figurative languages of a given text. Influenced by Modernist commitments, these critics aimed at "objective" critical praxis and whilst lyrics were often their favoured quarry, Shakespeare's tragedies did enter the frame on occasions. Spurred on by the work of Spurgeon amongst others, Brooks in *The Well-Wrought Urn* (1947) explored the organic unity of selected texts through close attention to their figurative motifs and included one discussion on *Macbeth* which concentrated upon the structural implications of the recurring motifs (infancy and clothes) in its imagery. The idiosyncratic William Empson resisted the label "New Critic," but his attention to detailed textual analysis, semantics, and aporia means that he often shared similar goals to the New Critics. Like M. M. Mahood's later *Shakespeare's Wordplay* (1957), his landmark study *Seven Types of Ambiguity* (1930) was enormously influential upon post-structuralist critics in the final decades of the century. Empson's close reading of the implications of rhetorical strategies of punning, irony, paradox, analogy, antithesis, and so on clearly looks forward to the work of later post-structuralist critics seeking to expose the problems of linguistic indeterminacy and textual crises of interpretation at work in Shakespearean drama.

However, the analytic models promoted by the "New Criticism" were resisted in some corners even during its ascendancy. Like Bradley's *Shakespearean Tragedy*, E. M. W. Tillyard's highly selective historicist study *The Shakespearean World Picture* has been much criticized by subsequent generations of readers but it remains a strategic referent for those working in the field. Its promotion of a conservative Shakespeare obsessively promoting the interests of a rigorously hierarchized social order and riddled with anxieties over the possible crumbling of the political *status quo* was widely read decades after its first publication and shaped for many in the post-war period the ways in which Shakespeare's tragic writing was understood. Clearly influenced by research into theatrical conventions and stage history conducted by critics like Bradbrook before the war, Anne Righter (Barton) explored issues of early modern authorship and most specifically that of the dramatist in *Shakespeare and the Idea of the Play* (1962). The Canadian critic Northrop Frye ranged across narrative modes and time periods in the endeavour to highlight archetypal narratives and their relations to the development of dramatic genre. Frye spent much more time focusing upon the Shakespearean genres of comedy and romance than the more "individualizing" tragedy, but in his *Fools of Time: Studies in Shakespearean Tragedy* (1967) he continued to turn critical attention away from character and rhetoric to "kinds" of plot: this led him to identify in the tragedies permutations of an *agon* focused on the superhuman hero and animated by forces of order, seduction, and resistance.

Responding keenly to European movements of existentialism, absurdism, and Artaud's theatre of cruelty along with the political climate engendered by totalitarianism in Cold-War Europe, Jan Kott's *Shakespeare Our Contemporary* (1964, first published in French) became an enormously influential analysis of Shakespearean tragic and historical writing in terms of its representation of political power mechanisms and its enquiries into the implications of state violence and social hierarchy. In Kott's vision, Shakespeare's fascination with brutality and victimization rendered him a worthy forefather to Brecht and Beckett. Politicizing the drama in a rather different manner, Leslie Fiedler's *The Stranger in Shakespeare* (1972) was clearly influenced by Jungian and earlier Shakespearean archetypal or mythopoeic criticism as expressed in the work of Wilson Knight and Frye. With its interest in the textual productions of (racial, sexual, and social) alienation and cultural violation in dramas such as *Othello*, it clearly looks forward to the work of post-colonial critics at the end of the century.

Seeking to challenge Tillyard's emphasis upon literary foreground and historical background and profoundly influenced by the thinking of Michel Foucault, Stephen Greenblatt emerged after the publication of *Renaissance Self-Fashioning* (1988) as a presiding force over a growing critical movement which sought to reintegrate hitherto "literary" early modern texts into the wider print culture of the sixteenth and seventeenth centuries and to attend to the specificities of cultural discourses (past and present) which control our enquiries into an "alien" early modern past. His publications and those of his fellow critics (for example, Louis Montrose, Leonard Tennenhouse, Stephen Orgel, Steven Mullaney) renegotiated the terms in which works such as Shakespeare's tragedies were to be understood. Readers were asked to interrogate vigorously the possibility of human agency and to ponder the ways in which subjects and indeed practices such as playmaking might be shaped by and respond to institutionalized discourses of power. A perceived unwillingness amongst New Historicist critics to envisage cultural power in terms other than those of remorseless oppression and containment inevitably generated dissent in some quarters. In Britain, figures such as Jonathan Dollimore, Alan Sinfield, and Catherine Belsey combined an understanding of Foucault with a much greater emphasis upon the inheritances of Marxist thinking. They became associated with the label of Cultural Materialism—which had been a term first coined by Raymond Williams. These critics shared the New Historicists' commitment to reverse the academic privileging of the "literary" text for study and to politicize our understanding of such works as Shakespeare's tragedies by inscribing them in a host of cultural narratives (concerning rank, economics, gender, education, patronage and government, for example). However, they also wished to expose the ways in which human and textual agency might be constituted through the resisting, interrogating and rescripting of the experience of cultural power.

Studies such as Dollimore's *Radical Tragedy* (1984), Dollimore and Sinfield's *Political Shakespeare* (1985), *Alternative Shakespeares* (1985) edited by John Drakakis and Catherine Belsey's *The Subject of Tragedy* all in their different ways sought: to debunk cultural appetites for trans-historical literature and political doctrine; to ponder the ideological pressures at work in early modern literature (often in terms of the cultural markers of gender, class, work, religion, and community); and to consider the multifarious ways in which cultural power may be produced. For these critics, the production of subjectivity in the tragedies was perceived as a site (rather than an effect) of cultural pressure points where competing discourses of power could be analysed. Although not associated with the project of Cultural Materialism in this period, another British critic, Terry Eagleton, also positioned Marxist thinking centrally in his analyses of the plays in *William Shakespeare* (1986). In this study Eagleton concentrated predominantly upon dramatic narrative as a response to early modern crises of economic transition: a decaying feudalism giving way to a more energetic proto-capitalist economy. The foregrounding of Marxist thinking in Shakespearean analysis also characterizes later studies such as Ivo Kamps's *Shakespeare Left and Right* (1991), *Shakespeare and Gender: a History*, which he co-edited with Deborah Barker (1995), and Victor Kiernan's *Eight Tragedies of Shakespeare: a Marxist Study* (1996).

Feminist and gender-based criticism has remained one of the liveliest and most popular areas of criticism on Shakespeare's tragedies in recent decades. A concern with elisions in literary and historical narratives, with gender stereotyping and cultural theorizing, with critical neglect and omission, with early modern practices of anatomy, medicine, law and inheritance, government, education, labour, leisure, authorship, and performance and so on— all these considerations have preoccupied feminist and gender-based scholarship and have certainly enormously revised the encounters of students and audiences with Shakespeare's tragedies in recent decades. An optimistic Juliet Dusinberre in *Shakespeare and the Nature of Women* (1975) championed a progressive bard who was "feminist in sympathy." However, this view was unsurprisingly challenged by subsequent critics. Whilst much research in the 1970s and early 1980s was devoted to images-of-women in the tragedies (most especially Ophelia and Gertrude) frequently in terms of (ahistorical) schemes of gender expectation, there were studies such as Linda Bamber's *Comic Women, Tragic Men: a Study of Gender and Genre in Shakespeare* (1982) which embraced considerations of narrative mode—in this instance, however, the binary organization of Bamber's discussions often served to reinforce the very essentialist oppositions she was seeking to attack. Elsewhere, Madelon Sprengnether in "Annihilating Intimacy in *Coriolanus*" (1986), for example, argued that a major axis around which to consider generic questions of tragedy was the discourse of gender. Feminist and gender critics such as Coppélia Kahn (*Man's Estate: Masculine Identity in Shakespeare* [1981]), Peter Erickson (*Patriarchal Structures in Shakespeare* [1985]), Karen Newman (*Fashioning Femininity and English Renaissance Drama* [1991]) and Philippa Berry (*Shakespeare's Feminine Endings: Disfiguring Death in the Tragedies* [1999]) turned attention away from a fixation with character towards larger discursive questions of gender and cultural organization, exploring the ways in which these codes: pointed to the radical instability of selfhood in the early modern period; shaped performances of subjectivity as the plays unfolded; and urged many characters on into quests for cultural power. Studies such as Lisa Jardine's *Still Harping on Daughters* (1989), Stephen Orgel's

Impersonations: the Performance of Gender in Shakespeare's England (1996) and Bruce R. Smith's *Shakespeare and Masculinity* (2000) examined a wide selection of early modern documents, paying particular attention to the ways in which contemporary accounts of theatre staging and the cultural performance of gendered identities may enrich our understanding of Shakespearean drama. In "The Patriarchal Bard: Feminist Criticism and Shakespeare (*King Lear* and *Measure for Measure*)" (1985), Kathleen McLuskie encouraged her readers to consider discourses of gender expectation in Shakespearean drama within the much larger cultural system of patriarchal control of ideological representation and relations of power in the early modern period. (More recently in "Beyond Shakespearean Exceptionalism," Barbara Bowen has bemoaned the isolationism of academic studies of Shakespeare which unhelpfully maintains the heroic status of the bard and frequently fails to consider women writers "seriously as producers of knowledge.")[13]

Responding most particularly to feminist and cultural materialist scholarship, post-colonial critics have urged readers and audiences to reflect upon the cultural markers of race, nation, and identity as they are deployed in early modern literature. Ania Loomba, Anthony Barthelemy, Kim F. Hall, John Gillies, Margo Hendricks, Dympna Callaghan, Jack D'Amico, and Imitiaz Habib, for example, have all concentrated on early modern discourses of geographical otherness and inevitably (amongst the plays under consideration in this section) *Othello* and *Titus Andronicus* are afforded particular attention. In direct comparison with some of the research by Cultural Materialists, particular interest is reserved by these critics for the ways in which Shakespeare's texts are mediated through the modern educational system. Many of their studies, such as Loomba's *Gender, Race and Renaissance Drama* (1989), Barthelemy's *Black Face, Maligned Race* (1987), Hendricks and Patricia Parker's collection *Women, "Race," and Writing in the Early Modern Period* (1994) and Hall's *Things of Darkness. Economies of Race and Gender in Early Modern England* (1994), chart the ways in which value systems surrounding race and nation, for example, are renegotiated within and across early modern dramatic texts. In addition, these critics also frequently consider the continuities and discontinuities between cultural perceptions of identity politics across geographical and chronological divides.

In terms of psychoanalytic criticism, the critical field is very diverse and was surveyed as a tradition of scholarly activity relatively early by Norman Holland in *Psychoanalysis and Shakespeare* (1964); and then given a critical update, for example, in the collection *Representing Shakespeare: New Psychoanalytic Essays* (1980) edited by Murray Schwartz and Coppélia Kahn. Much of the research in this area is unsurprisingly anchored around a belief in the psychological intelligibility of the Shakespearean character and in the strategic importance of considering the formative environment of the dramatized subjectivity and the "psychic" drama embodied in language. Kay Stockholder's *Dream Works. Lovers and Families in Shakespeare's Plays* (1987) was eager to consider elements of dramatic narrative in terms of psychic projection and fraught quests of wish fulfilment; whereas Stanley Cavell's *Disowning Knowledge in Six Plays of Shakespeare* (1987) resurrected to a degree the image of Shakespeare as the philosopher-poet, but attends particularly to the language of erotic metaphor and the sexualizing of power relationships in his plays. Marjorie Garber's *Shakespeare's Ghost Writers* (1987) also privileged the study of symbolic discourses of sexual metaphor and the body in order to reflect upon Shakespearean drama in the light of Freudian psychoanalysis. More recently, Janet Adelman, in *Suffocating Mothers: Fantasies of Maternal Origin in Shakespeare's Plays, Hamlet to The Tempest* (1992), has focused upon the political and psychological pressures surrounding the family as a formative environment for the human subject, highlighting in this instance the cultural elisions and the fantasies of desire linked with mothering narratives in Shakespeare's Jacobean plays.

Finally, another expanding area of research considering Shakespeare's tragic writing is that of performance criticism. Often clearly influenced by earlier scholarship conducted by theatre historians and drama critics like J. L. Styan, Arthur Colby Sprague, Glynne Wickham, William Tydeman, and Andrew Gurr, figures such as Barbara Hodgdon, William B. Worthen, Jill Levenson, Anthony B. Dawson, and Russell Jackson privilege performance as a critical and interpretative mode. Their work analyses in close detail dramatic representations, thematic emphases of production, staging designs, actor records, and the theatrical editing of given texts over the centuries. More recently, particular attention has been devoted to production concepts, past and present, and the ways in which the plural nature of audience engagement with them (in both the theatre and cinema) may be theorized.

Pedagogic strategies

Unlike many of the texts discussed in this volume, in general Shakespeare's tragedies do not have to fight for their place on university syllabi—nonetheless, this is less the case for texts like *Titus Andronicus* or *Coriolanus* than it is for *Romeo and Juliet* or *Hamlet*. Given the constraints of time and space on any study programme, tutors are forced to make difficult choices but my experience is that students may actively seek inclusion of more Shakespearean tragedies on a given course if they feel the genre is under-represented.

Clearly, as the previous section has indicated, the enormously diverse tradition of scholarship on the tragedies can offer a rich fund of stimuli for analysis in an educational environment. More familiar angles of approach, such as the issues of tyranny, kingship, heroism, kinship, rebellion, victimization, and social hierarchy, for example, will find ample support in the main body of criticism on these plays over the centuries. Developments in contemporary critical theory and Shakespearean scholarship have also urged those working in this area to reformulate fields of enquiry and to embark on a host of alternative investigations. I offer here a brief list of some suggested avenues for discussion, each accompanied by a few examples of supporting critical material:

- *representing the body*
  Scholz, Susanne, *Body Narratives: Writing the nation and fashioning the subject in early modern England Body Narratives* (New York/Basingstoke: St. Martin's Press / Macmillan–now Palgrave Macmillan, 2000); Healy, Margaret, *Fictions of Disease in Early Modern England: Bodies, plagues and politics* (New York: Palgrave–now Palgrave Macmillan, 2001); Paster, Gail Kern, *Humoring the Body: Emotions and the Shakespearean stage* (Chicago: University of Chicago Press, 2004); Pile, Steve, *The Body and the City: Psychoanalysis, space, and subjectivity* (London/New York: Routledge, 1996—for an enlightening general theoretical consideration of the area); Enterline, Lynn, *The Rhetoric of the Body from Ovid to Shakespeare* (Cambridge/New York: Cambridge University Press, 2000).
- *nation and identity*
  Helgerson, Richard, *Forms of Nationhood: the Elizabethan writing of England* (Chicago: University of Chicago Press, 1992); Hadfield, Andrew, *Literature, Politics and National Identity: Reformation to Renaissance* (Cambridge/New York: Cambridge University Press, 1994); McEachern, Claire Elizabeth, *The Poetics of English Nationhood, 1590–1612* (Cambridge/New York: Cambridge University Press, 1996); Baker, David J., *Between Nations: Shakespeare, Spenser, Marvell and the Question of Britain* (Stanford, CA: Stanford University Press, 1997).
- *cultural space*
  Dubrow, Heather, *Shakespeare and Domestic Loss: Forms of deprivation, mourning, and recuperation* (Cambridge/New York: Cambridge University Press, 1999); Klein, Bernhard, *Maps and the Writing of Space in Early Modern England and Ireland* (New York: Palgrave–now Palgrave Macmillan, 2001); West, Russell, *Spatial Representations and the Jacobean Stage: From Shakespeare to Webster* (Basingstoke/New York: Palgrave–now Palgrave Macmillan, 2002); Hiscock, Andrew, *The Uses of This World: Thinking space in Shakespeare, Marlowe, Cary and Jonson* (Cardiff: University of Wales Press, 2004).
- *reception*
  Bate, Jonathan, *Shakespearean Constitutions: Politics, theatre, criticism, 1730–1830* (Oxford: Clarendon Press, 1989); Marowitz, Charles, *Recycling Shakespeare: Contemporary critical quarrels* (Basingstoke: Macmillan–now Palgrave Macmillan, 1991); Vickers, Brian, *Appropriating Shakespeare* (New Haven: Yale University Press, 1993).
- *race*
  Loomba, Ania, *Shakespeare, Race, and Colonialism* (Oxford/New York: Oxford University Press, 2002); Gillies, John, *Shakespeare and the*

Geography of Difference (Cambridge: Cambridge University Press, 1994); Vitkus, Daniel, *Turning Turk: English theatre and the multicultural Mediterranean 1570–1630* (Basingstoke: Palgrave–now Palgrave Macmillan, 2003); Shapiro, James, *Shakespeare and the Jews* (New York: Columbia University Press, 1996).

- *language and rhetoric*
  Donawerth, Jane, *Shakespeare and the Sixteenth-Century Study of Language* (Urbana: University of Illinois Press, 1984); Parker, Patricia, *Shakespeare from the Margins: Language, Culture* (Chicago: University of Chicago Press, 1996); Rhodes, Neil, *Shakespeare and the Origins of English* (Oxford: Oxford University Press, 2004).

- *gender expectation*
  Erickson, Peter, *Patriarchal Structures in Shakespeare's Drama* (Berkeley: University of California, 1985); Kahn, Coppélia, *Man's Estate: Masculine identity in Shakespeare* (Berkeley: University of California Press, 1981); Newman, Karen, *Fashioning Femininity and English Renaissance Drama* (Chicago: University of Chicago Press, 1991); Novy, Marianne, *Love's Argument: Gender relations in Shakespeare* (Chapel Hill: University of North Carolina Press, 1984).

- *the Court and courtliness*
  Kernan, Alvin, *Shakespeare, the King's Playwright: Theater in the Stuart Court, 1603–1613* (Cambridge, MA: Yale University Press, 1995); Holderness, Graham, et al., *Shakespeare: Out of Court: Dramatizations of Court Society* (Basingstoke: Palgrave Macmillan, 1990); Richards, Jennifer, *Rhetoric and Courtliness in Early Modern Literature* (Cambridge: Cambridge University Press, 2003).

- *representation in the media*
  Boose, Lynda, and Richard Burt (eds), *Shakespeare, the Movie: Popularizing the Plays on Film, TV, and Video* (London: Routledge, 1997); Cartmell, Deborah, *Interpreting Shakespeare on Screen* (Basingstoke: Palgrave Macmillan, 2000); Davies, Anthony, *Filming Shakespeare's Plays: the Adaptations of Laurence Olivier, Orson Welles, Peter Brook and Akira Kurosawa* (Cambridge: Cambridge University Press, 1990); Kliman, Bernice W., *Hamlet: Film, Television, and Audio Performance* (Madison: Fairleigh Dickinson University Press, 1988).

- *sexuality and desire*
  Traub, Valerie, *Desire and Anxiety: Circulations of Sexuality in Shakespearean Drama* (New York: Routledge, 1992); Summers, Joseph H., *Dreams of Love and Power: On Shakespeare's Play* (Oxford: Oxford University Press, 1984); Zimmerman, Susan, *Erotic Politics: the Dynamics of Desire on the English Renaissance Stage* (London: Routledge, 1992); Smith, Bruce R., *Homosexual Desire in Shakespeare's England: a Cultural Poetics* (Chicago: University of Chicago Press, 1991).

- *economics of drama*
  Agnew, Jean-Christophe, *Worlds Apart: the market and the theater in Anglo-American thought, 1550–1750* (Cambridge: Cambridge University Press,

1986); Leinwand, Theodore B., *Theatre, Finance and Society in Early Modern England* (Cambridge: Cambridge University Press, 1999); Bruster, Douglas, *Drama and the Market in the Age of Shakespeare* (New York: Cambridge University Press, 1992).

- *social mobility and class*
  Patterson, Annabel M., *Shakespeare and the Popular Voice* (Oxford: Blackwell, 1989); Berry, Ralph, *Shakespeare and Social Class* (Amsterdam: Brill Academic Publishers, 1988); Holbrook, Peter, *Literature and Degree in Renaissance England: Nashe, Bourgeois Tragedy, Shakespeare* (University of Delaware Press, 1994).

- *censorship*
  Dutton, Richard, *Mastering the Revels: Regulation and Censorship of English Renaissance Theatre* (Basingstoke: Palgrave Macmillan, 1991); Dutton, Richard, *Licensing, Censorship and Authorship in Early Modern England* (Basingstoke: Palgrave–now Palgrave Macmillan, 2000); Clare, Janet, *Art Made Tongue-Tied by Authority: Elizabethan and Jacobean Dramatic Censorship* (Manchester: Manchester University Press, 1999).

- *genre theory*
  Fowler, Alastair, *Kinds of Literature: an Introduction to the Theory of Genres and Modes* (Oxford: Oxford University Press, 1982); Kerrigan, John, *Revenge Tragedy: Aeschylus to Armageddon* (Oxford: Oxford University Press, 1996); Snyder, Susan, *The Comic Matrix of Shakespeare's Tragedies* (Princeton: Princeton University Press, 1979); Barroll, J. Leeds, *Shakespearean Tragedy: Genre, Tradition, and Change in Antony and Cleopatra* (New York: Folger Books, 1984).

- *functions of ceremony in drama*
  Dash, Irene G., *Wedding, Wooing and Power: Women in Shakespeare's Plays* (New York: Columbia University Press, 1981); Neely, Carol T., *Broken Nuptials in Shakespeare's Plays* (New Haven/London: Yale University Press, 1985); Bates, Catherine, *The Rhetoric of Courtship in Elizabethan Language and Literature* (Cambridge: Cambridge University, 1992); Woodbridge, Linda, and Edward Berry (eds), *True Rites and Maimed Rites: Ritual and Anti-Ritual in Shakespeare and His Age* (Urbana: University of Illinois, 1992); Hopkins, Lisa, *The Shakespearean Marriage: Merry Wives and Heavy Husbands* (Basingstoke: Palgrave Macmillan, 1998).

- *the City*
  Paster, Gail Kern, *The Idea of the City in the Age of Shakespeare* (University of Georgia Press, 1985); Smith, David, et al., *The Theatrical City: Culture, Theatre and Politics in London, 1576–1649* (Cambridge: Cambridge University Press, 1995); Twyning, John, *London Dispossessed: Literature and Social Space in the Early Modern City* (Basingstoke: Palgrave Macmillan, 1998).

- *cultural discourses*
  Bradshaw, Graham, *Shakespeare's Scepticism* (New York: St. Martin's Press–now Palgrave Macmillan, 1987); Hill, John Spencer, *Infinity, Faith and Time: Christian Humanism and Renaissance Literature* (Montreal: McGill-Queen's

University Press, 1997); Grady, Hugh, *Shakespeare, Machiavelli, and Montaigne: Power and Subjectivity from Richard II to Hamlet* (Oxford: Oxford University Press, 2002); Braden, Gordon, *Renaissance Tragedy and the Senecan Tradition: Anger's Privilege* (Princeton: Yale University Press, 1985).
* *theory and textual structures*
Mousley, Andrew, *Renaissance Drama and Contemporary Literary Theory* (London: Macmillan, 2000); Parker, Patricia and Geoffrey Hartmann (eds) *Shakespeare and the Question of Theory* (New York: Methuen, 1985).

One of the challenges surrounding these texts is how to "refresh" encounters in the university classroom with texts such as *Macbeth* or *Othello* when interpretative strategies may have become "fixed" by earlier encounters with the texts. One of the ways to reconsider questions of heroism, violence, social theory, gender expectation, sovereignty, and racial difference, for example, with reference to these plays is to introduce strategically: more neglected texts such as *Titus Andronicus*; more problematic texts generically such as *Troilus and Cressida* or *Timon of Athens*; clusters of texts with generic analogy— *Hamlet*, Marston's *The Malcontent*, Kyd's *Spanish Tragedy*; or to embed the study of *Othello*, for example, in a collection of (excerpted) early modern documents (the source tale from Cinthio's *Gli Hecatommithi*, *Titus Andronicus*, Peele's *Battle of Alcazar*, relevant extracts from Hakluyt's *Principal Navigations*, George Abbot's *A Brief Description of the Whole World*, or John Pory's contemporary translation of Leo Africanus's *Descrittione dell' Africa e delle cose notabili che ivi sono*). *Troilus and Cressida* can be rendered more "tractable" for student analysis by placing it in the larger satirical context of the so-called "War of the Theatres" with Jonson's *Poetaster* and Dekker's *Satiromastix*, for example. However, another possible route is to consider it within the larger cultural preoccupation with Trojan/national identity by working with extracts from the opening discussion of Camden's *Britain, or A chorographicall description*, and from Thomas Heywood's *The Second Part of the Iron Age*, Marlowe's *Dido, Queen of Carthage*, and George Peele's narrative poem *The Tale of Troy*, for example—this is quite apart from evocations earlier in the century in Elyot's *The Governor* or Surrey's and Douglas's translations of Virgil . . . if time allows. All these options can give birth to a hitherto unrevealed text in seminar discussions and collapse the often unhelpful isolation in which Shakespeare's tragedies are studied.

For those resourcing comparative literature programmes, there are again possibilities for pulling the tragedies out of a familiar (and reassuring) space for seminar discussion and pursuing a number of interesting culturally specific enquiries into genre, characterization, reception, theatre history, and conventions: *Antony and Cleopatra* can be made to rub shoulders with Racine's *Bérénice*; *Coriolanus* with Alexandre Hardy's *Coriolan* or Corneille's *Horace* or *Suréna*; *Othello* with Calderón's *El médico de su honra*. Interestingly, *Titus Andronicus* makes more reference to classical texts than any of the other tragedies in the Shakespeare canon and can prove an unexpected opportunity for students to explore (Tudor translations of) Senecan drama, for example.

Of course, another possible *modus operandi* is to refocus a Shakespearean tragedy in terms of Tudor antecedents: to consider *Macbeth*'s representations of tyranny, inheritance, sovereignty, masculinity, etc. not only in terms of Marlowe's *Tamburlaine*, but beyond to more didactic literatures with (extracts from) Preston's *Cambises, King of Persia*, Norton and Sackville's *Gorboduc* and to extracts from Holinshed's *Chronicles*, *The Mirror for Magistrates* and medieval representations of the Herod figure in the cycle plays. Similarly *Antony and Cleopatra* can be drawn together with (extracts from) Cary's *Tragedie of Mariam*, Mary Sidney's *Antonie*, North's *Plutarch*, Fulke Greville's account of the destruction of his own version of the play and the French playwright Etienne Jodelle's *Cléopâtre Captive*. If a programme or seminar is targeting a particular area of cultural enquiry, gender, religion, theatre performance, the city, there are a number of collections which helpfully bring together useful material to feed a more focused, historicized discussion such as Aughterson's *Renaissance Woman* (1995), for example, or her *English Renaissance* collection (1998), or John N. King's *Voices of the English Reformation* (2004). In terms of genre, it can be valuable to work in seminars with selected extracts from contemporary documents concerning tragedy such as Sidney's *Apology for Poetry*, William Webbe's *Discourse of English Poetrie*, Thomas Heywood's *An Apology for Actors*, or Harrington's preface to his translation of *Orlando Furioso*. If such texts are not readily available in institutional databases, many of them can be accessed in collections such as Brian Vickers's *English Renaissance Literary Criticism* (1999).

The setting of (often starkly) contrasting critical material in seminars devoted to a given text can have an emancipating effect on discussion and can produce lively results encouraging a plurality of response to critical scenes or to the plays as a whole. An obvious example would be to draw together for a seminar on *Othello* (pre-class preparation, group-work in seminar, individual presentation) for their frictional energies contrasting pieces such as: Bradley's *Shakespearean Tragedy*; T. S. Eliot's appreciation of the hero in the *Selected Essays*; Wilson Knight's 1930 essay on the "Othello Music"; F. R. Leavis's 1952 essay "Diabolic intellect and the noble hero"; Lynda Boose's 1975 essay "Othello's handkerchief . . ."; Michael D. Bristol's 1990 essay "Charivari and the Comedy of Abjection in *Othello*"; Emily C. Bartels's 1990 essay "Making More of the Moor . . ."; and Dympna Callaghan's "Othello Was a White Man . . ." from 1996. Moreover, there is every reason to diversify the media of the criticism being considered on a given play by including reference to video or live performance and adapting assessment modes accordingly.

An increasing amount of attention is being devoted by scholars and those managing university syllabi on early modern literature to complex issues of early modern textual transmission and changing priorities of more modern editing. I have found this to be an invaluable approach which can disconcert students initially and invariably leads them to revising the experience of very familiar texts such as Shakespeare's tragedies. Seminar discussion can point up the illusory nature of the master text, probe questions of early modern authorship and ownership, and uncover the instabilities of textual production in the period. This approach is more readily on offer in affordable volumes for Shakespeare's tragedies than perhaps for other texts considered in this collection. In the 1997 Norton Shakespeare, for example, the student is given the possibility of reading contrasting *King Lear*s. Similarly, by moving between the quartos of 1603, 1604–5 and the 1623 Folio text with *The three-text Hamlet* edited by Paul Benjamin Bertram and Bernice W. Kliman (New York: AMS Press, 1991), some relatively brief enquiries in seminars can lead to a radical interrogation of familiar features of characterization, plot development, theories of staging, and even the naming of the cast members.

Notes

1. Ben Jonson, *Ben Jonson*, vol. 8, ed. C. H. Herford, Percy and Evelyn Simpson (Oxford: Clarendon Press, 1947), p. 584.
2. Samuel Johnson, *Johnson on Shakespeare*, ed. Arthur Sherbo, in *The Yale Edition of the Works of Samuel Johnson*, vol. 7 (New Haven and London: Yale University Press, 1968), pp. 72–3, 77.
3. Johnson, *Yale Edition of the Works of Samuel Johnson*, vol. 8, p. 704.
4. *Yale Edition of the Works of Samuel Johnson*, vol. 8, pp. 1047, 836, 795, 783, 823.
5. Samuel Taylor Coleridge, *Samuel Taylor Coleridge. Shakespearean Criticism in Two Volumes*, ed. Thomas Middleton Raysor, vol. 1 (London: Dent, 1961 reprint), pp. 44, 49, 16.
6. William Hazlitt, *William Hazlitt. Selected Writings*, ed. Ronald Blythe (London: Penguin, 1982 reprint), p. 273.
7. Hazlitt, *Selected Writings*, p. 276.
8. Edward Dowden, *Shakespeare: a Critical Study of His Mind and Art* (London: Kegan Paul, Trench and Co., 1883), pp. 224, 226.
9. Harley Granville-Barker, *Prefaces to Shakespeare. 1st Series: Love's Labour's Lost, Julius Caesar, King Lear* (London: Sidgwick and Jackson, 1927), p. ix.
10. Granville-Barker, *Prefaces to Shakespeare*, p. 56.
11. G. Wilson Knight, *The Imperial Theme* (London: Methuen, 1965 reprint), pp. 63, 111, 221.
12. Lily B. Campbell, *Shakespeare's Tragic Heroes. Slaves of Passion* (Cambridge: Cambridge University Press, 1930), p. 109.
13. Lloyd Davis (ed.), *Shakespeare Matters* (Newark: University of Delaware Press, 2003), pp. 109–21.

Selective guide to further reading

Access to databases such as *Early English Books Online* and *Literature Online* is revolutionizing academic environments for scholars and students alike. Greater familiarity with early modern print culture is inevitably changing radically the ways in which texts such as Shakespeare's tragedies can be studied and understood by large numbers of university communities around the world.

With regard to the more traditional area of print, I have necessarily had to limit the range of my suggestions given the enormous range of scholarly research focused on these plays across the decades. I have tried to cover a lot of ground economically. After drawing attention to the generic questions of tragedy in the first short section, I have listed a number of wide-ranging studies or broad anthologies of modern critical work which have not been included in earlier discussions and which may act as a stepping stone into more specialized study of these plays.

Generic studies

Bushnell, Rebecca (ed.). *A Companion to Tragedy*. Oxford: Blackwell, 2005.

Drakakis, John, and Liebler, Naomi Conn (eds). *Tragedy*. London: Longman, 1998.

Draper, R. P. (ed.). *Tragedy, Developments in Criticism: a Casebook*. London: Macmillan, 1980.

Nevo, Ruth. *Tragic Form in Shakespeare*. Princeton: Princeton University Press, 1972.

Palmer, Richard H. *Tragedy and Tragic Theory: an Analytical Guide*. Westport: Greenwood Press, 1992.

Steiner, George. *The Death of Tragedy*. London: Faber and Faber, 1961.

Williams, Raymond. *Modern Tragedy*. Stanford: Stanford University Press, 1966.

Monographs and edited collections

Bayley, John. *Shakespeare and Tragedy*. London: Routledge and Kegan Paul, 1981.

Bloom, Harold (ed.). *William Shakespeare: the Tragedies*. New York: Chelsea House, 1985.

Callaghan, Dympna. *Woman and Gender in Renaissance Tragedy: a Study of King Lear, Othello, The Duchess of Malfi, and The White Devil*. Atlantic Highlands: Humanities Press International, 1989.

———. (ed.). *A Feminist Companion to Shakespeare*. Oxford: Blackwell, 2000.

Charlton, H. B. *Shakespearean Tragedy*. Cambridge: Cambridge University Press, 1952.

Chedgzoy, Kate (ed.). *Shakespeare, Feminism and Gender*. Basingstoke: Palgrave–now Palgrave Macmillan, 2001.

Dutton, Richard, and Howard, Jean E. (eds). *A Companion to Shakespeare's Works, Volume I: the Tragedies*. Oxford: Blackwell, 2003.

Garner, Shirley Nelson, and Sprengnether, Madelon (eds). *Shakespearean Tragedy and Gender*. Bloomington: Indiana University Press, 1996.

Heilman, R. B. (ed.). *Shakespeare: the Tragedies*. New Perspectives. Englewood Cliffs, NJ: PrenticeHall, 1984.

Leech, Clifford (ed.). *Shakespeare: the Tragedies: a Collection of Critical Essays*. Chicago: University of Chicago Press, 1965.

Leggatt, Alexander. *Shakespeare's Tragedies: Violation and Identity*. Cambridge: Cambridge University Press, 2005.

Lerner, Laurence (ed.). *Shakespeare's Tragedies: an Anthology of Modern Criticism*. Harmondsworth: Penguin, 1963.

Liebler, Naomi C. *Shakespeare's Festive Tragedy: the Ritual Foundations of Genre*. London and New York: Routledge, 1995.

Marsh, Nicholas. *Shakespeare, the Tragedies*. New York: St. Martin's Press–now Palgrave Macmillan, 1998.

McAlindon, Tom. *Shakespeare's Tragic Cosmos*. Cambridge: Cambridge University Press, 1991.

McEachern, Claire. *The Cambridge Companion to Shakespearean Tragedy*. Cambridge: Cambridge University Press, 2002.

Mehl, Dieter. *Shakespeare's Tragedies: an Introduction*. Cambridge: Cambridge University Press, 1986.

Muir, Kenneth. *Shakespeare's Tragic Sequence*. New York: Barnes and Noble, 1979.

Neill, Michael. *Issues of Death: Mortality and Identity in English Renaissance Tragedy*. Oxford: Clarendon Press, 1997.

Rackin, Phyllis. *Shakespeare's Tragedies*. New York: Ungar, 1978.

Ribner, Irving. *Patterns in Shakespearean Tragedy*. New York: Barnes and Noble, 1960.

Wofford, Susanne L. (ed.). *Shakespeare's Late Tragedies: a Collection of Critical Essays*. Upper Saddle River, NJ: Prentice Hall, 1996.

5
Shakespeare: the Comedies[1]

Susan Bruce

Chronology

See Chronology in Chapter 4, "Shakespeare: the Tragedies."

Critical overview

> No, no, they do but jest, poison in jest; no offence i' the world.
> *Hamlet* III.ii.220[2]

> Mr. Johnson did not like any one who said they were happy, or who said anyone else was so. "It is all *cant* (he would cry), the dog knows he is miserable all of the time."[3]

> . . . the end of a Comedy would often be the commencement of a Tragedy, were the curtain to rise again on the performers.[4]

It has become a commonplace that Comedy has no "lexicon" with which to designate its properties, nor any over-arching theory to anchor and define its form.[5] Beyond the bland assertions that comedy "entertains" or "amuses" its audiences, and that its actions "turn out happily"[6] there has been, over the centuries, relatively scant attention paid to what comedy actually *is* (although there is more, as we shall see, on what it does). Aristotle's *Poetics* offered a blueprint for tragedy (albeit one with tangential relation to Early Modern Tragedy) and a number of words with which to describe its properties—*catharsis, hamartia, peripateia*, for example. But he left us no such handbook with which to embark on an understanding of tragedy's irresponsible sibling, comedy, and no one since then has managed to fill that gap.

The reasons for this are not entirely clear, although they may derive from comedy's unenviable position towards the bottom of our hierarchies of genre, less "weighty" than tragedy, less "poetic" than the lyric, less "meaningful" than the realist novel. As Laura Quinney argues, it is also a commonplace observation that

> literature most likely to be seen as "deep" or "real" or "true" is tragic literature—not only tragedies *per se* but works of all genres that seem bent on impressing us with the dark view . . . The works at the top of the hierarchy have the prestige of serious, philosophical thought. They earn this prestige precisely because they adopt a bleak perspective and deny our hopes. A more optimistic view, indeed any view that resists this one, is represented as willful illusion.[7]

So, if tragedy is at the top of the generic hierarchy, and occupies that position precisely because of its bleak perspective, comedy, by similar definition, comes rather close to the bottom—in its extreme form of slapstick, one step up from nonsense verse, perhaps. And we can see that general sense of a belittlement of comedy everywhere we look, if we look hard enough. It is present in Dr Johnson's conviction of the antipathy between happiness and truth. It underlies the early twentieth-century perception of Shakespearean comedy as "escapist," suggestive as that phrase is of a greater and depressing "truth" which comedy affords us the opportunity of avoiding.[8] It is apparent in everyday language: "I was only joking" implies that a "joke" owns no "meaning" and hence can have no "poison" in it; notable also in the extraordinary historical durability of that assumption. "No offence i' the world," says Hamlet—although this airy denial of the possibility of "poison in jest" is undermined by Hamlet's signal failure syntactically to anchor that claim in any assertion or denial. And it is also evident in the teleology which underscores Meredith's wry reiteration of the assertion that where comedy ends is tragedy's beginning: the end of the story, the locus of ultimate meaning, lies, in that view, not in comedy's multiple marriages but in despair, disaster, and death. Anastrophe (a word adopted by Northrop Frye to describe the way comedy turns things upside down) is trumped by the catastrophe of tragedy. (This may be odd, in a culture dominated for so many centuries by belief in a redemptive Christianity, but it remains true.)

So there we have one possible explanation of the failure to "theorize" comedy to anywhere near the same degree as tragedy. Another may lie in the amorphousness of the genre. Comedy is (in Renaissance terminology) a hodge-podge, or gallimaufry, of diverse forms, encompassing "Old Comedy" which originated with Aristophanes, satirical in nature; the "New Comedy" of Menander and Plautus which influenced Shakespeare in *The Comedy of Errors*; romantic comedies (such as *A Midsummer Night's Dream*, or *As You Like It*); much darker plays such as *All's Well That Ends Well* and *Measure for Measure*; and the Romances—*Pericles*, *Cymbeline*, *The Winter's Tale*, and *The Tempest*. There are arguably more differences than similarities in sensibility (to resurrect an elderly, but still useful, critical term) between (say) *The*

Comedy of Errors and *Measure for Measure*: everyone of them may ostensibly resolve their conflicts in the closure afforded by multiple marriages, but the form apparently common to them all does not adequately encompass their differences in tone. We accept the multiple marriages—more exactly, betrothals—at the end of *As You Like It* more easily than we do those at the end of *All's Well* or *Measure*; only in the Romances is comic closure assisted by divine intervention (and the degree of that closure, as we will see in more detail in the second section of this chapter, is a matter of debate: for an argument[9] that it is complete, see Orgel's introduction to *The Winter's Tale*; for a claim that it is not, see Swinburne on the same text[10]).

We should note also the historical instability of the plays' classification into one genre or another. The First Folio (1623) divided Shakespeare's plays into Comedies, Histories, and Tragedies and did not observe the sub-genre (some might say the other genre entirely) of Romance, into which most critics today would place *Pericles*, *Cymbeline*, *The Winter's Tale* and *The Tempest*. *Cymbeline* was not counted by the First Folio as a comedy at all, but rather placed with the Tragedies. And there is nothing in the First Folio to tell us whether Shakespeare's contemporaries shared the unease of later critics regarding *All's Well* and *Measure*, which (with *Troilus and Cressida*—which many contemporary critics now view as a tragedy) have sometimes been together grouped as "Problem Plays." F. S. Boas, who borrowed the term in 1896 from the drama of Ibsen, coined it because he thought that "dramas so singular in theme and temper cannot be strictly called comedies or tragedies"—they did not, in other words, fit nicely into any genre, since "the issues [they raise] preclude a completely satisfactory outcome."[11] The term has shifted in and out of the critical lexicon ever since; a good account of its history is offered by Rossiter (1961) as is, in the same essay, an intelligent discussion of tragi-comedy which is quite different from the understanding of that term iterated by J. W. Lever, for instance, in his introduction to *Measure for Measure*.[12]

Questions regarding genre had, long before Boas, already exercised the Neo-Classicist critics whose theoretical tenets dominated criticism throughout the late seventeenth and most of the eighteenth centuries. Such criticism valorized Neo-Aristotelian conceptions of the importance of the dramatic unities (of time, space, and action), and "purity" of genre (the Neo-Classicists, in general, liked their comedies, as their tragedies, "straight up"), and thus was often troubled by Shakespeare's habit of playing fast and loose with both. "The necessity of winding up the underplot in *The Merchant of Venice* has tacked what would have been more proper for an Interlude to one of the most interesting Comedies of the immortal Shakespeare" complained one B. Walwyn in 1782:

> The compleat unity of action finishes with the trial. Hence, Shakespeare's powers cannot banish us from the unpleasing emotion which every person

of taste and sensibility must experience during the fifth act. It can only be compared to the necessity of turning our attention from the ocean to a fish-pond.[13]

But he applauded Shakespeare for the "naturalness" of his characters, and in this respect, his writing illustrates the way in which Neo-classical concerns are beginning at this juncture to give way to Romantic ones. For Walwyn here, Comedy was a "mirror of human nature" with a moral purpose (to "reflect our follies, defects, vices and virtues; so that we may laugh at the first, ridicule the second, satirize the third, and enforce the latter"). For that moral purpose to be successful, characters need to be universal in their appeal, possessed of "feeling" "borrowed from nature." Romantic critics held Shakespeare to be supreme in his capacity for "the invention of characters in nature"; Walwyn's claims here illustrate the transition between these two different approaches to the genre.[14]

If there is no *Poetics* of Comedy (that is: a description of what it is) there exists, similarly, no compelling historicist account of it (that is: a description of why it blossoms at some times and not at others). Marxists such as Raymond Williams have offered such accounts of tragedy that remain persuasive: tragedy, Williams argued, appears not when a society is secure in its beliefs, nor in periods of open conflict, but in the interim between those states, when diverse ideologies compete for hegemony: then, claimed Williams, great tragedy blossoms, expressing in aesthetic form the ideological contradictions of the political unconscious of a nation.[15] No account of comedy quite like this exists either, although Mikhail Bakhtin (see below) comes closest. The late nineteenth century, however, starts to produce some more productive reflections both on what comedy does, and what its social preconditions might be. George Meredith, for instance, offered in his *Essay on Comedy* (1898) some provocative observations on the relation between comedy and gender. Comedy, he claimed:

> is the fountain of sound sense . . . and . . . lifts women to a station offering them free play for their wit, . . . on the side of sound sense. The higher the Comedy, the more prominent the part they enjoy in it . . . The heroines of Comedy are . . . not necessarily heartless from being clear-sighted: they seem so to the sentimentally-reared only for the reason that they . . . are not wandering vessels crying for a captain or a pilot. Comedy is an exhibition of their battle with men . . . : and as [men and women] . . . however, divergent, both look on one object, namely Life, the gradual similarity of their impression must bring them to some resemblance. The Comic poet dares to show us men and women coming to this mutual likeness.[16]

This social, even proto-feminist, aspect of Meredith's essay on Comedy is not the one most usually remarked in rehearsals of pre-twentieth-century writing on the genre. More commonly remembered are his distinctions between Comedy, Satire, Irony, and (unexpectedly) Humour; for Meredith, Comedy teaches, but it does so, unlike those other modes, in a life-affirming, humanistic manner: "you may estimate your capacity for Comic perception," he claims, "by being able to detect the ridicule of them you love, without loving them less, and more by being able to see yourself somewhat ridiculous in dear eyes, and accepting the correction their image of you proposes."[17] Comedy such as Shakespeare's is not intended to make us *laugh*: "the laughter of Comedy," Meredith argued, "is . . . often no more than a smile. It laughs through the mind, for the mind directs it; and it might be called the humour of the mind . . . the test of true Comedy is that it shall awaken thoughtful laughter."[18]

Meredith offers here a useful riposte to a perennial student reaction to Shakespearean comedy ("it's not *funny*"); he is also one of the few critics explicitly to contest the familiar antithesis of comedy and thought. In this respect, as in two other features of his writing, his *Essay* is a forerunner of the approaches to comedy which proved so productive in the mid to late twentieth century. In holding that comedy "awakens" "thoughtful laughter"; that it is pre-eminently related to the social; and that it is the aesthetic iteration of the battle of the sexes, Meredith stands as the precursor of those Shakespearean critics who have more recently set the terms for the ways in which Shakespearean comedy is currently understood. To summarize the concerns of those critics here at any length would largely be to repeat the lectures that most students will encounter in their own institutions, as well as the plethora of useful introductions to contemporary criticism currently in print.[19] For this reason I offer only a brief resumé of the approaches to Shakespearean comedy most influential in current teaching. Academic readers will not need me to rehearse these; but student readers might begin their secondary reading with the texts and critics I now mention. Two critics, two theorists, and two theoretical approaches demand attention here: Northrop Frye, and C. L. Barber (the critics); Bakhtin and Foucault (the theorists), and Feminism and New Historicism (the theoretical positions).

Northrop Frye and C. L. Barber understood Shakespearean comedy as intimately related to archetypal myths (in Frye's case) and Elizabethan social rituals (in Barber's). For Frye, Shakespearean comedy possessed a characteristic tripartite structure which moves from disorder at the beginning, into a "green world" outside culture in the middle (Arden, for example, Illyria, or the forest in *A Midsummer Night's Dream*), returning, finally, to the courtly world of culture. This movement, Frye claimed, performs a social function, for in it society effects a kind of rebirth, to emerge at the conclusion reinvigorated, freed from the moral constraints represented in characters who present obstacles to the progress of comedy towards realization of the hero's desire.[20] Frye was not new in approaching comedy through a consideration of its relation to ritual,[21] but his emphasis on the structural manifestation of that relation in the drama was. In Frye's readings, the conflicts apparent in the drama are transcended by the trajectory towards social renewal imposed in that structure. And in this respect, as well as (arguably) in his insistence on the universality of the archetypes he saw invoked in the plays, he understands Shakespearean comedy as essentially conservative.[22] This approach to the comedies' politics is largely shared by C. L. Barber. Unlike Frye, Barber's account is a historicist one, in that Barber anchors his understanding of the play not in universal archetypes, but in the social rituals contemporary to Shakespeare's age. Influenced by the interest in rites of passage expressed in the work of anthropologists such as Van Gennep and Victor Turner, Barber saw Shakespeare as transforming entertainments hitherto populist and rural into the aestheticized language of a professional national theatre, and in so doing reaffirming the Renaissance social hierarchies temporarily inverted in the plays' centres.[23]

Is, then, a view of Shakespearean comedy as a conservative genre ubiquitous in the criticism of the twentieth century? Certainly, as Patterson amongst others has pointed out,[24] it is a view which unites different types of criticism, not only Frye and Barber, but also the writings of New Historicist critics such as Greenblatt, Montrose, Tennenhouse, and Wilson. New Historicism is as much a methodology as it is a theory: it "works," generally, by juxtaposing literary texts such as Shakespeare's plays with anecdotes, pamphlets, and other contemporary discourses. Such critics are influenced by the French theorist Michel Foucault, whose account of the relation between power and its subversion maintains that power does not exist solely in the grand institution(s) of the State, but pervades society at all levels, so that the subject internalizes the mechanisms of his or her own subjection. Consequently, New Historicist critics generally offer a picture of the plays as containing the subversion which they fleetingly express. But not all critics share this understanding of the relationship between power and subversion. For the Marxist theorist, Mikhail Bakhtin (who pre-dated Foucault), the relationship between the two is quite different. Like Barber, Bakhtin saw comedy as intimately related to the social ritual; but for Bakhtin, the carnivalesque spirit which erupts in comedy is liberational, more absolutely subversive of the hegemonic order, enabling the expression of energies otherwise repressed. For Bakhtin, the Renaissance was a key historical moment where "two types of imagery reflecting the conception of the world . . . meet at a crossroads": popular culture, expressed through the carnivalesque spirit, and especially through the grotesque, pits itself at one and the same time against the medieval belief in a "static unchanging world order" and the "bourgeois conception of the completed atomised being."[25] It is this utopian thrust towards acknowledgement of belief in the "possibility of a complete exit from the present order of this life" which, for Bahktin, underlies the eruption in Renaissance writing of the carnivalesque spirit, which challenges the sober rationality of the hegemonic order, and is not contained by it.

But arguably the most enduringly influential revision of our understanding of Shakespearean comedy to emerge from the writings of critics of the twentieth century was that enabled by the explosion, in the 1980s and 1990s, of feminist (and, more recently, gender) criticism. No methodology unites those critics, and no consensus of belief in the politics of the plays binds that criticism together: some see the plays as reaffirming gender hierarchies,[26] some as offering profound challenges to those orders.[27] Whatever its apprehension of the politics of Shakespeare's comedies, however, feminist criticism has indubitably offered us new ways to think about old texts. It would be difficult, for example, for any contemporary critic—or, indeed, student—to share Walwyn's opinion that an audience's reaction to the final act of *The Merchant of Venice* "can only be compared to the necessity of turning our attention from the ocean to a fish-pond": the insights of feminist criticism have allowed us to see that Portia's final lesson in that play, in teaching the men to "keep safe" the "rings" of their spouses, is anything other than indivisible from the action at its centre—its cross-dressings, its contracts, and its casket.

Literary criticism "speaks" (sometimes despite itself) as much about the society which produces it as it does about the subject it addresses,[28] but it is much easier to hear what it says about that society in the critical voices of the past than to comprehend that relation in the voices of the present. It is always difficult to see ourselves as the product of our own time, and unsettling to acknowledge that our own critical foci may be as transient as those (say) of the Neo-Classicists who spoke, centuries ago, with such absolute conviction. Yet not to attempt this would be to foreclose both on the "auto-interrogation" fundamental to our discipline[29] and on one of criticism's most progressive objectives: to interrogate the texts, and the theories we inherit to aid our understanding of them, in ways that encourage the formulation of ideas that challenge both. The following section of this chapter, then, aims to address several concerns. Most directly, it attempts to situate some (though not all) of the debates about comedy which I have covered above in the material context of the classrooms of today. But in so doing, it aims also to provoke debate about the interface between teaching and research, an interface currently beleaguered in Higher Education, and arguably (if contentiously) potentially further problematized by recent shifts in the critical landscape in Early Modern Studies. Students, past and present, are the ultimate "stakeholders" in the outcome of that debate. So my ideal (not to say idealistic) aim would be to establish the grounds in which the questions which "we" ought to ask— who are our students? what should we teach them? how should we teach it?—might be asked also by our students. We may not, right now, end up with the same answers, but that may not be such a bad thing. Higher Education, after all, ought always to be a contested space if it is to remain a vital one.

Pedagogic strategies

Thus, a real classroom, real students, a real—even a literal—debate. The occasion is my Third Year course, "Shakespeare: Problem Plays and Late Plays," taught, over ten weeks in two-hour weekly seminars, to twelve students. This has been a lively group, and the students in it have been engaged in discussion during the semester. Only one of them—let's call him John—has been uniformly silent (despite my repeated efforts to get him to participate). It is now week ten, and we are ending with a seminar on *The Tempest*, which we are (because this is the last class) conducting as a debate. The students have put themselves into two groups to propose and defend the motion, which runs something like this:

> This class believes that *The Tempest* paints Prospero not as an ideal ruler, but as a petty tyrant; Caliban not as a "savage and deformed slave," but someone exploited and wronged. In so doing, the play offers no conclusive rebuttal of Caliban's claim that "This island's mine, by Sycorax, my mother". (I.ii.332)

The students have been told that they must work in a team, that they must all talk (for fear of losing "points," awarded by me) and that their interventions must invoke the ideas we have considered over the rest of the semester. They must pay attention, in other words, not only to the representation of the principal characters, but also to issues such as: debates over questions of tyranny, right rule, and justice; the conventions of romance; questions of sexuality and succession, and so forth. And in this, the last seminar of the course, John finally engages with the text and his fellow students: in fact, he animatedly argues his case throughout the two hours' duration of this class.

Why begin a discussion of the pedagogical strategies of teaching Shakespeare's comedies with this particular anecdote? What does it offer, above and beyond a hint about a decent debate you can have with your students (or your fellow students, if you are a student reader of this chapter)? One might, after all, conduct almost any class, on almost any text, as a debate: on the nature of justice in *Measure for Measure*; on whether *Troilus and Cressida* is nihilistic or *All's Well* the only Shakespeare play to reward a woman's attempts to fulfill the demands of her own sexual desire; on whether the jealousies of Leontes and/or Posthumous are necessarily inflected as male, or the bonds between Antonio(s) and other men homosocial or homosexual; on whether the category of the problem play means anything; on whether the closure of romance is complete. The list of possible topics is limitless, although some plays and genres offer themselves more readily to this particular strategy than others, romantic comedies arguably provoking less vehement responses to their conflicts than do problem comedies or some of the romances. So long as the students are primed to push their arguments one step further than they might otherwise have done, cued, as it were, to think of some things in terms of some others: of kings in terms of fathers; of the events within a text in terms of the way the text turns out; of female agency in terms of genre. So long as this prescription applies, it can be a useful strategy. It is productive at the end of a course, where it can serve a formative purpose as something which, whilst being fun, demands the employment of many of the skills required in assessed work. And it can play a role in the middle of a semester, as a tactic to galvanize the less enthusiastic group, or encourage the participation of the more reticent student (both of which it does most successfully if the tutor remains relatively silent).

But is this all? I omitted one detail from my relation of the anecdote above. John, the silent member of this group, was not just the only male, but also the only black student in it. This detail obviously suggests that the content of that seminar was as instrumental in generating John's involvement as was its form (and that suggestion itself ought implicitly to contest claims that comedy is only "escapist," and that it necessarily acts to contain the subversion that it generates). Yet the occasion raised questions for me whose answers are rather less easy to determine. I wondered precisely why someone who showed at the eleventh hour that he could contribute so animatedly to discussion had not done so before. Was his earlier silence consequential on the fact that his was the only black voice in a white classroom, as seemed to be the case for his belated intervention? If so, why? Was he intimidated? Was he convinced that whilst *The Tempest* had something to say to him, the other texts on the course did not? If the latter was the case, whose "fault" was that (if anyone's—conceivably, it was just "true")? Was it mine? (Did I fail to engage that student enough?) His? (It'd be depressing to think that the only reasons to engage with a text are the immediate ones generated by identity politics.) And in more general terms, to what degree should (not to speak of "do") pedagogical strategies still pay attention to such political questions?

This is a question more pressing than ever, given the changes we are living through in Higher Education, and the relation of those changes to the interface between teaching and research. For the trajectories of Higher Education and that of research in the early modern period have taken divergent routes over the last ten years. On the one hand, we have witnessed a transformation of Higher Education quite unparalleled in recent decades. Many have written on what is sometimes (not euphoniously) termed the "massification" of Higher Education, wherein university education has been "opened" to many more students, in the absence of a concomitant extension of funding either of the student or of the institution. The results are familiar: a new generation of students who, dependent on jobs rather than grants for their funding, are *de facto* part time, but who have the same span of semesters to complete their degrees as did their more fortunate predecessors; a sense that for those reasons, the students come to university "differently" prepared—and read less whilst they are here; a diminishing ratio of staff to the students they teach; reduced contact time; standardization of modules and assessment and so on.

Any discussion of pedagogical strategies should pay explicit attention to the changing conditions under which those strategies operate; at the same time, it should also consider the current condition of the research environment, or, more directly, the interface between the two. Explicitly to conceptualize that interface as it currently exists is, I fear, to identify a problem. In our field, a rapidly changing teaching environment faces a research community which is also changing, leaving behind the critical concerns of the 1980s and 1990s, when questions of gender, race, and class were part of the fabric of literary criticism, to focus instead on the marginal, or "minor": the minor genre, the minor—less canonical—literature, the minor form, whose connection with transformative politics is tenuous at best. Put bluntly, Early Modern criticism is in the process of abandoning the political concerns of the late twentieth century at the very moment when we are enjoined to "train" students in the "skills" which will allow "us" to "compete" in a global "information economy," and at the juncture when those students arrive with less exposure to the canon, have less time to read and derive, in ever larger numbers, from "non-traditional" backgrounds. In this context, it seems to me to be a particularly ironic moment for us to embrace, without question, Greenblatt's enigmatic dictum that "there is subversion, no end of subversion, only not for us."[30]

This particular conjunction of a globalized change in education and a local move in research foci, raises issues which we—and in that "we" I include both students and academics—need consciously to address in any consideration of pedagogic strategies, for such strategies should, surely, take account not only of what is taught or how you teach it, but also why you teach it that way, and to whom. It would have been relatively easy to devote the entirety of this section of this chapter to the listing of some possible pairings of texts, and to an explanation of why such pairings might be pedagogically productive. I might have suggested juxtaposing, for example, Fletcher's *Rule a Wife and Have a Wife* or *The Woman's Prize* with *The Taming of a Shrew* to enhance student comprehension of patriarchy in the period; or to teach *As You Like It* with Lyly's *Galatea* to offer more than one authorial take on issues of same-sex desire. I might have suggested pairing *Pericles* with *The Malcontent* to complicate a student's understanding of the figure of the absent monarch. Or, I might have devoted more space to suggesting the pairing of a given play together with one or more of its sources or appropriations: *Measure for Measure* with Cinthio, for example, and/or Dylan's "Seven Curses"; or *The Winter's Tale* with Greene's *Pandosto* or Sheldon Deckelbaum's recent adaptation, *Mamillius*. Certainly any romance can be usefully paired with any number of fairy tales. Fairy tales are a useful pedagogical shorthand for the establishment of an understanding of ideology: a class discussion of the different "messages" of *The Princess and the Pea* and *Jack and the Beanstalk* is, for instance, an efficient and memorable way to indicate differences between aristocratic and mercantile ideologies of virtue. It allows students an immediate passage into their more sophisticated and complex representation in (say) *Cymbeline* as well as an avenue to begin consideration of more thorny questions (why do fairy tales with heroines generally rehearse aristocratic ideologies of virtue; those with heroes mercantile ones, and what does that observation entail for a discussion of, say, *All's Well?*)

Or, again, I might have devoted this part of the chapter to suggestions of ways in which theoretical material might usefully be paired with primary texts in order to effect an understanding of how one might bring disparate discourses together to provoke readings hitherto unconsidered by a student. One might, for instance, ask students to read *Measure* through an understanding of "Beyond the Pleasure Principle"; or encourage them to consider what "The Uncanny" might tell us about *The Comedy of Errors*; one might pair *A Midsummer Night's Dream* (or more locally, Hermia's nightmare) with an extract from *The Interpretation of Dreams*. One could ask students to consider the various gifts in *Twelfth Night* in the light of a reading of Marcel Mauss, or to think about *Pericles* in the context of anthropological accounts of kinship relations and incest. (In my experience, students learn more, and have more of a sense of discovery—in today's parlance, "ownership of their learning"—by having to make the connections themselves than they do when those connections are offered them ready made in the form of a published article which they may find both intimidating and "seamless.")

Or, yet again, I might have chosen here to concentrate on perennial pedagogic problems, such as how we address the internally contradictory attitude with which most students approach the literature of the past, holding as they frequently do both that human values are unchanging, and that "everyone in the Renaissance thought x" about (for instance) witchcraft. Asking such students to read *The Tempest* in the light of extracts from King James's *Daemonologie* (on the one hand) and Reginald Scot's *Discoverie of Witchcraft* (on the other) can unsettle both beliefs reasonably efficiently. So too might an exercise which asked students to formulate what they might have felt if faced with Isabella's dilemma (or indeed Angelo's) in all its immediacy, and then asking them to see if anything in *Measure* might pre-figure that response. And "we" are important here too, like it or not: if we wish to encourage students to interrogate the authority of the text, or a critical reflection on it, must we not also wish them to interrogate the ultimate authority, on whom their future depends: that is, *us*? One of my colleagues recently gave her class an article of her own to read, told them that she now disagreed with it completely, having now changed her mind, and encouraged them to criticize her own response to the play. It didn't, she reports, on that occasion, "work," but I may try that strategy next semester, and begin "Shakespeare: Problem Plays and Late Plays," by asking my students to read this, the chapter I am currently completing. There would, I think, be worse ways of kicking that course off. It might, after all, serve the purpose of getting the students consciously to reflect on what I have "chosen" to teach them, and they have "chosen" to learn. (But will I do that if the cohort again, as it did in the anecdote with which I began this section, includes a lone black student? In that case, might I not, despite my best intentions, write that student into an identity he or she might not have otherwise chosen to adopt, by virtue of the nature of the material I ask him or her to read?)

It does, however, seem as important to offer to student readers of this chapter some mode of understanding the debates which govern pedagogic choices as it is to offer pedagogical strategies to those who make those decisions. Twenty years ago, there would have been more immediate (if still contentious) answers to some of the questions which surround the design of our syllabi: one thinks of the debates over women writers which have resulted in Aphra Behn's more stable presence on courses on comedy of the seventeenth century, for instance. Such debates will never be "over": English literature is too rich to be adequately covered in any university syllabus, even if those syllabi were concentrated only on the already canonical. But old questions persist, and new ones are occasioned by the changing conditions of Higher Education and the current focus of research in the field. I do not pretend here to have the answers to them, but they must, I think, remain explicit in our pedagogical considerations.

Here, then, are some of the questions which underlie my own teaching. Notions of cultural literacy still inform our society. How, then, do we weigh the relative merits of exposing students to more Shakespeare plays, or of introducing them to less canonical cultural discourses? In a context where students may have had less prior exposure to Shakespearean comedy than they ever have had before, how might we defend the inclusion of *The Two Noble Kinsmen* rather than *Twelfth Night*, of *Galatea* rather than *As You Like It*? (I do *not* mean to imply by this that there is no such rationale, nor to advocate a revisionary return to a purely canonical syllabus, only to urge that we make our rationales explicit.) How much time should we allot to the reading of secondary sources? The emergent student voice is all too easily swamped under the weight of what other people think. This has always been an especial problem with the teaching of Shakespeare. But what if the students we teach are non-traditional, less confident of the validity of their own response to the primary text, more easily intimidated by the authority of the critical voice (in print, in the lecture hall). When is the best time to introduce *that kind of* student to the authoritative voice of the printed critical word? I instruct my students not to read *any* critical material before the tutorial, but to concentrate first instead on identifying what their response is to (say) *The Merchant of Venice* and the issues that it raises. I tell them that only when they have done that, and then tested their own reactions first against their peers' (and mine) should they seek to test it against published work on the play. Is that right?

There are countless such questions. So I return, in conclusion, to the question of "our" purpose. Darko Suvin, in a provocative recent article on what it means to be a member of an English Department, quotes Walter Benjamin, musing on the function of criticism. "The point," says Benjamin, "is not to present the written works in the context of their time, but to present in the time that they arose the time that is cognizing them—our time."[31] In the same article, Suvin hazards his own definition of the use-value of the intellectual: "people who interpret the past and the ongoing flow of cultural production as articulations of a beauty that keeps alive the necessity of justice."[32] That, without doubt, is a difficult task, and one which depends for its success on recognition from both teacher *and* student. But it is not an unworthy one.

Notes

1. I thank Karen Britland, Lucy Munro, and Roger Pooley, for discussing this chapter with me as I was writing it.
2. William Shakespeare, *Hamlet*, ed. G. R. Hibbard (Oxford: Oxford University Press, 1987).
3. Hester Thrale of Samuel Johnson, quoted in Laura Quinney, *Literary Power and the Criteria of Truth* (Gainesville: University Press of Florida, 1995), p. 73.
4. George Meredith, *An Essay on Comedy* (London: Constable, 1898), 16.
5. Jill Levenson, "Comedy," in *The Cambridge Companion to English Renaissance Drama*, ed. A. R. Braunmuller and Michael Hattaway, pp. 263–300 (Cambridge: Cambridge University Press, 1990), p. 263; Northrop Frye, *A Natural Perspective: the Development of Shakespearean Comedy and Romance* (New York: Harcourt, Brace, 1965); John A. Cuddon, *A Dictionary of Literary Terms*, rev. edn. (Harmondsworth: Penguin, 1982).
6. M. H. Abrams, *A Glossary of Literary Terms* (New York: Holt, Rinehart and Winston, 1957); Martin Gray, *A Dictionary of Literary Terms* (Harlow: Longman, 1984); Cuddon, *A Dictionary of Literary Terms*.
7. Quinney, *Literary Power and the Criteria of Truth*, p. xv.
8. See, for example, John Dover Wilson, *Shakespeare's Happy Comedies* (Cambridge: Cambridge University Press, 1938).
9. *The Winter's Tale*, ed. Stephen Orgel (Oxford: Oxford University Press, 1996).
10. Algernon Charles Swinburne, *A Study of Shakespeare* (London: Chatto and Windus, 1880).
11. F. S. Boas, quoted in A. P. Rossiter, *Angel with horns, and other Shakespeare lectures*, ed. Graham Storey (London: Longman, 1961), p. 109.
12. *Measure for Measure*, ed. J. W. Lever, Arden Shakespeare (New York: Vintage, 1965.
13. B. Walwyn, extracted in Brian Vickers, *Shakespeare: the Critical Heritage. Volume 6: 1774–1801* (London: Routledge and Kegan Paul, 1981), p. 325.
14. Walwyn, in Vickers, p. 327; for a more recent discussion of the claim that comedy reflects life and is a vehicle for moral instruction, see Leo Salingar, *Shakespeare and the Traditions of Comedy* (London: Cambridge University Press, 1974).
15. Raymond Williams, *Modern Tragedy* (London: Verso, 1979); although the phrase "political unconscious" is Jameson's: Fredric Jameson, *The Political Unconscious: Narrative as a Socially Symbolic Act* (Ithaca: Cornell University Press, 1981).
16. Meredith, *Essay on Comedy*, pp. 28–30.

17. Meredith, *Essay on Comedy*, p. 78.
18. Meredith, *Essay on Comedy*, p. 88.
19. Levenson (1990); Gary Waller, *Shakespeare's Comedies* (Harlow: Longman, 1991); Emma Smith, *Shakespeare's Comedies* (Oxford: Blackwell, 2004).
20. Northrop Frye, *Anatomy of Criticism* (Princeton: Princeton University Press, 1957), pp. 163–4.
21. See, for instance, F. M. Cornford, *The Origin of Attic Comedy* (Cambridge: University Press, 1934).
22. For a cogent attack on the notion that a belief in universal values is necessary conservative, however, see Robert N. Watson, "Tragedy," in *The Cambridge Companion to English Renaissance Drama*, ed. A. R. Braunmuller and Michael Hattaway, pp. 305–51 (Cambridge: Cambridge University Press, 1990).
23. C. L. Barber, *Shakespeare's Festive Comedy* (Princeton: Princeton University Press, 1959).
24. Annabel Patterson, *Shakespeare and the Popular Voice* (Oxford: Blackwell, 1989).
25. Mikhail Bakhtin, *Rabelais and His World* (Cambridge, MA: MIT Press, 1968), p. 275.
26. See, for example, Janet Adelman, *Suffocating Mothers: Fantasies of Maternal Origin in Shakespeare's Plays, "Hamlet" to "The Tempest"* (London and New York: Routledge, 1992); Linda Bamber, *Comic Women, Tragic Men: a Study of Gender and Genre in Shakespeare* (Stanford: Stanford University Press, 1982); Kathleen McLuskie, *Renaissance Dramatists* (Hemel Hempstead: Harvester Wheatsheaf, 1989); Valerie Traub, *Desire and Anxiety: Circulations of Sexuality in Shakespearean Drama* (London: Routledge, 1992).
27. See for instance Marianne Novy, *Love's Argument: Gender Relations in Shakespeare* (Chapel Hill: University of North Carolina Press, 1984), and Carol T. Neely, *Broken Nuptials in Shakespeare's Plays* (London and New Haven: Yale University Press, 1985).
28. R. A. Foakes, *Hamlet versus Lear: Cultural politics and Shakespeare's art* (Cambridge: Cambridge University Press, 1993).
29. Gayatri Chakravorty Spivak, "Theory in the Margins: Coetzee's *Foe* reading Defoe's *Crusoe/Roxana*," pp. 154–80, in Jonathan Arac and Barbara Johnson (eds), *Consequences of Theory* (Baltimore: Johns Hopkins University Press, 1991), p. 155.
30. Stephen Greenblatt, *Shakespearean Negotiations: the Circulation of Social Energy in Renaissance England* (Berkeley: University of California Press, 1988), p. 39.
31. Walter Benjamin, quoted in Darko Suvin, "To Laputa and Back: a missing chapter of *Gulliver's Travels*," *Critical Quarterly* 47 (2005): 142–64, p. 149.
32. Suvin, "To Laputa and Back: a missing chapter of *Gulliver's Travels*," p. 149.

Selective guide to further reading

Abrams, M. H. (1981). *A Glossary of Literary Terms*. 4th edn. New York: Holt, Rinehart, and Winston.

Adelman, Janet. *Suffocating Mothers: Fantasies of Maternal Origin in Shakespeare's Plays, "Hamlet" to "The Tempest"*. London and New York: Routledge, 1992.

Bakhtin, Mikhail, *Rabelais and His World*. Cambridge, MA: MIT Press.

Bamber, Linda. *Comic Women, Tragic Men: a Study of Gender and Genre in Shakespeare*. Stanford: Stanford University Press, 1982.

Barber, C. L. *Shakespeare's Festive Comedy*. Princeton: Princeton University Press, 1959.

Bergeron, David. *Shakespeare's Romances and the Royal Family*. Lawrence: University Press of Kansas, 1985.

Bristol, Michael D. *Carnival and Theatre: Plebeian Culture and the Structure of Authority in Renaissance England*. London: Methuen, 1985.

Collins, Michael J. *Shakespeare's Sweet Thunder: Essays on the Early Comedies*. London: Associated University Presses, 1997.

Cornford, F. M. *The Origin of Attic Comedy*. Cambridge: Cambridge University Press, 1934.

Cuddon, J. A. *A Dictionary of Literary Terms*. Rev. edn. Harmondsworth: Penguin, 1982.

Dover Wilson, John. *Shakespeare's Happy Comedies*. Cambridge: Cambridge University Press, 1938.

Dusinberre, Juliet. *Shakespeare and the Nature of Women*. 2nd edn. London: Macmillan, 1996.

Felperin, Howard. *Shakespearean Romance*. Princeton: Princeton University Press, 1972.

Foakes, R. A. *Hamlet versus Lear: cultural politics and Shakespeare's art*. Cambridge: Cambridge University Press, 1993.

Foucault, Michel. *Power/Knowledge, Selected Interviews and Other Writings 1972–1977*, ed. Colin Gordon. New York and London: Harvester Press, 1980.

French, Marilyn. *Shakespeare's Division of Experience*. New York: Summit Books, 1981.

Frye, Northrop. *The Myth of Deliverance: Reflections on Shakespeare's Problem Comedies*. Brighton: Harvester, 1938.

———. *Anatomy of Criticism*. Princeton: Princeton University Press, 1957.

———. *A Natural Perspective: the Development of Shakespearean Comedy and Romance*. New York: Harcourt, Brace and World, 1965.

Gray, Martin. *A Dictionary of Literary Terms*. Longman: Harlow, 1984.

Greenblatt, Stephen. *Renaissance Self-Fashioning: From More to Shakespeare*. Chicago: University of Chicago Press, 1980.

———. *Shakespearean Negotiations: the Circulation of Social Energy in Renaissance England*. Berkeley: University of California Press, 1988.

Hall, Jonathan. *Anxious Pleasures: Shakespearean Comedy and the Nation State*. Madison: Fairleigh Dickinson University Press, 1995.

Hopkins, Lisa. *The Shakespearean Marriage: Merry Wives and Heavy Husbands*. Basingstoke: Macmillan–now Palgrave Macmillan, 1998.

Jameson, Fredric. *The Political Unconscious: Narrative as a Socially Symbolic Act*. Ithaca: Cornell University Press, 1981.

Jardine, Lisa. *Still Harping on Daughters: Women and Drama in the Age of Shakespeare*. 2nd edn. Brighton: Harvester, 1983.

Jordan, Constance. *Shakespeare's Monarchies: Ruler and Subject in the Romances*. Ithaca: Cornell University Press, 1997.

Kahn, Coppelia. *Man's Estate: Masculine Identity in Shakespeare*. Berkeley: University of California Press, 1981.

Kott, Jan. *Shakespeare Our Contemporary*. 2nd edn. London: Routledge, 1967.

Knowles, James, and Jennifer Richards. *Shakespeare's Late Plays: New Readings*. Edinburgh: Edinburgh University Press, 1999.

Leggatt, Alexander. *Shakespeare's Comedy of Love*. London: Methuen, 1974.

Levenson, Jill. "Comedy," in *The Cambridge Companion to English Renaissance Drama*, ed. A. R. Braunmuller and Michael Hattaway, pp. 263–300. Cambridge: Cambridge University Press, 1990.

McCandless, David Foley. *Gender and Performance in Shakespeare's Problem Comedies*. Bloomington: Indiana University Press, 1997.

McLuskie, Kathleen. *Renaissance Dramatists*. Hemel Hempstead: Harvester Wheatsheaf, 1989.

Meredith, George. *An Essay on Comedy*. London: Constable, 1898.

Montrose, Louis Adrian. *The Purpose of Playing: Shakespeare and the Cultural Politics of the Elizabethan Theatre*. Chicago: Chicago University Press, 1996.

Neely, Carol Thomas. *Broken Nuptials in Shakespeare's Plays*. London and New Haven: Yale University Press, 1985.

Nevo, Ruth. *Shakespeare's Other Language*. London: Methuen, 1987.

Novy, Marianne. *Love's Argument: Gender Relations in Shakespeare*. Chapel Hill: University of North Carolina Press, 1984.

Palfrey, Simon. *Late Shakespeare: a New World of Words*. Oxford: Oxford University Press, 1997.

Patterson, Annabel. *Shakespeare and the Popular Voice*. Oxford: Blackwell, 1989.

Quinney, Laura. *Literary Power and the Criteria of Truth*. Gainesville. University Press of Florida, 1995.

Salingar, Leo. *Shakespeare and the Traditions of Comedy*. Cambridge: Cambridge University Press, 1974.

Shakespeare, William. *Measure for Measure*, ed. J. W. Lever. Arden Shakespeare. New York: Vintage Books, 1965.

———. *Hamlet*, ed. G. R. Hibbard. Oxford: Oxford University Press, 1987.

———. *The Winter's Tale*, ed. Stephen Orgel. Oxford: Oxford University Press, 1996.

Smith, Emma. *Shakespeare's Comedies*. Oxford: Blackwell, 2004.

Spivak, Gayatri Chakravorty. "Theory in the Margins: Coetzee's *Foe* reading Defoe's *Crusoe/Roxana*" pp. 154–80, in Jonathan Arac and Barbara Johnson (eds), *Consequences of Theory* (Baltimore: Johns Hopkins University Press, 1991).

Suvin, Darko. "To Laputa and Back: a Missing Chapter of *Gulliver's Travels*." *Critical Quarterly* 47 (2005): 142–64.

Swinburne, Algernon Charles. *A Study of Shakespeare*. London: Chatto and Windus, 1880.

Tennenhouse, Leonard. *Power on Display: the Politics of Shakespeare's Genres*. London: Methuen, 1986.

Tillyard, E. M. W. *Shakespeare's Problem Plays*. London: Chatto and Windus, 1950.

Traub, Valerie. *Desire and Anxiety: Circulations of Sexuality in Shakespearean Drama*. London: Routledge, 1992.

Vickers, Brian. *Shakespeare: the Critical Heritage. Volume 6: 1774–1801*. London: Routledge and Kegan Paul, 1981.

Waller, Gary. *Shakespeare's Comedies*. Harlow: Longman, 1991.

Watson, Robert N. "Tragedy," in *The Cambridge Companion to English Renaissance Drama*, ed. A. R. Braunmuller and Michael Hattaway, pp. 305–51. Cambridge: Cambridge University Press, 1990.

Wheeler, Richard P. *Shakespeare's Development and the Problem Comedies: Turn and Counter-turn*. Berkeley: University of California Press, 1981.

Williams, Raymond. *Modern Tragedy*. London: Verso, 1979.

Williamson, Marilyn. *The Patriarchy of Shakespeare's Comedies*. Detroit: Wayne State University Press, 1986.

Wilson, Richard. *Will Power: Essays on Shakespearean Authority*. London: Harvester Wheatsheaf, 1993.

6
Shakespeare: the Histories
David Ruiter

Chronology

See Chronology in Chapter 4, "Shakespeare: the Tragedies."

Critical overview

Most editions of Shakespeare's works divide the plays into four generic categories—comedy, tragedy, history, and romance. Of the four, one might make the case that history is the least well understood and, as a result, possibly also the least embraced. This is not to say that the history plays lack popular appeal or are less than important. Indeed, few Shakespearean characters are as well-loved as Falstaff, and fewer still as memorably frightful as Richard III; and Stephen Greenblatt's *Will in the World* has recently reminded a wide audience that in fact it was the *Henry VI* plays, history plays, that won Shakespeare the status among peers and audiences that would propel him forward to his famous and ever more influential career as author of works that continue to delight spectators of both performance and text.[1] Nonetheless, the issue of understanding the genre, much less how to teach it, often remains something of a conundrum. Therefore, giving priority to pedagogical concerns, I will start with a summary of the form, then consider the plays' critical reception, and ultimately provide three approaches that will aid an understanding of Shakespeare's dramatic "histories."

The genre

Shakespeare's ten history plays are now often grouped into two tetralogies (four-play sets) and two "stand alone" plays, *King John* and *Henry VIII*. The "First Tetralogy" (sometimes called the "First Henriad") consists of *1 Henry VI*, *2 Henry VI*, *3 Henry VI*, and *Richard III*; the "Second Tetralogy" (or "Second Henriad") includes *Richard II*, *1 Henry IV*, *2 Henry IV*, and *Henry V*. Critical reception has tended to focus most of its attention on the plays of the two tetralogies, but all ten, taken together, do add to the consideration of the genre.

Without question, there were English history plays before Shakespeare, among them Thomas Sackville and Thomas Norton's *Gorboduc*, as well as plays whose subjects are revisited in Shakespeare's plays, such as John Bale's *King Johan*, and the anonymous *Troublesome Reign of John* and *Thomas of Woodstock*; in fact, according to Larry Champion, there are potentially 39 "history plays" prior to Shakespeare's, though only some are extant, and fewer still bear generic resemblance to those of the Bard.[2] To some extent the genre was, therefore, already beginning to take shape before Shakespeare introduced his work to the scene with the *Henry VI* plays, the first of which was probably written around 1589–90. Nonetheless, it would be a misunderstanding to think that Shakespeare merely contributed to the vogue of the day; indeed, as Phyllis Rackin has demonstrated, Shakespeare experimented with the form to such an extent, and with such success, that we could reasonably say that he created it, at least as a viable dramatic genre.[3] However, and whatever the tenuous influence of the other "histories," he did have an important precedent for his creation in the English medieval mystery plays, relatively brief religious dramas depicting a great number of biblical highlights performed in extended and relatively sequential patterns (or "cycles"). These plays did much to establish a "historical" connection between God's plan as depicted in, for instance, the story of Noah, and the present reality of medieval England; in other words, the history of England was analogous to, or even an extension of, the story of God's plan of creation/salvation.

In comparison to these mystery plays, Shakespeare's historical drama is not as particularly (and certainly not as immediately) concerned with a fundamentally sacred perspective of England's past, as it is in bringing to life portions of the political history of the nation. Many reasons contributed to this shift in focus, not the least of which was the already established idea that studying the past might provide current peoples and their governments a useful guide to both avoiding historical errors and building upon past successes. The plays also add current political philosophies into the presentation of the past, and may be seen, as well, to sanction (or not) such philosophies and the governments who enacted or could enact them. Additionally, the fact that Shakespeare's history plays began to appear so closely on the heels of the English defeat of the Spanish Armada in 1588 suggests that a burgeoning sense of patriotism and a more secure sense of national identity, which might be further stabilized through an understanding and celebration of the nation's past, contribute to both the writing and the enjoyment of the plays. Significantly, Shakespeare did have several useful historical texts at hand, most notably a new edition of Raphael Holinshed's *Chronicles* (1587), a circumstance that might lead to the thought that the Shakespearean "birth" of the English history play had more than a little to do with his agile use of available resources, and probably with a certain established market for historical (re)presentations.

As Charles Forker makes clear—and of particular significance to a discussion of genre—Shakespeare's history plays, created mostly in the form of tetralogies, strongly adhere to an *open* literary structure, as opposed to a *closed* one in which plots come to defined moments of closure, as is often the case in his other dramatic forms (consider *Twelfth Night*, *Macbeth*, and *The Tempest*, for example).[4] This open structure, which has caused some critics to degrade the dramatic genre of history,[5] allows for the plays to leave matters unresolved to a greater extent than is true in other genres, and therefore may call on the audience for a greater degree of searching consideration, rather than uncritical acceptance, of the ideas presented in these works. For example, in *Richard II*, an established system of kingship by divine right is challenged by a new, more Machiavellian sense of rule by the capable and strong. While Bolingbroke (the capable) ultimately defeats Richard (the rightful), audiences through the ages have left the play puzzling over the relative values represented by each king.[6] Shakespeare dramatizes how Bolingbroke's kingship unfolds in the two parts of *Henry IV*, but the answer to the question of which political philosophy is best, or even better, remains a matter of opinion, open to debate. While this open quality may make for difficulty in terms of generic definition, it energetically retains the potential to engage the audience and can therefore be a fruitful aspect to emphasize in pedagogical contexts, as I will explain.

Critical approaches

The critical analysis of Shakespeare's history has been extensive, and not only more, but also more varied approaches continue to be generated from studies of this genre. It is not possible in this short space to cover the entire range of analysis of the plays; however, a summary of some of the critical highlights of the past and a nod toward possibilities that are beginning to emerge might prove useful, especially as they relate to the pedagogical approaches discussed later in this essay. I have chosen a selection of books, edited collections, and essays in an effort to provide an accessible and representative sample.

One would be hard-pressed to provide an overview of significant twentieth–twenty-first century approaches to the plays without starting with E. M. W. Tillyard's *Shakespeare's History Plays*, which first appeared in 1944.[7] In this book, Tillyard puts forward an important idea, stating, "Shakespeare turned the Chronicle [History] Play into an independent and authentic type of drama, and no mere ancillary to the form of tragedy."[8] This assertion, coupled with a bold argument for Shakespeare's providential view of English history, provided, in many respects, the springboard for the majority of subsequent historical approaches to the history plays, and, more importantly, strongly suggested that the genre itself had been unfairly considered lesser than and fundamentally indebted to the dramatic darlings of comedy and tragedy. Tillyard's perspective that a cohesive, historical strategy was at work within the unfolding of the plays, and especially in the tetralogies, was quickly followed by Lily Campbell's *Shakespeare's Histories: Mirrors of Elizabethan Policy* (1947) which holds that the plays provide a template for analysis of the current politics of Shakespeare's England.[9] While, generally speaking, the views of Tillyard and Campbell are no longer favoured in what is called the "post-structural" era of literary criticism, their contributions did much to establish the particular study of Shakespeare's "history plays."

The second major wave of analysis of the history plays focuses largely on political and historical matters, and three essays are especially illustrative of this critical movement. An excellent starting point, Jonathan Dollimore and Alan Sinfield's essay, "History and Ideology: the Instance of *Henry V*" (1985), destabilizes any particular political reading of the plays, even while asserting that "we might conclude that the ideology which saturates his texts, and their location in history, are the most interesting things about them."[10] Certainly, this assumption of ideology as "most interesting" permeates much of the criticism of the plays following the World Wars, and is a hallmark of Stephen Greenblatt's extraordinarily influential "new historical" essay, "Invisible Bullets" (1988), which focuses on the competing issues of early modern cultural subversion and containment as demonstrated in the two parts of *Henry IV* and *Henry V*.[11] R. L. Smallwood, in "Shakespeare's Use of History" (1986), builds beyond Tillyard's thesis concerning the unique character of the history plays, arguing that if "comedy is that form of drama which concerns itself with social man, and tragedy with moral or ethical man, then history is above all an exploration of human political behaviour."[12]

Other political and historical views abound. Among them, Michael Manheim, in *The Weak King Dilemma in the Shakespearean History Play* (1973),[13] brings sixteenth-century political philosophy, as seen in Shakespeare's plays, to a point of relevance in the late twentieth century, while Peter Saccio's *Shakespeare's English Kings: History, Chronicle, and Drama* (1977) provides a highly accessible view of many of the social, political, and cultural factors that potentially played into the creation of Shakespeare's characters and ideas.[14] Philip Edwards's *Threshold of a Nation* (1979) is extraordinarily helpful in terms of understanding the patriotic and nationalist content of the plays.[15] An excellent comment on the many attempts to understand the political/historical context of Shakespeare's plays, Phyllis Rackin's *Stages of History: Shakespeare's English Chronicles* (1990) also does much to make clear why such attempts, even if always partial, remain meaningful to our efforts to understand Shakespeare's works and our own historicized worlds.[16] Paola Pugliatti, in *Shakespeare the Historian* (1996), highlights "the contradictions which are inevitably connected with any historical enquiry," and demonstrates how Shakespeare's reading of medieval history, and our reading of

Elizabethan history, can meaningfully and arduously pursue historical truth, even if all such attempts are doomed to ultimate corruption.[17]

A profound development of the post-structural era of Shakespeare criticism, and an area I will emphasize in the pedagogical approaches, comes by way of feminist interpretations of the plays. Several pieces might serve as a collective starting point: Coppélia Kahn's *Man's Estate: Masculine Identity in Shakespeare* (1981) remains a compelling psychoanalytic reading;[18] Jean Howard and Phyllis Rackin's *Engendering a Nation: a Feminist Account of Shakespeare's English Histories* (1997) is the most thoughtful, extended, and specific feminist study of the genre;[19] and Kathryn Schwarz provides a somewhat more condensed, but nonetheless exemplary study in her essay entitled, "Fearful Simile: Stealing the Breech in Shakespeare's Chronicle Plays" (1998).[20] Geraldo de Sousa significantly expands the discussion of gender in the history plays in *Shakespeare's Cross-Cultural Encounters* (1999).[21]

The third wave of criticism of the history plays consists of recent work that attempts to plot somewhat different courses for extended study of the genre. In 1982, David Scott Kastan's *Shakespeare and the Shapes of Time* began by revisiting, and indeed revaluing, the work of Tillyard and others, and went on to provide a strong argument for the centrality of Time and historiographical process in defining the genre of the history plays.[22] Kastan's work does much to reopen the debate of a potential aesthetic unity inherent to the genre, a perspective that Robert Bennett (1987) adheres to in a fine essay on both the "shape" of each play of the Second Henriad, but also the "grand unity" that the tetralogy achieves when read as a set.[23] In 1996, John Velz strongly urged further analyses of the plays, beyond the brilliance found in the multiplicity of historical/political readings, and provided several "aesthetic" possibilities with his edited collection, *Shakespeare's English Histories: a Quest for Form and Genre.*[24]

In the last decade, there has indeed been some movement away from past-oriented perspectives on the history plays. In truth, such notable critics as Greenblatt, Rackin, Smallwood, and others had already articulated worries that any supposedly historical reading of the history plays is complicated by our existence in the *present*, or as Rackin says, that "what we see in those plays, like what we see in the past, reflects our own concerns."[25] And while Rackin warns against a sort of dehistoricizing process used to make the plays servants to our own "sermons,"[26] Hugh Grady (2000)[27] and Ewan Fernie (2005)[28] take far more positive approaches to this issue of a nearly inevitable "presentism," urging that as our historical and critical lenses shift in modern and postmodern directions, we might find further productive openings in the texts. Paul Dean (1997)[29] and Michael Goldman (1998)[30] each provide excellent essays demonstrating the reader's or audience's responsible participation in the discovery of historical process in the history plays. In addition, Brian Walsh (2004) articulates a highly accessible and productive understanding of the risks and rewards inherent in the *then* and *now* of Shakespeare's performative history-making.[31] Perhaps the most powerful statement *against* using the plays mostly as cultural artefact and *for* engaging them as lively historical and literary enterprises is provided by Kiernan Ryan in his essay, "The Future of History in *Henry IV*" (1995); Ryan states, "History, it is plain, is not simply what happened, but what gets made, misconstrued, disputed, and remodeled."[32] As students of Shakespeare's history plays, whatever their professional stature, continue to engage with the plays with eyes to the past, awareness of the present, and thought for the future, we might expect even more dramatic understandings of the plays to emerge.

Pedagogic strategies

As I have already suggested, the discussions of genre and criticism contained here have been constructed with an eye towards pedagogical concerns. Taken together, the critics above make use of a productive set of interpretative tools for thoughtful and exciting engagement with Shakespeare's history plays. What follows is another set, this time of possibilities for teaching the plays; the three techniques below aim to encourage the students themselves to employ a variety of strategies both to see interpretative opportunities within the texts and to articulate meaningful understandings of those discoveries.

One way to begin teaching a history play is to use a constructivist approach to the text. The idea for doing so first occurred to me via two sources. The first appears in Albert Cook's essay, "The Ordering Effect of Dramatized History: Shakespeare and Henry VIII";[33] here Cook explains a method of reading that involves the use of what he calls "ideological integers," which I'll explain in a moment by way of example. The second source for this approach comes by way of discussion with my colleague, the English Education specialist Keith Polette. Polette has written and presented extensively on how to start students on a path to "constructing" the meanings of literary texts, and part of this process involves making predictions at various points in the reading process.[34]

In the case of *1 Henry IV*, probably the most popular history play today, the constructivist approach can be especially useful. My students, when beginning the study of any history play, get a bit bogged down by the sheer number of characters, many of whom enjoy a variety of names and nicknames. The students end up keeping an account of the characters and their political affiliations, only to miss out on much of the lively drama of the play; one student complained that *Richard II* was "worse than a Russian novel" in this respect. In the past, I tried to alleviate some of this stress by providing students with character name-lists that included political and personal allegiances. This did help, but also had the effect of making the students feel that they were indeed right to focus most (or all) of their attention on the practical matter of Henry versus the rebels, still leaving much of the drama cloudy, or apparently unimportant, including much of the Falstaff material.

Using a constructivist approach, the students see not only the two-sided martial conflict, but also multiple "ideological integers" at play and at battle. Before they begin reading the play, students (individually or in groups) should be encouraged to work on a selection of characters, especially those that demonstrate strongly differing ideologies. To explain the idea, I'll use four of the most discussed characters: Henry IV, Hotspur, Hal, and Falstaff. Each student or group should initially be assigned one character, for instance Henry IV. They are then asked to read and study Henry's first speech—"So shaken as we are, so wan with care / Find we a time for frighted peace to pant . . ." (I.i.1–33).[35] The students are directed to read the speech as a way to gain some initial perspective on the character of Henry. They should also be asked to circle words in the speech that they find especially descriptive, and those that they feel are clues to characterization. Then a collective list should be made, drawing out as many student responses as possible. A resulting list might look like this:

"shaken"
"wan with care"
"frighted peace"
"daub her lips with her own children's blood"
"intestine shock"
"civil butchery"
"chase these pagans in those holy fields"

What do these words and phrases tell the reader about Henry and his situation? The students can easily see the anxiety about the continued violence of civil war, and the desire to pursue a strategic foreign war so as to ally the domestic factions in a common cause. They see that Henry is in charge of others; they see that he is long-winded.

At this point, assign students the tasks of looking at a longish speech from Hotspur, Hal, and Falstaff. I would recommend choosing passages found early in the play. In the case of Hotspur, his first words work well—"My liege, I did deny no prisoners . . ." (I.iii.29–68). Here the list of phrases might include:

"leaning upon my sword"
"With many holiday and lady terms / He questioned me"
"he made me mad"
"To see him shine so brisk, and smell so sweet / And talk so like a waiting-gentlewoman"

From these and others, the students might create a portrait of an emotional, sexist, rebel-warrior.

With Falstaff and Hal, a look over the play's second scene will do nicely to show a play of wits that reveals Falstaff as the humorous centre of the community, and Hal as the rebellious but nonetheless savvy politician and would-be king. Bear in mind that these are just initial "impressions" of the characters.

We make the characterization lists in class and put them up side by side on a board or screen, so that the students have a chance to debate the shared descriptions. Once the students reach a set of lists they can accept, I ask them to discuss how they assume the characters will get along with each other, based exclusively on the limited personality profiles we've created.

This approach produces many positive results. First, the students together work on specific characters and become aware of them as individuals rather than simply as members of one side or the other in the civil war. Second, in building the profiles, the students also make predictions about the characters and about how they will interact with each other; making such predictions creates a dynamic, invested reading situation, which leads to greater understanding and retention. Third, the students gain this level of dramatic investment *before* they go on to wrestle with the issues of historical and political ideologies; once they are invested, they are more willing to take on deeper challenges that the play presents. Fourth, the students begin to apprehend the idea that integers/characters are put into relation or conflict with each other as a means of creating the drama itself. Fifth, the students' sense of textual discovery is heightened, making them more able and likely to read critically rather than passively.

As stated, the method works well with the other histories, too. For example, with *Richard III*, the compelling opening speech—"Now is the winter of our discontent / Made glorious summer by this sun of York . . ." (I.i.1–40)— immediately allows for predictions, and especially so if the students are provided with definitions of the genres of both "history" and "tragedy." The speech also challenges some fundamental assumptions, such as: the essential nature of family loyalty; the belief that all share the opinion that peace is preferable to war; and the concept that the violent are simple-minded thugs. Having the students articulate concepts found in this one speech again makes possible a level of investment in the reading that leads to higher levels of engagement with the texts and various concerns within them.

The tetralogies

Teaching the tetralogies offers especially productive venues for the study of Shakespearean texts. Among the chief benefits of the studying the Second Henriad, for example, is that the four-play set can easily be used to consider definitions of three of the four major dramatic genres—tragedy, comedy, and history; as the students undertake this consideration, they will come to see generic tradition, and they will also gain participatory ownership within a process of generic construction.

In teaching the Second Henriad, the students are immediately confronted with a bit of a dilemma in the shape of the tetralogy's first play, *The Tragedy of King Richard the Second*. The students are likely to be familiar with other of Shakespeare's well-known tragedies, and they will therefore have some expectations for the play's trajectory, and possibly quite a lot of knowledge concerning the tragic genre and its basic considerations. But the play is also assuredly a history, so what to do?

One strategy for handling the multiple genres that this and other plays inhabit is to deal with them multilaterally. Because tragedy is a more defined genre than is history, and because tragedy is probably more familiar to the students, I would recommend starting with this one. The students will then be able to use their knowledge and contribute to the discussion with some confidence. However, before beginning to read or discuss *Richard II*, alert the students to the idea that the play functions within two generic spaces, tragedy and history: while the class will deal with the title genre first, they will later in the term be asked to use *Richard II*, in concert with the other three plays of the tetralogy, to form a working definition of the genre of Shakespearean "History Plays." In other words, the students will be asked to understand the highly constructed genre of tragedy, and they will later be asked to construct the definition of Shakespearean history. Such a strategy puts the onus on the students by asking them first to understand (or be reminded of) the concept of genre itself, and then to craft a genre by way of their collective reading experience. The students thereby gain a sense of ownership of and responsibility for the generic shape of the texts.

The same method can be usefully applied to the two *Henry IV* plays. As C. L. Barber and a host of his followers (including Gus Van Sant in his brilliant film, *My Own Private Idaho*) have made clear, these two history plays can be taught as a single *comedy*.[36] Again, the benefit of doing so, in pedagogical terms, is immediate, because the students are likely to have some experience with Shakespearean comedy through reading, film, or live theatre. Take advantage of this knowledge base, add to it, and challenge it. However, also be sure to point out that *1* and *2 Henry IV* are indeed two, *separate* history plays, with differing perspectives on a host of issues, and that those perspectives also differ from what was witnessed in *Richard II*.

At this point in the study of the tetralogy, consider taking time to brainstorm on what aspects the first three plays have in common, and discuss how these points of similarity can now be combined to provide a working definition of a Shakespearean "history play." That definition will shortly be challenged and supplemented by the reading of *Henry V*, a play that is neither tragedy nor comedy. In other words, have the students form a collective reading platform to use as they explore a text that is not comic-history or tragic-history, but just history.

In this way, *Henry V* can be used as a sort of measure of the genre itself. For example, the students may have decided, as stated earlier, that *Richard II* brings forward competing concepts of kingship and governance through the leading performances of Richard and Bolingbroke, and that the *Henry IV* plays complicate and clarify these positions while adding a third in the person of Prince Hal; therefore, the students may choose to list one of the working tenets of the genre of "history play" as a work that enacts multiple political perspectives. In reading the fourth play, the students see that the third perspective, that of Hal/Henry V, appears to be both gloriously affirmed and significantly questioned, not so much by a would-be successor but by the king's own behaviour and by the perspectives of the ruled, especially in the characters of Bates and Williams. This might well lead them back to a discussion concerning how the view that history is formed by the powerful/elite is challenged in each play by the ideas of supposed social/political inferiors, which might then be added as another possible tenet to the definition of the genre. As well, the students might attempt to understand the particular failures and abuses of each king, and how the humanity of each is challenged or supported by the level of power each possesses at a particular moment. The main point is to have the students construct the definition of the genre, and to prompt them to realize that Shakespeare himself was at work on this very construction even as he, in significant ways, wrote the genre into existence.

In the case of the First Tetralogy, the same idea of construction can easily be applied, and with an even greater sense of the beginning author's experimentation within an extraordinarily loose form. Observing what the form gains from play to play, and what ideas are apparently tried and subsequently disregarded can lead to thoughtful discussions concerning the process of the would-be "artist." Certainly, this would also be an appropriate time to deal with Shakespeare's reputation among his peers. Have the students consider Robert Greene's condescending remark, in his *Groatsworth of Wit* (1592), that the young Bard sees himself as the "only Shake-scene in a country" while in fact he is "an upstart crow, beautified with our [presumably his more educated fellow authors'] feathers."[37] Students might then be encouraged to compare Greene's opinion to that of Thomas Nashe, who uses Shakespeare's success in dramatizing history—bringing, Nashe claims, ten thousand audience members to tears over the death of Talbot in *1 Henry VI*—to argue his opinion that poetry (including drama) is superior to more dusty forms of history. Ask the students to comment on these statements in light of their own readings of the *Henry VI* plays. Do Shakespeare's early histories bear witness to an immature playwright who borrows his best material from other sources? Or do the plays of the First Henriad speak to a developing artist who turns dry historical accounts into the memorable action of a new dramatic genre?

These strategies ultimately have a single focus: to make the students come to gain ownership of a sense of dramatic and generic construction and tradition, especially in terms of Shakespearean history.

A single issue

One of the questions my students frequently ask about the history plays is "What about the women?" The question signifies a legitimate and necessary concern, especially as it takes only the briefest glance through the pages of the combined history plays to see the massive dominance of male voices as compared to female. Indeed, in *Engendering as Nation*, Jean Howard and Phyllis Rackin define these plays collectively as "a specifically masculine drama."[38] The label is not overly bold. Therefore, I would recommend planning to discuss this issue with the students, and a variety of strategies can be used to set up this discussion.

Briefly, I would like to address the benefit of dealing with a single issue, such as the place of women in the history plays, in the study of Shakespeare and really all of literature. The argument against doing so, of course, is that the issue then limits the plays and, furthermore, allows the instructor to use the texts to promote his or her own political agenda. Though these points are valid and should be acknowledged, the single-issue strategy also uniquely promotes a depth of analysis that allows the students an intellectual place to thrive in their reading and comprehension of texts.

When the students ask about the paucity of women in the plays, they are bringing into play two considerations—Shakespeare's text and their own thoughts on women's standing in society, politics, and culture as a whole. The tendency when teaching the Bard's work is always to start (and often end) with the text, a sort of *sola Shakespeara* approach. Many times, such a strategy works very well, though in this case we might consider beginning the conversation a bit away from Shakespeare's text, in an effort to create some shared parameters for a productive discussion of both the history plays and the larger issue of women and society.

Cheris Kramarae is a noted gender and communication theorist whose work provides many potential avenues for a discussion of the women in Shakespeare's history plays. Her book, *Women and Men Speaking*,[39] articulates several significant theoretical frameworks for evaluating how gender impacts upon language and discourse. As an example, in the first chapter, "Women as a Muted Group," Kramarae clearly summarizes the concept of muted group theory as follows:

> The language of a particular culture does not serve all of its members equally, for not all of its speakers contribute in an equal fashion to its formulation. Women (and members of other subordinate groups) are not as free or as able as men are to say what they wish, when and where they wish, because the words and the norms for their use have been formulated by the dominant group, men. So women cannot as easily or as directly articulate their experiences as men can. Women's perceptions differ from those of men because women's subordination means they

experience life differently. However, the words and norms for speaking are not generated from or fitted to women's experiences. Women are thus "muted." Their talk is often not considered of much value by men—who are, or appear to be, deaf and blind to much of women's experiences.[40]

Students might be given this summary and asked to respond to it in writing in preparation for the next class discussion period: a possible prompt for the assignment would have each student, in 300–500 words, describe a scene from his or her own life in which a portion of the above definition is either supported or refuted. Several students would then be encouraged to read out their pieces in class, in an effort to generate a dialogue on the issues that Kramarae presents. In my experience, students usually have much to say about ideas such as "muted groups."

After this introductory lesson, assign the reading of one of the history plays; any one of them will work well. Tell the students to keep in mind the principles of muted group theory as they read, and to keep a list of passages that might be especially useful as support for or opposition to the theory's major tenets. This list will provide the students a set of talking points, which will be useful to them in defending positions during classroom discussions. After the play(s) have been read and discussed, have each student write another short essay, this time focusing on how one character does or does not affirm muted group theory.

This assignment works especially well as an introduction to a feminist interpretation of either tetralogy. In terms of the Second Henriad, the approach might be used as a week's lesson following the reading of the four plays, and the students—singly or in groups—might focus on (for instance) the idea of "mutedness" in the characters of the Queen in *Richard II*, the wives of Hotspur and Mortimer in *1 Henry IV*, Mistress Quickly in *2 Henry IV* (complicated by her appearance in *Henry V*), and Katharine in *Henry V*. In this way, the students would be asked to revisit each play, realizing that each might offer differing or supplementary ideas to that initial question of "What about the women?" If groups are used for this assignment, I have found it useful to have them present their findings to the whole class for discussion.

In the case of the First Henriad, I would suggest a slightly different possibility. Have the students deal specifically with the idea of muted group theory in preparation for reading *1 Henry VI*, and revisit the issue again after the completion of *3 Henry VI*; the characters of Joan and Margaret are just too rich to pass up in such a discussion. However, at this point, it would be worthwhile to have them add a feminist literary analysis to the discussion, and I would suggest a section from Nina Levine's *Women's Matters: Politics, Gender, and Nation in Shakespeare's Early History Plays*[41] or an essay such as Phyllis Rackin's "Women's Roles in Elizabethan History Plays."[42] Adding the literary criticism at this moment will allow for the students to consider the issue within the context of the discipline of literary studies, and to understand how what they have seen in the plays might be translated into a full-scale interpretative argument.

A final note

Teaching Shakespeare's histories presents unique challenges. As I have indicated, the plays have an open structure, which can be disconcerting to some, but that also allows for rewarding possibilities in terms of student discussion and understanding. Probably the most important element in teaching the plays involves having the students understand that they need to take ownership of their interpretations. They might achieve this through reading and writing assignments, through discussion, through performance of scenes, through viewing live or taped performances, or through a variety of other creative strategies. Ultimately, if they can come to view the texts' openness as creating both responsibility and opportunity, their experience of the plays will be an enriching one.

Notes

1. Stephen Greenblatt, *Will in the World: How Shakespeare Became Shakespeare* (New York: Norton, 2004), pp. 197, 207.
2. Larry Champion, *Perspective in Shakespeare's English Histories* (Athens: University of Georgia Press, 1980), pp. 6–10.
3. Phyllis Rackin, *Stages of History: Shakespeare's English Chronicles* (Ithaca, NY: Cornell University Press, 1990), pp. 27–31.
4. Charles Forker, "The Idea of Time in Shakespeare's Second Historical Tetralogy," *The Upstart Crow* 5 (1984): 20–34.
5. E. K. Chambers, *Shakespeare: a Survey* (New York: Hill and Wang, 1963).
6. Famously, Shakespeare's own ruler, Queen Elizabeth, had serious concerns about the politics of the play, stating, "I am Richard II. Know ye not that?" Her anxiety was not unfounded: in 1601 supporters of the Earl of Essex commissioned a performance of a play about Richard (probably but not certainly Shakespeare's) shortly before his failed attempt to overthrow Elizabeth's monarchy.
7. E. M. W. Tillyard, *Shakespeare's History Plays* (London: Chatto and Windus, 1951).
8. Tillyard, *Shakespeare's History Plays*, p. 320.
9. Lily Bess Campbell, *Shakespeare's Histories: Mirrors of Elizabethan Policy* (San Marino, CA: Huntington Library, 1947).
10. Jonathan Dollimore and Alan Sinfield, "History and Ideology: the Instance of *Henry V*," in *Alternative Shakespeares*, ed. John Drakakis (New York: Methuen, 1985), p. 227.
11. Stephen Greenblatt, "Invisible Bullets," *Shakespearean Negotiations: the Circulation of Social Energy in Renaissance England* (Berkeley: University of California Press, 1988), pp. 21–65. A few versions of "Invisible Bullets" have been published in a variety of venues since 1981; I've chosen this listing because of the value of the other essays contained Greenblatt's book.
12. R. L. Smallwood, "Shakespeare's Use of History," in *The Cambridge Companion to Shakespeare Studies*, ed. Stanley Wells (Cambridge: Cambridge University Press, 1986), p. 147.

13. Michael Manheim, *The Weak King Dilemma in the Shakespearean History Play* (Syracuse, NY: Syracuse University Press, 1973).
14. Peter Saccio, *Shakespeare's English Kings: History, Chronicle, and Drama* (New York: Oxford University Press, 1977).
15. Philip Edwards, *Threshold of a Nation* (Cambridge: Cambridge University Press, 1979).
16. Rackin, *Stages of History*.
17. Paola Pugliatti, *Shakespeare the Historian* (New York: St. Martin's Press–now Palgrave Macmillan, 1996), p. 21.
18. Coppélia Kahn, *Man's Estate: Masculine Identity in Shakespeare* (Berkeley: University of California Press, 1981).
19. Jean Howard and Phyllis Rackin, *Engendering a Nation: a Feminist Account of Shakespeare's English Histories* (New York: Routledge, 1997).
20. Kathryn Schwarz, "Fearful Simile: Stealing the Breech in Shakespeare's Chronicle Plays," *Shakespeare Quarterly* 49 (1998): 140–67.
21. Geraldo de Sousa, *Shakespeare's Cross-Cultural Encounters* (New York: Palgrave–now Palgrave Macmillan, 1999).
22. David Scott Kastan, *Shakespeare and the Shapes of Time* (Hanover, NH: University Press of New England, 1982).
23. Robert B. Bennett, "Four Stages of Time: the Shape of History in Shakespeare's Second Tetralogy," *Shakespeare Studies* 19 (1987): 61–85.
24. John W. Velz (ed.), *Shakespeare's English Histories: a Quest for Form and Genre* (Binghamton, NY: Medieval and Renaissance Texts and Studies, 1996).
25. Rackin, *Stages of History*, p. 36.
26. Rackin, *Stages of History*, p. 36.
27. Hugh Grady (ed.), *Shakespeare and Modernity: Early Modern to Millennium* (New York: Routledge, 2000): 1–19.
28. Ewan Fernie, "Shakespeare and the Prospect of Presentism," *Shakespeare Survey* 58 (2005): 169–84.
29. Paul Dean, "Shakespeare's Historical Imagination," *Renaissance Studies* 11 (1997): 27–40.
30. Michael Goldman, "History-Making in the Henriad," in *Shakespearean Illuminations: Essays in Honor of Marvin Rosenberg*, ed. Jay L. Halio and Hugh Richmond, pp. 203–19 (Newark: University of Delaware Press, 1998).
31. Brian Walsh, "'Unkind Division': the Double Absence of Performing History in *1 Henry VI*," *Shakespeare Quarterly* 55 (2004): 119–47.
32. Kiernan Ryan, "The Future of History in *Henry IV*," in *Henry IV Parts One and Two*, ed. Nigel Wood, pp. 92–125 (Philadelphia: Open University Press, 1995).
33. Albert Cook, "The Ordering Effect of Dramatized History: Shakespeare and *Henry VIII*," *Centennial Review* 42 (1998): 5–28.
34. Keith Polette, *Read and Write It Out Loud: Guided Oral Literacy Strategies* (Boston: Allyn and Bacon, 2005).
35. This and all references to Shakespeare's texts are from *The Complete Works of Shakespeare*, ed. David Bevington, updated 4th edn (New York: Longman, 1997).
36. C. L. Barber, *Shakespeare's Festive Comedy: a Study of Dramatic Form and its Relation to Social Custom* (New York: Meridian, 1963), pp. 192–221.
37. From "Greene's Groatsworth of Wit Bought With a Million of Repentance" (1592), in the anthology *The Renaissance in England: Non-dramatic Prose and Verse of the Sixteenth Century*, ed. Hyder E. Rollins and Herschel Baker, pp. 851–5 (Prospect Heights, IL: Waveland Press, 1992), p. 855.

38. Howard and Rackin, *Engendering a Nation*, p. 47.
39. Cheris Kramarae, *Women and Men Speaking: Frameworks for Analysis* (Rowley, MA: Newbury House, 1981).
40. Kramarae, *Women and Men Speaking*, p. 1.
41. Nina Levine, *Women's Matters: Politics, Gender, and History in Shakespeare's Early Modern Plays* (Newark: University of Delaware Press, 1998).
42. Phyllis Rackin, "Women's Roles in Elizabethan History Plays," in *The Cambridge Companion to Shakespeare's History Plays*, ed. Michael Hattaway, pp. 71–85 (Cambridge: Cambridge University Press, 2002).

Selective guide to further reading and resources

General: Shakespeare's history plays

Berry, Edward. "Twentieth Century Shakespeare Criticism: the Histories." *The Cambridge Companion to Shakespeare Studies* ed. Stanley Wells, pp. 249–56. Cambridge: Cambridge University Press, 1986.
Bloom, Harold (ed.). *William Shakespeare: Histories and Poems*. New York: Chelsea House, 1986.
Dutton, Richard, and Howard, Jean (eds). *A Companion to Shakespeare's Works: the Histories*. Malden, MA: Blackwell, 2005.
Hattaway, Michael (ed.). *The Cambridge Companion to Shakespeare's History Plays*. Cambridge: Cambridge University Press, 2002.
Wikander, M. H. *The Play of Truth and State: Historical Drama from Shakespeare to Brecht*. Baltimore: Johns Hopkins University Press, 1986.

Internet resources

The Folger Shakespeare Library <http://www.folger.edu/welcome/htm>
Shakespeare in the Classroom <http://www.pbs.org/shakespeare/educators>
William Shakespeare and the Internet <http://shakespeare.palomar.edu/>

Teaching Shakespeare: two recent aids to context and strategy

Fernie, Ewan, Wray, Ramona, Thornton Burnett, Mark, and McManus, Clare (eds). *Reconceiving the Renaissance: a Critical Reader*. Oxford: Oxford University Press 2005.
Palfrey, Simon. *Doing Shakespeare*. London: Arden Shakespeare, 2005.

7

Ben Jonson

Matthew Steggle

Chronology

1572	Ben Jonson born in London. His father, who died a month before Jonson was born, was a church minister. Jonson's mother remarries to a bricklayer.
1580s	Jonson attends Westminster School, studying under the scholar William Camden.
1589	Jonson apprenticed as a bricklayer.
early 1590s	Jonson serves as a soldier in the Low Countries, killing a man in single combat.
1594	Jonson marries Anne Lewis, whom he later described as "a shrew yet honest."[1] Jonson becomes involved in theatre, as an actor and a writer.
1597	*The Isle of Dogs*, a (now-lost) comedy co-written by Jonson and the satirist Thomas Nashe, is performed. The authorities order it banned and arrest all involved.
1598	*Every Man in His Humour* performed, Jonson's first major success and an early example of "humours comedy." Jonson kills his fellow-actor Gabriel Spencer in a duel. Jonson is sentenced to death for murder, and escapes the gallows only by pleading "benefit of clergy" and being branded on the thumb. Jonson converts to Catholicism while in prison.
1599	*Every Man Out of His Humour* performed, and printed the following year.
1600	*Cynthia's Revels* performed.
1601	*Poetaster* performed. *Poetaster* contains personal satire on Thomas Dekker and John Marston, and is part of the "War of the Theatres."
1602	Jonson is paid by Henslowe for writing extra scenes for Kyd's *Spanish Tragedy*.

1603	Jonson's tragedy *Sejanus* performed, leading to accusations against Jonson of Popery and treason.
	The Entertainment at Althorpe performed, marking the start of Jonson's career as a writer of courtly entertainments and masques.
	Jonson's son Benjamin dies of plague, commemorated in the poem "On my first son."
1605	Performance of *The Masque of Blackness* at court, a masque written by Jonson, with Inigo Jones as designer, for James I's wife Queen Anne.
	Jonson, George Chapman, and John Marston collaborate on *Eastward Ho!* Jonson is arrested on account of the play's satire against the Scots.
	Discovery of the Gunpowder Plot. A document survives suggesting that Jonson (who had had dinner with the conspirators a few weeks beforehand) was in some way involved in negotiations after the plot, and was asked to act as an intermediary in putting the government in touch with an unnamed Catholic priest.
1606	*Volpone* performed.
1609	*The Entertainment at Britain's Burse*, a recently rediscovered entertainment, staged to celebrate the opening of the New Exchange, a shopping centre in the Strand.
	Epicoene performed.
1610	*The Alchemist* performed.
	Jonson renounces Catholicism and returns to the Anglican faith.
1611	Jonson's tragedy *Catiline* performed on stage.
1612–13	Jonson travels in France, acting as a tutor to the son of Sir Walter Ralegh.
1614	First performance of *Bartholomew Fair*, at the Hope Theatre, also used for bear-baiting.
1616	Jonson publishes nine plays, numerous masques and entertainments, and a collection of poetry in his Folio *The Workes of Benjamin Jonson*. Jonson is the first Renaissance playwright to make such an implicit claim of literary merit.
	The Devil is An Ass performed.
1618	Jonson walks to Scotland and back. En route, he visits William Drummond of Hawthornden, and Drummond records in detail their conversations.
1623	Jonson's library largely destroyed in a fire (commemorated in his poem *An Execration upon Vulcan*).
	Jonson writes commendatory verse for the Shakespeare First Folio, published in this year, and modelled in many respects on Jonson's 1616 *Workes*.

1625	Death of King James, and accession of Charles. Jonson still engaged as a court masque-writer, but starts to become a more marginalized figure.
1629	Jonson suffers a stroke.
	The New Inn performed. It fails on the stage. Jonson writes the *Ode to Himself*, condemning the audience for being unworthy of the play.
1631	Final breakdown of Jonson's stormy relationship with Inigo Jones, chief designer for his masques.
1632	*The Magnetic Lady* performed.
1633	*A Tale of a Tub* performed.
1634	*Love's Welcome to Bolsover* performed, a masque written for his last and most loyal patron, William Cavendish.
1637	Death of Ben Jonson at Westminster.
1640	Posthumous publication of a new and expanded *Works*.

Critical overview

It is useful to think of Jonson's first literary critic as himself. Jonson's plays express an apparent certainty about their own literary worth, summed up in what the Epilogue of *Cynthia's Revels* reports Jonson as having said about his own play: "By—, 'tis good, and if you lik't, you may." This idea of drama as having literary merit is also symbolized by Jonson's unprecedented decision to publish his *Works*, in a thick and ample Folio aimed at the luxury market. Nor is this merely a matter of self-confidence: it is also a moral vocation. In various writings, poems, and even recorded conversations, Jonson outlines a view of the moral purpose of literature. Jonson believes that drama should bring wisdom to those who consume it, and that being a poet (under which heading he certainly includes playwrights) is almost a religious calling: "If men will impartially and not asquint look towards the offices and function of a poet, they will easily conclude to themselves the impossibility of any man's being the good poet without first being a good man" (Epistle to *Volpone*).

This view of an ethically engaged and autobiographically frank literature is interestingly out of step with many modern ideas about how literature works, something which itself might make an interesting teaching opportunity. Another thing that makes Jonson's literary manifesto interesting is the tension between theory and practice. Jonson's own life could not unfairly be called turbulent, rather than obviously displaying the serenity one might expect from the manifesto from *Volpone*. Jonson's plays, which one might expect to be worthy tracts on virtue, are in fact far more complicated than this, since the world depicted in Jonson's comedies, and in his two tragedies, is not necessarily one in which justice and morality win out. Rather, it is often anarchic, sometimes almost absurdist, and, in the right pedagogical circumstances, extremely entertaining.

Another long-influential construction of Jonson, and another one which raises as many problems as it clarifies, is that which started to crystallize in the decades after the Restoration, and which remains in some respects still prevalent today. This is Jonson as a foil to Shakespeare, typically in a formula in which Shakespeare is praised for naturalness, honesty, and authenticity, while Jonson is condemned for academic stuffiness and lack of basic human emotion. This pairing, in which, as Mick Jardine has written, Jonson is the "Other" against which writers identify the "Self" of Shakespeare, and *vice versa*, is dramatized, for instance, in the scene imagined by Thomas Fuller, of Shakespeare and Jonson trading witticisms in a tavern: Jonson is "solid and slow," like a Spanish galleon, and no match for the quick-witted and naturally gifted Shakespeare.[2]

This comparison, unfavourable to Jonson, also extends to the dramatists' respective treatment of character. Jonson works within a style, which he pioneered, of "humours comedy," where every character has one obvious comically exaggerated trait—a psychological imbalance, a compulsion, or an obsession. In addition, Jonson's plays draw attention to their own artificiality, explicitly declaring that they are working within that style, for instance, in the Induction to *Every Man Out of His Humour*. Having made that declaration, of course, Jonson promptly subverts it, delivering a play in the course of which all the characters are driven out of their particular humour. Shakespeare is less theoretically explicit (although Shakespearean comedies repay scrutiny as if they were humours comedies), and critics have long perceived his plays as more "authentic" as a result. Comparisons such as Fuller's, starting from an imagined biographical truth, always work to the denigration of Jonson's plays. A more modern critical approach, suspicious of biographical extrapolation, and aware of the difficulties in interpreting the plays that make up the Shakespeare canon as simply the product of an untaught genius warbling his native wood-notes wild, might therefore by corollary be suspicious of an approach that considered the plays of Jonson purely in terms of their (undoubtedly impressive) learning.

A third critical stereotype of Jonson, once again problematic but once again interesting to teach with, is represented by Edmund Wilson's essay "Morose Ben Jonson," in *The Triple Thinkers: Twelve Essays on Literary Subjects* (1948), which presents Jonson in psychoanalytical terms as a miserly anal neurotic.[3] Wilson's essay is a good pairing with the work of L. C. Knights (*Drama and Society in the Age of Jonson* [1937]),[4] who locates Jonson's plays much more in the context of a culture rather than an individual psyche, and the interplay of these two paradigms for viewing Jonson has continued up until the present day.

No survey of critical approaches to Jonson would be complete without consideration of the 11-volume edition of Jonson by C. H. Herford, Percy Simpson, and Evelyn Simpson published by the Oxford University Press between 1925 and 1952. For many students, the green-and-gold library buckram of Herford and Simpson, and the ragged-edged or even still partially uncut pages of the volumes, condition their experience of Jonson as an old-fashioned dinosaur of the literary canon. Herford and the Simpsons assume readers who are not deterred by Latin numerals, old spelling, and imitation of Renaissance typographical practice; who are accustomed to working with two, or even more, of the volumes open at once, comparing text and commentary; and who are fluent in Latin and Ancient Greek, neither of which languages the editors feel the need to translate. Herford and the Simpsons also, notoriously, privilege Jonson's Folio over all other early witnesses to the text of the plays, in the service of their vision of the Jonson canon as a unified, authorially polished *oeuvre*. Until the arrival of the imminent and much-needed *Cambridge Works of Ben Jonson* (forthcoming 2007), it remains the case that there is no complete substitute for the Oxford edition, but considered from the perspective of teaching—particularly teaching at first-year level—the great edition has become, in effect, a liability. Fortunately, editions like Helen Ostovich's *Four Comedies* (1997) and the Revels Plays series, which now includes many of Jonson's major plays, make it possible to engage with Herford and Simpson as a critical phenomenon in its own right, rather than as the only means of access to the text.

More recent work on Jonson develops both the psychoanalytical approach represented by Wilson and the contextualizing work of Knights. Work particularly worth mention includes the biographies of David Riggs (*Ben Jonson: a Life* [1989]), and W. David Kay (*Ben Jonson: a Literary Life* [1995], perhaps the best single-volume life of Jonson currently available to students).[5] A revival of interests in masque in general has paid particular dividends for Jonson studies, with work including essays collected by David Lindley in *The Court Masque* (1984).[6] Long written off as "tied to rules of flattery," Jonson's masques are now getting more and more attention as much more complex negotiations of the power relations of a court. Monographs in this area include Robert C. Evans's monograph *Ben Jonson and the Poetics of Patronage* (1989), and Lesley Mickel's *Ben Jonson's Antimasques: a Study of Growth and Decline* (1999).[7] The new directions in which Jonson studies is starting to move are indicated by the titles, and the contents, of two excellent recent collections of essays: Julie Sanders, Kate Chedgzoy, and Susan Wiseman (eds), *Refashioning Ben Jonson: Gender, Politics, and the Jonsonian Canon* (1998), and Martin Butler (ed.), *Re-Presenting Ben Jonson: Text, History, Performance* (1999).[8] *Refashioning Ben Jonson* is particularly interesting in that it reopens debate on Jonson and gender. Jonson has long been seen as a chauvinist, indeed, often used as a foil to set off Shakespeare's perceived proto-feminism, but the essays in this volume pay more attention to the subtleties of figures such as Frances Fitzdotterel (from *The Devil is An Ass*) or *The New Inn*'s Pru.

Among other monographs, Richard Dutton's *Ben Jonson: Authority: Criticism* (1996) explores the whole question of Jonson and the critical act, and Joseph Lowenstein, *Ben Jonson and Possessive Authorship* (2002) also addresses the question of how Jonson constructs, and in some accounts invents, the role of author.[9] Julie Sanders's *Ben Jonson's Theatrical Republics* (1998) takes forward the question of how Jonson's plays figure politics, in all its forms.[10] Bruce Thomas Boehrer's *The Fury of Men's Gullets: Ben Jonson and the Digestive Canal* (1997), a highly useful text for undergraduate teaching, tackles Jonson's interest in all stages of the digestive process, from first till last.[11]

Pedagogic strategies

The opening of *The Alchemist* offers an emblematic example of the problems, and opportunities, inherent in teaching Jonson:

> *Act* I. *Scene* I.
> FACE, SVBTLE, DOL Common.
>
> BEleeu't, I will.
> **SVB.**
> Thy worst. I fart at thee.
> **DOL.**
> Ha' you your wits? Why gentlemen! for loue—
> **FAC.**
> Sirrah, I'll strip you—
> **SVB.**
> What to doe? lick [f]igs
> Out at my—
> **FAC.**
> Rogue, rogue, out of all your sleights.
> **DOL.**
> Nay, looke yee! Soueraigne, Generall, are you mad-men?
> **SVB.**
> O, let the wild sheepe loose. Ile gumme your silkes
> With good strong water, an'you come.
> **DOL.**
> Will you haue
> The neighbours heare you? Will you betray all?
> Harke, I heare some body.
> **FAC.**
> Sirrah—
> **SVB.**
> I shall marre
> All that the taylor has made, if you approch.
> *The Alchemist*, I.i.1–10

It is probably not controversial to argue that one of the main tools for investigating a text in a seminar situation is a read-through. The above passage is, equally uncontroversially, one that ought to respond well to such a treatment: fast-moving and surprising. In close analysis, it can be seen to adumbrate some interesting themes of the play to follow: the interest in costume, the complicated, competitive, and shifting three-cornered relationship between Subtle, Face, and Doll Common, and the use of the language of politics (Sovereign, General), to describe that venture. Indeed, the notorious fart of the first line can be seen as a pre-echo of the explosion at the climax of the play, opening up opportunities to discuss the episode as, structurally, almost as a musical overture to the play to follow.

And yet, working with the scene in the version presented here, students may well struggle, in ways that instructors may not fully foresee, to deliver a read-through that helps their colleagues develop discussion of these issues. For example, asked to read through this passage, the student reading Face may well fail to recognize the first speech as belonging to them, the speech-prefix being concealed within the unfamiliar convention which Jonson takes over from Renaissance Latin editions of Terence. More insidious effects of this convention include the use of speech-headings on a separate line from the following speech, which visually breaks the scene down into a series of discrete utterances rather than overlapping and interrupting speeches. Even the use of "SVB" as a speech-heading for Subtle is an extra layer of noise that a student has to mentally filter out.

Further problems will result from the old spelling, so that, for instance, "Soueraigne" may well be unfamiliar enough to take all the pace off the speech when sight-read aloud, and this problem is compounded by to the specifics of the unfamiliar language. But above all, the lack of context and lack of explicit reference to stage movement or inflection makes it hard for students to imagine the scene as they go along as more than a disconnected sequence of speeches. The above version is taken from the full-text transcription of the 1616 Folio in *Early English Books Online*, and while extreme, it is not untypical of plain-text transcriptions of the play that students might obtain over the Internet. Indeed, some, such as a version downloadable through the University of Michigan's Humanities Technology Initiative,[12] and designed for use in a lexicographical corpus, are even less suitable for classroom use, breaking the text down entirely into a series of discrete single lines. Contrast these texts with the same scene in Helen Ostovich's 1997 edition of the play:

Act 1 Scene 1

[Enter] Face [and] Subtle [quarrelling violently, followed by] Dol Common [attempting to quiet them]

FACE [*Threatening with his sword*] Believe't, I will.
SUBTLE   Thy worst! I fart at thee!

DOL   Ha' you your wits? Why, gentlemen! For love—
FACE   Sirrah, I'll strip you—
SUBTLE   What to do? Lick figs
           Out at my—
FACE   Rogue, rogue, out of all your sleights!
DOL   Nay, look ye! Sovereign, General, are you madmen?
[*She holds Face back*]
SUBTLE   O, let the wild sheep loose! I'll gum your silks
           With good strong water, an' you come.
[*He threatens Face with a flask*]
DOL   Will you have
           The neighbours hear you? Will you betray all?
           Hark, I hear somebody!
[*Pause. The quarrel continues in hoarse whispers*]
FACE   Sirrah—
SUBTLE   I shall mar
           All that the tailor has made if you approach.

It is not merely that the modern-spelling version is easier to understand, or that the excellent on-page footnotes give a much richer sense of the play's meanings than the noteless versions available electronically (including the *EEBO* transcription above). These factors apply to all early modern texts in teaching situations. But Ostovich's layout makes the text much easier to read *as a piece of drama*. Thus, a student reader may well notice the way that the staccato, chaotic rhythms are still unobtrusively contained within the blank verse, because Ostovich's layout builds this in. Ostovich makes very extensive use of supplied stage directions, most of which are amplified from "implied stage directions" in the text itself, such as the emblematic opposition of Face's sword and Subtle's flask. The emblematic opposition itself is interesting, and productive of good debate, but so is the question of where in the text the editor has conjured these details from, or whether it is conjecture based on modern performances, and if the latter is the case, whether there is any validity to that type of performance evidence. Even where a student might be inclined to question Ostovich's square-bracketed additions—are we sure that there's a pause at line eight? Couldn't we have Face ignore Doll entirely for the moment, and continue to get louder?—the very presence of those additions is providing the material for a profitable debate about the performance possibilities of a scene.

If this scene is to be taken seriously in the seminar room as a piece of drama, it is necessary too to give it more time than one might usually allot for the read-through of a section of poem, or even of a tragedy, of comparable length. (On the usual seminar dynamics of read-throughs, see Matthew C. Hansen, "Learning to Read Shakespeare: Using Read-Throughs as a Teaching and Learning Strategy."[13]) The interesting things in this scene reside, not so much in the individual speeches, as in the relationships between them, and in the implied timing and movement. While the realities of seminar room layouts, and seminar group dynamics, often make impossible any sort of fully elaborated performance, a text like *The Alchemist* may well repay exhaustive re-rehearsed read-through of a short fragment of text better than a more normally paced read-through of a larger section. None of this is to deny the basic proposition that students should be aware of the materiality and unfamiliarity of the texts as they appeared in their early modern editions; merely to argue that, from the point of view of making a seminar on Jonson work, consideration of such material difficulties should be temporarily delayed.

In short, selection and vigorous recommendation of an appropriate edition is particularly critical when teaching Jonson, but the right edition can open up a profitable debate in terms of, in effect, performance criticism approaches to the plays. Such an approach can also draw on excellent recent publications on Jonson in performance, such as Richard Cave, Elizabeth Schafer, and Brian Woolland's *Ben Jonson and Theatre: Performance, Practice, and Theory* (1999), which includes interviews with directors and actors as well as more conventional academic pieces, or Brian Woolland (ed.), *Jonsonians: Living Traditions* (2003), a later collection of essays exploring performance approaches to Jonson.[14]

However, another factor with teaching Jonson is the selection of appropriate texts beyond the obvious ones. Almost invariably, Jonson is taught in terms of the "big four" comedies, *Volpone, Epicoene, The Alchemist*, and *Bartholomew Fair*, and this fact tends to reflect the priorities of syllabus design in which Jonson is invoked as a foil to Shakespeare. As well as their undoubted status as masterpieces, these four plays are convenient in that they are close in time to Shakespeare. Indeed, *Bartholomew Fair* refers to Shakespeare's *The Tempest* explicitly, and *The Alchemist* appears to do so implicitly, as David Lucking has argued in "Carrying Tempest in His Hand and Voice: the Figure of the Magician in Jonson and Shakespeare" (2004).[15] Given that there seems little prospect of dethroning Shakespeare from his central place in British culture, and that teaching priorities will continue to reflect a tendency to locate other early modern authors relative to Shakespeare, one possible strategy would be to pair a Shakespeare and a Jonson play together. This raises some interesting possibilities to venture beyond Jonson's most canonical comedies: possible pairings might include *Cynthia's Revels* and *A Midsummer Night's Dream*, *Sejanus* and *Julius Caesar*, and *The New Inn* and *The Tempest*. The first of these pairings takes perhaps the most neglected play in the Jonson canon, which features "live" magical effects on stage, supernatural characters, and an Ovidian interest in transformation. Like *A Midsummer Night's Dream*, it concludes with a fifth-act play-within-a-play which is partly a travesty of a "proper" entertainment, but which is also not entirely lacking in its own mythic and potentially transformative power. The second of the pairs would move Jonson's tragedy away from the usual stereotypes in terms of which it is discussed—Jonson and James, Jonson and seriousness—and locate it, for students, much more richly in terms of Renaissance dramatic representations of raw political power. *The New Inn*, performed in 1629 and often written off as one of Jonson's "dotages," is now increasingly seen in terms of a romance to set alongside Shakespeare's late plays, with its interest in reunion and the power of love. As far as I know, no one has yet attempted to use the surviving 110-line fragment of *Mortimer His Fall*[16] as a companion piece to Marlowe's *Edward II*, but the technique in general is a good one.

Nor need Jonson's drama be represented, in such pairings, only by full-length plays, thanks to the large number of much shorter texts in the canon. There are many texts with obvious pedagogical possibilities among Jonson's masques and entertainments, particularly in pairings with Shakespearean plays. *The Masque of Blackness* and *The Masque of Beauty* tend to head such lists, for their fascinating portrayals of the intersection of gender, blackness, and role-playing, but also worth attention are texts such as *Oberon, The Fairy Prince*, or *The Golden Age Restor'd*, short, complete, and provocative texts which, as their titles sufficiently indicate, bear on big questions of Renaissance culture. One particular short text is worth special mention, by virtue of being new to the Jonson canon. *The Entertainment at Britain's Burse*, rediscovered in 1995 thanks to the archival work of James Knowles, is interesting to teach with partly simply because it is not in Herford and Simpson. It is a short entertainment commissioned in 1609 to celebrate the opening of the New Exchange on the Strand, London's first purpose-built luxury shopping centre. This short and lively piece, much of which is given over to description of the goods on offer there, is ideal for focusing discussion of the marketplace in early modern London, and the place of drama in that marketplace. Its most obvious connections are with *Epicoene*, a play written at almost exactly the same time, but its representations of travel and the exotic give it a much wider interest. And, at merely three hundred lines in length, it would make an appropriate *lagniappe* to accompany a larger text on a student reading list.

Notes

1. *Conversations*, 254. Cited in *Ben Jonson*, ed. C. H. Herford, Percy Simpson, and Evelyn Simpson (Oxford: Clarendon Press, 1925–52), vol. 1, p. 139.
2. Mick Jardine, "Jonson as Shakespeare's Other," in *Ben Jonson and Theatre: Performance, Practice, and Theory*, ed. Richard Cave, Elizabeth Schafer, and Brian Woolland (London and New York: Routledge, 1999).
3. Edmund Wilson, "Morose Ben Jonson," in E. Wilson, *The Triple Thinkers: Twelve Essays on Literary Subjects* (London: Oxford University Press, 1938).
4. L. C. Knights, *Drama and Society in the Age of Jonson* (London: Chatto and Windus, 1937).
5. David Riggs, *Ben Jonson: a Life* (Cambridge, MA: Harvard University Press, 1989); W. David Kay, *Ben Jonson: a Literary Life* (Basingstoke: Macmillan—now Palgrave Macmillan, 1995).

6. David Lindley (ed.), *The Court Masque* (Dover, NH and Manchester: Manchester University Press, 1984).
7. Robert C. Evans, *Ben Jonson and the Poetics of Patronage* (Lewisburg: Bucknell University Press / London: Associated University Presses, 1989); Lesley Mickel, *Ben Jonson's Antimasques: a Study of Growth and Decline* (Aldershot, UK and Brookfield, VT: Ashgate, 1999).
8. Julie Sanders, Kate Chedgzoy, and Susan Wiseman (eds), *Refashioning Ben Jonson: Gender, Politics, and the Jonsonian Canon* (Basingstoke: Macmillan–now Palgrave Macmillan, 1998), and Martin Butler (ed.), *Re-Presenting Ben Jonson: Text, History, Performance* (Basingstoke: Macmillan–now Palgrave Macmillan, 1999).
9. Richard Dutton, *Ben Jonson: Authority: Criticism* (Basingstoke: Macmillan–now Palgrave Macmillan, 1996); Joseph Loewenstein, *Ben Jonson and Possessive Authorship* (Cambridge: Cambridge University Press, 2002).
10. Julie Sanders, *Ben Jonson's Theatrical Republics* (Basingstoke: Macmillan–now Palgrave Macmillan, 1998).
11. Bruce Thomas Boehrer, *The Fury of Men's Gullets: Ben Jonson and the Digestive Canal* (Philadelphia: University of Pennsylvania Press, 1997).
12. http://www.hti.umich.edu/
13. Matthew C. Hansen, "Learning to Read Shakespeare: Using Read-Throughs as a Teaching and Learning Strategy," *Working Papers on the Web* 4 (2002): 5 <http://www.shu.ac.uk/wpw/renaissance/hansen.htm>
14. Richard Cave, Elizabeth Schafer, and Brian Woolland (eds), *Ben Jonson and Theatre: Performance, Practice, and Theory* (London and New York: Routledge, 1999); Brian Woolland (ed.), *Jonsonians: Living Traditions* (Aldershot: Ashgate, 2003).
15. David Lucking, "Carrying Tempest in His Hand and Voice: the Figure of the Magician in Jonson and Shakespeare," *English Studies* 85 (2004): 297–310.
16. Ben Jonson, *Ben Jonson*, vol. 8, pp. 60–2.

Selective guide to further reading and resources

Jonson, I have argued, has been in many ways a prisoner of his editions, and to an extent, the availability of new web resources makes it easier than ever to allow students to explore this towering author. This final section reviews editions; journals; and online resources, both subscription and free-to-air. For an overview of recent books and articles I refer the reader back to pages 110–11 above.

Editions

Ben Jonson, *Ben Jonson* ed. C. H. Herford, P. Simpson, and E. Simpson, 11 vols (Oxford: Clarendon Press, 1925–52). Large, maddening, but still indispensable for some purposes.

Ben Jonson, *Four Comedies*, ed. Helen Ostovich (London: Longman, 1997). The best single-volume edition of the major plays.

Ben Jonson, *Epicene* [*sic*], ed. Richard Dutton (Manchester: Manchester University Press, 2003). This play is on the list partly as a representative of the excellent series of which it forms part, which now includes many of Jonson's full-length plays, and partly too because it contains an annotated edition of the *Entertainment at Britain's Burse* discussed above.

Journals

The Ben Jonson Journal. Currently in its twelfth year of publication, this is the only journal devoted solely to Jonson, and is an important resource for anyone working in the field. Abstracts of articles from past issues are available online at http://www.geocities.com/benjonsonjournal/benjonsonjournal.htm.

Electronic resources (subscription)

For Jonson, the main subscription-based electronic resources are the same as for other early modern dramatists. *Literature Online* <http://lion.chadwyck.co.uk> and *Early English Books Online* <http://eebo.chadwyck.com> have full-text transcriptions of most of Jonson's work, while the latter also contains page images of every page of every pre-1700 printing of Jonson.

Electronic resources (free-to-air)

Jokkinen, Aniina. *Ben Jonson (1572–1637)*
   <http://www.luminarium.org/sevenlit/jonson/>, part of the *Luminarium* website <http://www.luminarium.org/>. This site does what its title claims: it illuminates Jonson, by including a short biography and online editions of many texts, derived from William Gifford's nineteenth-century edition, and links to editions of many others. It also contains an excellent listing of the scholarly articles on Jonson which are available electronically without subscription.
Holloway, Clark J. *The Holloway Pages Ben Jonson Page,*
   <http://www.hollowaypages.com/Jonson.htm>. This marvellous site presents an online edition of Jonson based mainly on the 1692 Folio. Transcription completed so far includes all Jonson's plays, Jonson's poetry, and Jonson's earlier masques.
McLean, Adam. *The Alchemy Web Site*
   <http://www.levity.com/alchemy/home.html>. This site earns its mention on the list as a wonderful teaching resource for work on *The Alchemist*. An enormous repository of alchemical texts and illustrations.
Project Gutenberg, <http://www.gutenberg.org>. Contains several texts of Jonson plays, mainly derived from Felix Schelling's edition of 1910. Conveniently in modern-spelling.
The Schoenberg Centre for Electronic Text and Image,
   <http://dewey.library.upenn.edu/sceti/>. Includes a beautiful colour photographic fascimile of Jonson's 1616 Folio.
Thorndike, Ashley H. "Ben Jonson," in *The Cambridge History of English and American Literature* (1907–21), online at *Project Bartleby,*
   <http://www.bartleby.com/216/ index.html>. A complete, synoptic, and usefully old-fashioned account of Jonson.
"Ben Jonson," from Charles Wells Moulton (ed.), *The Library of Literary Criticism* (1901), online at <http://www.geocities.com/litpageplus/jonsonmoul.html>, as part of Robert C. Evans's *Litpage* project. Invaluable anthology of brief critical remarks from the seventeenth to nineteenth centuries, ideally suited for the preparation of seminar handouts.

8
Marston and Chapman

Rick Bowers

Chronology

Marston

1576	7 October, baptised at Wardington, Oxfordshire.
1594	BA, Brasenose College, Oxford.
1595–1606	In residence, Middle Temple, London.
1598	*The Metamorphosis of Pigmalions Image and Certain Satyres* and *The Scourge of Villainie*.
1599	1 June, Marston's satires, along with sundry other offensive and allegedly subversive pamphlets burned in public by order of the Bishops' Ban.
1599	*Antonio and Mellida* performed by the Paul's Boys.
1600	*Antonio's Revenge.*
1601	*What You Will.*
1604	*The Malcontent*, performed at Blackfriars Theatre by the Queen's Revels Boys and later by the King's Men.
1605	Collaborated with Jonson and Chapman on *Eastward Ho!* Performed at the Blackfriars.
1605	*The Dutch Courtesan.*
1606	*Sophonisba.*
1608(?)	*The Insatiate Countess*, unfinished, performed at Whitefriars Theatre.
1609	Ordained deacon and priest at Stanton Harcourt, Oxfordshire.
1616	Granted the incumbency at Christchurch, Hampshire.
1634	25 June, died at Aldermanbury, London; interred in the Temple Church.

Chapman

1559	Born at Hitchin, Hertfordshire.
1585–94	In military service abroad.

1596	*The Blind Beggar of Alexandria*, performed by the Admiral's Men at the Rose Theatre.
1597	*An Humorous Day's Mirth*.
1598	Continuation of Marlowe's *Hero and Leander*.
1601	*All Fools*, performed at Blackfriars Theatre.
1602	*The Gentleman Usher*.
1604	*Bussy D'Ambois*, Paul's Theatre.
1604	*The Widow's Tears*, Blackfriars.
1605	*Monsieur D'Olive*.
1605	Collaborated with Jonson and Marston on *Eastward Ho!* Performed at the Blackfriars.
1605	Briefly imprisoned with Jonson due to offensive material in *Eastward Ho!*
1608	*The Conspiracy and Tragedy of Charles Duke of Byron*, Blackfriars.
1610	*The Revenge of Bussy D'Ambois*, performed at Whitefriars Theatre.
1612(?)	*The Tragedy of Chabot*.
1616	Publication of Chapman's *The Whole Works of Homer*.
1634	12 May, died in London; interred at St Giles-in-the-Fields.

Critical overview

As playwrights, Marston and Chapman (along with Ben Jonson) intersect in 1605 with the notorious performance and publication of *Eastward Ho!* for which two of the three collaborators (not Marston) served time in gaol. Marston was best known to his contemporaries as a satirist while Chapman was perhaps better known and longer-lived as a classicist (it was his Homer that Keats "looked into"). Hazlitt, who first focused critically on the two playwrights in his third lecture on the Age of Elizabeth, describes them this way: "Next to Marston I must put Chapman, whose name is better known as the translator of Homer than as a dramatic writer. He is, like Marston, a philosophic observer, a didactic reasoner: but he has both more gravity in his tragic style, and more levity in his comic vein."[1] Although somewhat honorific, Hazlitt's observations also anticipate more modern perspectives in perceiving a burlesque energy about Marston's work: "Marston is a writer of great merit, who rose to tragedy from the ground of comedy, and whose *forte* was not sympathy, either with the stronger or softer emotions, but an impatient scorn and bitter indignation against the vices and follies of men, which vented itself either in comic irony or in lofty invective. He was properly a satirist."[2] However, the drama of both Marston and Chapman registers protest against contemporary disparities concerning social inequity and political corruption, making their work especially conflicted, radical, and assertive.

Indeed, Jonathan Dollimore detects the emergence of "radical tragedy" in Marston's *Antonio* plays even as he credits dangerous knowledge and dissident desire as foundational to anti-humanist critique. Herein, a play such as

Bussy D'Ambois features prominently in terms of de-centring the tragic subject itself. Marston and Chapman, then and now, assert social and psychic disjunctions that make readers, playgoers, and humanist thinkers uncomfortable in their received complacencies. Principled defiance, psychological conflict, self-destruction, and malcontent improvisation—all four and more register themselves within the distressed anti-humanist subject as indicative of the contingencies spoken to in tragedy that is truly radical. Crediting Nietzsche's view of the artist and philosopher as powerfully disquieting and subversive, Dollimore relates oppositional energies of self-destruction and agonized perception within the heroes of early modern English drama and quotes the character Tamyra from Chapman's *Bussy D'Ambois*:

> . . . Fear, fear and hope
> Of one thing, at one instant fight in me:
> I love what most I loathe, and cannot live
> Unless I compass that which holds my death.
> (II.ii.168ff)[3]

Dollimore appreciates the sheer energy of these dramas with regard to inversions of power in cultural and political terms, and his perspectives relate also to complications within performance.

A more philosophically humanist literary critic such as Geoffrey Aggeler sees these playwrights in terms of morality, philosophy, and didacticism. Hence, Aggeler unifies the two under the critical rubric of Neostoic Calvinism, as applied to Marston, and Stoic-Sceptic dialecticism with regard to Chapman.[4] Both playwrights marshal some elements of post-Montaigne scepticism, but it seems less clear—biographically, critically, and culturally—that Marston wrote his plays under some sort of Stoic moral duress. Outrageously histrionic, over the top, and sensational, Marston's plays seem altogether too extroverted and overstated for traditional moral regard. As T. F. Wharton, in his introduction to *The Drama of John Marston*, argues, "Possibly the most productive lines of enquiry that recent critical theory offers lead in exactly the opposite direction from moralism. Whether we address literature's commercial interchanges or the transactions of Bakhtinian 'Carnival' or Barthean *jouissance*, the discourse of criticism is now highly attuned to play and inter-play between text and audiences."[5] Marston's plays seem to be especially conscious of their ludic theatricality and ironic reflexivity in relation to audience complacency and expectation.

Chapman finds fuller Stoic equipoise in his dramatic verse, especially in his most famous work *Bussy D'Ambois*. But such equipoise is strictly metaphorical, and to put this tragedy in touch with Marston's "harsh comedy" *The Malcontent* is to highlight themes of defiance and assertion that are sharply attuned to irony in both plays. As the Malcontent himself avers, "Discord to malcontents is very manna" (I.iv.38). Bussy, likewise, declares,

"Who to himself is law, no law doth need" (II.i.203). In both cases more "discord" and "law" ensues than the characters can handle or even imagine. While such ironic and self-referential sense of "presentation" informs Chapman's drama, it suffuses Marston's plays. In *Bussy D'Ambois* ironic contests represent a philosophical competition between public service and private dignity that is metaphorically "played" in front of others. In the *Antonio* plays and *The Malcontent* irony asserts itself from the outset as a theatrical competition between public performance and private assertion that is literally "played" before others. Chapman's metaphorical theatre distances effect to elicit compassion; Marston's literalist theatre asserts effect to stimulate self interest. At all points, these plays are less about moral broadcasting and more about theatrical exchange. Their playfulness represents their theatrical power and their lasting value for classroom consideration. Unlike Chapman, Marston is usually disparaged as an authority on *any*thing, but he put readers right later in his preface to *Parasiter, or The Fawn*: "The life of these things consists in action," even as he challenged readers from the outset of his early satire *The Scourge of Villanie*: "Hee that thinks worse of my rimes then my selfe, I scorne him, for he cannot, he that thinks better is a foole."[6]

If Chapman confronts ideas within his plays, Marston clearly confronts audiences with his plays. Consider the aggressively disjunctive opening of *The Malcontent*: "*The vilest out-of-tune music being heard, enter* BILIOSO *and* PREPASSO." In a scene of only ten lines, two courtiers angrily remonstrate against the very conditions of music and action in which they find themselves: "Why, how now? are ye mad, or drunk, or both, or what?" Annoyed and defiant, Prepasso spurts: "You think you are in a brothel-house, do you not? This room is ill-scented" And immediately: "*Enter one with a perfume*." This ludicrous stage direction seems bent on providing literal atmosphere as Prepasso engages with it directly, "So, perfume, perfume; some upon me, I pray thee." Onstage, an extra with a huge oversized atomizer (perhaps bellows-sized?), complies to try and overcome the stench of corruption *in* and *of* this play. Through voice, music, and action, the opening scene suggests forms of loud and confused improvisation. Throughout, Marston's plays aggressively literalize and assert their own theatricality.

In like manner, the early stage action of *Antonio's Revenge* overleaps audience expectation with surprising theatrical excessiveness. Consider the abrupt stage direction with which the play opens: "*Enter* PIERO *unbraced, his arms bare, smeared in blood, a poniard in one hand, bloody, and a torch in the other,* STROTZO *following him with a cord*." Piero, homicidal maniac and villain of the piece, outside of his daughter Mellida's bedroom at 2:00 a.m., crows in triumph as he instructs his henchman to bind the body of a dead courtier to the body of his own living daughter Mellida. He intends to implicate both in fornication, thereby frustrating her true love, Antonio, against whom Piero aims his murderous revenge. Granted, Piero is as preposterous as he is insane. But these incredible actions make perfect sense to him, as they do within the play itself wherein notions of sanity and society and the bonds that purport to hold society together get deconstructed through unremittingly ridiculous and disjunctive theatrical self-consciousness.

Mark Thornton Burnett—who recently paired Marston and Chapman with regard to the figure of the malcontent—cites performance and anthropological critics elsewhere in the following shrewd observation: "Marston experiments with performative styles to demonstrate the effect on individuals of a repressive society in which the use of language is strictly regulated."[7] Presumably Marston's fellow student at the Middle Temple, John Manningham, noted the same tendency in Marston, to judge by the following anecdotal entry in his diary for 21 November 1602:

> Jo. Marstone the last Christmas when he daunct with Alderman Mores wifes daughter, a Spaniard borne, fell into a strang commendacion of her witt and beauty. When he had done, shee thought to pay him home, and told him she though[t] he was a poet. "'Tis true," said he, "for poetes fayne, and lye, and soe dyd I when I commended your beauty, for you are exceeding foule."[8]

The anecdote relates the obverse of fashioning an acceptable self. Instead, the figure of Marston in the story fashions an unacceptable self that both revels in and insists on the shocked attention it elicits. Moreover, he uses language with all the violence of blunt force trauma. To be at the centre of such retailed gossip, Marston either *did* insult the young woman as described or was eminently capable of doing so. The anecdote reads like an urban myth wherein the warning is implicit but nevertheless clear: beware of this funny, sarcastic bastard. He means to offend against comfortable sensibilities, his language is brutal, and he smashes through restraint even in the most innocuous of situations.

Small surprise then that Dollimore grants pride of place to *Antonio's Revenge* as a capital "R" "Radical Tragedy" in his book of the same name because of the play's insistent breakdown of coherent human subjectivity and displacement of comfortable providentialism. Through linguistic outrageousness, musical surprise, Senecan quips, disconnected outbursts, and extremely contrived dramatic situations, figures in the play call attention to their artifice. Again and again, they step outside their roles to comment on the action of the play, make comments totally inappropriate to the action involved, or disavow any sense of human rationality or social connectedness. In doing so, they connect most outrageously with the audience itself. The audience gets enlisted literally within the terms of the artifice as Piero rants in self-conscious realization:

> The bulk of man's as dark as Erebus,
> No branch of reason's light hangs in his trunk;

> There lives no reason to keep league withal,
> I ha' no reason to be reasonable.
>
> (I.iv.25–8)

In other words: stop making sense; nothing makes sense in any case.

Piero's thematic opposite is Pandulpho, the ostensible voice of Stoic endurance in the play, but he likewise "sees the light" of his situation in words even more self-referential:

> Man will break out, despite philosophy.
> Why, all this time I ha' but played a part,
> Like to some boy that acts a tragedy,
> Speaks burly words and raves out passion;
> But when he thinks upon his infant weakness,
> He droops his eye.
>
> (IV.v.46–51)

Of course the speakers of the above-quoted lines really *are* boys playing excruciatingly dramatic parts. They pitch themselves at a surprising level of ironic, self-conscious expression, a level at which Pirandello and Artaud would operate. Indeed Wharton, in *The Critical Fall and Rise of John Marston*, credits the twentieth-century Theatre of the Absurd for awakening readers critically to Marston's forms of theatrical disaffection. Likewise attuned to the burlesque reflexivity of these plays, R. A. Foakes took Marston at his own word in referring to them as "fantastical."[9]

From the first, Marston asserts absurd theatrical effects, including comic inflation and deflation, and reflexive realizations onstage that emphasize even as they subvert the very genre of revenge. Consider the Pirandello-like Induction to *Antonio and Mellida* where the child actor playing Antonio frets about his ability to double as an Amazon, but is quickly set straight on the duplicity of human nature: "Not play two parts in one? away, away; 'tis common fashion. Nay, if you cannot bear two subtle fronts under one hood, idiot go by, go by, off this world's stage" (73–6). Utterly incapable of subtlety, Piero asserts such disjunction at the outset of *Antonio's Revenge* where, blood-soaked and raging, he contemplates, momentarily, Antonio's newly widowed mother and exclaims:

> By this warm reeking gore, I'll marry her.
> Look I not now like an enamorate?
> Poison the father, butcher the son, and marry the mother—ha!
>
> (I.i.102–4)

This from a villainous figure whose moral awareness is constantly shown to be farcially shallow. Having murdered Pandulpho's son, Piero feels a twinge of guilt in Pandulpho's presence and shares his "remorse" matter-of-factly with the audience: " 'Fore heaven he makes me shrug; would 'a were dead" (II.ii.26). Piero even gleefully manipulates his henchman Strotzo into a theatrical confession of all the killings, promising to exonerate him publicly at the last. The two of them take fulsome pleasure in the enormity of the histrionic effects they hope to create—elaborating on the contrived emotion of their rhetoric, the duplicities of their presentation, and the bogus sincerity of Piero's magnanimous forgiveness—only to have Piero strangle Strotzo in front of all assembled immediately upon receipt of his public confession. Conventional expectations are constantly undercut, as when Antonio, agitated by Pandulpho along with the ghosts of his Father and others, vows finally and emotively, "Fright me no more; I'll suck red vengeance / Out of Piero's wounds, Piero's wounds" (III.ii.78–9). And Piero immediately enters "*in his nightgown and nightcap*," a touchingly ironic and harmless picture of concerned parenthood.

Such forced theatricality stresses the ludicrously reflexive energy of performance, as Piero does in *Antonio and Mellida* when he intercepts Antonio's letter to Mellida and goes off his head with panicked stuttering imperatives:

> Run to the gates; stop the gondolets; let none pass the marsh; do all at once. Antonio his head, his head! Keep you the court; the rest stand still, or run, or go, or shout, or search, or scud, or call, or hang, or do-do-do, so-so-so-something. I know not who-who-who-what I do-do-do-nor who-who-who-where I am. (III.ii.171–7)

He then launches into passionate idiomatic Italian verse as surprise foretaste of Antonio and Mellida who are together in the following scene, performing in Italian for some twenty lines in the manner of a passionate operatic duet. At the lovers' exit, a lone page remains onstage apologizing directly to the audience for this "confusion of Babel," and speculating as follows: "But howsoever, if I should sit in judgment, 'tis an error easier to be pardoned by the auditors" than excused by the author's' (IV.i.224–6). That is: judgement remains to be exercised by the audience, *not* by the author—he presumably has none.

Of course, malcontents and revengers often operate within a realm of passionate intensity that is rich in radical action but poor in conservative judgement. Such disparity explains a good deal of their theatrical appeal— what Michael Scott, in relation to Marston, identifies distinctly as " 'critic-proof' 'theatre machines', confronting the literary conventionalist and defying dominant ideologies."[10] Confrontation and defiance certainly attend the revenge actions of *Antonio's Revenge* in the murder of Piero's little son Julio. The resonances of the scene run as deeply through blood feud and human sacrifice as they do through stage horror and romantic excessiveness. Extremity generates extremity, as consanguine associations of "brother," "father," and "sister" sung from the mouth of the innocent Julio only further enrage Antonio and compel his vengeance. The scene retains and stresses overstated theatrical imperatives, as Antonio ignores Julio's infantile pathos—"Pray you do not hurt me. And you kill me, 'deed, / I'll tell my father" (III.iii.27–8)—ostensibly to kill that part of Piero that resides within his son. With Julio murdered onstage, the theatre itself reacts to the horror: "*From under the stage a groan*" (50 s.d.), just as Antonio conversely revels in blood:

> Lo, thus I heave my blood-dyed hands to heaven,
> Even like insatiate hell, still crying; "More!
> My heart hath thirsting dropsies after gore!"
>
> (67–9)

At this point, the paradoxical construction and stressed rhyme of "heaven/ hell" and "more/gore" generate the whole overstated nature of the play in miniature. Ethical applications collide with and engender further theatrical possibilities. Moreover, such histrionic possibilities constantly redouble themselves as the life blood of theatre.

As if to accent and disperse the excruciating theatricality of the preceding scene, Balurdo enters "*with a bass viol*" (III.iv.16) intent on serenading Maria on behalf of Piero. The instrument is neither romantic nor solo, creating an unusual visual effect of irony. But then the viol is manipulated by the same Balurdo who entered Act II "*with a beard half off, half on*" (II.i.20), character-istically accentuating his ironic artifice. Let us recall too that in the middle of *Antonio and Mellida*, Balurdo entered "*backward, DILDO following him with a looking glass in one hand and a candle in the other hand*" (III.ii.116), suggesting the misdirected, well-lit ludicrousness of this figure within the context of forced histrionics. As the protagonist, Antonio presents the most extreme example of this mode, as noted by the stage direction that begins Act IV of his revenge: "*Enter ANTONIO in a fool's habit, with a little toy of a walnut shell and soap to make bubbles.*" This strategy goes beyond a formal "antic disposition" to accentuate the metadramatic situation of boy actors involved in the the-atrical construction of the play. His costume and props visually shout his disposition, and Antonio shouts it too in determined ironic resolve: "He is not wise that strives not to seem fool" (IV.i.25). Moreover, Balurdo promised the same absurd function from the very first, significantly capping a discussion of performance art in the Induction to *Antonio and Mellida* as follows:

> GALEATZO. [To Balurdo] Well, and what dost thou play?
> BALURDO. The part of all the world.
> GALEATZO. "The part of all the world." What's that?
> BALURDO. The fool.
>
> (28–31)

Discounting seriousness, the fool asserts a new seriousness of the world, a parallel, theatrical seriousness in line with malcontents and reformers everywhere.

Chapman's *Bussy* plays provide a parallel, if somewhat forced, opposition to the effects of Marston's drama. The high seriousness of Chapman's neo-classical verse imagery and rhetoric is often seen to collide with the low cunning of Marston's more prosaic physical and theatrical assertions. However, both express opposition to political complacencies. Like Antonio, Bussy enters the theatrical space alone, poor, and prostrate. While Antonio's prostrate grief represents a repeated sight gag, Bussy's position is one from which to arise metaphorically even as he conveys the same reversed and disappointed understanding of the world as Marston's drama. Consider Bussy's famous opening lines:

> Fortune, not Reason, rules the state of things,
> Reward goes backwards, Honour on his head;
> Who is not poor is monstrous; only Need
> Gives form and worth to every human seed.
>
> (I.i.1–4)

Like Antonio with bubbles or Piero enraged, Bussy, within the perverse and disappointing contingencies of the material world, has "no reason to be reasonable." In a characteristic extended simile, he considers himself lost at sea, adrift within "the waves / Of glassy Glory and the gulfs of State" but looking to "Virtue" as guide (28–9, 32). Nonetheless, "Virtue" for Bussy manifests itself as both internal drive and external tactic. Self-assured, he wonders aloud about learning "a great man's part" at Court, only to be both denigrated and promoted by Monsieur who answers, "No, thou need'st not learn, / Thou hast the theory, now go there and practise" (103–5). The "role" of aesthetic, chivalric masculinity is at once socially conditioned and theatrically performed.

Bussy arrives at the French court like the surging elemental force of the sea itself. He destroys the henchmen of rivals even as he insists on the assertive feminizing of "Virtue" in relation to himself: he states directly, "He that will win, must woo her; she's not shameless" (I.ii.66). Self-confident and unabashed, he recklessly demeans the Duke of Guise and Count of Montsurry, and proceeds to seduce Tamyra, Countess of Montsurry, crediting himself: "Who to himself is law, no law doth need, / Offends no King, and is a King indeed" (II.i.203–4). Like Bussy, Tamyra is a malcontent force at Court and they mount new forms of opposition that dynamically and amorally counter received values.

As figures intent on power, however, they pursue predictably male and female prerogatives. Bussy is granted "impartial words" (III.ii.1) as the king's "Eagle" (4), and he proceeds at length in the manner of an attacking raptor to discredit corrupt politicians, clergymen, and lawyers everywhere for their crimes. He summarily puts Montsurry in his place even in the presence of Tamyra, occasioning the king's blindly overstated praise for his spirit, state, judgement, and nerve—"The genius and th' ingenuous soul of D'Ambois" (III.ii.107). Perhaps his finest ironic moment as malcontent occurs later in the scene in the form of a flyting match with Monsieur, his erstwhile supporter, wherein the two exchange polite but cutting insults. In response to Monsieur's aggressively mocking non-invitation to kill the king, Bussy verbally and directly attacks the arch aristocrat, expanding for some forty lines on Monsieur's treacheries, perjuries, violence, cruelty, even atheism, only to have the corrupt courtier debunk and conclude all in a single line: "Why now I see thou lov'st me, come to the banquet" (412), and they exit together. The king might continue to idealize Bussy, but Bussy's rhetorically powerful ideals are decidedly fragile when involved within the fluid positions, co-options, ironies, and subversions of court intrigue.

The same modes may be witnessed within the drama of court sexual intrigue with Tamyra. As a woman, she is malcontented within a world of masculine political prerogatives, but she is a Countess and therefore a political figure too. Like Bussy, she exercises desire configured as "virtue" and suffers for it within a political system that—through gross over-reaction—validates such desire. Such excessiveness gets literalized in Tamyra's demeanings by both Montsurry and Monsieur, culminating in that extreme scene of onstage torture where she is stabbed multiple times, forced to write a letter in blood, and even put to the rack (V.i). In *Horrid Spectacle*, Deborah Burks reads the scene with accuracy: "When he puts his wife on the rack, Montsurry uses for his private purposes a device that was among the most terrifying torments employed by European states for political interrogations."[11] More figuratively, the drama involves the supernatural complications of "Behemoth" and his confused devils as well as the impotently loquacious ghost of Friar Comolet. Such theatricality looks back to *Doctor Faustus* or *The Spanish Tragedy*, even as Bussy, also loquacious in the throes of death, makes a classical attempt to solidify his reputation:

> Prop me, true sword, as thou hast ever done:
> The equal thought I bear of life and death
> Shall make me faint on no side; I am up
> Here like a Roman statue; I will stand
> Till death hath made me marble.
>
> (V.iii.141–5)

At the same time, Guise and Monsieur cynically oversee all from a position on the upper stage formerly occupied in theatres by ghosts and supernaturals.

The appeal to Senecan heroism embodied in Chapman's Bussy D'Ambois relates curiously to contemporary French history with all of the political terror it represented for a complacent English audience.[12] "Ghostly" French Friars might be considered rather unreliable as conclusive moral commentators, yet Chapman, in characteristic sententiousness, attempts to convey high seriousness through just such a character at the conclusion of the play. The finale of *Antonio's Revenge* is more nonchalant. Having brought to a close a ludicrous onstage bloodbath, Antonio defers to a previously unmentioned couple of Senators who enter officially to thank Antonio and his revengers for their act of revenge. It might seem reductive to contrast Chapman's contrived poetic sensibility with Marston's contrived theatrical verve, but both are working within the material contingencies of drama with all the possibilities for creative tensions of performance.

Dollimore identifies the hero D'Ambois as torn in two directions and thus vacating an already vanishing humanist middle, as signalled before of the court when Bussy declares, "None can be always one" (IV.i.25). In this regard, consider also the very middle of the play when the King attempts détente between Bussy and the Guise through the "Hermean rod" (III.ii.108) of his own hand. Such a middle way, even—or perhaps especially—as facilitated by a king is impossible. In Marston's *The Malcontent* a providentialist compromise gets theatrically ejected by the title character who, having restored himself as Duke, kicks his rival in the ass with the telling line "Hence with this man: an eagle takes not flies" (V.vi.160). In Chapman's play, "Eagle" D'Ambois is more pathetic in a dying speech that relates his inner organs to volcanic mountains that "Melt like two hungry torrents: eating rocks / Into the Ocean of all human life, / And make it bitter, only with my blood" (V.iii.185–7). He finally recognizes limitation even as his words ascend to the empty space of performance. This takes place despite his more characteristically hopeful assertion: "Justice will soon distinguish murderous minds / From just revengers" (II.i.168–9). Not in this play; not in Marston's play; nor anywhere else.

Throughout, Marston's drama asserts physical action, graphic expression, and theatrical self-consciousness. Chapman's work, by contrast, privileges rhetorical expansion through highly figurative verse, stage movement, and assertion of poetic imagery. If Chapman engaged with the classics retrospectively as enabling background for his Senecan dramatic material, Marston parodied the classics through linguistic self-consciousness, Senecan quips, surprise reversals, and disconnectedly ludicrous present-tense actions. The two met for a moment in unlikely collaboration with Ben Jonson in *Eastward Ho!* after which they departed separately under strained circumstances. The scholarly convenience that has forced them together since the time of Hazlitt might well let them go their separate ways again.

Pedagogic strategies

Marston's plays are made of "play" and are best understood through emphasizing visual and kinetic possibilities. Focus especially on theatrical elements by having students themselves take parts as in the induction scenes of *Antonio and Mellida* or *The Malcontent*. Or, launch immediately into blocking out a few short scenes such as *The Malcontent* (I.i), beginning "*The vilest out-of-tune music being heard, enter BILIOSO and* PREPASSO." Let students choose or perform the music—the louder and viler the better. Stress self-consciousness, role play, physical blocking, ludicrous energy, and radical overstatement, as in *Antonio's Revenge* (V.v) where all the revengers—male and female—arrive to torment Piero. Accent the parody of the revenge scenes through their overstated performances. Let the students improvise the final dance scene in *The Malcontent* (V.vi.67ff.), or have them realize *Antonio and Mellida*'s stage direction (III.ii.115). Have students identify Marston's word coinages and strained usages (see *Antonio's Revenge* Appendix B) and acquaint them with Ben Jonson's distaste for Marston's vocabulary. Invite them to invent a few words themselves.

Chapman's work is better absorbed through exploration of poetic imagery. In line with—or as a challenge to—Brooke's editorial observation that "it is easier to grasp the total effect than grasp the modulating images" (143), have students rewrite and paraphrase highly figurative passages such as *Bussy D'Ambois* I.i.5–33, III.i.1–41, III.ii.375–411, IV.i.7–20, or V.iii.1–25. Let students share their paraphrases aloud, share the meanings that they discern, and then read Chapman's lines aloud. Focus on similes and pursue what exactly is being "likened" to what and why. Relate Chapman's theatrical effects of the supernatural to Marlowe's *Doctor Faustus*. Stage Bussy's interaction with Tamyra, Behemoth, and Comolet: IV.ii.128–73, or the extreme action of Montsurry and Tamyra: V.i.38–146.

Such physical interaction with, and recognition within, these works will foreground teachable moments in the texts of Marston's *Antonio* plays and *The Malcontent* along with Chapman's *Bussy D'Ambois* to force reconsiderations regarding physical satire, social critique, gender expectations (especially with regard to heroism), and theatrical representation (especially with regard to play). These radical dramas get taught most effectively through engagement, through de-emphasizing "explanations" in favour of "explorations."

Notes

1. P. P. Howe (ed.), *The Complete Works of William Hazlitt*, 21 vols. (London: Dent, 1931), vol. 6, p. 230. For a recent discussion regarding the authorship of *Eastward Ho!* see Suzanne Gossett, "Marston, Collaboration, and *Eastward Ho!*" *Renaissance Drama* 33 (2004): 181–200.
2. Howe, *Complete Works of William Hazlitt*, vol. 6, p. 224.
3. Jonathan Dollimore, *Radical Tragedy: Religion, Ideology and Power in the Drama of Shakespeare and his Contemporaries*, 3rd edn. (Durham, NC: Duke University Press, 2004), p. xxxiii.
4. Geoffrey Aggeler, *Nobler in the Mind: the Stoic-Skeptic Dialectic in English Renaissance Tragedy* (London: Associated University Presses, 1998).

5. T. F. Wharton (ed.), *The Drama of John Marston: Critical Re-Visions* (Cambridge: Cambridge University Press, 2000), pp. 3–4.
6. *The Poems of John Marston*, ed. Arnold Davenport (Liverpool: Liverpool University Press, 1961), p. 101.
7. Mark Thornton Burnett, "'I will not swell like a tragedian': Marston's *Antonio's Revenge* in Performance," *Neuphilologische Mitteilungen* 90 (1989): 319. See also Mark Thornton Burnett, "Staging the Malcontent in Early Modern England," in *A Companion to Renaissance Drama*, ed. Arthur F. Kinney (Oxford: Blackwell, 2002), pp. 336–51.
8. Robert Parker Sorlien (ed.), *The Diary of John Manningham of the Middle Temple, 1602–1603* (Hanover, NH: University Press of New England, 1976), p. 133.
9. See R. A. Foakes, "John Marston's Fantastical Plays: *Antonio and Mellida* and *Antonio's Revenge*," *Philological Quarterly* 41 (1962): 229–39. *Antonio and Mellida* is dedicated to "the most honorably renowned Nobody," and Marston in mock humility offers up his work as follows: "Since it hath flow'd with the current of my humorous blood to affect (a little too much) to be seriously fantastical, here take (most respected Patron) the worthless present of my slighter idleness."
10. Michael Scott, "Ill-mannered Marston," *The Drama of John Marston: Critical Re-visions*, ed. T. F. Wharton (Cambridge: Cambridge University Press, 2000), p. 224.
11. Deborah G. Burks, *Horrid Spectacle: Violation in the Theater of Early Modern England* (Pittsburgh: Duquesne University Press, 2003), p. 119.
12. See Andrew M. Kirk, *The Mirror of Confusion: the Representation of French History in English Renaissance Drama* (New York: Garland, 1996), esp. pp. 155–67.

Selective guide to further reading

Aggeler, Geoffrey. *Nobler in the Mind: the Stoic-Skeptic Dialectic in English Renaissance Tragedy*. London: Associated University Presses, 1998.

Burks, Deborah G. *Horrid Spectacle: Violation in the Theater of Early Modern England*. Pittsburgh: Duquesne University Press, 2003.

Burnett, Mark T. "'I will not swell like a tragedian': Marston's *Antonio's Revenge* in Performance." *Neuphilologische Mitteilungen* 90 (1989): 311–20.

Chapman, George. *Bussy D'Ambois*. Ed. N. S. Brooke. Manchester: Manchester University Press, 1979.

Dollimore, Jonathan. *Radical Tragedy: Religion, Ideology and Power in the Drama of Shakespeare and his Contemporaries*. 3rd edn. Durham, NC: Duke University Press, 2004.

Foakes, R. A. "John Marston's Fantastical Plays: *Antonio and Mellida* and *Antonio's Revenge*." *Philological Quarterly* 41 (1962): 229–39.

Gossett, Suzanne. "Marston, Collaboration, and *Eastward Ho!*" *Renaissance Drama* 33 (2004): 181–200.

Hazlitt, William. "Lecture III: On Marston, Chapman, Deckar, and Webster." *The Complete Works of William Hazlitt*, ed. P. P. Howe, vol. 6, pp. 223–48. London: Dent, 1931.

Kirk, Andrew M. *The Mirror of Confusion: the Representation of French History in English Renaissance Drama*. New York: Garland, 1996.

Marston, John. *The Poems*. Ed. Arnold Davenport. Liverpool: Liverpool University Press, 1961.

———. *Antonio and Mellida*. Ed. G. K. Hunter. Lincoln: University of Nebraska Press, 1965.

———. *The Malcontent*. Ed. G. K. Hunter. London: Methuen, 1975.

———. *Antonio's Revenge*. Ed. W. Reavley Gair. Manchester: Manchester University Press, 1978.

Pascoe, David. "Marston's Childishness." *Medieval and Renaissance Drama in England* 9 (1997): 92–111.

Rowe, Katherine. "Memory and Revision in Chapman's *Bussy* Plays." *Renaissance Drama* 31 (2002): 125–52.

Scott, Michael. "Ill-mannered Marston." *The Drama of John Marston: Critical Re-visions*, ed. T. F. Wharton, pp. 212–30. Cambridge: Cambridge University Press, 2000.

Wharton, T. F. *The Critical Fall and Rise of John Marston*. Columbia, SC: Camden House, 1994.

———. (ed.). *The Plays of John Marston: Critical Re-Visions*. Cambridge: Cambridge University Press, 2000.

9
City Comedy
Alizon Brunning

Chronology and context

City comedy is frequently described as "Jacobean City Comedy" and so the reign of James I (1603–25) may be considered to provide a set of temporal boundaries for the genre. Although some city comedies were written before the accession of James,[1] most of the major city comedies were written in the "long decade" between 1600 and 1613. The term "Jacobean" in this context is often used to describe a mood as much as a historical period. This mood is prevailingly dark and satirical and its content is dominated by sexual obsession, financial rapaciousness, social mobility, and exploitation.

Whether city comedy presents an accurate reflection or mirror of the time is subject to some debate but the "realistic" settings of city comedy (that is their urban framework, contemporary reference, and focus on the materiality of seventeenth-century life) has led many critics to read the plays as analogues of early modern experience. The plays have been identified as a response to, or a reflection of, a society in transition: moving in basic terms from one cultural ideology based on inherited status and degree to one based on the accumulation of wealth and possessions. Critical disagreement arises over the question of whether the playwrights were critical of such change or implicated in it.

The playwrights who wrote city comedy (John Marston, Ben Jonson, Thomas Middleton, Thomas Dekker and Thomas Heywood, Francis Beaumont and George Chapman) all contributed to the genre at the same time as writing tragedies, masques, civic entertainments, and other cultural forms. For a useful insight into other works of these dramatists, the reader is urged to refer to the relevant chapters in this volume.

Critical overview

Criticism of city comedy, as Susan Wells has noted, has followed "two major lines of investigation . . . the sociological criticism of L. C. Knights and the generic criticism of Brian Gibbons."[2]

Brian Gibbons's seminal study defined city comedy as a distinct genre which can be seen as having "a recognizable form, style and subject matter" and by which the plays

> may be distinguished from the other kinds of Jacobean comedy by their critical and satirical design, their urban settings, their exclusion of material appropriate to romance, fairytale, sentimental legend or patriotic chronicle.[3]

While not the first critic to use the term city comedy, as Douglas Bruster points out, Gibbon's devotion of a single study to the genre stimulated great critical interest in the plays.[4] This has led to the creation of "something like a city comedy canon" which, Bruster suggests, provides a convenient label for later critics such as Susan Wells, Gamīnī Salgādo, Wendy Griswold, and Lee Bliss.[5]

The urban setting is a key element of city comedy which as the name suggests is defined by location. Usually the location of the play's action is London but it can be set in Italy or, indeed, in a mixture of locations. In these dramas, the countryside is often presented as an absent other, an idealized landscape to be exploited for the purpose of advancing one's social status.

The material presence of the city is an important factor in these plays, with place names providing textually what Bruster calls "topographical building blocks."[6] In Gail Kern Paster's study the city takes on almost anthropomorphic qualities becoming "the City as Predator."[7] However, as well as its concrete material presence, the city is also an imaginative space. Both Middleton and Jonson were involved in civic entertainments where the city was presented as a form of civic ideal and in the satirical environment of city comedy we are often presented with an "urban atmosphere in which aggressive individualism has become an accepted behavioural norm."[8] Susan Wells recognizes this tension as a central element of city comedy and links it closely to London's commercial development. In this genre, she argues, two contradictory aspects of the marketplace confront each other dramatically: the marketplace is both a festive and a commercial space in which older forms of organic communal festivity are juxtaposed with newer forms of commercial exchange.[9] In this way the writers of city comedy may be seen to express the relations of exchange and accumulation through a larger ongoing dramatic spectacle which can celebrate or call into question these relations.[10] In a more recent work Ceri Sullivan explores the relationship between city comedy and the mercantile credit economy by reading the plays in relation to merchant handbooks.[11]

Although Wells has set up the distinction between generic study and sociological criticism in this area, the two invariably overlap because the city is both an imaginative creative theatrical construction and a real historical locus of social transformation. Indeed, most criticism before Gibbons tended to focus on the plays as forms of social realism.[12] Consequently, sociological criticism (following Knights) has largely focused on issues of class and society. Critics such as Levin, Paster, Wells, Leggatt, Bruster, Griswold, and Bliss have addressed the presentation of the city and its citizens in terms of developing market relations in different ways. Debate has tended to focus on whether the play texts were critical of such social transformation offered by nascent capitalism, as argued by Knights,[13] or complicit with it in a more complex way, as suggested by Leinwand and Wayne.[14]

One of the key areas of sociological criticism over recent years has been that of class relations. Definition of class, like definitions of both the city and comedy, remains a slippery concept. In Alexander Leggatt's character-based study, he proposes that city comedies are "set in a predominantly middle class social milieu."[15] Others such as Theodore Leinwand argue for the importance of recognizing the theatre's role in *staging* social constructions, rather than simply reflecting "real" class relations. He suggests that the theatre created a complex repertoire of characters, a "self conscious staging of the clearly inadequate roles and types which Londoners tolerated for the purposes of identifying one another."[16]

The relationship between "reality" and dramatic form is always a complex one and we need to be aware, as Leinwand reminds us, that although the plays are "informed by the social and economic reality in which the play-wrights found themselves . . . this does not mean that we turn to these dramatizations for a mirror image of the time."[17] The relationship between the theatre and extra-theatrical reality is, he argues, more subtle than this; it is shaped by aesthetic representation and has "passed through the filters of tradition."[18] Bruster also argues that creating categories of analysis (like class and genres and subgenres such as citizen or city comedy) "can obscure the more complex ways literature manages to incorporate social content."[19]

The most recent study which focuses on city comedy as a separate genre is *Plotting Early Modern London*, edited by Dieter Mehl, the title of which sug-gests a convergence of drama, historical period, and place.[20] Divided into six parts, each section addresses a different aspect of city comedy. In part one, "Bourgeois Domestic Drama," the role of the family is a focus for discussion by Alan Brissenden and Matthias Bauer. Part two, "The Culture of Credit," focuses on changing market relations with essays on the crises of credit by Richard Waswo and on the concept of "Risk as Romance" by Anne-Julia Zwierlin. Part three, "Playhouse Politics," looks at social allegiances and audience participation in essays by David Crane and Andrew Gurr. Part four addresses a rather unexamined area, that of the relationship of the plays to their religious contexts. Angela Stock examines the relation between ritual, theatre, and satire in Jacobean civic pageantry; and Alizon Brunning dis-cusses the ambivalent treatment of religious conversion in several plays. Approaching fairly uncharted territory, part five examines "City Comedy and Shakespeare," with an argument made by Dieter Mehl for *The London Prodigal* as a Shakespearean city comedy and an essay by Ruth Morse on possible crossovers between Jonson's *Every Man In His Humour* and Shakespeare's *Twelfth Night*. Finally, in part six, essays by Robyn Bolam and Deborah Cartmell suggest that modern film directors are conflating city comedy and Shakespeare by creating urban Shakespeares which appeal to a young generation. This final chapter suggests exciting contemporary transactions between productions of contemporary Shakespeare and the genre of city comedy.

Pedagogic strategies

Quite often a course on Renaissance or Early Modern Literature may include one or two city comedies as an acknowledgement that Shakespeare's contemporaries existed. More rarely, there might be a course on Middleton or Jonson in which the city comedies appear as a part of a study of the author's overall *oeuvre*—here the emphasis might be more on the author than the genre. Even more rare will be the course that is solely devoted to city comedy. In many cases students will only experience one or two city comedies at most. It may be that on a course which aims to cover a lot of ground, the teacher has as little as two hours contact time with students to spend on a city comedy. Consequently, it becomes necessary to identify the key difficulties raised and to find strategic ways of overcoming these with limited classroom resources.

The challenges in teaching city comedy are several and raise many questions about the best way to teach and understand the plays. The genre is a hybrid one appropriating, mixing, and parodying many literary and non-literary sources. The plays' dominant tones are satire and irony, but it is not always clear what is being satirized. The topical references can often be overwhelming and students may feel little connection with the context. Furthermore, the complex plots of city comedy can be confusing, characters do not seem to have the depth of Shakespearean drama, dialogue is fast paced with little use of extended speeches of the sort familiar elsewhere in early modern drama. Isolating scenes or even speeches is not always helpful. How then are we to introduce students to this wonderful but complex genre?

As space is limited I am going to suggest ways of introducing students to a specific city comedy, Thomas Middleton's *A Chaste Maid in Cheapside*. Two sessions are suggested which include a series of workshop activities, individual worksheets, and contextual study. These are designed to engage students, alert them to key themes and issues, open discussion and debate, and to prepare them for further study. These strategies would be equally valid for the study of other plays.

Session one

In the first workshop students are introduced to three key elements common to most city comedy: money, sex, and status. As they work through these issues, students who are studying Shakespeare alongside city comedy might be asked how treatment of these issues differs to that witnessed in Shakespearean comedy and tragedy—and possibly, if it is part of the syllabus, in Jacobean tragedy. Seeing the plays is often the best introduction to complex plots, but performances are rare. Acting out scenes can also be a productive but time-consuming way of bringing a play to life. However, not all students are happy to act and some may be reluctant to participate. This workshop overcomes this by developing a series of dramatic tableaux that visually present the series of exchanges that take place in the play.

Have the students read the text before class and divide them in advance into five groups each representing "family" or character units. Three groups would represent the families and would consist of the would-be socially mobile Yellowhammers, the gentry, the Kixes, and the materialist Allwits. The other two groups would represent units that are the catalysts of transformation, and include Sir Walter Whorehound and the Touchwoods—Senior and Junior.[21] As they are reading the play, students should be given a worksheet which asks them to focus particularly on their unit taking into account the following questions: what is the status of my character/family and does this status change? What does my character or family have possession of and what does it lack? What does it desire? How does it seek to transform itself? On the worksheet they should jot down key scenes or speeches that demonstrate this.

In the session set the first three groups on one side of the classroom and the other two opposite; have a number of key icons of status prepared to represent each group. These could be drawn on pieces of paper or card and, if time allows, the students could make these themselves, perhaps drawing on iconography used in art. Each icon should also have a corresponding symbol of lack, the object drawn with a cross through it. You would need several sets of icons to represent money, land/nobility, material possessions, honour, children, love, lust, and chastity. You may also wish to introduce the idea of cuckoldry by making or drawing a few sets of horns!

Having worked independently through the play, students now work in groups and agree on icons that represent their group's possessions, lacks, and desires. It should look something like this:

- The Yellowhammers have money and children but no honour.
- Moll Yellowhammer has love and chastity.
- The Allwits have children and riches but no honour.
- The Kixes have riches but no children. They have title but their kinsman Whorehound will inherit the family estate unless they produce an heir.

On the other side of the room:

- Sir Walter has some money and some land. He stands to inherit land if the Kixes remain infertile. He does have children too (seven by Mrs Allwit) but they are a secret.

- Touchwood Senior has too many children. He has no money.
- Touchwood Junior has nothing but he has love for Moll.

Now working through the play generally (not necessarily in strict scene order), create a series of tableaux that represent the financial and sexual exchanges made in the play. The groups can begin to swap icons:

- The Yellowhammers want to exchange their daughter for title and honour while Walter wants more money and sex with a virgin. They want to exchange their son in a similar arrangement with the Welsh Widow.
- Moll and Touchwood Junior exchange their love.
- Allwit exchanges his wife's sexual favours with Whorehound for material goods/money. Whorehound gives him children. His lustful wife gets pleasure.
- Touchwood Senior exchanges his fertility with the Kixes' money.

This final exchange brings about a collapse in the chain of exchanges. Lady Kix's impregnation by Touchwood senior disinherits Sir Walter and he loses his title and land. He in turn is unwanted by both the Yellowhammers and the Allwits and is rejected.

Using these visualization techniques the students should have a more physical sense of the text's dramatic energy and can now begin developing their textual study. As a class they can now work through the play together using their worksheets to identify scenes or speeches that are used to demonstrate sexual, social, and financial status and the key moments of exchange which bring about transformation. Here are some suggestions (I have italicized pivotal moments):

The Yellowhammers

(I.i) Their attitude to marriage: " 'tis a husband solders up all cracks" (31). Hints at their sexual looseness: "when I was of your youth I was lightsome and quick, two years before I was married" (8–9).
(III.i) Their attitude to Moll's elopement with Touchwood Junior: "I will lock up this baggage / as carefully as my gold; she shall see as little sun, / If a close room or so can keep her from the light on't" (43–5).
(IV.i) On hearing Allwit's description of Whorehound as a womanizer and father of illegitimate children:

> The knight is rich, he shall be my son-in-law
> No matter so the whore he keeps is wholesome
> My daughter takes no hurt then; so let them wed,
> I'll have him sweat well e'er they go to bed.
>
> (278–81)

(IV.ii) Maudline Yellowhammer on capturing the runaway Moll: "I have brought your jewel by the hair" (64).

(V.ii) Moll's "death" and the Yellowhammers' reaction to it: "Twill be our shame then" (2). Her brother Tim's reaction: "Gold to white money was never so changed, / As my sister's colour to paleness" (20). Maudline to her daughter on her "deathbed": "Look but once up, thou shalt have all the wishes of thy heart / That wealth can purchase" (95). The Yellowhammers plan to stay away from the funeral for fear of public shame but cheer up when they realize that they can still marry Tim to the Welsh widow: "Mass, a match! / We'll not lose all at once, somewhat we'll catch" (115).

Moll

(III.i) To Touchwood Junior after being separated from her lover by her father: "Thou violence keep me, thou canst lose me never, / I am ever thine although we part for ever" (50–1).

(IV.ii) After her second attempt at elopement and near drowning, and hearing she must be married to Whorehound the next day: "O bring me death tonight, love pitying fates, / Let me not see tomorrow up upon the world" (79–80).

(V.ii) Moll's deathbed song (41–8).

The Kixes

(II.i) Their childless state (and hint at Oliver's sexual impotence) Oliver: "I'd give a thousand pound to purchase fruitfulness" (144).

> Tis our barrenness puffs up Sir Walter—
> None gets by your not-getting, but that knight;
> He's made by th'means, and fats his fortunes shortly
> In a great dowry with a goldsmith's daughter.
>   (II.i.159–62)

Touchwood Senior as a potential solution to the infertility: (II.i.186–204) *(III.iii) Marital problems as Sir Oliver is "not given to standing" (136). Lady Kix's "cure" must be taken lying down (165–71).*

The Allwits

(I.ii) Their materialism: of his pregnant wife "my wife's as great as she can wallow, Davy, and longs for nothing but pickled cucumbers and his (Whorehound's) coming" (I.ii.6–7). The key speech by Allwit (I.ii.12–57). Mrs Allwit's sexual longing and lust for Whorehound—the father of her children (134–6).

The Christening scene: (III.ii).

(IV.i) Allwit tries to persuade Yellowhammer that Whorehound is unsuitable for his daughter (231–70).

(V.i) On hearing firstly about Sir Walter's "murder" of Touchwood Junior and secondly of his disinheritance by Lady Kix's pregnancy (and with great irony as Whorehound has fathered his seven children):

> I must tell you sir,
> You have been somewhat bolder in my house
> Than I could well like of; I suffered you
> Till it stuck here at my heart; I tell you truly
> I thought you had been familiar with my wife once.
>
> (152–5)

Sir Walter Whorehound

(I.i) Attitude to women as commodity: "A goldsmith's shop sets out a city maid" (100).
(IV.ii) On his impending marriage to Moll:

> I never was so near my wish, as this chance
> Makes me: ere tomorrow noon,
> I shall receive two thousand pounds in gold,
> And a sweet maidenhead
> Worth forty.
>
> (90–4)

(IV.ii) His "fatal" duel with Touchwood senior (106).
(V.i) Sir Walter Whorehound's conversion and rejection of the Allwits (1–115). Lines 115–16: A servant reports that Touchwood Junior is dead. Whorehound's potential rejection by the Allwits who fear he will lose his lands if executed. A second announcement from a servant that Lady Kix is pregnant and he is now disinherited (143) is the final straw.

Touchwood Senior

(II.i) The burden of fertility: the parting between Touchwood senior and his wife—"some can only get riches and no children, / We can only get children and no riches" (11–12)—begins as a scene of married love but then descends into his accounts of frequent adultery.
(III.iii.50–171) The "cure" of Lady Kix's barrenness—a vial of almond milk for Sir Oliver and a physic which must be taken lying down for Lady Kix.

Touchwood Junior

(I.i) refers to women in hunting images (139–44 and 167). Sexual imagery of fingers and rings (191–6).
(III.iii) Devotion to Moll and persuasion of his brother to impregnate Lady Kix and thus disinherit his rival Whorehound (1–49).
(IV.ii) His "fatal" duel with Whorehound (100–14).

Having achieved an overall understanding of the central elements of status, sex, and money, and having identified the exchanges that lead to transformation in the play, the students might start to think about the tone of the play. As city comedy is supposed to be satirical what exactly is being satirized here and how? Where are moments of irony? How does the romantic love plot of Touchwood Junior and Moll fit into the rest of the plot? Does their love seem romantic or does it seem like a parody of other romantic comedies?

At this point it would be an idea to begin some comparisons with Shakespeare and to move toward some critical analysis. Some key parallels might be the conflation of Moll with jewels and gold in this play and the same comparison Shylock makes of Jessica in *The Merchant of Venice* (II.viii) and Barabas of Abigail in Marlowe's *The Jew of Malta* (II.i). The "death" and "resurrection" of Hero in *Much Ado about Nothing* (IV.i, V.iii, V.iv) and the treatment of Hermione in *The Winter's Tale* (III.ii, V.i, V.iii) provide a contrast as these women "die" because they are accused of being unchaste, whereas Moll "dies" because her father values the market value of her chastity more than her virtue. The "Willow song" of Desdemona in *Othello* (IV.iii) would also make useful comparisons with the "swan song" of Moll. However, I think the most useful play to compare *A Chaste Maid in Cheapside* with is not a comedy at all but a tragedy which most students are familiar with: *Romeo and Juliet*. Despite being a tragedy *Romeo and Juliet* follows the plot of a romantic comedy that goes wrong at the end because the lovers do not awake in time to be "resurrected." The mock death of Juliet (IV.iii), also betrothed to an unwanted suitor, Paris, the scene in which her father mourns his dead daughter (IV.v) and the final scene wherein the couple are "resurrected" after death by replacement with a golden statue (V.iii) provide a useful contrast with the plot of Middleton's play. Students could be encouraged to think about key differences and similarities which would illuminate not only their readings of city comedy, but also of Shakespeare, who presents the same themes of status, sex, and money but in different ways. This would be a useful moment to introduce students to some key elements of romantic or "festive" comedy.

Before the second session students would be given some critical reading to prepare them to analyse the text and the genre in more detail.

Session two

Northrop Frye identifies the comic plot as consisting of "a movement from threatening complication to a happy ending."[22] This movement is in three parts: the first, the suggestion of a lost ideal state in the play's past; secondly, a rebellious and disharmonious state which may begin the play; and finally, the restoration or imitation of the earlier harmonious past. The rebellious stage is often centred on the desire of a young man for a young woman and is complicated by the resistance or opposition to this desire by parents or parental figures. This is followed by a period of conflict moving towards a point of crisis that may involve the near death of the hero or heroine or some kind of ritually symbolic death. This is then resolved by some twist in the plot which may centre on the miraculous resurrection of the protagonist/s and the subsequent transformation of the social community. At the end of the play a new society is formulated around the couple. The creation of this new society is usually signalled by a party or festive ritual often including weddings and communal dancing which suggests that the future society will be fruitful and regenerating.

This core structure is based on Roman New Comedy, an acknowledged source for city comedy, and also for Shakespeare's "Festive Comedy." The dramatic form of such comedy, according to C. L. Barber and his followers, is closely related to social customs of the period and is structured in a similar way to rites of passage rituals such as marriage.[23] In these plays social harmony is promised at the end by feasting and dancing.

However, as Susan Wells and other critics have noted, city comedy is displaced from Barber's "Green World" to the dirty, noisy, rapaciously materialist society of Early Modern London. The result of this in many cases is what R. B. Parker has called a "soiled saturnalia."[24] It is at this point that the identification of the key issues of sex, status, and money can be discussed with a framework of comedy. Transformation through marriage is a key element of festive comedy and students can begin to consider how far the economic situation of the marketplace creates some moments of tension, as suggested by the oxymoronic title *A Chaste Maid in Cheapside*. While students are encouraged to think about the difference location makes to the presentation of comic ideals, they may also be encouraged to think about the temporal setting of the play. The battle between Carnival, the force of comedy, and its anti-festive antithesis Lent is made problematic in that the materialism of the citizens takes place within the Lenten period itself. Students can be asked to consider whether this might be a critique of the characters' spiritual bankruptcy or a criticism of outdated laws which have economic, rather than religious, motivations and which ignore real issues of poverty and hunger. Again useful comparison can be made with Shakespeare with *Twelfth Night*'s Sir Toby Belch and Malvolio being one example, and possibly even Falstaff and Hal in *II Henry IV*.

In worksheets or through class discussion students could be asked to consider the following questions:

- How do the exchanges discussed in session one impact on both the comic form and tone?
- Where does material enjoyment differ from materialism?
- Can too much fertility be a bad thing?
- What evidence is there in the play of social bonding and community?
- Does the ending provide a satisfactory resolution in Frye's terms?
- Is there a point where the transformation is more than superficial, that is, does it bring about real change?
- What is being satirized? Is it the materialist society or comedy itself?

Further key scenes to study in tandem with critical reading might be:

- (I.ii) Allwit's celebration of his kept status.
- (II.i) The scene where Touchwood has to abandon his family because he just can't stop procreating.
- (II.iii) The scene where spies are on the look out for banned meat and are outwitted by Allwit with his "what cares colon for Lent" and by the cast-off mistress of Touchwood senior who tricks them into confiscating her unwanted baby in the belief that it is a quarter of lamb.
- (III.ii) The Christening scene in which Allwit's anti-hospitality and the Puritans hypocrisy are both hilarious and problematic.
- (V.iv) The final scene in which the Yellowhammers celebrate the fact that they can save money as one feast will serve both their children's marriages.

Rather than overwhelm students with critical reading it is suggested that some key journal articles (many available online) are read along side the workshop activity with a further bibliography supplied for independent study. These might include:

Bowers, Rick. "Comedy, Carnival and Class: *A Chaste Maid in Cheapside.*" *EMLS* 8, 3 (January 2003). <http://www.shu.ac.uk/emls/08–3/bowecome. htm>

Chatterji, Ruby. "Theme, Imagery and Unity in *A Chaste Maid in Cheapside.*" *Renaissance Drama* 8 (1965), 106–16.

Frassinelli, Pier P. "Realism, Desire and Reification: Thomas Middleton's *A Chaste Maid in Cheapside.*" *EMLS* 8, 3 (January 2003). <http://extra.shu. ac.uk/emls/08-3/fraschas.html>

Horwich, Richard. "Wives Courtezans and the Economics of Love in Jacobean City Comedy." *Comparative Drama* 7 (1973): 291–309.

Jenstad, Janelle D. " 'The City cannot hold you': Social conversion in the Goldsmith's Shop." *EMLS* 8, 2 (September 2002). <http://extra.shu.ac.uk/ emls/08-2/jensgold.html>

Marotti, Arthur. "Fertility and Comic Form in *A Chaste Maid in Cheapside.*" *Comparative Drama* 3 (1969): 65–74.

Paster, Gail K. "Leaky Vessels: the Incontinent Women of Jacobean City Comedy." *Renaissance Drama* 18 (1987): 43–65.

Wells, Susan. "Jacobean City Comedy and the Ideology of the City." *ELH* 48 (1981): 37–60.

Yachnin, Paul E. "Reversal of Fortune: Shakespeare, Middleton and the Puritans," *ELH* 70, 3 (Fall 2003): 757–86.

Notes

1. Jonson's *Every Man in His Humour* (1598) and *Every Man Out of his Humour* (1599) might be considered early city comedies.
2. Susan Wells, "Jacobean City Comedy and the Ideology of the City," *English Literary History* 48 (1981): 37–60, p. 37; respectively, L. C. Knights, *Drama and Society in the*

Age of Jonson (London: Chatto and Windus, 1937) and Brian Gibbons, *Jacobean City Comedy* (Cambridge, MA: Harvard University Press, 1968).

3. Brian Gibbons, *Jacobean City Comedy: a study of Satiric plays by Jonson, Marston and Middleton* (London: Methuen 1968), p. 11.
4. Wells, "Jacobean City Comedy"; Douglas Bruster, *Drama and the Market in the Age of Shakespeare*, Cambridge Studies in Renaissance Literature and Culture (Cambridge: Cambridge University Press 1995). Both attribute the definition of city comedy to Gibbons, although Bruster recognizes the term's earlier genesis. Bruster, p. 31.
5. Wells, "Jacobean City Comedy"; Gamīnī Salgādo, *Four Jacobean City Comedies* (Baltimore and Harmondsworth: Penguin, 1975); Wendy Griswold, *Renaissance Revivals: City Comedy and Revenge Tragedy in the London Theatre 1576–1980* (Chicago: Chicago University Press, 1986); and Lee Bliss, *The World's Perspective: John Webster and the Jacobean Drama* (New Brunswick: Rutgers University Press, 1983).
6. Bruster, *Drama and The Market*, p. 35.
7. Gail Kern Paster, *The Idea of the City in the Age of Shakespeare* (Athens: University of Georgia Press 1985), p. 152.
8. Paster, *The Idea of the City*, p. 152.
9. Wells, "Jacobean City Comedy," p. 37.
10. Wells, "Jacobean City Comedy," p. 54.
11. Ceri Sullivan, *The Rhetoric of Credit: Mercantile Texts and City Comedy* (London: Association of University Presses, 2002).
12. Bruster, *Drama and The Market*, p. 31.
13. L. C. Knights, *Drama and Society in the Age of Jonson* (London: Chatto and Windus, 1937).
14. Theodore Leinwand, *The City Staged: Jacobean Comedy 1603–1613* (Madison: University of Wisconsin Press, 1986); Don E. Wayne "Drama and Society in the Age of Jonson: an Alternative View," *Renaissance Drama* 13 (1982): 103–30.
15. Alexander Leggat, *Citizen Comedy in the Age of Shakespeare* (Toronto: University of Toronto Press 1973), p. 3.
16. Leinwand, *The City Staged*, p. 18.
17. Leinwand, *The City Staged*, p. 3.
18. Leinwand, *The City Staged*, p. 4.
19. Bruster, *Drama and The Market*, p. 37.
20. Dieter Mehl, et al., *Plotting Early Modern London* (Aldershot: Ashgate, 2004).
21. If you have enough time and students you could add Davy and the Welsh Widow to the list but I have excluded them for the sake of some simplicity.
22. Northrop Frye, *Anatomy of Criticism: Four Essays* (Princeton: Princeton University Press, 1957), p. 162.
23. C. L Barber, *Shakespeare's Festive Comedy: a Study of Dramatic Form in Relation to Social Custom* (Princeton: Princeton University Press, 1959); Edward Berry, *Shakespeare's Comic Rites* (Cambridge: Cambridge University Press, 1986); Michael D. Bristol, *Carnival and Theatre: Plebeian Culture and the Structure of Authority* (New York: Methuen, 1985); François Laroque, *Shakespeare's Festive World: Elizabethan Seasonal Entertainment and the Professional Stage* (Cambridge: Cambridge University Press, 1993).
24. R. B. Parker, introduction to Thomas Middleton, *A Chaste Maid in Cheapside* (London: Methuen, 1969), p. lix.

Selective guide to further reading and resources

The overview on pages 132–5 provides a thorough, if not comprehensive, list of key texts on city comedy. However, other useful work has been written on individual authors who may be referenced elsewhere in this volume. Journal articles on individual texts can also be invaluable and online journals, such as *EMLS*, and e-databases, such as *JSTOR* and *MUSE*, make access to these much easier. Many of the monographs on city comedy give a good guide to historical context as do individual editions of plays. *EEBO* has made access to a wider range of primary sources recently more available for undergraduate study. *Bartleby.com* also provides useful introductions to topical prose writers such as Nashe, Dekker, Deloney, Greene, and Munday.

Editions of city comedy

Beaumont, Francis. *The Knight of the Burning Pestle*. Ed. Sheldon P. Zitner. Revels. Manchester: Manchester University Press 2004.

Dekker, Thomas. *The Honest Whore Part I and II*. London: Routledge, 1999.

Jonson, Ben. *The Alchemist*. New Mermaids. London: A. and C. Black, Andrew Brodie Publications, 2004.

———. *The Alchemist and Other Plays*. Oxford: Oxford Paperbacks, 2004; includes *Volpone* and *Epicene*.

———. *Bartholomew Fair*. Ed. Suzanne Gossett. Revels. Manchester: Manchester University Press, 2000.

———. *The Devil is an Ass*. Ed. Peter Happé. Revels. Manchester: Manchester University Press, 1996.

———. *Every Man In His Humour*. Ed. Robert N. Watson. New Mermaids. London: A. and C. Black, 2003.

———. *Every Man Out of His Humour*. Ed. Martin Seymour Smith. New Mermaids. London: Ernest Benn, 1988.

———. *Every Man Out of His Humour, Cynthia's Revels and The Poetaster: The Works of Ben Jonson Part Two*. Montana: Kessinger, 2004.

———. *Volpone*. Ed. Robert Watson. New Mermaids. London: A. and C. Black, 2003.

———, George Chapman, John Marston. *Eastward Ho*. Ed. R. W. van Fossen. Revels. Manchester: Manchester University Press, 1998.

Marston, John. *The Dutch Courtesan*. Ed. David Crane. New Mermaids. London: A. and C. Black, 1997.

Middleton, Thomas. *A Chaste Maid in Cheapside*. Ed. Alan Brissenden. New Mermaids. London: A. and C. Black, 2002.

———. *A Mad World My Masters* and other Plays. Ed. Michael Taylor. Oxford: Oxford World Classics, 1998; includes *A Trick to Catch the Old One* and *Michaelmas Term*.

Bibliography

Bliss, Lee. *The World's Perspective: John Webster and the Jacobean Drama*. New Brunswick: Rutgers University Press, 1983.

Bruster, Douglas. *Drama and the Market in the Age of Shakespeare*. Cambridge Studies in Renaissance Literature and Culture. Cambridge: Cambridge University Press, 1995.

Chakravorty, Swapan. *Society and Politics in the Plays of Thomas Middleton*. Oxford, Clarendon Press, 1996.

Covatta, Anthony. *Thomas Middleton's City Comedies*. Lewisburg: Bucknell University Press, 1973.

Gibbons, Brian. *Jacobean City Comedy*. London: Methuen, 1968.

Griswold, Wendy. *Renaissance Revivals: City Comedy and Revenge Tragedy in the London Theatre 1576–1980*. Chicago: Chicago University Press, 1986.

Heinemann, Margot. *Puritanism and Theatre: Thomas Middleton and Oppositional Drama under the Early Stuarts*. Cambridge: Cambridge University Press, 1980.

Knights, L. C. *Drama and Society in the Age of Jonson.* London: Chatto and Windus, 1937.
Leggatt, Alexander. *Citizen Comedy in the Age of Shakespeare.* Toronto: University of Toronto Press, 1973.
Leinwald, Theodore. *The City Staged: Jacobean Comedy 1603–1613.* Madison: University of Wisconsin Press, 1986.
Levin, Harry. "Notes Towards a Definition of City Comedy." *Renaissance Genres: Essays on Theory, History and Interpretation,* ed. Barbara Lewalski. Cambridge: Harvard University Press, 1986.
Mehl, Dieter, et al. *Plotting Early Modern London.* Aldershot: Ashgate, 2004.
Paster, Gail Kern. *The Idea of the City in the Age of Shakespeare.* Athens: University of Georgia Press, 1985.
Salgādo, Gamīnī. *Four Jacobean City Comedies.* Baltimore and Harmondsworth: Penguin, 1975.
Sullivan, Ceri. *The Rhetoric of Credit: Mercantile Texts and City Comedy.* London: Association of University Presses, 2002.
Wayne, Don E. "Drama and Society in the Age of Jonson: an Alternative View." *Renaissance Drama* 13 (1982): 103–30.

Further reading

Agnew, Jean-Christophe. *Worlds Apart: the Market and the Theater in Anglo American Thought.* New York: Cambridge University Press, 1986.
Barber, C. L. *Shakespeare's Festive Comedy: a Study of Dramatic Form in Relation to Social Custom.* Princeton: Princeton University Press, 1959.
Berry, Edward. *Shakespeare's Comic Rites.* Cambridge: Cambridge University Press, 1986.
Bristol, Michael D. *Carnival and Theatre: Plebeian Culture and the Structure of Authority.* New York: Methuen, 1985.
Frye, Northrop. *Anatomy of Criticism: Four Essays.* Princeton: Princeton University Press, 1957.
Laroque, François. *Shakespeare's Festive World: Elizabethan Seasonal Entertainment and the Professional Stage.* Trans. J. Lloyd. Cambridge: Cambridge University Press, 1991.
Pollard, Arthur. *Satire.* Critical Idiom. London: Methuen, 1970.
Rowe, George E., Jr. *Thomas Middleton and the New Comedy Tradition.* Lincoln: University of Nebraska Press, 1979.
Slights, William. "The Incarnations of Comedy." *University of Toronto Quarterly* 51, 1 (Fall 1981): 13–27.
———. "Unfashioning the Man of Mode: Comic Countergenre in Marston, Jonson and Middleton." *Renaissance Drama* ns 15 (1984): 69–80.
Smith, David, et al. *The Theatrical City: Culture, Theatre and Politics in London 1576–1649.* Cambridge: Cambridge University Press, 1995.
Stallybrass, Peter, and White, Allon. *The Politics and Poetics of Transgression.* London: Methuen, 1986.

10
Thomas Middleton
Ceri Sullivan

Chronology

1580	Born in London to a freeman of the Tilers' and Bricklayers' Livery Company.
1586	Father died, mother, Anne, remarried but the match turned sour and Anne forced to go to law to protect her children's inheritance.
1598	Enters Queen's College, Oxford.
1599	*Micro-Cynicon: Six Snarling Satires* published.
1601	Reported to be in London with players.
*c.*1602	Marries Mary Marbeck. *Blurt Master Constable, The Family of Love.*
*c.*1603	*The Phoenix.*
*c.*1604	Son Edward born. *The Puritan, The Honest Whore (part 1).*
*c.*1605	*A Mad World, My Masters, Michaelmas Term, A Trick To Catch The Old One.*
*c.*1607	*Your Five Gallants.*
*c.*1608	*The Roaring Girl.*
*c.*1611	*A Chaste Maid in Cheapside, The Second Maiden's Tragedy, Wit at Several Weapons.*
1612	*No Wit, No Help Like a Woman's.*
1613	*The Triumphs of Truth* (Lord Mayor's pageant).
1614	*The Masque of Cupid* (lost).
*c.*1615	*The Witch, More Dissemblers Besides Women.*
*c.*1616	*The Mayor of Quinborough or Hengist King of Kent, The Widow, The Nice Valour, Civitatis Amor* (Lord Mayor's pageant).
1617	*A Fair Quarrel, The Triumphs of Honour and Industry* (Lord Mayor's pageant).
*c.*1618	*The Old Law.*
1619	*Inner Temple Masque, World Tossed at Tennis, The Triumphs of Love and Antiquity* (Lord Mayor's pageant).
1620	Made City Chronologer for London (required to memorialize major events in the life of the city).

c.1621	*Anything for a Quiet Life, Women Beware Women, The Sun in Aries* (Lord Mayor's pageant).
1622	*The Changeling, The Triumphs of Honour and Virtue* (Lord Mayor's pageant).
1623	*The Spanish Gypsy, The Triumphs of Integrity* (Lord Mayor's pageant).
1624	*A Game at Chess.*
1626	*The Triumphs of Health and Prosperity* (Lord Mayor's pageant).
1627	Died.

Critical overview

Society's "great recorder" was T. S. Eliot's view of Middleton, speaking of him as a dispassionate writer who registered the flaws and virtues of society without either judging them or drawing attention to his own status as author. The mere possibility of such Olympian detachment—let alone either its correctness or its use in preparing to perform the plays—was challenged in the second half of the twentieth century by sceptical and politicized critics. The following discussion will split the reaction to Middleton's work into the three genres he principally worked in: city comedy, revenge tragedy, and topical writing.

Critics of the 1960s started with the premise that Middleton's city comedies were moral satires on lust and avarice, and arguments circled around how far he was engaged with what he purported to criticize. Readers pointed out that while the genre of the city comedy was stereotypical and formal (a young virgin or wife is wooed or confined by her rich but aged suitor or father, but eventually lost by a series of tricks to a spendthrift young gallant, who gives up his liaison with a good-hearted whore to win a wife and money in one), Middleton's comedies looked realistic in their locations, their characterization, and the details of everyday life that every Londoner could recognize. How could a satirist not be secretly attached to something he described with such panache? This consensus was sharply varied in the late 1960s by Margot Heinemann's influential study of Middleton's politics. She first threw light on the dramatist's links to the parliamentary puritan party. The city comedies, she went on to argue, opposed court values, especially the idea that rank and influence were the result of birth not merit, that social mobility was to be frowned on, that the middling sorts of London were financial resources for the court without an ethical or political stance of their own. Like the revenge tragedies, the comedies showed a society of already-damned individuals, savagely fornicating, hoarding, bribing, manipulating, eating each other. They were Calvinist sermons of disgust. This was a powerful vision, not dislodged until the 1980s when feminist critics such as Gail Kern Paster picked up the visceral obsessions of Middleton's comedies in Heinemann's work but read them as expressions of a synecdochical view of women in the period. Women were seen as parts to be split up and circulated around between desiring men. When moving out of these defined roles women cause the men considerable anxiety as they seep and leak, in speech and body, outside the magic circle. They work, travel, speak, select their own partners, and in doing so arouse admiration, desire, and fear. Equally, the impotent husbands and fathers who allow the gender hierarchy to become more fluid than it should be are derided for their effeminate inability to hold on to what is valuable (their masculinity, signalled by their possession of the woman). Such discussions held a particular element that interested critics in the 1990s such as Theodore Leinwand: circulation. This last analytical movement worked through the implications of credit as the basic mode of transaction in the early modern period, the idea of social credit where the value of an individual was inferred by his creditors in the signals he gave of dress, behaviour, and associates, and the idea of credit as a rhetorical strategy that creates belief in an assertion. Solid monetary gain could accrue from the wise manipulation of belief in one's value, which depended on tales told of oneself being circulated. The verbal dexterity of Middleton's tricksters and gallants entice credit then cash from their hoarding seniors.

The trajectory of comment on Middleton's tragedies was similar to the comedies, moving from ethics to gender to rank as constricting systems that are challenged or (in some views) ultimately affirmed by the tragedies. Once again, the discussion noted how the psychological realism of Middleton's local characterization and his particularity in dramatic action counter-pointed the stereotypical form of the revenge tragedy (incestuous, adulterous, or unsuitable liaisons, often promoted by cynically manipulative courtiers against the family interest, were followed by highly coloured revenges by wronged fathers, brothers, or husbands acting to restore the social order). The question of whether such spectacles reduced or inflamed sinful desires yielded to one of how far the central female figure was powerful in sin or a victim of the men around her, and this, in its turn, gave way to a study of how rank, cash, and sexual favours were swopped at court. Particular interest was shown in the metadramatic elements of these plays, which often paused or ended with masques, dumbshows, processions, and other self-consciously dramatic moments. Here, the real and the sign faced each other down, as early modern audiences and writers explored the striking technical possibilities of the new theatres, either enclosed public arenas or darkened private rooms.

Analysis of Middleton's work for the city of London started in tandem with the economic analysis of the city comedies, and particularly of the pageants he was paid by livery companies to write in celebration of the annual election of a Lord Mayor on 28 October each year. After the mayor had taken an oath of loyalty to the Crown at Westminster and returned to the city the pageant, consisting of five or more wagons, went through the streets pausing at significant spots to praise him (St Paul's churchyard, say, or the Standard in Cheapside which provided water for the area). The topography of London and its ritual spaces, how a merchant presented himself as worthy of honour and civic responsibility, and the relationship between the crown and the city in the run-up to the civil war, were the areas of comment.

Finally, the most recent work on Middleton has been on plays he wrote with other dramatists and the movement of these into print. These studies challenge romantic understandings of the writer as the origin of inspiration and authority, whose work expresses a single vision. In early modern drama the norm was to write on demand to a theatre company's needs—which meant speed and flexibility—which in turn meant collaborating in writing or adapting previously written plays, always with a forthcoming specific production in mind. This is of particular interest when, for instance, critics start to recognize collaboration by Shakespeare, eroding his bardic status as Great English Author, font of our language and values. Using biographical, stylistic, typographical, and literary methods Brian Vickers has shown that Middleton worked on *Timon of Athens* with Shakespeare. Moreover, since early modern plays emerged as the result of a printer's efforts to bring together authors' papers, actors' parts, and the theatre company's commercial intentions the early modern play text can prove as unstable as its authorship.

Pedagogic strategies

Readers new to Middleton might like to consider the city comedy *The Roaring Girl*, collaboratively written by Middleton and Dekker for the large public theatre, the Fortune, which counterpoints the celebration of the city in the mayoral pageant *The Triumphs of Truth*, written for the grocer Sir Thomas Myddelton. The questions raised by these come up again but in a different register in the revenge tragedy *Women Beware Women*. The following discussion will deal with five concerns in approaching Middleton: the staging, the language, key items or images, the social use of drama, and the physical text.

- Our post-modern understanding is that meaning is created by reception and medium as much as by the abstract "text." The early modern concept of the text also regarded itself as placed in a particular situation, one that passed power from the rhetorician to his audience. Focusing on staging ensures that both the political nature and the self-consciousness of early modern drama is forgrounded. Middleton's plays are peculiarly metadramatic and conscious of their audiences and performance spaces.
- Distinguishing the general features of early modern London English from a dramatist's personal speech habits (their idiolect) is difficult but necessary if one wants to see where their latter is deliberately varied. Middleton's idiolect registered his expensive education, his interests, and the people he was writing for on any one occasion.

- Since realism in early modern drama, either of plot or of characterisation, is not a primary concern, it can be helpful to look for the differences in the aesthetics of then and now by studying key items or images. In Middleton their repetition provides points to register changes in the themes and structures of the play. In his city comedies circulating items appear as fetishes which stand in for what everyone desires. In his civic entertainments the drama itself circulates. In his tragedies the act of revenge is repeated in a closed community in a potentially endless economic cycle.
- Unlike characteristic twenty-first century works, early modern fictional works did not set out to transcribe reality nor to express their authors' attitudes about their personal situations. They claimed to teach the reader the ideal, then move his will towards attaining it by delighting and entertaining him. This didactic function was expressed in work that took pleasure in formal shaping. This did not have to be expressive or realistic, but it had to be useful. Can Middleton's plays be said to move or teach their readers? Even the commercial or violent ones?
- Understanding the publication history of the three plays can lead to an understanding of the unstable nature of the early modern printed text and the role of the author in producing this. Middleton collaborated on the comedy and wrote to order on the pageant, mirroring today's commercially oriented texts such as films and magazines more than the solipsistic product of high literature. By contrast, the revenge tragedy was an elite work aimed at the niche market of private theatres.

A single scene from each drama will be used to consider these five issues. Since a new reader of Middleton is learning how to frame the questions that will allow her to move between texts the final scene from *Women Beware Women* will be presented as a series of short, pertinent points that could prompt her to engage with the tragedy as with the civic texts rather than modelling the discussion for her as will be done for the civic entertainments.

The Roaring Girl

The play's central device is to show how a young gallant gets permission to marry his love against the initial opposition of his father by pretending that he intends to marry a notorious cross-dressing woman, the Moll of the title. Most of the play's action, however, focuses on how the straight-talking, straight-dealing Moll scorns feminine wiles and preserves her virtue in the face of unwanted suitors. A subplot shows how three citizens' wives in London support gallants and yet maintain their marriage vows and check marital jealousy. Act II scene I opens with a row of shops in London selling consumer goods: tobacco, personal linen, and feathers. Mistresses Openwork, Tiltyard, and Gallipot entice four gallants (Goshawk, Greenwit, Laxton, and Trapdoor) to buy. On the strength of Mistress Gallipot's attachment to Laxton he borrows her husband's profits from the shop. When Moll walks down the street she is met with suspicion by Mistress Openwork who thinks her husband rather too civil to Moll, and sets up what seems to be an amorous liaison with Laxton at 3.00—though since later in the scene she also arranges to meet Trapdoor at the same time it becomes evident that these will be rencontres to fight, not make love.

In performing London's commercial sector to itself, since the bulk of the public theatre audience were merchants, freemen and apprentices, *The Roaring Girl* was being theatrically audacious. The unusually specific nature of Middleton's stage directions—he tells us that the shops are in a row, what they sell, and who is in them—and the opening bawled street cries make it clear that the division between on and off stage is to be eroded. The acting space is also the working space on-stage, prompting thought into how far selling off-stage is also a matter of coaxing along an "audience" for the goods. Even more intriguingly, there is a further layer of acting in Laxton and Mistress Gallipot's intrigue, which is hidden from the other gallants, and in Laxton's manipulation of Mistress Gallipot's affection (later revealed as an act to entice an attempt on her virtue so she can prove it inviolable). When Moll enters she acts the man, and Trapdoor acts the lover. Each character mumbles asides to the audience which allow the latter into the secret of whom to credit and who not. The knowledge that this is a fictional scene about social fictions is emphasized in what we would think of as cut-away shots, moving from shop to shop as characters' voices are raised then lowered as the next shop is focused on (one stage direction is "fall from them to another"). It is testing in reading to see who is being addressed, for example

> *[Laxton] blows tobacco in their faces*
> Greenwit [*and*] Goshawk: Oh, puh, ho ho.
> Laxton: So, so.
> Mistress Gallipot: What's the matter now, sir?
> Laxton: I protest I'm in extreme want of money.
> (II.i.68–71)[1]

Mistress Gallipot's concern seems at first to be for the gallants, as smoke gets in their eyes, and then turns out to be for Laxton. It seems likely that early on in the play's history the original of Moll, Mary Frith, appeared at the Fortune theatre to see the play, teased the audience about what they would find in her breeches, then played and sang to it. Frith—alias Moll Cut-purse—was a notorious figure in 1600s London, a swaggering cross-dresser whom the church was shortly to charge with drinking, swearing, and dressing as a male. MTV itself could not produce a more self-reflexive, split-screen media moment, signalled in II.i by the filmic stage direction that moves the eye from one booth to another "fall from them to the other."

The Londoners' speech is resonantly appropriate in its local and concrete reference, slight and swift dialogue, and competitive and easy movement in puns and images between one referent and another. The nooks of London appear: St Paul's where the bankrupts loiter, Mile End where the soldiers practise, Tyburn where the gallows are, Brainford, Staines, or Ware where the adulterers congregate, Gray's Inn Fields where are lawyers and footpads, St Antholin's where the bell for a morning sermon rang out at 5 a.m., the despised suburbs and licentious liberties outside London wall. Recent events come up: the tall German giving fencing lessons in the city, the rituals of chopping, mixing, and lighting with a coal the tobacco in the fashionable vice of smoking, the sauces in an ordinary or cheap eating house of mustard, oil, and vinegar. There is nothing abstract about the way they speak: pot-herbs, pipes, almanacs, angels . . . The imagery used is also concrete: pockets "cackle" when they lay the ha'penny "eggs" that are the only coins left after a night's debauch; Mrs Openwork was out before "such a snail as you crept out of your shell"; a cap "looks for all the world with those spangled feathers like a nobleman's bedpost." Bawdy references underlie most images.

> Goshawk: Oh sir, 'tis many a good woman's fortune, when her husband turns bankrupt to begin with pipes and set up again.
> Laxton: And indeed the raising of the woman is the lifting up of the man's head at all times.

Here we have moved from the sale of pipes of tobacco to recover a bankrupt's fortunes to the male "pipe" that raises a woman's belly. Laxton's response converts the bankrupt to the impotent husband unable to begin with a pipe, whose wife lifts his head with the horns of the cuckold. It is the sort of involved joke that modern actors feel impelled to mime. Characters compete to pack multiple meanings into single words (yard, pipe, shift, service, standing, riding, and so on). The repeated reminder is that money can be exchanged for sex if women are prepared to circulate like coins.

How "useful" is this scene? In noughties criticism the interest would lie in the way Moll has escaped the confines of gender, showing it for a social construction that wants to keep the power structure of masculine over feminine intact by claiming that the latter identity is necessarily the result of being a woman. In this scene Moll is the one with swagger and power, who thinks to test the citizens' wives' virtue, who picks fights, takes on servants, and appears to select her sexual partners. Her ability to determine her own way of living is mirrored on a minor scale by the wives, and counterpointed by the femininity of the gallants, who trifle with linen and feathers, fall at Moll's feet, get paid by the wives, and chatter amongst themselves. In Middleton's own time such plays were alternately regarded as inducements to vice (the public house audience containing a good proportion of impressionable teenage apprentice boys) or an entertainment that assuaged through fantasy desires that could not be enacted in public. Audience interest might be aroused by Moll's musing that Londoners cannot know if the women are honest because they are rarely tempted greatly by the gallants. Is the play therefore like a fairy tale that tests its heroine, and is Moll herself to be tempted to be as unchaste as her masculine dress suggests she is to Trapdoor and Laxton? Preachers in the 1600s denounced women cross-dressing as scandalous to the law of God, and popular attention found them as titillating as cross-dressing men are found today—so what lies behind the latter men's sudden sexual interest in Moll? Do they long on their own account to invert the social and religious orderings?

The collaboration between Dekker, a prolific dramatist and pamphleteer, and Middleton is so close that editors are mostly unable to assign scenes to either dramatist with any confidence. The usual split of each play was by plot line or by types of action, and dramatists would become known for their handling of elements in the play. By thinking in terms of Hollywood script conferences rather than tortured lonely writers in cottages or garrets we might get closer to how the early modern playwright thought. *The Roaring Girl*'s II.i is usually given mainly to Middleton but not wholly so. One can reasonably infer that both men read through and made suggestions for the other's scenes, and both were working to a common framework, in which their own ideas and those of the acting company that commissioned the play were mixed, but the details of co-writing are the key. Did they write their allocated sections separately but simultaneously, and sew them together later? How much was specified before starting work? Did each man write with the other's style in mind? At what stage did the other revise his partner's work? And—beyond this—how far does the 1611 text reflect what the authors wrote, what Prince Henry's men acted, or what the printer found profitable? Again, a comparison with the production and distribution structures of our own relatively new entertainment industry is provocative in shaking the fallacy of the originary text. What is the original of a film—the shooting script? The rushes? The director's cut? The film released to the Americas—or the different version European markets get? The DVD? The television showing mid-afternoon? Since some of Shakespeare's plays are currently assumed to have been part written by Middleton—a scene in *Macbeth* and substantial parts of *Timon of Athens*—the discussion becomes more intense when the organic results of Shakespeare's unique genius need to be protected from the "interpolations" of his collaborator.

The Triumphs of Truth

After the newly appointed mayor emerges from the Guildhall, on the morning of the day he takes the oath of loyalty and service to the city and the monarch, a trumpet sounds and "a grave, feminine shape" representing London welcomes him. She lists the care "in government, in wealth, in honour" she has given him and asks in return that he does not follow the courses of her disobedient "sons," who show no service to the city. The mayor is to take no bribes and keep the city, "the king's chamber," free of pollution. The mayor departs for Westminster to take the oath, being met at the riverside by five barges, dressed as "Indian spice-islands." On his return to Baynard's Castle Truth's Angel and his champion Zeal salute him with the warning that Error is about to attack him—which, as the procession moves on to the chain that marks the boundary of St Paul's Cathedral churchyard, duly happens. Error and his champion Envy welcome the mayor ecstatically, for now "will and appetite" can govern the city in deceit, the sale of offices, overlooking offences, and simple sloth and gluttony (as members of the crowd can attest). Zeal hastily forces Error and Envy back.

Civic pageants in the 1600s recreated London's streets as theatrical spaces. The streets were already presentation spaces, of course, since this was a small city by our standards (*c.*200,000), with recognized areas for services and types of people, and everyone knew their neighbours' business. Where current walkers through London can fade into invisibility, no such comfortable alienation was available four hundred years earlier—Londoners were always on show. The rueful self-awareness about the city's follies and quirks that drives the city comedies is multiplied as praise in the civic dramas. Take, for instance, the figure of London, "on her head a model of steeples and turrets," who speaks for London in the streets of London wearing a model of London. The city's real image-consciousness is twice-removed, in the figure and in its headgear. Even more, Mother London addresses the person who has been selected to represent London to the crown, and does so by asking him to reflect on how he came from her, and so should mirror her. Though there is some evidence that actors repeated speeches as the procession wound about not all the audience who lined the route could have heard the actors speak from the pageant wagons, so the costumes of the participants were read with as much interest and knowledge by the spectators as a plate of fish and chips is by cultural semioticians today—the "champion of Truth, in a garment of flame-coloured silk, with a bright hair on his head, from which shoot fire-beams . . . his right hand holding a flaming scourge, intimating thereby that as he is the manifester of Truth, he is likewise the chastiser of Ignorance and Error." Of course.

The register Middleton uses for these pageants of praise is more formal than the city comedy since this is a public celebration of city values, a cere-monial that confers honour on the commercial space it moves through. There are speeches at the new Mayor, Sir Thomas Myddelton, not dialogue with him; the are few concrete references, suggestions, and criticisms of past irregularities are kept tactfully and prudently general. The assault on Myddelton's will by Error is through his passions, any appetite for power, envy, or sloth; fortunately in Truth's Angel, his reason, and in Zeal, his holy fervour for good, he finds strength to resist. The battle implied in Myddelton's will (a psychomachia) is visualized by the pageant, but no specific schemes are mentioned. Thus Error does not tell Sir Thomas that he should make the most of a large engineering enterprise Myddelton's brother Hugh had completed the same year, 1613, of bringing a fresh water supply to London.

Rather, he instructs the mayor to "Let not thy conscience come into thine eyes / This twelvemonth, if thou lov'st revenge or gain,"[2] and leaves the audience to conjecture the means how. Similarly, Error's boast that he can run over "Back-ways and by-ways, and fetch in my treasure / After the wishes of my heart, by shifts, / Deceits, and slights"[3] turns him into the trickster of city comedy, but leaves out the local reference. Yet this very mild form of warning (partnered as it was by the other tactful mode of advice, praise for the virtues demanded by a civic post which was urbanely assumed the mayor would have) was not to the city governors' taste. *The Triumphs of Truth* and the previous year's pageant by Dekker were the only two to have this dramatic element to them.

These pageants were financed by the merchants who made up the livery company that the mayor belonged to. Myddelton belonged to the wealthy Grocers' Company, which oversaw the city's trade in importing, wholesaling, and retailing all luxury consumables such as sugar and spices. Where the extravagance of court masques showed the glory of the king in stage machines, blazing lighting, and rich costumes, the Grocers left more pragmatic reminders. Later in the 1613 pageant lucky spectators might have caught the little parcels of nutmeg, pepper, and cinnamon that were tossed into the crowd. Later still, those influential people whom the Grocers wanted to impress got a printed version of the pageant. Once again one is left with a question about what the "text" of his display is: the notes the author read to the Company, their revisions, the *ad hoc* requirements of production on the day, the bits that got left out because of rain or a rush, the speeches that a spectator could not hear as the pageant moved on, the official record sent on after the event?

Women Beware Women

The pivotal scene for the play, act II scene ii, starts with a quiet conversation between the widow Livia and the Duke of Florence's pander. Livia offers to draw to the palace the young gentlewoman Bianca (a recently married factor's wife) since Bianca's beauty has caught the eye of the duke. While the two wait another "client" of Livia's appears: her brother, who is anxious to marry his daughter Isabella off to a rich but idiotic ward, the latter trying to make sure he's getting a good bargain in Isabella's looks. When the factor's mother appears she is persuaded to call Bianca to the palace. While the mother and Livia play chess below, Bianca is enticed upstairs to view the palace's monument—and is raped by the Duke. When she descends she whispers revenge on Livia and the pander, promises that are later to be gloriously fulfilled in the play's bloody final scene, where multiple murders and a suicide come in the guise of a court entertainment. *Women Beware Women* was based on two stories circulating during Middleton's teens: that of Bianca Capello, who became the mistress then wife of the Duke of Tuscany before her death in 1587, and a French tale of incest published in 1597. It is not known where the play was first performed, nor the exact date of composition.

The following points may awake a reader's interest in the comparison and contrasts available with the city texts to produce more extended commentary themselves.

- *Metadrama*: the Duke lusts after Bianca when he sees her as he processes through the streets. The pander attempts to rouse her sexually by showing her erotic pictures. There is a grim comedy in the simultaneous games of rape in the Monument and chess between the widows. The scene cuts rapidly between the selection by Ward and Duke of women.
- *Language*: Bianca is initially hoarded for the use of her factor husband until she is brought into circulation. The terms of exchange ("ladies' ware" for cash) are as rigorously gone through by the Ward and his companion as they are enumerated by the Duke to Bianca. The women start to bargain on their own account, so one deed will be requited by another.
- *Repeated moments*: three related groups of ideas structure the scene, namely honour (look for the words reputation, credit, belief, rumour, faith, courtesy, advancement, patron), wit (find folly, experience, youth, age, advice, wisdom, plan, cunning, treachery, subtlety), and the sexual innuendo as a sign not of plenty but of obsession.
- *Didactic elements*: the separation of male and female is muddled by Livia's cynical energy in satisfying two men's lusts and her brother's foolish sweating bustle over the wedding. There is an anxious emphasis, even by the raped woman, that her virtue lies in physical chastity not adultery. The combination of sexual licence and physical violence may arouse the immoderate audience as it does the Duke or make them regard it with as much as bitterness as Bianca.
- *Publication history*: the play was not published until 1657. It is uncertain where it was played. In 1989 Howard Barker rewrote the parts of the play to emphasize the "sexual stock exchange"; his title page boasting collaboration "with" Middleton.

Notes

1. *The Roaring Girl*, ed. Elizabeth Cook, New Mermaids (London: A. C. Black, 1997).
2. *The Triumphs of Truth and the Entertainment at the Opening of the New River*, in *The Works of Thomas Middleton*, ed. A. H. Bullen, vol. 7, pp. 227–66 (London, 1886), p. 242.
3. *Works of Thomas Middleton*, vol. 7, p. 243.

Selective guide to further reading and resources

General

Middleton's complete works were edited by A. H. Bullen in eight volumes, including the prose, verse, and city entertainments (London, 1885–86). The projected complete Oxford edition under Gary Taylor is imminent. Individual plays appear in the Revels and New Mermaid series. All the plays, including the pageants, can be accessed on Early English Books Online (subscription web-service that provides digital images of the majority of books published between 1473 and 1700). *Early Modern Literary Studies* 8, 3 (2003) is a special issue on Middleton (http://www.shu.ac.uk/emls/08-3/08-3toc.htm). In terms of productions, there was a 1968 film of *Women Beware Women* which is not commercially available, but nothing filmed on the city pageant or comedy.

Chakravorty, Swapan. *Society and Politics in the Plays of Thomas Middleton.* Oxford: Clarendon Press, 1996.

Friedenreich, Kenneth (ed.). *"Accompaninge the Players": Essays celebrating Thomas Middleton.* New York: AMS Press, 1983.

Heinemann, Margot. *Puritanism and Theatre: Thomas Middleton and opposition drama under the early Stuarts.* Cambridge: Cambridge University Press, 1980.

Limon, Jerzy. *Dangerous Matter: English Drama and Politics in 1623/4.* Cambridge: Cambridge University Press, 1986.

Steen, S. J. *Ambrosia in an Earthern Vessel: Three centuries of audience and reader response to the works of Thomas Middleton.* New York: AMS Press, 1993.

Vickers, Brian. *Shakespeare Co-author. A historical study of five collaborative plays.* Oxford: Oxford University Press, 2002.

Yachnin, Paul. "Reversal of fortune: Shakespeare, Middleton, and the puritans." *ELH* 70, 3 (2003): 757–86.

The Roaring Girl

DiGangi, Mario. "Sexual slander and working women in *The Roaring Girl*." *Renaissance Drama* 32 (2003): 147–76.

Forman, Valerie. "Marked angels: counterfeits, commodities, and *The Roaring Girl*." *Renaissance Quarterly* 54, 4 (2001): 1531–60.

Leinwand, Theodore. *Theatre, Finance and Society in Early Modern England.* Cambridge: Cambridge University Press, 1999.

Paster, Gail Kern. "Leaky vessels: the incontinent women of city comedy," *Renaissance Drama* 18 (1987): 43–65.

Rose, Mary Beth. "Women in men's clothing: apparel and social stability in *The Roaring Girl*." *English Literary Renaissance* 14 (1984): 367–91.

The Triumphs of Truth

Bergeron, D. M. *English Civic pageantry 1558–1642.* London: Edward Arnold, 1971.

Sergei Lobanov-Rostovsky's words, "*The triumphes of golde*: economic authority in the Jacobean Lord Mayor's show." *ELH* 60 (1993): 879–98.

Smith, D. L., Strier, R. and Bevington, D. (eds). *The Theatrical City: Culture, Theatre and Politics in London 1576–1649.* Cambridge: Cambridge University Press, 1995.

Women Beware Women

Barker, Howard (with Thomas Middleton). *Women Beware Women.* London: Calder, 1989.

Brooke, Nicholas. *Horrid Laughter in Jacobean Tragedy.* London: Open Books; New York: Barnes and Noble, 1979.

Eliot, T. S. "Thomas Middleton" [1927], in *Selected Essays.* London: Faber, 1932.

Holdsworth, R. V. (ed.). *Three Jacobean Revenge Tragedies.* Basingstoke: Macmillan–now Palgrave Macmillan, 1990.

Neill, Michael. *Issues of Death: Mortality and Identity in English Renaissance Tragedy.* Oxford: Clarendon Press, 1997.

11
Webster and Ford

Rowland Wymer

Chronology and context

John Webster was born in about 1578. His father was a well-to-do coach-maker whose business included providing the carts used to carry prisoners to execution. Webster's known work in the theatre dates from 1602 to about 1626, making it almost exactly coterminous with the reign of James I (1603–25). His earliest surviving plays are relatively undistinguished collaborative works, *The Famous History of Sir Thomas Wyatt* (1602), *Westward Ho!* (1604), and *Northward Ho!* (1605), all written with Thomas Dekker. His final plays were also written collaboratively and have likewise failed to arouse much critical enthusiasm. They include *Anything for a Quiet Life* (*c*.1621) with Middleton, *A Cure for a Cuckold* (*c*.1625) with Rowley, and *Appius and Virginia* (*c*.1626) with Heywood. In between he wrote, unaided, the two tragedies on which his reputation depends, *The White Devil* (1612) and *The Duchess of Malfi* (1613–14), plays which Hazlitt and many subsequent critics have thought "come the nearest to Shakespear[e] of any thing we have upon record."[1] His third independently written work was the flawed but fascinating tragicomedy *The Devil's Law-Case* (*c*.1617). The dates of his two tragedies place them at the precise moment when Shakespeare was retiring from the theatre, and close to the mid-point of James's reign. Since both plays contain ferocious outbursts against court life ("O happy they that never saw the court, / Nor ever knew great man but by report" (*The White Devil* V.vi.261–2)), it has seemed natural to many critics and teachers to situate them primarily within a Jacobean political context and to see them as exemplifying the growing hostility to the Stuart court which, a generation later, would help to cause the Civil War which began in 1642.

One of the problems with this easily "teachable" account is that it overlooks the way that many great plays, and certainly Webster's two tragedies, have been built out of previous plays, written and performed within a different political context. No one would deny the enormous influence of *Hamlet* (*c*.1601) on Webster's vision of court life as poisoned by "some curs'd example"

(*The Duchess of Malfi* I.i.14) at the very fountainhead and source of power, so that the state becomes, in the view of the malcontent commentator who channels our perceptions of it, a "prison," peopled by spies and flatterers and haunted by secret murders. It is easy to forget, however, that *Hamlet* was an Elizabethan play which reflects some of the deep discontent with the Elizabethan court in the last years of the sixteenth century (one symptom of which was the failed Essex rebellion of 1601). *Hamlet* and other successful Elizabethan plays generated an artistic momentum which carried on beyond 1603, creating a brief vogue for political tragedy which was already subsiding by the time Webster was writing his major plays. Paradoxically, however, serious dissatisfaction with James I and his policies did not really develop till the second half of his reign.[2]

The most sensational and "theatrical" of Jacobean court scandals, the trial and conviction of James's favourite Robert Carr, Earl of Somerset, and his wife Frances Howard for the poisoning of Sir Thomas Overbury did not take place till 1616, though Overbury's death, at first declared to be natural, had occurred in 1613 while Webster was writing *The Duchess*. It is in fact difficult to draw precise topical inferences from Webster's tragedies, which are both set in sixteenth-century Italian courts, powerfully mythic locations for writers of tragedy since Marston's *Antonio's Revenge* (1600). Although *The Devil's Law-Case* also has an Italian setting, it seems a much more determinedly "topical" play, filled with contemporary allusions and apparently bent on making a contribution to a current debate about women which had been triggered by Joseph Swetnam's misogynist pamphlet *The Araignment of Lewde, Idle, Froward and Unconstant Women* (1615).

The two tragedies are clearly also deeply interested in the behaviour of women within a patriarchal society but they seem generally to avoid this kind of topicality. However, the Duchess of Malfi's secret and fatal marriage has some striking parallels with the case of Arbella Stuart, James's cousin and a possible heir to the throne, who, at the time Webster was writing, was imprisoned in the Tower for having contracted a secret marriage in 1610 to William Seymour against the express wishes of James. She was to die in 1615, driven mad by grief. It is also possible that the death in November 1612 of Prince Henry, James's son and heir, who had been a focal point for the hopes of many who were opposed to James's style of government, casts a shadow over the ending of *The Duchess*. The surviving son of Antonio and the Duchess, who inherits the dukedom in the last scene, is the same boy whose horoscope had foretold a "short life" and a "violent death" (*The Duchess of Malfi* II.iii.63). Webster had probably interrupted his writing of *The Duchess* to compose an elegy to Prince Henry titled *A Monumental Column*, which was published within weeks of his death.

The implication of what I have been saying so far is that, despite some suggestive historical connections, the most important context for the study of Webster's plays is the development of Elizabethan and Jacobean theatre in the first decade of the seventeenth century. Webster clearly owes a great deal to Shakespeare and the sequence of major tragedies which he had written for the King's Men at the Globe between 1599 and 1608. After *Hamlet, Othello* (*c.*1603) certainly proved the most influential upon Webster. *The White Devil* seems like a sustained exploitation of the paradoxical symbolism of black and white which underpins Shakespeare's play, while the part of Ferdinand in *The Duchess* gave Richard Burbage the chance to reprise his performance of a man driven to insane extremes of jealousy. Webster also, in the "Note to the Reader" which prefaces *The White Devil*, pays explicit tribute to Chapman and Jonson, referring primarily to their political tragedies, such as *Sejanus* (1603) and *Bussy D'Ambois* (1604). Both these plays, written at the moment of transition from Elizabeth to James rather than out of any substantial experience of Jacobean court life, gave Webster some of the atmosphere and rhetoric he needed to represent the court vividly as "a rank pasture" (*The Duchess of Malfi* I.i.306) (though the particular force of the adjective "rank" comes from *Hamlet*).

I have already mentioned the name of the remaining playwright whose work is essential to an understanding of Webster. John Marston wrote plays for the children's companies when they resumed playing in 1599 at small indoor theatres and, for a short period, became serious rivals to the adult companies playing at the large open-air theatres. The more satirical and self-conscious style which Marston developed for these boy actors was a challenge to the more straightforwardly heroic and passionate repertoire of the adults and Webster's art is a brilliant fusion of these different styles. From the very beginning of his career he worked for both adult and children's companies, both outdoor and indoor theatres. His place at the cross-over point between the "public" and "private" theatre traditions is epitomized by his contribution to Marston's tragicomedy, *The Malcontent* (1602–4). This was originally written for the Chapel Children, to be played at the indoor Blackfriars, but when the King's Men acquired it and performed it at the Globe, Webster wrote a new Induction for it. When the King's Men themselves began playing at the indoor Blackfriars, during the winter months from 1609 onwards, there was a further confluence of the two traditions. The title page of *The Duchess of Malfi* tells us that, like other King's Men plays, it was performed both at the Globe and the Blackfriars, though it seems to have been written with the latter playhouse chiefly in mind.

In summary, I would conclude that the single most important date for an understanding of Webster's plays is 1599, the year Shakespeare began his major sequence of tragedies and the year in which Marston began writing for the Paul's Boys. It was the theatrical developments between 1599 and 1609 rather than any specifically Jacobean political events which determined his art, though it is obvious that his plays register a general cultural unease, Elizabethan as much as Jacobean, about the power relations (including those between men and women) which structure society.

Ford was born in 1586, only eight years after Webster, but he probably did not begin writing for the theatre till he was in his late thirties and is normally seen as belonging to a later generation. His best plays all date from around 1630, making him the most important writer of tragedy during the reign of Charles I (1625–49). Like Webster, he began by collaborating with other dramatists and, indeed, the careers of the two men briefly overlapped when, on two occasions, they were members of the same writing team. The first of these was a lost domestic tragedy, *The Late Murder of the Son upon the Mother* (1624), and the second a tragicomedy mainly written by John Fletcher, *The Fair Maid of the Inn* (1626). Ford's other collaborative work includes *The Witch of Edmonton* (1621), *The Spanish Gypsy* (1623), *The Welsh Ambassador* (1623), and *The Sun's Darling* (1624), all written with Dekker, sometimes as co-author and sometimes as part of a larger team.

Ford's first independently written play, a tragicomedy called *The Lover's Melancholy* (1629), is also the first play in which his distinctive verse style emerges, a style which is capable of suggesting emotional depth and nuance through subtle rhythmic variation rather than any particular complexity of vocabulary or syntax. It was succeeded by his four major tragedies, whose precise order and date of composition is uncertain, but which may well be as follows: *The Broken Heart* (1629), *'Tis Pity She's a Whore* (1630), *Love's Sacrifice* (1631), and *Perkin Warbeck* (1632). The first of these was written for the King's Men at the Blackfriars and the remaining three for Queen Henrietta's Men, playing at the other major Caroline indoor theatre, The Cockpit (or Phoenix) which had been built in 1616. His last two plays were the tragicomedies *The Fancies Chaste and Noble* (*c.*1635) and *The Lady's Trial* (1638). A third independently written tragicomedy, *The Queen*, is of uncertain date and may belong to either the beginning or the end of his career.

Ford's best plays were written and performed during a period of considerable political conflict when Charles I was attempting to rule without recourse to Parliament and was therefore constrained to find other ways, often quasi-legal and unpopular, of raising the money he needed. Historians differ over whether the period of "personal rule" (1629–40) marked an inevitable slide towards civil war but one would expect to find symptoms of social and political conflict in the drama of the time. In Ford's case, however, it is quite difficult to contextualize his plays in this way or to identify what his own political or religious values might have been. One of the most important books on the politics of Caroline drama, Martin Butler's *Theatre and Politics 1632–42* (1984), has almost nothing to say about Ford. An ambitious subsequent attempt to argue that Ford's plays should be seen as addressed to a coterie of Catholic sympathizers was made by Lisa Hopkins in *John Ford's Political Theatre* (1994) but I remain to be convinced by it.[3]

Love's Sacrifice certainly alludes to the cult of Platonic love fostered by Charles's Queen, Henrietta Maria, and the story of the royal "pretender" Perkin Warbeck seems designed to provoke reflection on the nature of kingship.

A relevant context for the latter play may be the peace treaty with Spain which was signed in 1630 and which left Charles's brother-in-law, Frederick of Bohemia, without any chance of reclaiming his kingdom, reduced to the status of a "pretender" to his own throne. The more potent implication, that Charles himself is little more than a "royal actor,"[4] is more difficult to confirm from the play. In his Prologue to *The Lady's Trial*, printed only three years before the outbreak of civil war, Ford attacked playwrights "who idly scan affairs of state," confirming perhaps that he was more interested in psychological than political conflict.

As in the case of Webster, the most important context within which to understand Ford's plays is that of the overall map of Elizabethan, Jacobean, and Caroline theatre. Like Webster, Ford had high literary ambitions and saw himself as primarily writing for the more discriminating theatre-goer, the kind who could more reliably be found among "private" theatre audiences. Yet, also like Webster, he had collaborated with Dekker and written plays which were designed to please the less select audiences at the large open-air theatres. Both men drew effectively on the different theatrical styles available and both shared the problem of trying to write tragedies which would wring an emotional response from audiences who had already been exposed to Shakespeare's major plays. The most important thing to remember about Ford is not so much the specific dates of previous successful plays but that most of these plays were still in circulation, still in repertory. This is one reason why it is valid to treat the whole body of English Renaissance drama from the late 1580s to 1642 synchronically as well as diachronically. Shakespeare may have died in 1616 but he was still Ford's contemporary.

Critical overview

The critical reputation of both dramatists has been very uneven but has followed a similar pattern. The three plays most often revived today, *The White Devil*, *The Duchess of Malfi*, and *'Tis Pity She's a Whore*, all seem to have been popular enough to have been kept in repertory up until the closing of the theatres by Parliament in 1642. This was despite an unsuccessful first performance of *The White Devil* which Webster ascribed to the limitations of the open-air Red Bull Theatre and its clientele, as well as to the time of year ("so dull a time of winter" [*The White Devil* 'To the Reader']), which combined to deprive him of "a full and understanding auditory" (ibid.). During the Commonwealth period there is some evidence that, for a minority at least, Webster was acquiring a certain amount of literary cult status. When playgoing began again at the Restoration all three plays were performed on more than one occasion before a major shift of taste in the late seventeenth century saw virtually all of Shakespeare's contemporaries, apart from Jonson and Fletcher, disappear from the stage.

The Romantic period saw a major revaluation of both writers as great tragic poets rather than as crafters of performable plays, poets who were capable of expressing the extremes of human emotion in richly figurative language. Charles Lamb's *Specimens of English Dramatic Poets* (1808) anthologized substantial extracts from both playwrights, and Lamb's enthusiasm was continued by other important nineteenth-century critics like Hazlitt and Swinburne. The most influential critic of the early twentieth century, T. S. Eliot, was also extremely responsive to the poetry of these plays. Despite Eliot's frequent attacks on Romanticism, there is something deeply Romantic about his appreciation of the capacity of their language to express and provoke "the deepest terrors and desires."[5] Eliot, more than anyone else, ensured that these plays were to be incorporated in English literature syllabuses as higher education expanded in the second half of the twentieth century, whether or not they were ever performed or even considered performable.

The revival of interest in both Webster and Ford as poets was often accompanied by serious doubts about whether their plays could ever hold the attention of a modern audience. If one began with naturalistic assumptions about what constituted a "well-made" play, both dramatists could be accused of creating creaky plots, obscurely motivated characters, and scenes which were impossible to present in the theatre with any degree of plausibility. Bernard Shaw, and Shaw's admirer William Archer, were two of the most important critics to express this view repeatedly. Some of their objections derive from a sense of moral and aesthetic decorum about the representation of violence on stage which now seems old-fashioned, but their criticisms could not be fully challenged until there was more evidence available of successful modern revivals. The landmark production in this respect was that of *The Duchess of Malfi* at the Haymarket Theatre in 1945. This was directed by the legendary George "Dadie" Rylands, incidentally perhaps the only person ever to have played all three of the play's leading parts (The Duchess, Ferdinand, and Bosola). For audiences who were beginning to read in their newspapers of the full horror of the Nazi camps, the play seemed much more "real" than it had to William Archer. The strategies employed by Ferdinand to break the Duchess's spirit, seen by Shaw and others as absurd and melodramatic, were in fact closely replicated by the Gestapo when they showed the teenage son of a Czech partisan, under interrogation following the assassination of Heydrich, the head of his mother floating in a fish tank.

Since 1945 there have been major professional productions of most of these plays, which have taught us a great deal about how well they can work in the theatre. I would argue that academic critics have not yet benefited as much as they should have done from the opportunities they have been given, for the first time in over three hundred years, to see first-class actors tackle these difficult but immensely rewarding texts. We are sometimes told that it was the new historicist and materialist forms of criticism which developed in the 1980s which rescued these plays from critical disapproval and marginalization by refocusing attention on their capacity to embody the contradictory social discourses of their period rather than achieve any aesthetic transcendence or resolution of these contradictions. Interesting though some of these historical approaches have been, they seem to me less critically significant in the long term than the testing out of these plays in an appropriate playing space like the Swan at Stratford. In a similar way, Deborah Warner's 1987 production of *Titus Andronicus* at the Swan did more to rehabilitate that famously abused play than any amount of academic scholarship.

Most of the older critical issues relating to Webster can be reviewed by looking at one or more of the collections of critical essays (or passages) edited by G. K. and S. K. Hunter (1969), Brian Morris (1970), R. V. Holdsworth (1975), or Don D. Moore (1981). The more recent critical preoccupation with historicized questions of gender and power relations is well represented in Dympna Callaghan's New Casebooks volume (2000) which includes a version of Frank Whigham's important essay "Sexual and Social Mobility in *The Duchess of Malfi*" (1985). There are two good collections of essays on Ford by D. K. Anderson (1986) and Michael Neill (1988) which both serve to summarize the previous critical history and point in a number of new directions. My own *Webster and Ford* (1995) also includes some reflections on the critical reputations of both dramatists but is more aesthetically oriented than a good deal of recent criticism and tries to make a strong case for the plays to be appreciated for the kind of intense experience they can provide in the theatre.

Pedagogic strategies

The only two plays by Webster normally studied at undergraduate level are *The White Devil* and *The Duchess of Malfi*, which are both easily available in a number of good single-play editions, such as those by John Russell Brown (Revels Plays) or Elizabeth Brennan (New Mermaids). If a tutor wishes to explore *The Devil's Law-Case* or *A Cure for a Cuckold*, then the obvious edition to use would be the Oxford World's Classics *The Duchess of Malfi and Other Plays* (1998), edited by René Weis. Deciding which of the two major tragedies to focus on depends to some extent on the kind of argument one wants to make about Webster's relationship to Shakespeare. If one wants to suggest that he is attempting a very different kind of tragedy, one which is less concerned with the "old stable ego of character" than with the breakdown of a whole society, then one would pick *The White Devil*. If instead one wants to argue that Webster was playing interesting variations on the Shakespearean norm without departing from it radically, then one would pick *The Duchess*. In both plays the tragic centre of gravity has shifted away from the "great men" who dominate Shakespeare's plays towards the women and dependants who are destroyed by them but in *The Duchess* there is a much greater, and recognizably Shakespearean, compassion evoked for both the title character and for Bosola. *Hamlet, Othello,* and *King Lear* can all be paired effectively with either play and a number of other interesting Shakespearean comparisons also suggest themselves. The mockery of the steward Malvolio in *Twelfth Night* for dreaming that he might marry his mistress has an element of ideological conservatism which contrasts interestingly with Webster's more romantic and daring treatment of the same situation.

The most usual Ford play to select for undergraduate study is *'Tis Pity She's a Whore* which exists in a number of single-play editions. A good affordable one is the Revels Student Edition (1997) by Derek Roper, based on his earlier Revels edition (1975) but with an updated introduction. *The Broken Heart, Perkin Warbeck,* and *Love's Sacrifice* are all potentially teachable as well and the first two, along with *The Lover's Melancholy,* can be found in the Oxford World's Classics *'Tis Pity She's a Whore and Other Plays* (1995), edited by Marion Lomax. There is a good, but expensive, single-play edition of *Love's Sacrifice* (2002) by A.T. Moore in the Revels series but otherwise the only real option would be to get students to consult the original quarto on *Early English Books Online.*

Once again, the choice of play depends on what kind of point one is trying to make about Ford's relationship with earlier drama. *'Tis Pity* looks very much like an attempt to rewrite *Romeo and Juliet* by raising the stakes considerably, mixing a sympathetic treatment of young love with the horror of incest and giving the male protagonist some of the heterodox intellectual arrogance of Marlowe's Faustus. If there is some loss of Shakespeare's lyric voice, there is also arguably a gain in tragic intensity, some of which comes from the additional influence of Webster's *Duchess of Malfi.* There is a fiercely emotional "objectivity" about Ford's play that can make *Romeo and Juliet* look sentimental.

Perkin Warbeck clearly harks back to Shakespeare's history plays, and *Richard II* in particular. A sustained comparison between the two plays is by no means entirely to Ford's disadvantage. If there is once more some loss of lyricism, there is a good deal of compensation to be found in Ford's sophisticated development of the "player king" motif in such a way that the foundations of human identity and existence itself come into question. This "pretender" who never concedes he is pretending reminds one irresistibly of a remark by Jean Cocteau which Sartre brooded over endlessly: "Victor Hugo was a madman who thought he was Victor Hugo." A good twentieth-century play with which to compare *Perkin* is Pirandello's *Henry IV* and this pairing raises many of the same existential questions. It is also worth looking at reviews of the only major modern production of Ford's play to date, the 1975 Royal Shakespeare Company performance.

The Shakespearean prototype for *Love's Sacrifice* is *Othello* and here it is less easy to make a case for Ford improving in any way upon Shakespeare, which is why I would be less interested in setting up a comparison, even without the problem of obtaining an affordable text. By contrast, *The Broken Heart* is quite unlike any play by Shakespeare or indeed any previous English Renaissance tragedy. It has always been recognized as Ford's most distinctive play but its emotional delicacy has sometimes seemed over-literary and unlikely to be realized effectively in performance. A number of revivals in the 1990s, pre-eminently the magnificent Royal Shakespeare Company production of 1994, have validated it as a theatre piece. There is a strong case for teaching it as a successful example of a completely *un*Shakespearean type of tragedy, and for exploring how and why it might nevertheless work in the theatre.

This discussion of which texts to select has made clear that I do not believe in teaching Shakespeare separately from his fellow dramatists and nor do I believe in starting from an assumption that he must be superior to them in every respect, however much they do indeed owe to him. Having seen very fine productions of most of these plays and, in some cases, been deeply moved by them, I want to get my students to engage with them aesthetically and emotionally and not merely historically. I want to find ways of over-coming the "distance" which often exists between students and what they are reading, without sacrificing a historical perspective. The sophisticated forms of historical contextualization which have dominated the academic criticism of Renaissance drama since the early 1980s seem to me to overlook some of the more basic difficulties which undergraduate students often have in engaging with these plays. They find the language, Webster's in particular, quite hard, and they find the plots difficult to follow, as indeed they are on a first reading.

Whether giving a lecture or a seminar, I usually begin with some kind of map of the characters and their relationships and some kind of summary of the essentials of the plot. Without these, all the more sophisticated points one might wish to make tend to float in a void. I also like to begin by focusing on the openings of plays and the way in which the audience, which initially knows no more than the student who has just picked up the play, is drawn into initial judgements about the characters and the societies in which they live, judgements which might have to be qualified or even reversed at a later point. One practical advantage of focusing on the openings of the plays is that the student who has failed to complete the required reading for the seminar will not be totally lost.

After initial concentration on Act I, I usually try to identify one or more key scenes and analyse them in detail before attempting any overall discussion of the play. Kate Aughterson's *Webster: the Tragedies* has some good examples of the kinds of close reading of particular scenes which would be productive in a seminar. Obvious choices would include the trial scenes from *The White Devil* (III.ii) and *The Devil's Law-Case* (IV.ii), the whole of Act IV from *The Duchess of Malfi*, the Soranzo-Annabella quarrel scene (IV.iii) from *'Tis Pity*, the encounter between Perkin and Frion (IV.ii) in *Perkin Warbeck*, and the final scene of *The Broken Heart*.

Much the best way of dealing with problems of language difficulty is to make sure that passages which one wishes to discuss in detail actually get read out in class (or heard from an audio or video recording). The failure of many students to hear in their heads the lines of poetry they are silently reading is one of the chief sources of their comprehension problems. Moreover, basic issues of comprehension modulate interestingly into more subtle questions of tone and effect as soon as one reads anything out. In what precise tone of voice does the dying Annabella say "farewell, / Brother, unkind, unkind" (*'Tis Pity She's a Whore* V.v.92–3)? How would it affect our understanding of their relationship and of the play as a whole? In what tone of voice does Bosola tell the Duchess "Look you, the stars shine still" (*The Duchess of Malfi* IV.i.100)? It is possible to argue that one's understanding of his character, his relationship to the Duchess, and one's interpretation of the whole play hangs entirely on the tone of voice here, whether brutal, compassionate, or simply offhand. If one asks what does the famous "I am Duchess of Malfi still" (Ibid., IV.ii.142) actually *mean*, one can talk about aristocratic pride, a Senecan assertion of the self ("Medea superest"), the contradictory senses of "still" ("always" or "for the moment"), or the absence of any personal name, but the answer can never be a secure one because the line can be delivered in quite different tones of voice and with quite different body language. It can sound ringingly defiant, plaintive, or simply exhausted. It can be delivered from a standing position, a kneeling position, a prone position, or, as in the 1996 Cheek by Jowl production, in a feisty pose, with one hand on hip and a cigarette in the other.

Having experienced, as I have said, some memorable performances of most of these plays, I always want students to get an understanding of how they work in the theatre, which is not just a matter of explaining particular pieces of stage business but of being alert to the emotional nuances which particular lines might carry, or not carry, depending on the actor's delivery. One of the fascinations, but also frustrations, of a performance-orientated approach is not only the obvious fact that different actors do quite different things with the same role but also that reviewers react in quite different ways to the same performance. The Royal Shakespeare Company 2000 production of *The Duchess of Malfi* was an extreme example of this, producing completely contradictory comments on all the main performances. For example, Tom Mannion as Bosola either "fails to communicate any inner conflict" (*Times Literary Supplement* 1 December 2000) or "makes the character's fits of conscience convincing" (*Guardian* 13 November 2000).

It is perhaps the instability of all evidence relating to performance which drives most teachers back into a more historical approach, despite their paying lip service to the fact that most historical evidence is also textual and hence not nearly as stable as it seems. For the majority of students (and on English courses most of these tend to be women) the most immediately engaging form of historical approach is a broadly feminist one. Most of these plays represent women either forced into marriage, prevented from marrying, accused of being a whore, or murdered. It is actually often easier to get a class to engage emotionally and intellectually with their predicaments than it is with the more famous (male) protagonists of Shakespearean tragedy. Once that initial engagement with the text has been achieved, it becomes possible to open up some of the complicated historical and theatrical factors governing the representation of women and their choices in the early seventeenth century. One can do this by using specific interpretative essays, such as those anthologized by Dympna Callaghan, or extracts from a collection of relevant primary material like Kate Aughterson's *Renaissance Woman: a Sourcebook*, or indeed the primary sources themselves on *Early English Books Online*.

My hope would always be to integrate this historical material with a critical response which remains sensitive to emotional nuance and the impact of performance. When these things are missing and one finds oneself seriously out of sympathy with an eminent academic critic, one has to trust one's own judgement. A good tutor is not someone who has read plenty of recent criticism and can ventriloquize it fluently. It is someone who has engaged as fully as possible with the plays themselves, both in their original historical and theatrical context and in the endlessly renewable context of modern performance, and who can lead students towards a similar level of engagement, an engagement which is aesthetic and emotional as well as intellectual and historical.

Notes

1. William Hazlitt, "Lectures Chiefly on the Dramatic Literature of the Age of Elizabeth," in *Webster: the Critical Heritage*, ed. Don D. Moore (London: Routledge, 1981), p. 60.
2. I have written at greater length about this seeming paradox in "Jacobean Pageant or Elizabethan Fin-de-Siècle? The Political Context of Early Seventeenth-Century Tragedy," in *Neo-Historicism: Studies in Renaissance Literature, History and Politics*, ed. Robin Headlam Wells, Glenn Burgess, and Rowland Wymer, pp. 138–51 (Cambridge: D. S. Brewer, 2000).
3. My reservations about the overall argument of her book are set out at some length in my review of it in *Medieval and Renaissance Drama in England* 10 (1998): 310–15. However, the book remains valuable for some of its detailed and perceptive comments on the plays.
4. The phrase is used, ambiguously, by Marvell when describing the execution of Charles I in "An Horatian Ode upon Cromwell's Return from Ireland." See *Andrew Marvell: the Complete Poems*, ed. Elizabeth Story Donno (Harmondsworth: Penguin, 1972), p. 56.
5. T. S. Eliot, "Ben Jonson," in *Selected Essays*, 3rd edn (London: Faber, 1951), p. 155.

Selective guide to further reading

Anderson, D. K. (ed.). *"Concord in Discord": the Plays of John Ford 1586–1986*. New York: AMS Press, 1986.

Aughterson, Kate (ed.). *Renaissance Woman: a Sourcebook*. London: Routledge, 1995.

——. *Webster: the Tragedies*. Basingstoke: Palgrave–now Palgrave Macmillan, 2001.

Callaghan, Dympna (ed.). *The Duchess of Malfi*. New Casebooks. Basingstoke: Macmillan–now Palgrave Macmillan, 2000.

Cave, Richard Allen. *"The White Devil" and "The Duchess of Malfi": Text and Performance*. Basingstoke: Macmillan–now Palgrave Macmillan, 1988.

Clark, Ira. *Professional Playwrights: Massinger, Ford, Shirley, and Brome*. Lexington: University Press of Kentucky, 1992.

Holdsworth, R. V. (ed.). *"The White Devil" and "The Duchess of Malfi": a Casebook*. London: Macmillan, 1975.

Hopkins, Lisa. *John Ford's Political Theatre*. Manchester: Manchester University Press, 1994.

Hunter, G. K. and S. K. (eds). *John Webster* (Penguin Critical Anthologies). Harmondsworth: Penguin, 1969.

Lomax, Marion. *Stage Images and Traditions: Shakespeare to Ford*. Cambridge: Cambridge University Press, 1987.

McCabe, Richard A. *Incest, Drama and Nature's Law, 1550–1700*. Cambridge: Cambridge University Press, 1993.

Moore, Donald D. (ed.). *Webster: the Critical Heritage*. London: Routledge, 1981.

Morris, Brian (ed.). *John Webster*. London: Benn, 1970.

Neill, Michael (ed.). *John Ford: Critical Revisions*. Cambridge: Cambridge University Press, 1988.

Sturgess, Keith. *Jacobean Private Theatre*. London: Routledge, 1988.

Wymer, Rowland. *Webster and Ford*. Basingstoke: Macmillan–now Palgrave Macmillan, 1995.

Useful information on the stage history of these plays can be found in most good modern editions. The fullest account for Webster's two tragedies is by David Carnegie in David Gunby et al. (eds), *The Works of John Webster: an Old-Spelling Critical Edition*, vol.1 (Cambridge University Press, 1995). There is a good essay by Roger Warren on "Ford in Performance" in Michael Neill (1988) and one by Alan Dessen on *"'Tis Pity She's a Whore*: Modern Productions and the Scholar" in D. K. Anderson (1986). Richard Allen Cave's "Text and Performance" volume (1988) has a detailed discussion of four selected performances of Webster's tragedies. There are similarly full accounts of the RSC productions of *The Broken Heart* (1994) and *The White Devil* (1996) in *Shakespeare and His Contemporaries in Performance*, ed. Edward J. Esche (Aldershot: Ashgate, 2000). Kathleen McLuskie and Jennifer Uglow have edited a "performance text" of *The Duchess of Malfi* (Bristol: Bristol Classical Press, 1989), with details from various productions given opposite each page of text. Some of the original staging conventions are intelligently and interestingly discussed in the books by Marion Lomax and Keith Sturgess.

Basic information about recent productions can be obtained from *Plays and Players*, The Royal Shakespeare Company Performance Database on the Shakespeare Birthplace Trust website, and the archive section of the National Theatre website. Reviews of modern productions can be tracked down by consulting *Theatre Record* (formerly *London Theatre Record*), *Research Opportunities in Medieval and Renaissance Drama*, or the annual roundup of performances, both Shakespearean and non-Shakespearean, in *Shakespeare Survey*. Internet sources for reviews include *UK Newspapers Online* (or simply the *Guardian Online* if your institution does not subscribe to the larger database), *Shakespeare Bulletin* (which covers US as well as UK productions), *Early Modern Literary Studies*, and *The Times Literary Supplement Centenary Archive*. *TLS* reviews are usually particularly detailed and informative.

The single most useful thing one can do when teaching a Renaissance play is to take students to a good modern performance. Failing that, any film or television version or adaptation which one can get hold of has considerable educational value. The BBC screened quite good performances of *The Duchess of Malfi* in 1972 and *'Tis Pity She's a Whore* in 1980, but neither tape is now easily obtainable. The BBC has recently made all of its complete Shakespeare series available on DVD and it would be doing a great service to us all if it did the same for its backlist of non-Shakespearean plays. The 1973 Italian film of *'Tis Pity She's a Whore*, directed by Guiseppe Patroni Griffi, used to be much more readily obtainable, but is currently out of print in the UK, though still available for hire in the US. There is some discussion of it in an online article of mine titled " 'The audience is only interested in sex and violence': Teaching the Renaissance on Film" (2002) <http://www.shu.ac.uk/wpw/renaissance/wymer.htm>.

Mike Figgis's *Hotel* (2001) is about a group of actors in Venice who are making a film of *The Duchess of Malfi* and contains a number of extracts from the play, adapted by Heathcote Williams, who also plays Bosola. Interesting in a different way (but not available commercially) is *Quietus* (2002), an hour-long film "adapted from texts by John Webster," written and directed by Peter Huby, which transposes some elements of the story of *The Duchess of Malfi* to rural Yorkshire in the early seventeenth century, and uses a number of lines from both of Webster's major plays. These last two examples give an idea of the hold which Webster, as both poet and dramatist, continues to exercise over a certain kind of creative imagination, as he once did over both Swinburne and T. S. Eliot.

12
John Fletcher

Carol A. Morley

Chronology and context

John Fletcher (1579–1625) was born in Rye, Sussex, where his father Richard was an Anglican minister. John was the fourth of nine children in a family of staunch Protestant divines and was no doubt also destined for ordination from an early age. His cousin Phineas Fletcher was a notable poet in the "Spenserian" fashion. His uncle Giles was also a writer, but although literary and learned, the family had no previous connection with the professional theatre.[1]

John matriculated at his father's old college, now Corpus Christi, Cambridge in 1591. (Beaumont was also sent to the University of Oxford at the early age of twelve.) Fletcher's childhood and student days spanned the years of his father's upwardly mobile prosperity. He was eighteen, however, when disaster struck. From Rye, his father had been promoted to the position of Dean of Peterborough. He gained a certain notoriety for his severity as Protestant chaplain presiding over the execution of Mary, Queen of Scots in 1587 and was subsequently made Bishop of Bristol, then Worcester and finally London. Shortly after this last promotion, he lost the Queen's favour, his post, and his fortune by marrying a widow, Mary Baker, apparently notorious for promiscuity. One frequently reprinted libellous verse, "On Bishop Fletcher," runs:

> We will divide the name of Fletcher
> He, my Lord F.; and she, my Lady Letcher.[2]

He died in 1596. Two years later, John gained his MA from Cambridge. The head of the family was now his uncle Giles, who was himself subsequently disgraced in connection with the Essex rebellion of 1601. This combination of family circumstances effectively prevented John from following any profession which might depend upon family fortune or social status. By 1606 he had begun to work as a playwright, from the start collaborating with another newcomer, Francis Beaumont.

Francis Beaumont (1584/5–1616) was the third son of Francis Beaumont, a judge. His parents' families were prosperous members of the landed gentry and were notable for Catholic recusancy, being extensively fined for their religious non-conformity. Beaumont's uncle Gervase was tortured in the Tower of London in 1601, suspected of harbouring Jesuits, but neither Beaumont nor his father seems to have upheld the family tradition of recusancy to the detriment of their social status.[3] In 1597 Beaumont went to Oxford, but left a year later on his father's death. He resumed student life in 1600 at the Inns of Court in London (another family tradition). Here he began to write and, like Fletcher, soon gravitated to the professional theatre.

How Beaumont and Fletcher met and why they decided to work together is unknown. How exactly they collaborated can only be roughly deduced from their surviving plays. Reduced expectations in both cases strongly suggest an economic rationale for adopting the theatre as a career. Their family backgrounds, too, included some sensational scandals, reversals, and downfalls on both sides. This should be borne in mind when reviewing much older criticism of their writing as contrived and implausible, trivial and sensational. Their partnership became legendary throughout the seventeenth century, both for their plays, and for their unique working symbiosis. Aubrey, writing long after their deaths, notes that the friends:

> lived together on the Banke side, not far from the Play-house, both batchelors; lay together; had one wench in the house between them, which they did so admire; the same cloathes and cloake, &c. betweene them.[4]

Between 1606 and 1608 the men collaborated on two comedies and a tragedy. Meanwhile, both playwrights, working solo, had disasters with the boys' company, the Children of the Queen's Revels. After Beaumont's *Knight of the Burning Pestle* and Fletcher's *Faithful Shepherdess* were soundly rejected by their respective audiences, the writers teamed up for their first joint hit, *Philaster* (1608–10), for Shakespeare's company, the King's Men. The 1610 publication of *Faithful Shepherdess* enabled Fletcher to justify the literary credentials of his pastoral and denounce the flawed judgement of its audience. His "Epistle to the Reader" includes his own definitions of pastoral and tragi-comic drama: the latter has been much debated in relation to Fletcher's later plays in that genre.

> A tragi-comedy is not so called in respect of mirth and killing, but in respect it wants deaths, which is enough to make it no tragedy, yet brings some near it, which is enough to make it no comedy, which must be a representation of familiar people, with such kind of trouble as no life be questioned; so that a god is as lawful in this as in a tragedy, and mean people as in a comedy.[5]

Other writers (Jonson, Chapman, Field, and Beaumont) contributed enthusiastic poems showing their support for the play. From this early stage, Fletcher was clearly established as a significant fellow-poet/dramatist by his peers.

Fletcher may have married, in 1612, a Joan Herring, in Bankside's parish church (now Southwark cathedral).[6] This tends to contradict traditional biographies, which have Beaumont being the partner who broke up the ménage by marrying in 1613, and retiring from the theatre. Evidence now suggests that Beaumont suffered a serious apoplexy (stroke) the same year as his marriage, and that he lived on for three years as a melancholy invalid.[7] He died in London in 1616, aged only 32, and received the tribute of a burial in Westminster Abbey, in what is now known as Poets' Corner.

Fletcher had continued to work alone on several plays during their partnership; after Beaumont's retirement he continued to combine solo writing with other collaborations. Nathan Field appears to have been his next choice as a new collaborator, but he died in 1619/20. Having already written a sequel to Shakespeare's *Taming of the Shrew* (*The Tamer Tamed, or The Woman's Prize*), Fletcher also worked with Shakespeare on *Henry VIII, Two Noble Kinsmen* and the lost play *Cardenio*. After Shakespeare's retirement, Fletcher became the chief playwright of the King's Men, where he worked till his death (of the plague) in 1625. By then, he had collaborated on as many as seventeen plays with his own eventual successor, Philip Massinger. Massinger and, in turn, James Shirley continued work on plays unfinished at his death or which they felt to need revision for later productions. This elusive chain of authorship demonstrates the pragmatic nature of playhouse practice, long at odds with a scholarly preference for clear-cut authorship and imputed "intentionality" in literary criticism. A prolific, innovative, and prodigiously successful dramatist, Fletcher's chosen working methods frequently resist the precise analysis possible with single-authored plays. Elusive to the last, the location of Fletcher's grave in what is now Southwark Cathedral is unknown, though tradition maintains that Massinger was eventually buried with him.

The folio editions of works by commercial playwrights served to elevate the status of their work to that of contemporary classics. This was already the case for Jonson and Shakespeare and the 1647 First Folio performed the same service for Fletcher (and Beaumont). Plays, created for the ephemeral world of the theatre, became established as worthy of attention and study as "literature." It is also worth noting that the original context of the publication of the 1647 Folio, during the English Civil War, reflects a wholehearted nostalgic adoption of "Beaumont and Fletcher" as Royalist totems.

Fletcher and collaboration

The fame of his partnership with Beaumont served for a long time to eclipse an appreciation of John Fletcher's single-authored work as well as that written with other collaborators. Revisions of several plays after Fletcher's death further complicate our understanding of the wide network of authorial contributions to the plays originally (and traditionally) attributed to "Beaumont and Fletcher." A talented partnership, sustained over anywhere from six to a dozen plays, was long celebrated as a prodigious union in the joint composition of more than 50. Scholars have long neglected these plays, being perhaps deterred and, it may be argued, in denial over the huge body of writing which survives, and what to say about it. The following table therefore provides the full canon of known plays and the massive complexity of attributions.[8]

Table 12.1: Known canon of Fletcher's dramatic writings (including collaborations and other relevant playtexts) (Key: B = Beaumont, F = Fletcher, M = Massinger, Sh = Shakespeare)

Authors	Probable date	Title	Genre	Notes
B & F	1606–25	Loves Cure	comedy	revised by M after F's death?
B & F	1606–7	The Woman Hater	comedy	Children of Paul's
B & F	1607–8	Cupid's Revenge	tragedy	Children of the Queen's Revels
F	1608–10	The Faithful Shepherdess	pastoral	Children of the Queen's Revels
B	1607–8	Knight of the Burning Pestle	comedy	Children of the Queen's Revels
B & F	1608–10	Philaster	t-comedy	King's Men: all following plays
B & F	1608–10	The Scornful Lady	comedy	
B & F	1609–12	The Captaine	comedy	
F	c.1610–13	Monsieur Thomas	comedy	
B & F	1611	A King and No King	t-comedy	
B & F	1611	The Maid's Tragedy	tragedy	
F	c.1611	The Night Walker	comedy	revised by Shirley
F	c.1611	The Woman's Prize	comedy	(or The Tamer Tamed)
F	1611–14	The Tragedy of Bonduca	tragedy	
B & F	1612	The Coxecombe	comedy	
B	1612–13	The Maske of the Inner Temple and Grays Inn		
F	c.1612–14	The Tragedy of Valentinian	tragedy	
F & Field	c.1612–15	Four Playes, or Moral Representations in One	entertainment	
F, M & Field	1613	The Honest Mans Fortune	t-comedy	
Sh & F	1613	Henry VIII	history	
Sh & F	c.1613	Two Noble Kinsmen	t-comedy	
F	c.1614	Wit without Money	comedy	revised by Shirley
F, Middleton, Rowley	c.1614	Wit at Several Weapons	comedy	
F & Middleton	1615–16	The Nice Valour	comedy	(or The Passionate Madman) (LitOnline attrib. to M solo)
F (& B)	c.1615–16	Loves Pilgrimage	t-comedy	

(B), F & M	c.1616	*The Tragedy of Thierry*	tragedy	(or *Thierry and Theodoret*)
F, M & Field	c.1616	*The Knight of Malta*	t-comedy	
F	1616–17	*The Mad Lover*	t-comedy	
F & Field	1616–17	*The Queene of Corinth*	t-comedy	
E, M & Field	1617	*Rollo Duke of Normandy*	tragedy	(or *The Bloody Brother*)
Jonson & Chapman				
F	c.1617–25	*The Chances*	t-comedy	
F	1618	*The Loyal Subject*	t-comedy	
F & M	1619	*Sir John van Olden Barnavelt*	tragedy	(first published 1883)
F & M	1619–20	*The False One*	t-comedy	
F & Ford	c.1619–23	*The Lawes of Candy*	t-comedy	(LitOnline attrib. to Ford solo)
F	c.1619–23	*Women Pleased*	t-comedy	
F & M	c.1619–23	*The Little French Lawyer*	comedy	
F & M	c.1619–23	*The Custome of the Country*	comedy	
F	c.1619–25	*The Humerous Lieutenant*	t-comedy	
F	c.1621	*The Island Princesse*	t-comedy	
F	c.1621	*The Wilde-goose Chase*	comedy	
F & M	c.1621	*The Double Marriage*	tragedy	
F	c.1621	*The Pilgrim*	comedy	
F & M	1621–2	*The Spanish Curate*	comedy	
F & M	1622	*The Prophetesse*	t-comedy	
F & M	c.1622	*The Sea Voyage*	t-comedy	
(B), F & M	c.1622	*The Beggars Bush*	comedy	
F & M	c.1623	*The Lovers Progresse*	t-comedy	
F & Rowley	c.1623	*The Maide in the Mill*	comedy	
F	1623–4	*Rule a Wife and Have a Wife*	comedy	
F	c.1624	*A Wife for a Month*	t-comedy	
F & M	1624–5	*The Elder Brother*	comedy	revised by M after F's death?
(B), F & M	c.1625	*The Noble Gentleman*	comedy	revised by M?
F & M	c.1625	*The Faire Maid of the Inne*	t-comedy	revised by M?
F & M	perf. 1634	*A Very Woman*	t-comedy	(LitOnline attrib. to M solo)
Shirley	1635	*The Coronation*	comedy	attrib. B & F in 1679 folio

At least one other collaboration with Shakespeare, *Cardenio*, is lost, as is *The Jeweller of Amsterdam*, co-written with Field.

Critical overview

A first century of high esteem is witnessed in frequent performances, publications, and adaptations of Fletcher's work. Then there followed a decline in demand for revivals, which reflected the eighteenth century's preoccupation with refined and sentimental drama. After that developed a progressive overshadowing of Fletcher with the emergence of Shakespeare as England's unrivalled "Bard," together with Victorian distaste for the plays' frequent overt sexual themes and bawdy wit. The following quotations are not unrepresentative of the changing cultural climate. John Dryden (1688) asserted:

> I am apt to believe the English Language in them arrived to its highest perfection . . . their Playes are now the most plesant and frequent entertainments of the Stage; two of theirs being acted through the year for one of Shakespeare's or Jonson's. The reason is, besides there is a certain gayety in their Comedies, and Pathos in their more serious Playes, which suits generally with all mens humour. *Shakespeares* language is likewise a little obsolete, and *Ben Johnsons* wit comes short of theirs.[9]

Samuel Taylor Coleridge (*c*.1811) compared Beaumont and Fletcher (a "well-arranged bed of flowers") unfavourably with Shakespeare ("an Indian fig-tree, all is growth, evolution . . . "), adding that, "Shakespeare is the height, bredth and depth of Genius. Beaumont and Fletcher the excellent mechanism, in juxtaposition and succession of Talent."[10] Coleridge also expressed the political objections that Beaumont and Fletcher were "the most servile jure divino royalists" and "high-flying passive-obedience Tories."[11] Such conclusions derived from his reading of individual characters' expressions of loyal subservience to various tyrannical, absolutist rulers in the plays as authorial propaganda. He therefore dismissed the writers as reactionary monarchists out of tune with his own radical views and Romantic aspirations. Sandra Clark blames Coleridge's negativity for the "extraordinary invisibility of so vast a corpus" from his day to ours.[12]

T. S. Eliot (1919) chose not to devote a separate chapter to Beaumont and Fletcher, but in his discussion of Jonson took Coleridge's floral metaphor further: "the blossoms of Beaumont and Fletcher's originality draw no sustenance from the soil, but are cut and slightly withered flowers stuck into sand." He defined their appeal as writers: "clever . . . hollow . . . superficial with a vacuum behind it."[13] Waith (1952) countered this with his own definition: "artificial flowers which cannot wither," and Finkelpearl (1990) rounded off the sequence of botanical metaphors with "Beaumont and Fletcher are the vast unexplored Amazonian jungle of Jacobean drama."[14]

Fletcher's reputation is now rising as theatres rediscover the potential of plays in performance. Academic interest is also gaining momentum. Fletcher is emerging as a significant author of the European Baroque, and a previously underrated voice worthy of debate in gender/women's studies. (Many of his neglected plays have intriguing dominant females, to counter his more frequently discussed victimized/exploited heroines.)[15] The main areas of critical debate are:

- *Collaboration.* The scholarly challenge to identify and isolate disparate hands in co-authored plays once dominated the field. Ernest Oliphant and the various Cambridge editors, notably Cyrus Hoy, have all argued their best guesses. In Fletcher's collaborations with Shakespeare, he was until recently seen as an intruder, polluting the purity of Shakespeare. Bardolatry dies hard, despite our better understanding of early modern theatre practice.
- *Tragi-comedy.* "The third genre," popularized, if not invented by Beaumont and Fletcher, became the dominant genre of Stuart commercial theatre. Marston's *Malcontent* (1604) is an important precursor in the genre, as are Shakespeare's "problem plays": *Troilus and Cressida, All's Well* and *Measure for Measure* (all 1602–5). It is worthy of note that the 1679 second Folio statement ("The Book-sellers to the Reader") boasts the addition of seventeen plays absent from the first and adds, "thus every way perfect and compleat have you, all both Tragedies and Comedies, that were ever written by our Authors." In this folio tragi-comedy is not distinguished as a separate category. Indeed, the Prologue to *The Captaine* teases the audience with the elusiveness of easy generic definitions:

> For to say truth, and not to flatter ye,
> This is nor *Comody*, nor *Tragedy*,
> Nor *History*, nor anything that may
> (Yet in a weeke) be made a perfect play.

- *Restoration influence.* The more of Fletcher's work we read, the harder it becomes to see Restoration comedy as anything other than a continuation of earlier theatrical fashions, largely established by Fletcher and partners. The absence of good critical texts has long obscured our awareness of the risqué plotting and humorous verbal obscenity of some Fletcher plays; thus sophisticated bawdry has long been identified as a Restoration innovation.
- *Intertextuality.* Shakespearean echoes in Fletcher could be put down to plagiarism, and were. That artistic influence worked in both directions may have been harder for Shakespearean purists to stomach, but is clearly demonstrable. Our understanding of the widespread working practice of multiple collaboration is likely to overtake the analytical discipline of attribution studies in academic importance.

Pedagogic strategies

This section offers a selection of teaching strategies for six plays from the Beaumont and Fletcher canon. It provides suggestions for comparative readings of contemporary plays on related themes by various other writers and a range of useful background reading relating to Fletcher's use of historical and literary sources, together with his exploration of topical issues and dramatic forms. Questions for class discussion or essay work are also suggested.

A King and No King

A popular tragi-comedy centred on an unstable young king with tyrannical tendencies. A delightfully convoluted backstory of secret adoption provides an eleventh-hour solution for King Arbaces' incestuous obsession with his "sister."

- Discuss the consequences of absolutism, given the fictional scenario when the ruler, "above the law," proposes to break the most serious of social taboos. The topical relevance of "Divine Right" can be examined using King James's recent speech to Parliament (1609) on the nature of kingship, beginning:

  The State of Monarchy is the supremest thing upon earth . . . Kings are justly called Gods, for that they exercise a manner or resemblance of divine power upon earth . . . [16]

- Contemporary with *The Winter's Tale*, and also set in Sicily. Read the plays in parallel, comparing Leontes' sudden jealousy of his wife (I.2) with Arbaces' equally sudden desire for his "sister" (III.1). The combination of emotional intensity here, followed by frankly implausible plot devices which provide happy endings, can be discussed using Fletcher's own definition of tragi-comedy. Have critics who prefer to distinguish Shakespeare's late plays as "Romances" simply denied the possibility that he was influenced to participate in the "new genre" as a result of Fletcher's influence?
- Could also be read with Ford's *'Tis Pity She's a Whore* as a tragedy of consummated incest, to invite discussion of the different genres. Compare, for example, IV.4. with *'Tis Pity* I.3, where both "brothers" declare their passion. Arbaces and Giovanni are also both given significant soliloquies where they debate their desire, temptation, and guilt. Discuss the theatrical convention of the soliloquy (also using *Richard III* and *Hamlet* if required). Does the character talk to himself, or does the actor address the audience directly? What are the consequences of the latter, where the spectators are made complicit in the secret?

Bonduca

This is the tragedy of Boudicca (Boadicea) and her rebellion against the Roman occupation of Britain. A good start would be a discussion of the class's preconceived ideas about Boudicca in history and iconography.

- The play challenges its audience to confront an opposition of their patriotic and cultural values (British v. Roman) at a point in history where they collided. The constant recourse to ancient Rome by many writers other than Shakespeare is a useful theme for introducing the dominance of "Romanitas" in early modern education, literature, and art, as well as performance. A broad canvas for opening up investigation of Renaissance values.
- Fletcher's use of his historical source, Holinshed, offers the basis of an exploration of his "Shakespearean" methodology in adapting and freely altering the story he found there. For example, Holinshed gives the Queen a vigorous speech to her troops reminiscent of Queen Elizabeth's famous rhetoric at Tilbury before the battle against the Spanish Armada.[17] It provides a ready-made dramatic climax, but Fletcher omits the speech from the play: why?
- Bonduca is an exemplary virago, inviting discussion of her status and treatment as a widowed queen regnant. That her agency is subverted throughout the play by the inclusion of the anachronistic Caratach (Caratacus) possibly demonstrates Fletcher's creative freedom and political perspective to best effect. Read III.1, where Fletcher stages the women at prayer, proclaiming their legitimate grievances. Caratach's brutal indifference to the rape of the daughters invites discussion of early modern attitudes to sex. Whose viewpoint would the audience support here?
- Both *Antony and Cleopatra* and *Cymbeline* can be read in conjunction with *Bonduca*, the former in respect of its tragic heroine, the latter for a tragicomic take on Roman colonization. Consider the strategy of "othering" in the plays. In *Antony and Cleopatra*, clearly, the queen of Egypt is the exotic alien and the audience is invited to identify with Roman values, however austere. Where the conquered "natives" are British (as in *Cymbeline*), the signals are confused. Note that Shakespeare never wrote a tragedy with an autonomous female heroine. Is Fletcher making a significant innovation?

The Chances

A perfect example of a Fletcher comedy which anticipates the cheerful indecency, plot-intricacy, and downright absurdity of Restoration comedy. Fletcher here shows himself to be a master of farce, and indebted to Jonson's style of city comedy. Two innocents abroad are intent on enjoying all the vices available in a permissive city. The adventures of one night lead one of the duo to return to their lodging with a mysterious baby, the other with an anonymous lady in distress. The assumption that the former is Don John's bastard, the latter Don Frederick's whore is shared by everyone but the audience. Fletcher adds a noblemen's feud, a duel, a borrowed hat, a real whore sharing the same name as the heroine and a fake necromancer, to provide chaotic entertainment.

- A highly successful play with a long afterlife. Adapted in the Restoration (by Villiers), in the eighteenth century (by Garrick) and in the nineteenth as a comic operetta. Fletcher's own source was a story by Cervantes. Discuss our modern assumptions that stories should be "original" against the early modern conventions of imitation and intertextuality. Jonson outlines an aesthetic principle quite alien to our ideas of creative authorship:

  The third requisite in our *Poet*, or Maker, is *Imitation*, to bee able to convert the substance, or Riches of another *Poet*, to his owne use. To make choise of one excellent man above the rest, and so to follow him till he grow very *Hee*: or, so like him, as the Copie may be mistaken for the Principall.[18]

- Is the play still funny today? A Hollywood pitch for this story might mention "buddy movie," "grossout comedy" and probably "road trip." III.2 provides a set-piece of the wounded Antonio quarrelling with his surgeon. The contemporary treatments on offer are bizarre and unpleasant. Does the scene exaggerate for satirical effect, or reflect early modern practice?
- Dame Gillian (the landlady), early dismissed as a stereotypically drunken crone, is revealed as the ingenious tier-up of everyone's loose ends, as well as the moral conscience of the story. What does her surprising agency reveal about the preconceptions of both the protagonists and audience?
- The final scene (V.3) shows a mock séance, arranged by Gillian's brother, in order to reconcile events. Compare with the confidence tricksters in Jonson's *Alchemist* (especially V.2: Dol as the Queen of the Fairies), and Falstaff's ordeal in the final scene of *Merry Wives*. What does this tell us about the gullibility and superstition of the "victims"? Also discuss the moral purpose of early modern comedy—the importance of vice being seen to be corrected/ridiculed by virtuous characters.
- Both *Comedy of Errors* and Aphra Behn's *The Rover* can demonstrate a continuous tradition of popular comic plot devices: innocents abroad; mistaken identities; master–servant interplay; sexual temptations; grotesque caricatures of "foreign" eccentrics. Find the stock characters and situations (which may be traced back in theatre history, including *commedia del' Arte* and Greek/Roman comedy).

The Faithful Shepherdess

The play's eventual success demonstrates how far ahead of theatrical fashion Fletcher had been. By 1634, when the King's Men revived it at court for

Queen Henrietta Maria, the pastoral genre had become established as an élite vehicle for theatrical symbolism to complement the masque. The play was finally translated into Latin by Richard Fanshawe as a testament to its enduring importance, to him, as a nostalgic icon of the lost world of élite Caroline performance.[19]

- Fletcher's "Epistle to the Reader" can be studied in full, noting not only his definitions but also his downright indignation. Other writers' poems commending the play, from the first edition, demonstrate their approval of his daring to experiment with an *avant garde* dramatic form imported from Italy. Sample the first pastoral, Tasso's *Aminta* (1575) and Guarini's *Il Pastor Fido* (1589, English translation, 1602).[20]
- Pastoral verse is a starting point for understanding the literary conventions Fletcher ambitiously brought to the stage. Lots to choose from, for example: Samuel Daniel, "A Pastoral" ("O happy golden age . . ."), Marlowe's "The Passionate Shepherd to his Love" and Ralegh's response, "The Nymph's Reply." Sidney's *Arcadia* demonstrates that the Elizabethan reading public welcomed the lengthy prose narrative and revelled in its complex plotting, convoluted adventures, and lyrical interludes. Does this tell us something about our differing attention spans, lack of access to then-familiar classical references, or even preference for different types of fantasy in fiction?
- *The Winter's Tale* most probably includes a riposte from Shakespeare, showing the new boy how much, or little, Arcadian lyricism a London audience was prepared to stomach at the time. Compare the sheep shearing scene (IV.4) and Perdita's role (where idealism is both played on and subverted). Note that Shakespeare chose never to write a full pastoral of his own, and that Fletcher never tried again.
- The play is solidly indebted to *A Midsummer Night's Dream* for much of its language, characterization, and comic complexity. Is it in part an over-ambitious *homage*? Fletcher gives us a Puck-like satyr, magical interventions, censorious elders, and multiple loving couples running, at times berserk (but completely chaste), through a moonlit forest. To the *Dream*, Fletcher adds malicious lechery, attempted murder, an irredeemable malcontent, and a coherent pagan religious system for his pastoral society. Is the play simply too long, too lyrical, too complicated?
- Amarillis's storyline reveals the profound shift in taste and expectation between early modern audiences and our own. Where Aspatia (*Maid's Tragedy*) may seem morbidly self-indulgent to us, the original audience sympathized with the pathos of her fate and her choice of self-sacrificial death. Any student who has been frustrated by the passivity of Ophelia and Desdemona may find a converse excitement in the amorous adventures of the feisty, determined Amarillis in her reckless pursuit of Perigot (who loves Amoret). That she is made to see the errors of her lust, and repent (after being rescued from rape) to embrace chastity clearly demonstrates

Fletcher's determination to portray the polarity of virtue and evil in purely sexual terms. This accords with all available source materials outlining the early modern norms of acceptable female behaviour. Her promise to conform hereafter fits the moral purpose of the comedy, but her outrageous adventures provide the dramatic core of our interest. Does Fletcher give us a heroine we love to hate simply in order to demonstrate her reformation, or to relish the theatricality of her transgressions?

The Maid's Tragedy

This is Beaumont and Fletcher's most famous tragedy, and probably their most anthologized and discussed play to date, as well as most frequently revived in performance.

- See *A King and No King*, for discussion of divine right. This tragedy develops an extreme scenario where it becomes possible to discuss the possibility, even permissibility of regicide/tyrannicide.
- Read with Middleton and Rowley's *Changeling* and Ford's *'Tis Pity* as a triumvirate of Jacobean tragedies centring on the perceived danger to men of the perverse sexuality of women. Or, possibly, the susceptibility of men in placing the fulfilment of sexual desire before the moral codes decreed by society.
- The Masque (I.2). This brings an exclusive form of royal entertainment to the public stage of the Globe: the original audience would most likely have never been privileged to see one for themselves before. Compare the shorter, interrupted masque scene in Shakespeare's contemporary *The Tempest* (IV.1). Beaumont's own *Masque of the Inner Temple and Grays Inn* for the marriage of the king's daughter in 1612 is an enlightening real-life example of the conventions of performance.[21]
- The wedding night scene (II.1) is a *tour de force* of staging and dialogue, shockingly disturbing the audience's expectations. Donne's "Epithalamium made at Lincoln's Inn" and "Elegie: Going to Bed" can be compared to demonstrate the social acceptability of *marital* erotica. Discuss the very public celebration of these rites of passage in society generally.
- Who is the "maid" of the title? Aspatia, the ousted bride, who suffers and laments her humiliating rejection, eventually deciding to commit "suicide by duel" with her former fiancé. He subsequently also commits suicide. Both Aspatia and Amintor are virgins ("maids" not being restricted to females in early modern usage). Or is it Evadne, the king's mistress, who is forced to confront the moral horrors of her degradation? At first, she is a complicit concubine, later an adulterous wife. Stress that she was chaste before the king seduced her. Does she have our sympathy, and the status of a tragic heroine?
- Cross-dressed heroines. Aspatia disguised herself as her own brother to die at Amintor's hands. Combine with *Philaster* or a themed study of the motif.

The idea derives popularity from both *Faerie Queen* and *Arcadia*, but remains both useful and titillating, due to the stage reality of boy-actors-playing-women-playing-boys. Students may think that Shakespeare's use of the motif is exclusive to him, in Viola, Portia, Rosalind, *et al*. It is widespread and crosses all genres. None of Shakespeare's cross-dressed heroines ever dies. Is Fletcher pushing an established stage convention into experimental territory?

Philaster

Here the writers have no single source: they build suspense and surprise on an original plot, although it is greatly indebted to a long tradition of romance literature, *Arcadia* in particular. It achieved and sustained great success.[22]

- Discuss Andrew Gurr's assertion:

  Philaster is one of the most ambitious works of literary collaboration ever written. Its aim was no less than the translation of the higher literature and educational design of Sidney's *Arcadia* into commercial drama . . . at a time when only the lowest potboiling third of the dramatic repertory was produced by multiple authorship.[23]

- Fletcher's "Epistle to the Reader" in *Faithful Shepherdess* can be used to discuss his declared intentions for the ingredients of a tragi-comedy. In this most popular of their plays, does he follow his own rules?
- The play is contemporary with *Cymbeline*, but it is impossible to say which influenced the other. Discuss their parallels: imperilled princesses, tormented heroes and scheming viragos. Female cross-dressing is a feature of both (see notes above for the motif in *Maid's Tragedy*). Euphrasia does not reveal her identity until the final scene. As the page Bellario, she has included the audience amongst the people she deceives, a notable break with convention. How surprised were the students at her revelation? Both plays have implausible resolutions: are they flaws, or part of the comedy?
- The influence of *Hamlet* is clear. Both plays have disinherited princes as heroes. Philaster's madness, violence, and tormented love can all be compared with Hamlet's behaviour. In both cases the hero's popularity with the mob deters the usurping king from overtly harming him. How do Philaster's characterization and circumstances diverge to enable a happy ending to take place?
- Political topicality: King James was pursuing a possible Spanish match for his eldest son, Prince Henry. Discuss anti-Spanish feeling in England, recalling Queen (Bloody) Mary and the Armada, as well as contemporary events on the Continent. Is Philaster's rival, Pharamond, just a caricature playing to the audience's predictable hostility? Compare the Prince of Aragon (*Merchant of Venice*, II.9) or Don Armado (*Love's Labours Lost*).

Notes

1. See the full *Oxford DNB* entries for all the Fletchers.
2. Quoted by J. F. Danby, *Poets on Fortune's Hill* (London: Faber and Faber, 1952), pp. 154–5, and attributed to Bishop Goodman, who added, "I think he had a check from the Queen, and died for sorrow."
3. Philip J. Finkelpearl, *Court and Country Politics in the Plays of Beaumont and Fletcher* (Princeton, NJ: Princeton University Press, 1990), p. 11.
4 Aubrey, *Brief Lives*, late seventeenth century (MSS left at his death in 1697, unpublished until 1948). Variously anthologized, and available online, e.g. at *Twilight Pictures*, quoting ed. Oliver Lawson Dick (London: Secker and Warburg, 1958), pp. 21–2.
5. John Fletcher, "Epistle to the Reader," from the first edition of *The Faithful Shepherdess* (1610), reprinted in various editions and online sources.
6. Andrew Gurr (ed.), *Philaster* (Manchester: Manchester University Press, 1969; reprinted 2003), p. xxi. The *Oxford DNB* online entry makes no reference to this, however.
7. See the "Elegie" on Beaumont in *The Poems of Thomas Pestell*, ed. Hannah Buchan (1940), pp. 71–4; *DNB* gives a fuller account of biographical details contained in the poem; under separate headings the full biographies of all Fletcher's listed collaborators can be found.
8. Genres after *Literature Online*, collaborators after Bowers, vol. 10, pp. 751–2. He stresses the "tentative" attributions in many cases.
9. John Dryden, *Of Dramatic Poetry and Other Critical Essays*, 2 vols (London: Dent, 1967), p. 251. Widely available in other editions, and online at <http://www.rpo.library.utoronto.ca>. G. E. Bentley, *The Profession of Dramatist in Shakespeare's Time* (Princeton, NJ: Princeton University Press, 1971), p. 210, provides the statistics to back this up: between 1616 and 1642, the King's Men played Beaumont and Fletcher at court 42 times, Shakespeare 18 and Jonson 7.
10. Coleridge's marginalia jotted in an 1811 edition of Jonson and Beaumont and Fletcher plays. Quoted in Roberta F. Brinkley (ed.), *Coleridge on the Seventeenth Century* (Durham, NC: Duke University Press, 1955), p. 664.
11. Quoted by Brinkley, *Coleridge on the Seventeenth Century*, pp. 655 and 656 respectively.
12. Sandra Clark, *The Plays of Beaumont and Fletcher: Sexual Themes and Dramatic Representations* (Hemel Hempstead: Harvester Wheatsheaf, 1994), p. 2.
13. T. S. Eliot, "Jonson": first printed in *The Sacred Wood* (1919), frequently reprinted in collections, e.g. *Selected Essays* (London: Faber, 1932) and *Elizabethan Dramatists* (London: Faber, 1963), and available at <http://www.bartleby.com>.
14. Waith, Eugene M., *The Pattern of Tragicomedy in Beaumont and Fletcher* (New Haven: Yale University Press, 1952), p. 40; Finkelpearl, *Court and Country Politics*, p. 245.
15. "It is surprising that the re-examination of early modern sexuality now taking place in so many areas of thought has not already extended to their work." Clark, *Plays of Beaumont and Fletcher*, p. 153.
16. Frequently anthologized, also available online at: <http://www.royal.gov.uk> and <www.luminarium.org/sevenlit/james>.
17. Raphael Holinshed, *Chronicles: the Historie of Englande* (London: John Harrison, 1577), Book 1, pp. 60–1, also available on *EEBO*. Elizabeth's Tilbury speech is widely available for comparison.

18. Ben Jonson, *Workes*, vol. 2, *Timber: or, Discoveries*, p. 127, frequently anthologized and available on *EEBO*. Also quoted by Eve Rachele Sanders, *Gender and Literacy on Stage in Early Modern England* (Cambridge: Cambridge University Press, 1998), p. 61.
19. Richard Fanshawe, ["F.F"], trans., *La Fida Pastora* (London: G. Bedell, 1658).
20. Available for example in Elizabeth Story Donno (ed.), *Three Renaissance Pastorals*, Medieval and Renaissance Texts and Studies 102 (Binghampton, New York: 1993). *Aminta* was not published in translation until 1628 but Fletcher may have read the English edition of both plays in the original, printed in 1591. His Latin and Spanish were fluent, so we may assume his ability to cope with Italian.
21. Available on *EEBO* and online, for example, at Twilight Pictures. It supplies an eye-witness description of the event, gives "the Argument" of the action followed by the text.
22. See Peter W. M. Blayney, "The Publication of Playbooks," in *A New History of Early English Drama*, ed. John D. Cox and David Scott Kastan (New York: Columbia University Press, 1997), pp. 383–422. Here the play is the only Beaumont and Fletcher entry in his top eleven, although much could be done with the interpretation of statistics relating to early editions to argue for the equal popularity of both *A King* and *Maid's Tragedy* as their undisputed "top three."
23. Gurr, *Philaster*, p. xxv.

Selective guide to further reading and resources

Bowers, Fredson (gen. ed.). *The Dramatic Works in the Beaumont and Fletcher Canon*, 10 vols. Cambridge: Cambridge University Press, 1966–96. Provides comprehensive critical old-spelling bibliographical apparatus. Hard reading for a student expecting the user-friendly critical apparatus provided by single-volume editions of early modern drama.

Clark, Sandra. *The Plays of Beaumont and Fletcher: Sexual Themes and Dramatic Representations*. Hemel Hempstead: Harvester Wheatsheaf, 1994.

Cone, Mary. *Fletcher without Beaumont: a Study of the Independent Plays of John Fletcher*. Saltzburg: *Studies in English Literature*, 60, 1976.

Danby, John F. *Poets on Fortune's Hill*. London: Faber and Faber, 1952.

Finkelpearl, Philip J. *Court and Country Politics in the Plays of Beaumont and Fletcher*. Princeton, NJ: Princeton University Press, 1990.

McMullan, Gordon. *The Politics of Unease in the Plays of John Fletcher*. Boston: University of Massachusetts Press, 1994.

Oliphant, E. H. C. *The Plays of Beaumont and Fletcher. An Attempt to Determine their Respective Shares and the Shares of Others*. Oxford: Oxford University Press, 1927.

Palmer, Daryl W. *Writing Russia in the Age of Shakespeare*. Aldershot: Ashgate, 2004. Background on Fletcher's uncle Giles's travels to Russia as the Queen's Ambassador. Chapter 8 discusses Fletcher's Russian play, *The Loyal Subject*.

Waith, Eugene M. *The Pattern of Tragicomedy in Beaumont and Fletcher*. New Haven: Yale University Press, 1952.

Wilson, John Harold. *The Influence of Beaumont and Fletcher on Restoration Drama*. New York: Haskell House, 1969.

Web resources

Literature Online: full transcriptions of all the plays.

EEBO (Early English Books Online): full facsimiles of all early editions, and other early books cited for comparison and contextual reading.
<http://eebo.chadwyck.com/home>

Oxford Dictionary of National Biography: Provides short-cut links between Fletcher and Beaumont as a matter of course, but not to Massinger.
<http://www.oxforddnb.com/>

<http://www.gutenberg.org>: provides e-book versions of all the plays.

<http://www.theatredatabase.com/17th_century/beaumont_and_fletcher_001.html>: a handy site, but treat the 1927 reprint article with caution and compare, for example *DNB* or Finkelpearl for more current biographical interpretations.

<http://www.uq.edu.au/emsah/drama/fletcher> (Twilight Pictures): a dedicated Beaumont and Fletcher site, which eventually aims to provide the complete works on line, together with background materials.

<http://www.luminarium.org/sevenlit>: another useful selection of plays, poems and articles.

<http://Bartleby.com>: has *Philaster*; also provides a link to G. C. Macaulay's critical essay from vol. 6 of the *Cambridge History of English and American Literature* (18 vols, 1907–21). An example of the late Victorian climate of censorious expostulation which afflicted Beaumont and Fletcher studies for generations. Here they are given responsibility for initiating "a general relaxation of moral and intellectual fibre" in the drama. Linking their popularization of tragi-comedy and alleged neglect of tragedy to a "lowering of moral standards" generally, this pernicious, reactionary drivel is an excellent example of the old prejudices still included in state-of-the-art databases.

13
The Masque

Richard Dutton

Chronology and context

No aspect of early modern drama better reflects the changes in the ways we study Shakespeare and his contemporaries than the court masque, that arcane and elaborate form of entertainment which featured in court life from the time of Henry VIII but flourished most particularly in the reigns of James I and Charles I. As recently as 1995, David Lindley could write that "despite a thin trickle of major studies over the years, the court masque remains marginal to the study of the great age of English drama."[1] Yet the volume in which that remark appeared partly belied it: a selection of eighteen masques, published by a major press and aimed to sell to students in paperback. Thirty years before it would have been unthinkable. What changed?

When I was an undergraduate, in the late 1960s, the masque was not taught in English departments, nor were there texts available from which to teach it. The issue was still essentially as it had been when T. S. Eliot wrote on Ben Jonson, the leading writer of English masques, in 1919: "But [his] masques, an important part of his work, are neglected . . . The masques can still be read, and with pleasure, by anyone who will take the trouble—a trouble which in this part of Jonson is, indeed, a study of antiquities—to imagine them in action, displayed with the music, costumes, dances, and the scenery of Inigo Jones."[2] As Eliot saw it, modern readers were too lazy to take the trouble. Indeed, even though Jonson was already one of my favourite authors, I did not read his masques until I was well advanced in my graduate studies. Eliot contrasted the neglect of Jonson with the continuing readership for Milton's Ludlow masque, commonly known as *Comus* (1634), which *was* (and is) widely read and taught: "There are hundreds of people who have read *Comus* to ten who have read the *Masque of Blackness*."[3] But *Comus* is radically different from most of the court masques of the period, in ways Eliot deplored, castigating it as "the death of the masque . . . literature cast in a form which has lost its application."[4] Even today it is rarely taught alongside other drama, getting by largely on Milton's prominent canonical position, with minimal emphasis on its formal characteristics. *Comus* is the exception which proves the rule that no one back then read masques. And by the same token I shall not be considering it here.

The general neglect of the masque is not difficult to explain. Masques are barely drama in the sense that we usually understand that term: they have little in the way of plot, action, or character-development. They usually comprise a sequence of relatively static tableaux, interspersed with songs and dances. The words are generally sparse and repay little close attention—certainly not the kind of attention recommended by the New Criticism or Practical Criticism which then still dominated English classrooms on both sides of the Atlantic, approaches which valued richness and density of language, and such qualities as ambiguity and paradox. There is little of that in masques, in large part because the words were in effect secondary to non-verbal features, such as scenery, staging, costume, dancing, and music. At that time the study of theatre as a discipline in its own right, where such matters are legitimate concerns, was only in its infancy and had little influence within English departments. The subject-matter of these entertainments, moreover, is almost always mythology of an arcane and, to most modern minds, impenetrable nature, which did not recommend them to undergraduate classrooms: even a confirmed classicist like Eliot recognized it as "a study of antiquities."

Furthermore, court masques were invariably written for very specific occasions in the life of the court—New Year celebrations, marriages, the visit of a foreign dignitary, the elevation of someone to a particular honour—in ways that seemed to contain their meaning and significance within very narrow bounds. (Even at the time, Francis Bacon conceded "these things are but toys."[5]) More generally, these lavish entertainments, celebrating the royal family and senior members of the aristocracy, were widely seen as symptoms of much that was wrong with English political life in the first half of the seventeenth century. They were self-indulgent, self-congratulatory, inward-looking exercises in flattery, which ignored much of what was going on in the country outside the charmed circle of the court. (Beaumont and Fletcher's *The Maid's Tragedy* described masques as "tied to rules of flattery."[6]) As such they were thought part of a decadence that beset the culture of the early Stuart regimes, stepping stones on the road to the Civil War. That same court culture was widely held to have sapped the vitality of Elizabethan drama in general, monopolizing the talents of the leading actors and dramatists, and estranging them from their popular and quasi-democratic roots. Masques were commonly stigmatized as symptoms of all these developments.

And there was one other reason that masques did not find their way on to the curriculum: William Shakespeare never wrote one. Many of his Jacobean contemporaries did, including Jonson, Beaumont, Chapman, Daniel, and (rather later) Shirley. But the absence of Shakespeare from the roster, the supreme embodiment of the vigour of Elizabethan drama, only reinforced the stigma attached to them. Either because he was never asked or because he showed no inclination, he did not write in this form. Or rather, did not write precisely in this form. It is widely recognized that Shakespeare's late plays—including *Pericles, Cymbeline, The Winter's Tale* and (pre-eminently) *The Tempest*—contain masque-like features, including an intensified use of spectacle, music, and dance. Indeed, as we shall see, Prospero in *The Tempest* stages a masque of sorts. And *Henry VIII* enacts the staging of a famous masque in history, in which the king himself performed at Cardinal Wolsey's palace.[7] But none of this stirred more than an incidental interest in masques for their own sake at that time.

Forty years later, the situation has changed out of all recognition. Court masques are widely studied and taught. Perhaps the best single measure of this is the fact that texts of Jonson masques now feature as indispensable items, not only in specialist anthologies of Renaissance drama, but in those bedrocks of English literature survey courses, *The Norton Anthology of English Literature* (8th edn, 2006), which contains *The Masque of Blackness*, and the *Longman Anthology of British Literature* (2nd edn, 2003), which contains *Pleasure Reconciled to Virtue*. Another crude but indicative measure is to search for "masque" and "Jonson" on the online *MLA International Bibliography*, which in late 2005 listed 184 items, of which 129 were since 1980, 77 since 1990, and 29 during the current millennium—significant rates of recent productivity. At least one of these, pointedly sub-titled "Introducing Undergraduates to Stuart Masques and Enjoying It,"[8] even offers advice on how to teach a masque.

This chapter attempts to explain how and why that change happened, firstly in general terms and secondly with reference to two particular texts, Jonson's *Masque of Blackness* and the masque of Ceres in *The Tempest*. As I indicated earlier, this offers an insight into changing critical fashions in respect of early modern drama as a whole.

Critical change

The seeds of change were being sown even while I was an undergraduate. And many were being sown by one remarkable scholar, Stephen Orgel.[9] His *The Jonsonian Masque* (1965) was the first comprehensive study of its subject; his modern-spelling edition of *The Complete Masques* appeared in 1969 (with a paperback *Selected Masques* the following year, the first realistic attempt provide for classroom use); with Roy Strong he published Inigo Jones's complete masque designs in *Inigo Jones: the Theatre of the Stuart Court* (1973); an extremely influential small book, *The Illusion of Power*, followed in 1975.[10] Running through all of these was an emphasis on the masque not as a literary text, but as a quasi-theatrical event of which words were only one element, while the distinctive staging (usually, throughout the early Stuart period, devised by Jones) also contributed significantly to the meaning. Central to

Jonson's masques was the figure of King James, for whose court he wrote most of them. James himself, unlike his wife and children, never actually performed in these masques. But he is always in a critical sense their central subject: their mythology, imagery, and organization are focused on praising him. Once Jones had introduced the proscenium arch into Britain, and with it perspective scenery (*Oberon*, 1611, is usually thought to be the earliest instance of such staging) James was even literally the focus of the event, since the perspective illusion created by the scenery was only entirely true from the location of his "state" or royal chair.

Masques were thus intimately associated with royal magnificence and power, projecting it (through those few fortunate enough to be present) both abroad and at home. In Orgel's analysis, therefore, the masque could only be understood in relation to the wider culture of which it was a part, and in relation to its audience, whose consumption of it was an essential part of its meaning. Indeed, at the point in the proceedings known as the revels, the masked aristocrats in the show danced with those who were only watching, dissolving the distinction between performers and audiences/spectators. It is for that reason that we should hesitate to label masques simply as "drama," which normally requires a separate aesthetic space within which a fiction unfolds. In the masque, the "fiction" (that is, the words of the text) is never entirely separate from the wider context of its performance. So that, in order to study masques, we cannot simply study words but must understand the whole cultural event of which they are only a part. This emphasis on *context* and on *audience reception* was entirely alien to New or Practical Criticism, which insisted that meaning was entirely contained within the "verbal icon" of the text itself.[11] It was, however, entirely consonant with some new models of literary theory, particularly those based on structuralism and on reader-response theory, which around 1970 began to register on Anglophone consciousness.

With hindsight we can see that Orgel's work (and especially *The Illusion of Power*) was most influential in setting the stage for the New Historicism of the 1980s and 1990s, a critical fashion commonly said to have been inaugurated by Stephen Greenblatt's *Renaissance Self-Fashioning* (1980).[12] For the New Historicists literature was significant as the product of sociological pressures in a culture (rather than as the invention of specially gifted individuals) and required a wider reading of that culture. They focused on what Greenblatt dubbed "the circulation of social energy," highlighting issues of power and patronage relations—within literary texts and as generated/transmitted by them—over traditional themes like love, faith, or the formal qualities of texts.[13] It is no exaggeration to say that they approached all literature very much as Orgel had analysed the apparently unique form and condition of the court masque, though they brought to it a poststructuralist sensibility specifically informed by the writings of Michel Foucault on issues such as personal identity and social control.

The most distinctive work on the masque in this mode is Jonathan Goldberg's *James I and the Politics of Literature* (1983), where he argues that all Jacobean literature reflects and propagates the authority of the presiding monarch, an authority textually expressed in King James's own writings.[14] But the masque as developed by Jonson is the paradigmatic genre, the "mysteries" of this "elitist, abstruse, exclusive"[15] form perfectly reflecting the mysteries of state in an absolute monarchy:

> The masque presents its "more removed mysteries" for the king, holding up a mirror of his mind. In its form, the masque provides a mirror, too, for it elucidates the spectacle that the king presents sitting in state. The mysteries of the masque reflect the monarch's silent state: the masque represents the king. The king observes and is observed; as much as the masquers themselves, he is onstage.[16]

The poet, in effect, identifies totally with his royal subject:

> For Jonson, then, the performed masque aimed at the condition of writing. This was an implicitly royal and royalist aim. Text and monarch stood in the same relationship to the performance onstage . . . The invention of the masque is translated into the flesh of the king. Printed, the masque gains an everlastingness, a royal imprimatur. The king is dead, long live the king: the king, too has the permanence of a text.[17]

Nothing expresses more comprehensively the Foucauldian pessimism of New Historicism, its conviction that power is everywhere and all-encompassing, while all attempts to resist only reinforce its authority. Not surprisingly, the court masque offered little to the (mainly British) cultural materialists, heirs of sophisticated Marxists like Raymond Williams and Louis Althusser, who looked to historical texts precisely *in order to resist*. They looked to find the *flaws* in the illusion of power, cracks in the surface of the text, from which to build a subversive resistance to absolute power (of Stuart kings or of President Reagan and Prime Minister Thatcher). But there were others, less doctrinaire than the cultural materialists, sometimes dubbed revisionists, who found ways round the totalitarian edifice imagined by Goldberg. While recognizing that all court masques generically defer to the monarch, they argued that "local readings" of particular masques (for example, finding implicit allusions to current issues, observing factional alliances among those taking part, or taking at face value some of the "dissension" generally present in antimasques) revealed less-than-univocal "texts," writers and audiences.

Three early items by Leah Marcus (1979 on *Pleasure Reconciled to Virtue*, 1981 on "Masquing Occasions," and 1985 on *The Golden Age Restor'd*) on the local "occasions" of masques demonstrated what was possible in that mode, and they were followed by substantial contributions from David Norbrook (1984 on "The Reformation of the Masque," 1986 on *The Masque of Truth*), David Lindley (1986 on *Hymenaei* and *A Challenge at Tilt*, 2000 on *The Memorable Masque*), Paul Sellin (1986 on *Newes from the New World*), Martin Butler (1991 on *The Gipsies Metamorphosed*, 1992 on *Pan's Anniversary*, 1993 on Caroline masques, and 1998 on "Courtly Negotiations"), Lindley and Butler together (1994 on *The Golden Age Restor'd*), Russell West (2003 on "Court and Contestation in the Jacobean masque"), and MacIntyre (2004 on *Oberon*).[18] Lindley's collection of essays, *The Court Masque* (1984) brought together a range of essays in his mode, beside other contributions. By concentrating, often on a single masque and its context—but not reading them within a set Foucauldian or Althusserian pattern of power-relations—such essays showed how masque-events could speak with a mixed voices simultaneously. David Lindley observes in his 1995 edition of masques "that many works were presented *to* the monarch in the interests of the politics and ambitions of the nobles who performed or commissioned them."[19] Even in works paid for by the monarch himself, though they "needs must present an 'illusion of power', careful attention to their detailed political context reveals that the apparently sycophantic panegyric may often be part of a work anxiously engaged in negotiation between court and king and between different political factions within the court itself."[20] He concludes: "For the modern reader, then, the court masque can profitably be studied, not simply as the mouthpiece of absolutist ideology, but as a stage where many of the contradictions of that ideology were consciously or unconsciously played out."[21]

Lindley is thinking here of politics, but what he says applies equally well to gender, which is also an ideological construct. Reflecting on "the illusion of power," feminist critics began to consider what masques might reveal about early modern attitudes to women. Suzanne Gossett's early " 'Man-maid, begone!' Women in Masques" (1988) highlights Jonson's misogynistic attitude towards the women for whom he wrote, and the "complication of having male and female 'women' in the same fiction."[22] It was problematic to mix the public stage convention of men playing women (for speaking parts), while aristocratic women played idealized versions of themselves on the same stage; she suggests the issue was resolved by the 1608 introduction of the antimasque, able to contain unruly men-women (typically witches and hags) in a separate sphere. But others quickly recognized the potential within masques (despite their male authors) to challenge some standard assumptions about the all-male early-modern stage and to provide a platform for female empowerment. The very fact that women could perform in masques at court, whereas they could not act in the public theatres, and that they might have a significant hand in their composition, created unique spaces for them in the culture which was elsewhere so uniformly patriarchal.

The key figure here is Anna of Denmark, James's consort.[23] Anna was the figure around whom many of the masques in the first decade of James's reign were constructed. And while she did not labour on them in the sense that Daniel, Jonson, and Jones did, she had a significant input into their construction; the idea that the ladies in *The Masque of Blackness* should appear in black-face was hers, as was the suggestion that *The Masque of Queens* should have an antimasque.[24] Indeed, the Venetian ambassador reported that she was "the authoress of the whole work," a phrasing which highlights a distinctive early modern relationship between a patron and creative artists. The implications of this relationship have been worked over exhaustively since Gossett's article, with significant inputs from Hardin Assand (1992), Marion Wynne-Davies (1992), Barbara Kiefer Lewalski (1993), Leeds Barroll (1996, 1998), and Clare McManus (1998, 2002, 2003).[25] Although much of this work celebrates Anna's authority and female agency, nagging doubts persist. To a large extent these matters are only accessible via male-authored texts, which may indeed be misogynistic in spirit; and while the women might pose and dance, they did not speak—the dialogue and songs were reserved for professional actors. Even in *The Masque of Queens*, the most splendid of the entertainments in which Anna and her ladies performed and the one in which Jonson credited her with the most significant input, doubts abound. A central theme of the masque is witchcraft which, as everyone knew from his *Daemonologie*, was an abiding concern of the king, while Jonson presented a handsomely annotated holograph copy of the masque not to the Queen who graced its performance, but to her son, Prince Henry.[26] It may be argued from this that the female agency apparent in the masque is always contained by male authority, patriarchal and authorial. But what cannot be doubted is that the masque has become a central site for discussion of the role of women in early modern society.

By the same token, it has also become a significant site for the study of other contentious issues, often cutting across the matters of court politics and female agency which, as we have seen, are central to its current standing. Chief among these would be issues of race; of colonization; of nationhood; and of what we might collectively call "the other." As already noted, Queen Anna herself directed Jonson to construct *The Masque of Blackness* around the motif of herself blacked up as an Aethiopian (while the *Masque of Beauty* was to show her and her ladies again in white skins, "blanched" by the sun of Britannia). This invites comparison to canonical dramatic texts, like *Titus Andronicus* and *Othello*, where racial colour is conspicuously an issue.[27] While, as Siddiqi points out, colour is also an issue in other masques, it is in *The Masque of Blackness* that it has been most exhaustively studied; I have more to say, below, about the general reception of this masque.

Colonization is often but not always closely related to issues of colour; masques several times address the colonies in the New World (most notably Chapman's *The Memorable Masque* of 1613[28]). But England (in the process of expanding into Britain) also had colonies closer to home in Ireland, as Jonson's *The Irish Masque* reminded the court.[29] This, then, is entirely typical of current responses to the court masques. Once dismissed as arcane ephemera, with little intrinsic literary merit, they are now enthusiastically studied for what they reveal about the early modern world—when the world as we now know it took shape—in such intensely topical areas as gender, race, politics, and colonialization. They address all of these in ways that the more familiar commercial drama of the era never could, since they were expressly written for the ruling elite, inviting their identification and participation. We no longer worry whether they are "great" literature: such aesthetic categories have largely been ignored since "theory" did so much to challenge how and what we read. And while we still recognize that much of their imagery and mythology is arcane, we are content to demystify it as far as we can; just as we largely settle for understanding the mechanics—what the antimasque and revels are, how perspective scenery works, and so on—only as far as we need to in order to grasp the topical material they deal with. In such ways, a revolution in taste has been effected in half a lifetime. In forty years the deadest of dramatic dodos has been revived and (as if by some miracle of DNA engineering) firmly installed within the literary canon.

The Masque of Blackness

In looking for a single masque to exemplify this revolution in taste, we are really faced with a choice of two: by far the lion's share of attention has focused fairly equally on *The Masque of Blackness* (1605) and *The Masque of Queens* (1609), both Queen Anna masques which naturally evoke feminist interest. But *Blackness* also raises racial questions: it is the convergence of these two issues which has raised it as high as canonical inclusion in *The Norton Anthology of English Literature*. As Lesley Mickel puts it: "The fact that this particular masque has merited such extended attention must be due to its status as Ben Jonson's first experimentation with the form which he dominated for so long and to the fact that the masque's governing trope resonates with continuing critical preoccupation with the issues of race and gender."[30]

Stephen Orgel's early work on Jonson's masques actually finds little of particular interest in this piece beyond its being his first essay in the genre and his first collaboration with Inigo Jones, who placed the action on a raised stage: earlier court masques had been on the same floor level as their audiences, with less division between participators and spectators. This occasioned Dudley Carleton's distinction in one of the most quoted of all eye-witness accounts of masques: "At Night we had the Queen's Maske in the Banquetting-House, or rather her Pagent."[31] A pageant is to be watched, not to take part in; the masquers did descend for the revels dancing, but this distinction remained a feature of Jones staging. Carleton went on to ridicule the costuming: "Their Apparell was rich, but too light and Curtizan-like for such great ones. Instead of Vizzards, their Faces and Arms up to the elbows, were painted black, which was Disguise sufficient, for they were hard to be known; *but it became them nothing so well as their red and white, and you cannot imagine a more ugly Sight, then a Troop of lean-cheek'd Moors.*"[32] Orgel initially made little of this, recognizing that disguising in black-face had a long history in masquing, not least at James and Anna's earlier Scottish court: "Queen Anne's bright idea for a 'masque of blackness' was by 1605 a very old one."[33] The masque was performed by Anna and her ladies, but it essentially celebrated the power of the British monarch, the sun whose cleansing rays they sought, King James.

This was broadly the received view until Gossett (1988) highlighted the centrality of women performers in these masques, noting how uncomfortably they fitted in a patriarchal world which either condescended to women or was outrightly misogynistic: "The writers lived in a world profoundly ambivalent about women."[34] James himself was notoriously more interested in his male favourites than in his wife, while "Jonson's attitude toward women, an ambivalence verging on antipathy, is evident in the structure and commentary of his masques from *Blackness* on."[35] Hardin Assand (1992) carries this forward in arguing for "the unique status that *The Masque of Blackness* possesses as a mimetic document of Queen Anne's marginal existence in the Jacobean court."[36] He argues for reading "the text as an 'event,' as a document encoded with linguistic and cultural clues of its historical significance"[37] and from that identifies it as

> a supremely feminine masque, insisting on Britannia's affairs and rejecting the notion that noble women defer to a masculine definition of their existence, challenging typical Renaissance notions of power which insisted on masculine incarnations that denied a role for independent noble women.
>
> As an aesthetic object, Queen Anne responded to the vehicle of the masque by subverting the properly decorous and chaste symbols for a blackness which, in Renaissance eyes, conveyed a sexual lustiness, a spiritual depravity, and a permanent ethnicity impervious to royal modulation.[38]

Yet he argues that this struggles against the grain of the courtly event, dominated by her royal husband and his male writer: "The masque tortuously celebrates the margins of power"[39] and in that way is true to the marginality of Anna herself at James's court.

Others have read Anna's situation much more positively. Barbara Kiefer Lewalski (1993) and Leeds Barroll (1996, 1998) have emphasized the autonomy of her court and Anna's separate political agenda, into which the masque played.[40] Lewalski argues for its subversive potential within the patriarchal king's court, while Barroll demonstrates "how the masque attests to Anna's continuing and persistent efforts to promote her circle, to establish her presence at court and to establish a context for the exercise of her own politics."[41] This line of thinking, which refuses to see Anna as a trapped victim, has found its fullest expression in Clare McManus's *Women on the Renaissance Stage*, which sees in *Blackness* a paradigmatic text for her masquing agenda: "The structure of the court masque, a synthesis of disparate genres of art and performance into a unified whole, left it vulnerable to a destabilization which was compounded by Anna's active contribution to a feminine representative strategy. An examination of *Blackness* demonstrates the nature of female performance and of cultural agency as they related to the demands of the masque form, and reveals the controversial status of such performance with Jacobean society."[42] Key to McManus's own analysis is the emphasis on Jonson's words as a "performance" text, not a literary one. His poetry (which for Jonson preserves the "spirit" of the masque, while the "carcass" of performance is abandoned) speaks within the discourse of the king's court; but other aspects of the performance are not so confined. Masquers did not speak, so they developed silent languages of disguise and of dance to express themselves: "The physicalisation of language in *Blackness* demonstrates not that the corporeal female masquer was excluded from linguistic expression but rather that this resulted in the physicalisation of language itself and the textualisation of the performing female body. This performance denies Jonson's dichotomy of carcass and spirit, suggesting that this polarity is both redundant and reductive."[43] And this is not only an achievement in itself; it marks a decisive step towards wider female performance on the English stage: "From the moment when women stepped on to the stage which Jones brought into the masque genre in *Blackness*, female performance assumed a greater theatricality."[44]

Alongside this interest in *Blackness* as a text about female agency runs a concern with what it says about race. Assand largely thinks about colour as a metaphor for female marginality, but Kim F. Hall—while also exploring that territory[45]—relates it to questions of the place of James's new Britain in the world. She suggests that *Blackness* "inaugurated a new era in the English court which demonstrated a renewed fascination with racial and cultural differences and their entanglements with the evolving ideology of the state . . . Interest in the importance of this first collaboration of Ben Jonson and Inigo Jones ignores the very central political question of why such a landmark production involves bringing 'Africa' (albeit a European version) to the English court."[46] She argues that this is linked to problems of political identity both within the newly-created state and in relation to the early developments of the first British empire: "Traditional notions of 'Englishness' and concomitant problems of social disorder were being interrogated and threatened on all sides by the growing pains of imperialism . . . In court entertainments, tropes of racial and cultural difference are used to represent [the] seat of political authority as the center of a stable, ordered, and ultimately English world. However, such manipulations reveal that race is indeed 'a dangerous trope,' which highlighted the problematic differences of the Jacobean court even as it helped to create the illusion of power."[47]

Hall's argument is expressly a postcolonial "take" on the beginnings of the colonial moment: Edward Said's *Orientalism* is specifically invoked. Mary Floyd-Wilson, by contrast, relates its interest in race to the era's own conceptualization of such matters: "*Blackness'* sustained focus on the relationship between external temperature and physiology clearly connects the work to prevalent climate theories of the period . . . [it] endeavors to establish Britannia as a temperate 'world divided from the world' and to fashion whiteness as the dominant complexion, but in the process it is compelled to acknowledge England's somewhat marginalized northern position."[48] The tensions identified in the masque are thus less to do with either marginalized women or colonies and empires, but with a traditional perception of the British Isles as remote from the centres of classical culture (which, not accidentally, were blessed with ideal climates) and its peoples physiologically diminished by the northern location. This is the more fraught in that its most northerly region, Scotland, has been united with England in King James's "Great Britain." Jonson seeks to counter these tensions by his tactful depiction of Britannia as an embodiment of ancient virtues: "By representing Britannia as an ancient union of southern wisdom and northern 'beauty', Jonson's masque 'revives' the island's ancient history and establishes the land and its people as 'temperate'."[49]

Similar issues are addressed from a geographical perspective by Richmond Barbour (1998), who suggests that court masques "provided signal occasions for a nascently imperial British court to consider its relations to the encompassing world," while *Blackness* in particular "offers an arresting formulation of early Stuart England's geography: the masque celebrates Britain's difference from distant, 'darker' worlds."[50] Barbour explores Jonson's geographical sources in the extensive annotation of the printed masque and then relates his use of "Britannia" to the authoritative account of the name and its origins in the 1586 *Britannia* by his old teacher at Westminster School, William Camden, which however identified the British with body-painting and pigmentation: "To recognize Jonson's indebtedness to Camden . . . is to understand the ideological labour in Jonson's celebration of 'Britannia' in *The Masque of Blackness*. To identify Britain with Albion, that 'white land,' and to naturalize an equation of whiteness with beauty and civility, the poet must suppress powerful contestatory discourses, alternate histories, that Camden derives from the name."[51] Jonson's labour is to find a geographic etymology which equates with the realities and aspirations of the Britannia made manifest at James's court. Jean MacIntyre complements Barbour's argument in suggesting that Jonson invokes the posthumous approval of Queen Elizabeth for this new regime and its agenda. She argues that *Blackness* "encodes the king's policy of peace with all nations and his 1605 effort to make the union of the Scottish and English crowns in his person the kingdoms' union under the ancient name of Britain."[52] To reinforce this "Jonson evokes the symbolism of Elizabeth's lunar names. When Aethiopia rejoices that Britain's ancient name is restored, he implies that from the heavens Elizabeth approves the union brought about through James, the temperate sun that rose as she 'declined' and whose 'light sciential is'."[53]

This by no means exhausts everything that has been written about *Blackness* or is likely to be written about it. But it gives a flavour of the richness and variety now found in a text which, until very recently, was dismissed as inconsiderable. And it gives some indication of the range of views possible about what such a text can tell us about such matters as court politics, gender, and race.

Shakespeare's masque in *The Tempest*

There is, inevitably, a long tradition of commentary on Prospero's masque of Juno, Ceres, and Iris in *The Tempest*, one of Shakespeare's most popular plays. But interest in it *as a masque*, as a specific dramatic form, only parallels the interest in the court masque which we have already traced. So in 1965 Northrop Frye could summarize its significance from a quasi-anthropological perspective, without reference to its formal characteristics: "What the wedding masque presents is the meeting of earth and heaven under the rainbow, the symbol of Noah's new-washed world, after the tempest and flood had receded, and when it was promised that springtime and harvest would not cease . . . out of the cycle of time in ordinary nature we have reached a paradise (Ferdinand's word) where there is a *ver perpetuum*, where spring and autumn exist together."[54] Nor is he interested in the fact that the masque is rudely interrupted, in effect by Prospero himself, remembering "that foul conspiracy / Of the beast Caliban" (IV.i.139–40).[55] Even Frank Kermode, in his classic 1954 Arden edition of the play, while faithfully detailing many of the technical aspects of the masque, sees little dramatic point to it and its interruption, finding it a minor distraction within the play's neo-Terentian classical structure: "In the third act the turbulence is intensified, according to the formula for the *epitasis*; the fourth act continues the *epitasis*, with the direct threat of intervention from Caliban, but also prepares for the comic catastrophe, by the union of Ferdinand and Miranda. The apparently unnecessary perturbation of Prospero at the thought of Caliban may be a point at which an oddly pedantic concern for classical structure causes it to force its way through the surface of the play."[56] And when Inga-Stina Ewbank offered an overview of masques in Elizabethan and Jacobean plays she saw little remarkable in Shakespeare's use of the form here: "In *The Tempest* the ultimate function of the masque is as a symbol of evanescence rather than of social ethics. We see in this play Shakespeare's uniqueness in being able to use the masque on so many levels at once"—she lists "the betrothal of Ferdinand and Miranda," the "stress on nature and fertility" and "the idea of the masque [as] a comment on all reality"—"The very delight of the masque provokes the thought of its own short-livedness and hence of the impermanence of all things."[57] The interest is entirely thematic, not functional.

But in 1975 Glynne Wickham signalled a change, arguing that Shakespeare "incorporated the fully developed Jonsonian masque, complete with antimasque, into the fabric of the play," pointing to such features as the use of symbolic persons, arcane mythology, the "antic" qualities of Stephano, Trinculo, and Caliban, panegyric and epithalamic passages, and especially the use of stage machinery for Juno's descent (IV.i.72ff). He particularly argues that the banquet scene in which Ariel, "like a harpy," confronts the "three men of sin" (III.iii.53) acts formally as an antimasque to the masque proper which follows it, outlining the human and political discord which the show of Juno, Ceres, and Iris is to resolve.[58] That same year Stephen Orgel addressed *The Tempest* in *The Illusion of Power*, emphasizing the combination in Prospero of political power and of masque-authorship, the illusions of the latter feeding the authority of the former: "Prospero's awareness of time comprehends both masque and drama, both seasonal cycle of endless fruition and the crisis of the dramatic moment. The awareness of both his art and his power, producing on the one hand his sense of his world as an insubstantial pageant, and on the other, his total command of the action moment by moment."[59] So for Orgel, although Prospero becomes unusually disturbed at the point where the masque breaks off, there is no essential rupture in his power, which simply switches to other modes. To this extent, Orgel's analysis follows the traditional assumption (inherent in all the critiques discussed earlier) that the play in essence endorses Prospero's view of everything that happens—that he is an enlightened, essentially benign ruler, whose authority we naturally support. Orgel resists the absolutist political implications of all this, even as he is among the first to register them openly, but he does not see significant resistance within the text. The play endorses what its courtly audience would expect, the "triumph of an aristocratic community . . . [with] a belief in hierarchy and a faith in the power of idealization."[60]

But Ernest B. Gilman begs to differ. Drawing partly on the reader-response theory of Wolfgang Eiser, and what this tells us of how readers/audiences react to rhythms and narrative expectations generated by a text, he argues a very different effect in the ending of the masque: "The jolt of such an abrupt dispersal is felt by any audience, surely, but its full significance will be understood by an audience alert to the context of court spectacle here invoked. For in the sequence of the disrupted masque, followed by the sudden reappearance of Caliban's 'foul conspiracy,' Shakespeare engineers an exact reversal of the order of events in a Jacobean masque."[61] By focusing on the *audience* as the determiners of meaning, rather than the play's masque-author, Gilman identifies important differences and reversals in the text: "The complete contrary to Ferdinand's rapt wonder is the sense—again opened up for us retrospectively—that the masque is a delusion and a trap for those who would 'live here forever' . . . We re-place our hypothetical view of the revels-as-culmination with a revised understanding of the revels-as-prologue to a moment as yet unfinished."[62] And so to the Epilogue, which confirms this sense of the audience's power: "As Prospero's magic was greater than Sycorax's, so ours is now greater than his in that he must be 'confined' inside the island until we 'release' him from his 'bands'."[63] Gilman sees the process of the play as a "lesson" for Prospero, as well as for the audience.

John Gillies—well into the era of New Historicism and cultural materialism—marks a distinct shift in *Tempest* criticism towards a more critical understanding of its Jacobean significance, especially in relation to colonization.[64] Starting from the "coincidence that Shakespeare's spectacular and exotic play *The Tempest* was performed at court with Chapman's similarly exotic *Memorable Masque* for the marriage, in February 1613, of the princess Elizabeth to the Elector Palatine,"[65] he compares the two works. Chapman's masque is, as he puts it, "self-consciously Virginian" and he uses this to license a reading of the play as also essentially about American colonization. In particular he argues that *The Tempest* addresses a very specific moment in the history of Virginia colonization (1608–10), when the whole project was very much in doubt: the Bermuda shipwreck, on which Shakespeare indisputably draws, was only one of several setbacks and old dreams of El Dorado (which Chapman's masque seems to endorse) needed to be replaced with something more realistic if the venture was to go forward: "I want to suggest two things. First, that two important Shakespearean motifs, the ideas of temperance and fruitfulness, are identifiably Virginian. This is to say that the play translates into poetic and dramatic terms a pair of rhetorical *topoi* that are crucial in forming the official portrait of Virginia. Second, I want to show that these Virginian motifs, culminating in the masque of Ceres, take on distinctly Ovidian form. Here, I will argue that though Ovid may seem to lead us away from Virginia, he really leads us back to the informing principle of her discursive being—the principle of the moralized landscape."[66] So the masque embodies the culmination of an argument about colonization not as about idleness and sudden riches, but about fruitful agricultural labour. And its sudden truncation is "hardly illogical"—Caliban can be thought of as "Shakespeare's version of the unreclaimed natural forces that resist the power of Ovid's Ceres . . . a hunter-gatherer of wild fruits rather than a planter of agricultural 'foison'."[67] Gillies's reading of the play in the context of colonial plantation squares with the almost unchallenged assumption in the late 1980s/early 1990s that the play is largely about the American experience. It has certainly been challenged since: Bermuda shipwrecks were doubtless in Shakespeare's mind as he wrote *The Tempest*, but very little that is specifically American surfaces in the text and the Mediterranean context is also very strong.

James Knowles takes the argument about the play's masque in a different direction by re-examining its formal characteristics and so its ideological connotations. He suggests that it owes far less to Jonson's court masques than is often (because of their familiarity) assumed. He specifically challenges Glynne Wickham's 1975 arguments (noted above), pointing out for example that the mythology of Juno, Ceres, and Iris is far from arcane; that descents from the stage "heavens" were more a tradition of the public theatres than of Inigo Jones stagings, requiring far from elaborate technology; and that an act-break between III.iii and IV.i, filled with music at the Blackfriars theatre, would reduce the antimasque/masque relationship of the "harpy" banquet and Prospero's masque proper. It is also significant that the masque is performed by "spirits," not by aristocratic humans; that Prospero offers a commentary of sorts on his own creation, which is not in the spirit of the Jonson/Jones entertainments; and that it involves the use of none of the architectural scenery, with its wonder-inducing transformations, which had become the hallmarks of those shows.

It has been commonplace to argue that Shakespeare nevertheless evoked what he could of the Jonson model, despite the limited resources at his command. But Knowles argues for "a different interpretation of Prospero's masque, which does not align the play with the Jonsonian masque or with royal ideology" and seeks "to resituate *The Tempest* within a much more diverse and polyvalent conception of aristocratic rather than court or royal culture."[68] Rather than the Jonsonian court masque, he finds echoes of "the mythological pageants of late Elizabethan public theatre" and of Daniel's *Vision of the Twelve Goddesses* (1604), the first of the Jacobean court masques but very different in style from what Jonson introduced the following year. And he particularly argues that "[g]enerically, Prospero's masque is closer to the hybridity of Marston's *Entertainment at Ashby*, the only other known example of a betrothal masque"[69]—as distinct from a marriage one. In his view, therefore, it is a mistake to use the masquing element in the play to identify it with the Jacobean court, as the Jones/Jonson masques were inevitably identified. In this he stands out against a wider strain of recent criticism of *The Tempest*, represented most clearly by Alvin Kernan's *Shakespeare: the King's Playwright*, which sees the play as primarily of and for James's court.[70]

David Norbrook similarly resists the identification of the play with the Jacobean court, arguing that its status as a product for the commercial theatre allowed it a quasi-Bakhtinian capacity to voice multiple discourses, not merely that of the ruling elite: "Despite their royal label, the King's Men owed most of their revenue to public performances; Shakespeare's plays were thus able to pit different discourses against each other with far greater freedom than courtly literature."[71] In such a context "the writer as agent could achieve a degree of independence from the prevailing structures of power and discourse . . . The play is not overtly oppositional or sensationally 'subversive'; but it subjects traditional institutions to a systematic, critical questioning."[72] This questioning extends to the nature of Prospero's authority and to his special creation, the masque: "Shakespeare's questioning of legitimacy extends even to the genre *par excellence* of the naturalisation of authority, the court masque . . . The aim of the masque was to naturalise the king's name, to turn courtiers into gods and goddesses; Prospero dissolves his masque and its courtly language melts into air, leaving . . . 'a strange hollow and confused noise', an undifferentiated roaring that undercuts the confident marks of social difference. The pageants are 'insubstantial'."[73]

David Bevington similarly starts his consideration of the *Tempest* masque with the fact that it is written for a commercial play, and that Shakespeare himself is distinctive in the Jacobean era for not having written a court masque. But he stops far short of Norbrook's radical politics (which look for signs "of a possible republican sub-text in the play").[74] Like Gillies, he compares Shakespeare's masque with one of those written for the wedding of Princess Elizabeth and the Elector Palatine, this time Campion's *The Lord's Masque*, noting multiple differences:

> the masque in *The Tempest* presents itself as a version of a courtly masque at one remove: not for the court in the first instance (though the play was taken to court) and not for the actual wedding of Elizabeth and Frederick, but for a paying audience interested in what a court wedding masque would be like. Prospero plays at being the royal master who has ordered the occasion; Ariel is his producer, his Inigo Jones and Thomas Campion all rolled into one . . . Ferdinand and Miranda stand in for the royal couple whose marriage is being celebrated. Their marriage is "real" enough, of course in the fiction of the play, but it is not a mere allegory for the royal wedding of 1613.[75]

Bevington's whole analysis outlines this sense of being "at one remove." "Staging of this masque is manifestly simpler than that of *The Lord's Masque*, and yet it capitalizes on resemblances to the more elaborate courtly entertainments that would be produced for the royal wedding" and so on.[76] It is within this "remove" that Bevington discerns a Shakespeare of some independence, critical of the king even as he broadly approves the politics of the royal wedding:

> The masque in *The Tempest* is a demonstration of, and a tribute to, dramatic art and poetry of the imagination. The ultimate authority is not a royal spectator surrounded by his courtiers and bridal couple but the dramatist in his own theatre, speaking to the patrons who signal their approval by their paid admission and their applause . . . Shakespeare's politics of masquing, in this play that is insistent upon public performance and that also suggests some implicit criticism of James as a "wise fool" even while it appears to mirror patriotic approval of the Protestant marriage of James's daughter, is a politics of independent artistry.[77]

We have travelled a long way from the idea that Shakespeare's masque is almost a distraction from the real structure of *The Tempest*, or at most simply of a piece with its general thematics: it is now regarded as an essential, almost defining moment of the play. We can see that thinking about the masque has in fact paralleled general criticism of the play, which has radically problematized the figure of Prospero and what is often seen as his colonial project. The authority of the ruler, like the authority of the dramatist, has repeatedly been fought over—and still hangs in the balance.

Pedagogic strategies

The principal challenge in teaching *The Masque of Blackness* is to make the words come alive. Even by the standards of other court masques this seems a particularly inert affair, with hardly any of the qualities we normally look for in drama—character, action, conflict. *The Masque of Queens* does at least have the conflict between the antimasque and the masque proper, an obvious point of entry. The issue here, therefore, is to find other points of engagement and excitement in what many students will find a particularly impenetrable text: Jonson's description of the whole affair seems especially formal and pedantic.

I suggest that a general point of entry is the description of the fans held by the women masquers.[78] As they advance in pairs one holds a fan with both of their adopted names, the other "a mute hieroglyphic, expressing their mixed qualities." So the first two, Queen Anna and the Countess of Bedford, have chosen the names *Euphoris* and *Aglaia* and their "mute hieroglyphic" is "A golden tree, laden with fruit." "Which manner of symbol," Jonson explains, "I rather chose . . . as well for strangeness, as relishing antiquity." Why "strangeness"? Why should that be an issue here? If they know any Shakespeare, students may recall Hippolyta's response to the "story of the night" of the lovers in *A Midsummer Night's Dream*, which for her "grows to something of great constancy; / And howsoever, strange and admirable" (V.i.23–7). Or Alonso in *The Tempest*, as the resolution of the play unfolds: "These are not natural events; they strengthen / From strange to stranger" (V.i.229–30). The key point is that what is going on is deliberately remote, not readily understood: the symbols need to be decoded, the puzzles to be understood. So there are obvious questions: why are the adopted names in classical Greek rather than English? What does "antiquity" add to the proceedings? Editions will probably help them to translate: *Euphoris* is "abundance," *Aglaia* is "splendour." Why should these qualities have been the ones specifically associated with the queen and her friend? And why this "hieroglyphic"? The more answers we can offer, the less "mute" the whole text is.

So we establish that this is not a work to be passively received, but one we need to read as if it is a puzzle, one we need to decode. This point can be reinforced by looking at dramatic texts which present masque-like occasions, showing how audiences react to them (often very badly!). In *Love's Labour's Lost* (V.ii) the king and his male courtiers present a surprise "Russian masque" for the princess and her ladies, and the ladies rise to the challenge of "reading" the symbolism of the disguises, partly repaying the men in kind by disguising themselves. Shortly thereafter both royal parties observe the show of the Nine Worthies mounted by Holofernes, Armado, and Co. This is not a true masque, but shows something of the expected audience/performance relationship. The problem is that the courtiers can read the clumsy efforts of the lower orders all too readily; but in deriding this well-meant offering they show that they do not absorb all of its import: its heroic figures are examples they are implicitly exhorted to emulate. In stooping to laughter (Holofernes protests "This is not generous, not gentle, not humble": V.ii.626) they in fact debase themselves, rather than rising to the imaginative challenge. Masques within Elizabethan and Jacobean plays often in fact show the on-stage audience (and performers) getting lost and confused, so that the event descends into bloody mayhem: see, for example, *The Spanish Tragedy*, *The Revenger's Tragedy* and *Women Beware Women*. This as it were inverts what is expected of the true audience (and indeed performers) of a court masque, who are urged to rise above the confusion, to understand the symbolic messages, extolling the court of which they are all a part, and to take them to heart. In this respect, Ferdinand in *The Tempest* is the paradigmatic masque-viewer: "This is a most majestic vision, and / Harmonious charmingly . . . / So rare a wondered father and a wife / Makes this place Paradise" (IV.i.118–24). Of course, in a true court masque he would be one of the performers, but he takes effortlessly to his role as audience, recognizing the majesty and solemnity of the event, its overpowering aesthetic affect ("harmonious" underscores the critical role of the music, while "charmingly" partly implies "like magic") and how it relates to his planned role as Miranda's bridegroom.

One approach to making Ferdinands of our students is to emphasize the collaborative nature of masques, involving not only a poet but a stage-designer, musicians, dance-masters, lighting experts, and so on. On the same model, students can be broken up into groups to find out about particular features of the work, which they can eventually share in class. Some of this will require library work, but much of it can be done on the Internet, which might have been designed for the task. Firstly, the surroundings in which the event took place. The Banqueting Hall where *Blackness* was staged no longer exists, but the much grander one that eventually replaced it does—the splendid neoclassical "double cube" of a building, designed by Inigo Jones, who staged this masque. Many images of this are available on the net. Why is it a particularly appropriate space for mounting events like *Blackness*? What is the significance of the magnificent Rubens painting on the ceiling? It in fact depicts King James (the king for whom *Blackness* was performed) ascending to heaven after his death. The space is thereby made sacred to the whole

Stuart dynasty—and one feature of this masque, as of every other one, is to exalt monarchy as an institution and the Stuarts in particular. What do they know of kingship in this era?

Secondly, can they get a handle on the staging, which Jonson describes in considerable detail?[79] Do they appreciate how special this must have seemed, when public theatres used next to no scenery and no machinery of the kind that imitated waves? Can they imagine (even reconstruct) how the wave machine would have worked or how the moon could be made to appear so conspicuously?[80] A group might be delegated to produce a collage which would reproduce the key visual elements: a good starting point, to stir the imagination, would be Botticelli's *The Birth of Venus* (widely available on the net), since it depicts a character floating on a shell—clearly the "shell" in *Blackness* must have been much bigger, but the symbolic effect may well have been similar. It is also easy to retrieve the image of a "daughter of Niger" as sketched by Jones for this masque (try googling [images] "masque blackness"—a lot of useful material will come up): substitute that for Venus—and produce variations on the theme to get all twelve masquers (some of Jones's other masque designs may suggest analogous visual elements: another group might be delegated to track them down). Anyone especially interested in art or design in the class might be asked to work through the implications of the representation of the "vast sea . . . from the termination or horizon of which (being the level of the state, which was placed in the upper end of the hall) was drawn, by lines of perspective, the whole work, shooting downwards from the eye."[81] Why is perspective important to some artists (especially Renaissance artists like Leonardo da Vinci and Rubens) but not to others (Ancient Egypt, Picasso)? Why does it matter that the horizon is at the level of the "state," the chair where the king sat?

Thirdly, is it possible to reconstruct anything of the music and dancing which was so central to the experience of the masque? We know that Alfonso Ferrabosco the younger wrote the music for this masque, and while we cannot identify specific items much of his music has survived and is available on CD, played by the early instruments. With those rhythms in our mind we can begin to imagine what the dancing was like: again, there is much information on the net and elsewhere, and a group ought to be able to find reasonable explanations of "measures" and "corantos."[82] It is perhaps more important that the students have a grasp of the symbolic resonances of music and dance in the era, and there is no better context for learning that than Sir John Davies's 1596 poem, *Orchestra* (accessible in a useful selection on the *Luminarium* website, for example). This may be a long stretch but it is worth remembering that our students have grown up with pop videos as staples of their imaginative lives: the relationships between music, dancing, and the world more generally are something they know a lot about—if they can be brought to analyse what they know.

Fourthly, who were the people taking part in this event, and who were those watching? The key watcher, of course, was King James—until 1603 King of Scotland and now also King of England. What do we know of him and his interests? The online *Oxford Dictionary of National Biography* offers such information succinctly and also gives a picture. His accession to the English throne now meant that the island of Britain had a single ruler for the first time in history (though popular myth suggested it had also had such rulers in the distant past). This is why the text plays so conspicuously with the name "Britannia," a resurrection of Roman usage which was not yet commonly used. Why was that significant? Do students know *King Lear* or *Cymbeline* and how Shakespeare alludes to these subjects? A group could conduct similar searches in respect of three other key participants, who are of wider interest to students of Renaissance literature: Queen Anna, who was central to much of the masquing for the first ten years of James's reign (further sources are discussed in the essay above); Lucy, Countess of Bedford, who was Anna's close friend and a patron of poets like Donne and Jonson (what can we learn from their poems about her?); and Lady Mary Wroth, who herself wrote poems and a prose romance, *Urania*. These researches should quickly reveal that James and Anna were hardly a doting couple, though they deferred to each other's status in public. Feminists have tried to argue that these tensions, between the king who is ostensibly honoured by the masque and the queen and her ladies who actually perform it, are apparent in the text. Can students see anything of that?

Fifthly, set some students to read the symbolism a) of the sets; b) of the costumes; and c) of the spoken/sung text. What are the key themes and issues? Why sun? Why sea? Why sky and celestial bodies? What do we make of colours and appeals to the senses? Of geometrical bodies? Of geographical issues? Set someone to trace all the classical allusions. This is perhaps the point at which to begin to draw everything together, perhaps starting with the general question of why Jonson goes out of his way to make this such an impenetrable text. He impresses on us the solemn significance of the event, though we know from other sources that the night was in fact quite a raucous affair. He wants to distinguish the *idea* of the masque from some of the less decorous realities of its performance: if the course is discussing neo-Platonism that would offer a way in. Jonson also wants to separate the masque as much as possible from mere popular entertainment. If the masque is being studied alongside Jonson's theatrical career, that is another possibly useful angle.

I suggest those issues be addressed before confronting the question of race and colour. This is in many ways the biggest conceptual hurdle to leap. It is unthinkable these days that a Queen of England would appear in black-face, and difficult enough to imagine why anyone would want to. But Jacobean England did not have a history of colonization and black slavery—though it was on the brink of beginning one. Nor did it have memories of black-face minstrels, with their insensitive impersonations of African-American entertainers. Some of the articles cited earlier in this chapter have tried to locate racial colour in its historical context, and might be appropriate for more advanced students. Others rather run together questions of race and gender: is this appropriate? Alternatively it can be instructive to look at *Blackness* alongside *Othello*, where colour is also an issue. How are they the same, how different in this? *The Masque of Queens* can similarly be examined alongside the witches in *Macbeth*. *Pleasure Reconciled to Virtue* is an obvious pairing for Milton's *Comus*. In short, although masques can often seem at first inert and impenetrable, there are few of them that do not touch on themes familiar in more accessible Renaissance material, making it possible to open them up by comparison. And count yourself lucky that you live in the age of the Internet, when it is possible to bring so many of the "removed mysteries" of court masques to your students' desktop screens.

Teaching the masque in *The Tempest*

The masque in *The Tempest* hardly poses problems of the same order. Nevertheless, time permitting, students will come to it with a greater understanding of the issues if they first experience a true court masque in the ways suggested for *Blackness*. But that may not be the masque to choose expressly for this purpose: a true wedding masque like *Hymenaei* is a more obvious choice.[83] An examination of the significance to James I's court of the marriage of the young Earl of Essex and Lady Frances Howard would illuminate what Prospero attempts to do in the union of Ferdinand and Miranda. But if time does not permit a comparative approach, a useful way into the *Tempest* masque (again dividing questions among separate groups of students) is via the famous Hatfield or "rainbow" portrait of Elizabeth I, widely available (and discussed) on the Internet (try googling [images] "Elizabeth rainbow portrait"). Decoding that picture opens up the significance of Iris as a bridge between heaven and earth (compare the classical and biblical implications of the rainbow), one that is replicated in the relationship between a monarch and her subjects. This invites exploration of why Juno and Ceres should be the other deities involved—the one associated with marriage, the other with fruitfulness. Why is the Proserpina myth evoked here? Equally, why is it so significant that Venus and Cupid should be excluded? What do students make of the staging of Juno's descent? How spectacular might it have been at the Globe, at the Blackfriars, or at court? What is symbolized in the dance of the nymphs and the reapers? (My suggestions on looking at dance in *Blackness* may be helpful here.) Lastly, what is the significance of the masque breaking off, unfinished, and of Prospero's "distemper"?

Notes

1. David Lindley (ed.), *Court Masques: Jacobean and Caroline Entertainments, 1605–1640* (Oxford: Oxford University Press, 1995), Introduction, p. x.
2. T. S. Eliot, "Ben Jonson," quoted from *Selected Essays* (London: Faber, 1950), p. 139. Jonson was the single most influential writer of masques in England, writing more

and doing more to regularize their form than anyone else. It was Jonson who fastened on the spelling, "masque," when many contemporaries used "mask" (denoting the general use of masks in these shows); he also made the "anti-masque" a key feature of Jacobean and Caroline masques—his spelling denoting that he conceived of it as a "foil" or challenge to the main masque that followed, as distinct from "antemasque" (merely a prelude) or "antic/antique-mask," forms which involved grotesque or ludicrous figures.

3. Eliot, *Selected Essays*, p. 139.
4. Eliot, *Selected Essays*, p. 139.
5. Francis Bacon, *The Essays or Counsels*, ed. M. Kiernan (Oxford: Clarendon Press, 1985), p. 117.
6. Francis Beaumont and John Fletcher, *The Maid's Tragedy*, ed. T. W. Craik (Manchester: Manchester University Press, 1988), I.i.10–11.
7. Shakespeare also contrives that Romeo first sees Juliet at a masque at the Capulet house.
8. Randall Ingram, "*Pleasure Reconciled to Virtue*: Introducing Undergraduates to Stuart Masques and Enjoying It," in *Approaches to Teaching English Renaissance Drama*, ed. Karen Bamford and Alexander Leggatt (New York: Modern Language Association of America, 2002), pp. 180–5.
9. Orgel did not, of course, emerge from a vacuum. There had been significant scholarly work on the masque in Enid Welsford, *The Court Masque* (Cambridge: Cambridge University Press, 1927) and Allardyce Nicoll, *Stuart Masques and the Renaissance Stage* (Cambridge: Cambridge University Press, 1938) between the world wars, and later by D. J. Gordon, whose key essays were collected by Orgel himself as *The Renaissance Imagination* (Cambridge: Cambridge University Press, 1975), and John C. Meagher, *Method and Meaning in Jonson's Masques* (Notre Dame: Notre Dame University Press, 1966). The point is that it was Orgel's work that introduced masques to a much wider readership.
10. Stephen Orgel, *The Jonsonian Masque* (Cambridge MA: Harvard University Press, 1965); Orgel, *The Complete Masques* (New Haven and London: Yale University Press, 1969; Orgel, *Selected Masques* (New Haven and London: Yale University Press, 1970); Stephen Orgel and Roy Strong, *Inigo Jones: the Theatre of the Stuart Court* (London: Sotheby Parke Bernet, 1973); Orgel, *The Illusion of Power* (Berkeley: University of California Press, 1975).
11. This, of course, an allusion to the classic New Critical study, *The Verbal Icon: Studies in the Meaning of Poetry* by William K. Wimsatt (Lexington: University of Kentucky Press, 1954).
12. Stephen Greenblatt's *Renaissance Self-Fashioning* (Chicago and London: University of Chicago Press, 1980).
13. "The Circulation of Social Energy in Renaissance England" is the subtitle of Greenblatt's *Shakespearean Negotiations* (Oxford: Clarendon Press, 1988).
14. Jonathan Goldberg's *James I and the Politics of Literature* (Baltimore and London: Johns Hopkins University Press, 1983).
15. The adjectives derive from "Roles and Mysteries" in D. J. Gordon, *The Renaissance Imagination: essays and lectures*, ed. Stephen Orgel (Berkeley and London: University of California Press, 1975) p. 18.
16. Goldberg, *James I*, p. 57.
17. Goldberg, *James I*, pp. 58–9.
18. Leah S. Marcus, "The Occasion of Ben Jonson's *Pleasure Reconciled to Virtue*," *SEL* 19, 2 (Spring 1979): 271–93 (reprinted in *The Politics of Mirth: Jonson, Herrick, Milton,*

Marvell, and the Defense of Old Holiday Pastimes. Chicago: University of Chicago Press, 1987); Leah S. Marcus, "Masquing Occasions and Masque Structure," *Research Opportunities in Renaissance Drama* 24 (1981): 7–16; Leah S. Marcus, "City Metal and Country Mettle: the Occasion of Ben Jonson's Golden Age Restored," in *Pageantry in the Shakespearean Theater*, ed. David M. Bergeron, pp. 26–47 (Athens, GA: University of Georgia Press, 1985). David Norbrook, "The Reformation of the Masque," in *The Court Masque*, ed. David Lindley, pp. 94–110 (Manchester: Manchester University Press, 1984); David Norbrook, "'The Masque of Truth': Court Entertainments and International Protestant Politics in the Early Stuart Period," *The Seventeenth Century* 1, 2 (July 1986): 81–110. David Lindley, "Embarrassing Ben: the Masques for Frances Howard," *ELR* 16, 2 (Spring 1986): 343–59; David Lindley, "Courtly Play: the Politics of Chapman's The Memorable Masque," in *The Stuart Courts*, ed. Eveline Cruickshanks, pp. 43–58 (Stroud: Sutton, 2000). Paul Sellin, *The politics of Ben Jonson's Newes from the new world discover'd in the moone* (Berkeley: University of California Press, 1986). Martin Butler, "'We Are One Mans All': Jonson's The Gipsies Metamorphosed," *Yearbook of English Studies* 21 (1991): 252–73; Martin Butler, "Ben Jonson's Pan's Anniversary and the Politics of Early Stuart Pastoral," *ELR* 22, 3 (Autumn 1992): 369–404; Martin Butler, "Reform or Reverence? The Politics of the Caroline Masque," in *Theatre and Government under the Early Stuarts*, ed. J. R. Mulryne and Margaret Shrewing, pp. 87–117 (Cambridge: Cambridge University Press, 1993); Martin Butler, "Courtly Negotiations," in *The Politics of the Stuart Court Masque*, ed. David Bevington and Peter Holbrook, 20–40 (New York: Cambridge University Press, 1998); Martin Butler and David Lindley, "Restoring Astraea: Jonson's Masque for the Fall of Somerset," *ELH* 61, 4 (Winter 1994): 807–27. Russell West, "Perplexive Perspectives: The Court and Contestation in the Jacobean Masque," *Seventeenth Century* 18, 1 (Spring 2003): 25–43. Jean MacIntyre, "Prince Henry's Satyrs: Topicality in Jonson's Oberon," in *A Search for Meaning: Critical Essays on Early Modern Literature*, ed. Paula Harms Payne, pp. 95–104 (New York: Peter Lang, 2004).

19. Lindley, *Court Masques*, p. xv.
20. Lindley, *Court Masques*, p. xvi.
21. Lindley, *Court Masques*, p. xvi.
22. Suzanne Gossett, "'Man-maid, begone!' Women in Masques," *ELR* 18, 1 (Winter 1988): 96–113, p. 102.
23. Her name is often anglicized as Queen Anne, but the attention she has recently received, especially from those interested in her masquing, has prompted a revival of her own preferred style.
24. See C. H. Herford, Percy and Evelyn Simpson (eds), *Ben Jonson*, 11 vols (Oxford, 1925–52), vol. 7, pp. 169, 282.
25. Hardin Assand, "'To blanch an Ethiop, and revive a corse': Queen Anne and *The Masque of Blackness*," *Studies in English Literature* 32, 2 (Spring 1992): 271–95. Marion Wynne-Davies, "The Queen's Masque: Renaissance Women and the Seventeenth-Century Court Masque," in *Gloriana's Face: Women, Public and Private, in the English Renaissance*, ed. S. P. Cerasano and Marion Wynne-Davies, pp. 79–104 (Detroit: Wayne State University Press, 1992). Barbara Kiefer Lewalski, "Enacting Opposition: Queen Anne and the Subversions of Masquing," in *Writing Women in Jacobean England* (Cambridge, MA: Harvard University Press, 1993). Leeds Barroll, "Theatre as Text: the Case of Queen Anna and the Jacobean Court Masque," in *The Elizabethan Theatre* XIV, ed. A. L. Magnusson and C. E. McGee,

pp. 175–93 (Toronto: Meany, 1996); Leeds Barroll, "Inventing the Stuart Masque," in *The Politics of the Stuart Court Masque*, ed. David Bevington and Peter Holbrook, pp. 121–43 (Cambridge: Cambridge University Press, 1998). Clare McManus, "Defacing the Carcass: Anna of Denmark and Ben Jonson's *Masque of Blackness*," in *Refashioning Ben Jonson: Gender, Politics, and the Jonsonian Canon*, ed. Julie Sanders, Kate Chedgzoy, and Susan Wiseman, pp. 93–113 (New York: St. Martin's Press-now Palgrave Macmillan, 1998); Clare McManus, *Women on the Renaissance Stage: Anna of Denmark and Female Masquing in the Stuart Court (1590–1619)* (New York: Manchester University Press, 2002); Clare McManus (ed.), *Women and Culture at the Courts of the Stuart Queens* (New York: Palgrave Macmillan, 2003).

26. See Lawrence Normand, "Witches, King James, and *The Masque of Queens*," in *Representing Women in Renaissance England*, ed. Claude J. Summers and Ted-Larry Pebworth, pp. 107–20 (Columbia: University of Missouri Press, 1997).

27. See, for example: Joyce Green MacDonald, "'The Force of Imagination': the Subject of Blackness in Shakespeare, Jonson, and Ravenscroft," *Renaissance Papers* (1991): 53–74; Assand (1992); Yumna Siddiqi, "Dark Incontinents: the Discourse of Race and Gender in Three Renaissance Masques," *Renaissance Drama* 23 (1992): 139–63; Suzy Beemer, "Masks of Blackness, Masks of Whiteness: Coloring the (Sexual) Subject in Jonson, Cary, and Fletcher," *Thamyris* 4, 2 (Autumn 1997): 223–47; Kim F. Hall, "Sexual Politics and Cultural Identity in *The Masque of Blackness*," in *Critical Essays on Ben Jonson*, ed. Robert N. Watson, pp. 237–49 (New York: G. K. Hall; London, Prentice Hall, 1997); Mary Floyd-Wilson, "Temperature, Temperament, and Racial Difference in Ben Jonson's *The Masque of Blackness*," *English Literary Renaissance* 28, 2 (Spring 1998): 183–209; Bernadette Andrea, "Black Skin, the Queen's Masques: Africanist Ambivalence and Feminine Author(ity) in the *Masques of Blackness and Beauty*," *ELR* 29, 2 (Spring 1999): 246–81.

28. See John Gillies, "Shakespeare's Virginian Masque," *ELH* 53 (1986): 673–707; Karen Robertson, "Pocahontas at the Masque," *Signs: Journal of Women in Culture & Society* 21, 3 (Spring 1996): 551–83; and David Lindley, "Courtly Play."

29. See James M. Smith, "Effaced History: Facing the Colonial Contexts of Ben Jonson's Irish Masque at Court," *ELH* 65, 2 (Summer 1998): 297–321; Jim Sullivan, "'Language Such as Men Doe Vse': the Ethnic English of Ben Jonson's *The Irish Masque* at Court," *Michigan Academician* 31, 1 (April 1999): 1–22; and Thomas Rist, "Religious Politics in Ben Jonson's 'The Irish Masque'," *Cahiers Elisabéthains* 55 (April 1999): 27–34.

30. Lesley Mickel, "Glorious Spangs and Rich Embroidery: Costume in *The Masque of Blackness* and *Hymenaei*," *Studies in the Literary Imagination* 36, 2 (Fall 2003): 41–59, pp. 41–2.

31. Quoted from Herford and Simpson, vol. 10, p. 448.

32. Ibid.

33. *The Jonsonian Masque*, p. 65.

34. Gossett, "Women in Masques," p. 113.

35. Gossett, "Women in Masques," p. 99.

36. Hardin Assand, "Queen Anne and *The Masque of Blackness*," p. 271.

37. "Queen Anne and *The Masque of Blackness*," p. 273.

38. "Queen Anne and *The Masque of Blackness*," p. 280.

39. "Queen Anne and *The Masque of Blackness*," p. 283.

40. Barbara K. Lewalski, "Enacting Opposition," and Leeds Barroll, "Theatre as Text" and "Inventing the Stuart Masque."

41. Leeds Barroll, "Inventing the Stuart Masque," p. 132.
42. Clare McManus, *Women on the Renaissance Stage*, p. 3.
43. McManus, *Women on the Renaissance Stage*, p. 17. Lesley Mickel (2003) complements McManus on the language of dance with an analysis of the rich costumes the ladies wore, arguing that "in *Blackness* [they] obviously made a large contribution to its impact as a whole, [but] they are in some ways not typical of development in this area" ("Glorious Spangs and Rich Embroidery: Costume in *The Masque of Blackness* and *Hymenaei*," p. 54).
44. McManus, *Women on the Renaissance Stage*, p. 212.
45. See also Andrea, "Black Skin, the Queen's Masques," who reintegrates issues of racial stigma and women's behaviour: "This equation of feminine transgressiveness and denigrated blackness accordingly becomes a dominant motif in the Queen's masques," p. 252.
46. Kim F. Hall, "Sexual Politics," pp. 3–4.
47. Hall, "Sexual Politics," pp. 15–16.
48. Mary Floyd-Wilson, "Temperature, Temperament, and Racial Difference," pp. 186–7).
49. Floyd-Wilson, "Temperature, Temperament, and Racial Difference," p. 208.
50 Richmond Barbour, "Britain and the Great Beyond: *The Masque of Blackness* at Whitehall," *Playing the Globe: Genre and Geography in English Renaissance Drama*, ed. John Gillies and Virginia Mason Vaughan, pp. 129–53 (Madison, NJ: Fairleigh Dickinson University Press; London: Associated University Presses, 1998), pp. 129–30.
51. Barbour, "Britain and the Great Beyond," p. 147.
52. Jean MacIntyre, "Queen Elizabeth's Ghost at the Court of James I: *The Masque of Blackness, Lord Hay's Masque, The Haddington Masque,* and *Oberon*," *Ben Jonson Journal* 5 (1998): 81–100, p. 84.
53. MacIntyre, "Queen Elizabeth's Ghost," pp. 85–6.
54. Northrop Frye, *A Natural Perspective* (New York and London: Columbia University Press, 1965), pp. 157–8.
55. References to Shakespeare are to *The Complete Works of Shakespeare* (5th edn), ed. David Bevington (Pearson Longman: New York, 2004).
56. Frank Kermode (ed.), *The Tempest*, The Arden Shakespeare (London: Methuen, 1954), p. lxxv. Kermode does, however, argue convincingly that the masque was always part of Shakespeare's dramatic design. The second recorded performance of the play (the first was at court on November 1, 1611) was as part of the festivities for the wedding of Princess Elizabeth to the Elector Palatine, which spanned December 1612–February 1613) and there have long been those who argue that the masque as we have it reflects alterations for that performance. Kermode's argument certainly did not settle the matter to everyone's satisfaction: see Irwin Smith, "Ariel and the Masque in *The Tempest*," *SQ* 21 (1970): 213–23.
57. Inga-Stina Ewbank, " 'These Pretty Devices': a Study of Masques in Plays" in *A Book of Masques: In Honour of Allardyce Nicoll* [Festschrift], pp. 405–48 (Cambridge: Cambridge University Press, 1967), pp. 419–20.
58. Glynne Wickham, "Masque and Anti-masque in *The Tempest*," *Essays and Studies* 28 (1975): 1–14, p. 5.
59. Orgel, *Illusion of Power*, p. 47.
60. *Illusion of Power*, p. 40.
61. Ernest B. Gilman, " 'All eyes': Prospero's Inverted Masque," *Renaissance Quarterly* 33 (1980): 214–30, pp. 214–15.

62. Gilman, "Prospero's Inverted Masque," pp. 225, 226–7.

63. "Prospero's Inverted Masque," pp. 228–9.

64. John Gillies, "Shakespeare's Virginian Masque."

65. Gillies, "Shakespeare's Virginian Masque," p. 673.

66. "Shakespeare's Virginian Masque," pp. 676–7.

67. "Shakespeare's Virginian Masque," p. 698.

68. James Knowles, "Insubstantial Pageants: *The Tempest* and Masquing Culture" *Shakespeare's Late plays: New Readings*, ed. Jennifer Richards and James Knowles, pp. 108–25 (Edinburgh: Edinburgh University Press, 1999), p. 109.

69. Knowles, "Insubstantial Pageants," p. 120.

70. Alvin Kernan, *Shakespeare: the King's Playwright* (New Haven and London: Yale University Press, 1995).

71. David Norbrook, "'What cares these roarers for the name of king?' Language and Utopia in *The Tempest*," in *The Tempest: Contemporary Critical Essays*, ed. R. S. White, pp. 167–90 (Basingstoke: Macmillan–now Palgrave Macmillan, 1999), p. 183.

72. "Language and Utopia in *The Tempest*," p. 172.

73. "Language and Utopia in *The Tempest*," p. 181.

74. David Bevington, "*The Tempest* and the Jacobean court masque," *The Politics of the Stuart Court Masque*, ed. David Bevington and Peter Holbrook, pp. 218–43 (Cambridge: Cambridge University Press, 1998); Norbrook, "Language and Utopia in *The Tempest*," p. 179.

75. Bevington, "*The Tempest* and the Jacobean court masque," p. 231.

76. "*The Tempest* and the Jacobean court masque," p. 232ff.

77. "*The Tempest* and the Jacobean court masque," pp. 237–8.

78. *Norton Anthology of English Literature* (8th edn, 2006), p. 1332.

79. Ibid., pp. 1327–8.

80. Ibid., p. 1331.

81. Ibid., p. 1296.

82. Ibid., p. 1333.

83. See Catherine M. Shaw, "*The Tempest* and *Hymenaei*." *Cahiers Elisabéthains* 26 (October 1984): 29–39.

Selective guide to further reading and resources

Andrea, Bernadette. "Black Skin, the Queen's Masques: Africanist Ambivalence and Feminine Author(ity) in the *Masques of Blackness and Beauty*." *ELR* 29, 2 (Spring 1999): 246–81.

Assand, Hardin. "'To blanch an Ethiop, and revive a corse': Queen Anne and *The Masque of Blackness*." *Studies in English Literature* 32, 2 (Spring 1992): 271–95.

Barbour, Richmond. "Britain and the Great Beyond: *The Masque of Blackness* at Whitehall." *Playing the Globe: Genre and Geography in English Renaissance Drama*, ed. John Gillies and Virginia Mason Vaughan, pp. 129–53. Madison, NJ: Fairleigh Dickinson University Press; London: Associated University Presses, 1998.

Barroll, Leeds. "Theatre as Text: the Case of Queen Anna and the Jacobean Court Masque." *The Elizabethan Theatre* XIV, ed. A. L. Magnusson and C. E. McGee, pp. 175–93. Toronto: Meany, 1996.

———. "Inventing the Stuart Masque." *The Politics of the Stuart Court Masque*, ed. David Bevington and Peter Holbrook, pp. 121–43. Cambridge: Cambridge University Press, 1998.

Beemer, Suzy. "Masks of Blackness, Masks of Whiteness: Coloring the (Sexual) Subject in Jonson, Cary, and Fletcher." *Thamyris* 4, 2 (Autumn 1997): 223–47.

Bergeron, David M. "Pageants, Masques, and History." *The Cambridge Companion to Shakespeare's History Plays*, ed. Michael Hattaway, pp. 41–56. Cambridge: Cambridge University Press, 2002.

Berry, Philippa, and Archer, Jayne Elisabeth. "Reinventing the Matter of Britain: Undermining the State in Jacobean Masques." *British Identities and English Renaissance Culture*, ed. David J. Baker and Willy Maley, pp. 119–34. Cambridge: Cambridge University Press, 2002.

Bevington, David. "*The Tempest* and the Jacobean court masque." *The Politics of the Stuart Court Masque*, ed. David Bevington and Peter Holbrook, pp. 218–43. Cambridge: Cambridge University Press, 1998.

———, and Holbrook, Peter (eds). *The Politics of the Stuart Court Masque*. New York: Cambridge University Press, 1998.

Boehrer, Bruce Thomas. "Great Prince's Donatives: MTV Video and the Jacobean Court Masque." *Studies in Popular Culture* 11, 2 (1988): 1–21.

Brock, D. Heyward. "Ben Jonson's First Folio and the Textuality of His Masques at Court." *Ben Jonson Journal* 10 (2003): 43–55.

Burley, Anne. "Courtly Personages: the Lady Masquers in Ben Jonson's *Masque of Blackness*." *Shakespeare and Renaissance Association of West Virginia—Selected Papers* 10 (Spring 1985): 49–61.

Butler, Martin. " 'We Are One Mans All': Jonson's *The Gipsies Metamorphosed*." *Yearbook of English Studies* 21 (1991): 252–73.

Butler, Martin. "Ben Jonson's Pan's Anniversary and the Politics of Early Stuart Pastoral." *ELR* 22, 3 (Autumn 1992): 369–404.

Butler, Martin. "Jonson's News from the New World, the 'Running Masque,' and the Season of 1619–20." *Medieval and Renaissance Drama of England* 6 (1993): 153–78.

———. "Reform or Reverence? The Politics of the Caroline Masque." *Theatre and Government under the Early Stuarts*, ed. J. R. Mulryne and Margaret Shrewing, pp. 87–117. Cambridge: Cambridge University Press, 1993.

———. "The Invention of Britain and the Early Stuart Masque." *The Stuart Court and Europe: Essays in Politics and Political Culture*, ed. R. Malcolm Smuts, pp. 65–85. Cambridge and New York: Cambridge University Press, 1996.

———. "Courtly Negotiations." *The Politics of the Stuart Court Masque*, ed. David Bevington and Peter Holbrook, pp. 20–40. New York: Cambridge University Press, 1998.

———. "Private and Occasional Drama." *English Renaissance Drama*, ed. A. R. Braunmuller and Michael Hattaway, pp. 131–63. Cambridge: Cambridge University Press, 2003.

———, and Lindley, David. "Restoring Astraea: Jonson's Masque for the Fall of Somerset." *ELH* 61, 4 (Winter 1994): 807–27.

Crouch, Patricia A. "Dissecting the Royal Subject: the King's Two Bodies and the Jacobean Court Masque." *Atenea* 22, 1–2 (December–January 2002): 17–30.

Cunnar, Eugene R. "(En)Gendering Architectural Poetics in Jonson's *Masque of Queens*." *Lit: Literature, Interpretation, Theory* 4, 2 (1993): 145–60.

Dundas, Judith. " 'Those Beautiful Characters of Sense': Classical Deities and the Court Masque." *Comparative Drama* 16, 2 (Summer 1982): 166–79.

Ewbank, Inga-Stina. " 'These Pretty Devices': a Study of Masques in Plays." *A Book of Masques: In Honour of Allardyce Nicoll*, various editors, pp. 405–48. Cambridge: Cambridge University Press, 1967.

Faust, Joan. "*Queenes* and Jonson's Masques of Mirrors." *Explorations in Renaissance Culture* 28, 1 (Summer 2002): 1–29.

Finkelstein, Richard. "Ben Jonson on Spectacle." *Comparative Drama* 21, 2 (Summer 1987): 103–14.

Floyd-Wilson, Mary. "Temperature, Temperament, and Racial Difference in Ben Jonson's *The Masque of Blackness*." *English Literary Renaissance* 28, 2 (Spring 1998): 183–209.

Frye, Northrop. *A Natural Perspective*. New York and London: Columbia University Press, 1965.

Gillies, John. "Shakespeare's Virginian Masque." *ELH* 53 (1986): 673–707.

Gilman, Ernest B. "'All eyes': Prospero's Inverted Masque." *Renaissance Quarterly* 33 (1980): 214–30.

Goldberg, Jonathan. *James I and the Politics of Literature*. Baltimore and London: Johns Hopkins University Press, 1983.

———. "Fatherly Authority: the Politics of Stuart Family Images." *Rewriting the Renaissance: the Discourse of Sexual Difference in Early Modern Europe*, ed. M. W. Ferguson, M. Quilligan and N. J. Vickers, pp. 3–32. Chicago: University of Chicago Press, 1986.

Gossett, Suzanne. "'Man-Maid, Begone!' Women in Masques." *ELR* 18, 1 (Winter 1988): 96–113.

Hall, Kim F. "Sexual Politics and Cultural Identity in *The Masque of Blackness*." *Critical Essays on Ben Jonson*, ed. Robert N. Watson, pp. 237–49. New York: G. K. Hall; London, Prentice Hall, 1997.

Hees, Edwin. "Unity of Vision in Ben Jonson's Tragedies and Masques." *Theoria* 67 (October 1986): 21–32.

Ingram, Randall. "*Pleasure Reconciled to Virtue*: Introducing Undergraduates to Stuart Masques and Enjoying It." *Approaches to Teaching English Renaissance Drama*, ed. Karen Bamford and Alexander Leggatt, 180–5. New York: Modern Language Association of America, 2002.

Johnson, A. W. *Ben Jonson: Poetry and Architecture*. Oxford: Clarendon; New York: Oxford University Press, 1994.

Kermode, Frank (ed.). *The Tempest*. The Arden Shakespeare. London: Methuen, 1954.

Kernan, Alvin. *Shakespeare: the King's Playwright*. New Haven and London: Yale University Press, 1995.

Knowles, James D. "Masques in the 1619–20 Season." *Notes & Queries* 39, 3/237 (September 1992): 369–70.

———. "Insubstantial Pageants: *The Tempest* and Masquing Culture." *Shakespeare's Late plays: New Readings*, ed. Jennifer Richards and James Knowles, pp. 108–25. Edinburgh: Edinburgh University Press, 1999.

———. "'Tied / To Rules of Flattery?': Court Drama and the Masque." *A Companion to English Renaissance Literature and Culture*, ed. Michael Hattaway, pp. 525–44. Oxford and Malden, MA: Blackwell, 2000.

Lanier, Douglas. "Fertile Visions: Jacobean Revels and the Erotics of Occasion." *SEL* 39, 2 (Spring 1999): 327–56.

Lewalski, Barbara Kiefer. "Enacting Opposition: Queen Anne and the Subversions of Masquing." *Writing Women in Jacobean England*. Cambridge, MA: Harvard University Press, 1993.

Limon, Jerzy. *The Masque of Stuart Culture*. Newark: University of Delaware Press, 1990.

———. "The Masque of Stuart Culture." *The Mental World of the Jacobean Court*, ed. Linda Levy Peck, pp. 209–29. Cambridge: Cambridge University Press, 1991.

Lindley, David. "Embarrassing Ben: the Masques for Frances Howard." *ELR* 16, 2 (Spring 1986): 343–59.

————. "Courtly Play: the Politics of Chapman's *The Memorable Masque.*" *The Stuart Courts*, ed. Eveline Cruickshanks, pp. 43–58. Stroud: Sutton, 2000.

———— (ed.). *The Court Masque.* Dover, NH: Manchester University Press, 1984.

Loewenstein, Joseph. *Responsive Readings: Versions of Echo in Pastoral, Epic, and the Jonsonian Masque.* New Haven: Yale University Press, 1984.

————. "Printing and the 'Multitudinous Presse': the Contentious Texts of Jonson;s Masques." *Ben Jonson's 1616 Folio*, ed. Jennifer Brady and W. H. Herendeen, pp. 168–91. Newark: University of Delaware Press; London: Associated University Presses, 1991.

MacDonald, Joyce Green. "'The Force of Imagination': the Subject of Blackness in Shakespeare, Jonson, and Ravenscroft." *Renaissance Papers* (1991): 53–74.

MacIntyre, Jean. "Queen Elizabeth's Ghost at the Court of James I: *The Masque of Blackness, Lord Hay's Masque, The Haddington Masque,* and *Oberon.*" *Ben Jonson Journal* 5 (1998): 81–100.

————. "Prince Henry's Satyrs: Topicality in Jonson's *Oberon.*" *A Search for Meaning: Critical Essays on Early Modern Literature*, ed. Paula Harms Payne, pp. 95–104. New York: Peter Lang, 2004.

Marcus, Leah S. "Masquing Occasions and Masque Structure." *Research Opportunities in Renaissance Drama* 24 (1981): 7–16.

————. "City Metal and Country Mettle: the Occasion of Ben Jonson's *Golden Age Restored.*" *Pageantry in the Shakespearean Theater*, ed. David M. Bergeron, pp. 26–47. Athens, GA: University of Georgia Press, 1985.

————. "The Occasion of Ben Jonson's *Pleasure Reconciled to Virtue*". *SEL* 19, 2 (Spring 1979): 271–93. Reprinted in *The Politics of Mirth: Jonson, Herrick, Milton, Marvell, and the Defense of Old Holiday Pastimes*. Chicago: University of Chicago Press, 1987.

Marsh-Lockett, Carol. "Ben Jonson's *Haddington Masque* and *The Masque of Queenes*: Stuart England and the Notion of Order." *College Language Association Journal* 30, 3 (March 1987): 362–78.

Maurer, Margaret. "Reading Ben Jonson's Queens." *Seeking the Woman in Late Medieval and Renaissance Writings: Essays in Feminist Contextual Criticism*, ed. Sheila Fisher and Janet E. Halley, pp. 233–63. Knoxville: University of Tennessee Press, 1989.

McManus, Clare. "Defacing the Carcass: Anna of Denmark and Ben Jonson's *Masque of Blackness.*" *Refashioning Ben Jonson: Gender, Politics, and the Jonsonian Canon*, ed. Julie Sanders, Kate Chedgzoy and Susan Wiseman, pp. 93–113. New York: St. Martin's Press–now Palgrave Macmillan, 1998.

————. *Women on the Renaissance Stage: Anna of Denmark and Female Masquing in the Stuart Court (1590–1619).* New York: Manchester University Press, 2002.

———— (ed.). *Women and Culture at the Courts of the Stuart Queens.* New York: Palgrave Macmillan, 2003.

Meskill, Lynn Sermin. "Exorcising the Gorgon of Terror: Jonson's *Masque of Queens.*" *ELH* 72, 1 (Spring 2005): 181–207.

Mickel, Lesley. *Ben Jonson's Antimasques: a History of Growth and Decline.* Aldershot, UK and Brookfield, VT: Ashgate, 1999.

————. "Glorious Spangs and Rich Embroidery: Costume in *The Masque of Blackness* and *Hymenaei.*" *Studies in the Literary Imagination* 36, 2 (Fall 2003): 41–59.

Musgrove, S. "'Edified by the Margent': Dramaturgical Evidence in Jonson's Masques." *Parergon* 3 (1985): 163–72.

Norbrook, David. "The Reformation of the Masque." *The Court Masque*, ed. David Lindley, pp. 94–110. Manchester: Manchester University Press, 1984.

Norbrook, David. "'The Masque of Truth': Court Entertainments and International Protestant Politics in the Early Stuart Period." *The Seventeenth Century* 1, 2 (July 1986): 81–110.

———. "'What cares these roarers for the name of king?' Language and Utopia in *The Tempest.*" *The Tempest: Contemporary Critical Essays*, ed. R. S. White, pp. 167–90. Basingstoke: Macmillan–now Palgrave Macmillan, 1999.

Normand, Lawrence. "Witches, King James, and *The Masque of Queens.*" *Representing Women in Renaissance England*, ed. Claude J. Summers and Ted-Larry Pebworth, pp. 107–20. Columbia: University of Missouri Press, 1997.

Orgel, Stephen. *The Power of Illusion.* Berkeley: University of California Press, 1975.

———. "Jonson and the Amazons." *Soliciting Interpretation: Literary Theory and Seventeenth-Century English Poetry*, ed. Elizabeth D. Harvey and Katharine Eisaman Maus, pp. 119–39. Chicago: University of Chicago Press, 1990.

Over, William. "Familiarizing the Colonized in Ben Jonson's Masques." *Partial Answers: Journal of Literature and the History of Ideas* 2, 2 (June 2004): 27–50.

Palmer, Barbara D. "Court and Country: the Masque as Sociopolitical Subtext." *Medieval and Renaissance Drama in England: An Annual Gathering of Research, Criticism and Reviews* 7 (1995): 338–54.

Parry, Graham. "The Politics of the Jacobean Masque." *Theatre and Government under the Early Stuarts*, ed. J. R. Mulryne and Margaret Shewring. Cambridge and New York: Cambridge University Press, 1993.

Paster, Gail Kern. "The Idea of London in Masque and Pageant." *Pageantry in the Shakespearean Theater*, ed. David M. Bergeron, pp. 48–64. Athens, GA: University of Georgia Press, 1985.

Pugh, Syrithe. "'Rosmarine' in *The Masque of Blackness*: Jonson's Herbal *Medicamina Faciei*?" *Notes & Queries* 52, 2 (June 2005): 221–3.

Rist, Thomas. "Religious Politics in Ben Jonson's 'The Irish Masque'" *Cahiers Elisabéthains* 55 (April 1999): 27–34.

Robertson, Karen. "Pocahontas at the Masque." *Signs: Journal of Women in Culture & Society* 21, 3 (Spring 1996): 551–83.

Sanders, Julie, Kate Chedgzoy, and Susan Wiseman (eds). *Refashioning Ben Jonson: Gender, Politics, and the Jonsonian Canon.* New York: St. Martin's Press–now Palgrave Macmillan, 1998.

Schoch, Richard W. "(Im)pressing Texts and Spectacular Performance: the Quarrel between Ben Jonson and Inigo Jones." *Constructions* 9 (1994): 1–12.

Schwarz, Kathryn. "Amazon Reflections in the Jacobean Queen's Masque." *SEL* 35, 2 (Spring 1995): 293–309.

Shaw, Catherine M. "*The Tempest* and *Hymenaei.*" *Cahiers Elisabéthains* 26 (October 1984): 29–39.

Siddiqi, Yumna. "Dark Incontinents: the Discourse of Race and Gender in Three Renaissance Masques." *Renaissance Drama* 23 (1992): 139–63.

Smialkowska, Monika. "'Out of the Authority of Ancient and Late Writers': Ben Jonson's Use of Textual Sources in *The Masque of Queens.*" *ELR* 32, 2 (Spring 2002): 268–86.

Smith, Irwin. "Ariel and the Masque in *The Tempest.*" *SQ* 21 (1970): 213–23.

Smith, James M. "Effaced History: Facing the Colonial Contexts of Ben Jonson's Irish Masque at Court." *ELH* 65, 2 (Summer 1998): 297–321.

Sullivan, Jim. "'Language Such as Men Doe Vse': the Ethnic English of Ben Jonson's *The Irish Masque* at Court." *Michigan Academician* 31, 1 (April 1999): 1–22.

Thierry, Demaubus. "Ritual, Ostension and the Divine in the Stuart Masque." *Literature and Theology* 17, 3 (September 2003): 298–313.

Walls, Peter. *Music in the English Courtly Masque, 1604–1640.* New York: Oxford University Press, 1996.

West, Russell. "Perplexive Perspectives: the Court and Contestation in the Jacobean Masque." *Seventeenth Century* 18, 1 (Spring 2003): 25–43.

Wickham, Glynne. "Masque and Anti-masque in *The Tempest.*" *Essays and Studies* 28 (1975): 1–14.

Wynne-Davies, Marion. "The Queen's Masque: Renaissance Women and the Seventeenth-Century Court Masque." *Gloriana's Face: Women, Public and Private, in the English Renaissance*, ed. S. P. Cerasano and Marion Wynne-Davies, 79–104. Detroit: Wayne State University Press, 1992.

Yamada, Yumiko. "*The Masque of Queens*: Between Sight and Sound." *Hot Questrists after the English Renaissance: Essays on Shakespeare and His Contemporaries*, ed. Yasunari Takahashi, 255–67. New York: AMS, 2000.

<http://www.oxforddnb.com/>
<http://www.luminarium.org/lumina.htm>

14

Early Modern Women Dramatists

Karen Raber

Chronology

c.1553	Jane (or Joanna) Lumley writes translation of Euripides's play, *The Tragedy of Iphigenia*
1592	Publication of Mary Sidney's translation of Robert Garnier's *Tragedy of Antonie*
1603	Probable dates of composition of Elizabeth Cary's *The Tragedy of Mariam, Fair Queen of Jewry*
1613	Cary's *Tragedy of Mariam* entered into Stationers' Register
c.1621	Mary Wroth composes *Love's Victory*
1645	Lady Jane Cavendish and Lady Elizabeth Brackley collaborate on *The Concealed Fancies* and *A Pastorall*
1662	Margaret Cavendish, *Plays Written by the thrice Noble, Illustrious and Excellent Princess, the Lady Marchioness of Newcastle*
1668	Margaret Cavendish, *Plays Never Before Printed*
1663	Katherine Philips's *Pompey* is staged in Dublin and London, the first play by a woman to be performed during the Restoration.

Rest in peace, Judith Shakespeare: the real sisters of William and his peers are ready to take the stage. Nearly a century after Virginia Woolf invented her fictional doomed woman poet in her now much-anthologized essay, "A Room of One's Own," its suicidal protagonist may finally be ready for burial. Woolf's character, originally intended to draw attention to the absence of women from the canon, became in the latter part of the last century more of a bugbear for feminist scholars and critics working on women's plays in the period, and has unfortunately gone a long way toward convincing a couple of generations of undergraduates that there simply weren't *any* women poets or dramatists in Shakespeare's day. Initially embraced by feminist critics, reproduced in all kinds of collections, quoted obsessively in nearly every general essay on women dramatists (obviously including this one), and so famous that its title has become common parlance even among those who have never read the essay itself, Woolf's piece concludes that poor Judith, had she existed, would have been forced into an illegitimate pregnancy, gone mad, and drowned herself.[1] However, as Margaret Ezell has pointed out, Woolf's fantasy is precisely that—a fantasy, and one coloured by Woolf's own bias toward valuing a professional career and her romantic ideal of poetic creativity.[2] While it is true, as Ros Ballaster asserts, that no women wrote for the commercial theatre in the renaissance, it is *not* true that women did not write, and it is equally *not* true that they were unable to write drama.[3] Fortunately, as a consequence of decades of recuperation of texts and sustained assaults on critical assumptions and biases about early modern drama, women dramatists in the period are now impossible to ignore in nearly any type of undergraduate survey course, and figure prominently in specialized courses at all levels—there are numerous editions of early modern women's writing, editions of women writers' plays, and most survey anthologies like the Norton and Longman British Literature volumes include works by Elizabeth Cary and Margaret Cavendish at a minimum.

Yet problems with fully integrating the work of women dramatists into the curriculum remain: how does their work relate to the more familiar theatrical drama by Shakespeare, Marlowe, Jonson, and others? Is it more beneficial to students to emphasize how unusual such writing by women was, or should students be taught to read women's plays as part of a general, mainly theatrical tradition, thus possibly overlooking the significance of their coterie origins? Should a "female tradition" of dramatic composition be constructed, or should individual works by women be read in direct dialogue with plays by their male peers? How do we negotiate how women's sometimes very poetic and formally conservative drama is received by twenty-first century students who live in an increasingly visual and formally transgressive culture? In this essay I will briefly rehearse the history of critical treatment of early modern women's plays, summarizing the most recent and successful methods for understanding such works. I will conclude by suggesting a series of strategies for teaching the work of women writers, strategies that I hope will usefully "stage" the answers to the questions I have posed above.

Critical overview

Long before the Restoration opened the world of the commercial theatre both to female actresses and female theatrical dramatists, writers like Jane (or Joanna) Lumley, Mary Sidney, Elizabeth Cary, Mary Wroth, Jane Cavendish, and Elizabeth Brackley were contributing to a body of private dramatic works now usually called "closet drama." Even after the theatres were opened to female dramatic authors like Aphra Behn, Margaret Cavendish, Katherine Philips, and Anne Finch continued to experiment with the form. Like Shakespeare, they translated plots and conventions from classical and Contintental sources; like Kyd and Marlowe, they invented mad men and

bad women; like Jonson they generated witty dialogue and comical characters—
in other words, they explored the full range of possibilities drama offers the
poet. Some of their works were clearly influenced by Shakespeare's, and in
turn they may have influenced the more publicly accessible theatrical drama
of their male peers.[4] The one thing they did not do is offer their plays
directly to the theatre-going public by staging them in the large amphitheatres, or even in smaller and more restricted venues; such commercial transmission of women's writing would have incurred blame for its presumption,
and for the sexual connotations attached to any form of public transaction
by women. Yet they shared this limitation with many class-conscious male
writers as well, a fact that should remind us that even for Shakespeare and
other male playwrights, writing for the stage and writing drama were not
entirely synonymous.[5]

Critical work on women's plays in the period, however, languished for
nearly four centuries in part because of these genre constraints. For T. S. Eliot
and other early critics interested in sixteenth-century imitations of Senecan-
style drama, the "neo-Senecans" like Sidney (and Cary, although Eliot does
not specifically count her among the Sidney circle) could not transcend the
constipated nature of the form; these "shy recluses" wrote "travest[ies]" of
Senecan reserve and decorum and would have benefited from a good dose of
real blood and terror.[6] Cavendish, already branded "mad Madge" in her own
time by Dorothy Osborne, was roundly dismissed by Virginia Woolf as "a
vision of loneliness and riot," a "weed" in the garden of literature.[7] Most
plays by women, though, were simply lost to the oblivion of canonical marginality and (presumed) literary-historical irrelevance.[8] By the 1960s and
1970s when feminism opened debate on women's representation in all walks
of life, significant recuperative scholarship was necessary just to make the
names and accomplishments of early women writers available again. Nancy
Cotton Pearse in 1977 reintroduced Elizabeth Cary, and the 1980s saw an
avalanche of similar acts of restorative criticism by Catherine Belsey, Elaine
Beilin, Margaret Ferguson, Betty Travitsky, and others.[9]

These first steps usually focused on one or more of several issues in
women's plays: the establishment of female subjectivity, resistance to social
and political constructions of femininity and female roles, the domestic/
political divide, and revisions of the canon. The conditions in which women
began to write drama necessarily required a great deal of critical attention:
renaissance ideologies of order insisted that women were weak, fickle, irra-
tional beings whose proper place was in submission to male authority and
contained within the domestic sphere. At the same time, women's access to
the humanist education that made writing in "serious" genres possible (genres
like dramatic tragedy or lyric poetry as opposed to forms of writing that were
not indebted to strict traditions of form) was limited—while some few elite
women obtained a level of learning comparable to their male peers' through
access to tutors and family libraries, many women, even aristocratic women,

did not. Criticism in the 1980s and 1990s addressed both the fundamental conditions that disenfranchised women—like the paradigm of masculine subjectivity that excluded women by definition—and the specific strategies women writers used to negotiate their entry into print. Translation, the choice of decorous Senecan style, an emphasis on stoicism for female heroines, invocation of familial connections or circumstances to cloak personal ambition all mitigated the consequences of writing.[10] Critics influenced by New Historicism or with an interest in material history and culture broadened their purview to include the location of play-texts in the widest possible cultural contexts, examining the relationship between plays, institutions, and cultural developments. They examined ideologies of marriage, love, and motherhood and drew connections between the plays and the English country house, theatrical and non-theatrical spectatorship, patronage systems and coterie circulation, religious and political changes, civil war, and classical icons like the Amazon.[11] Most such criticism initially focused on Sidney, Cary, and Cavendish, whose works were increasingly prominent in print and pedagogy; but other women dramatists have garnered critical attention if sometimes only sporadically and with difficulty.

A number of interesting, and often contestatory, critical trends have emerged from the mid-1990s through the present. One involves the problematic relationship of women dramatists' work to the commercial theatre. Alison Findlay, Gweno Williams, and Stephanie Hodgson-Wright along with other participants in the Women and Dramatic Production project in England have attempted to correct what is, in their view, the false assumption that the reason early modern women's plays lack a dramatic history is because they are unperformable. Their goal is rescuing closet and coterie drama by women from an ongoing and inherent critical preference for staged plays: "Their voices ventriloquised, their bodies usurped and their potential as dramatists denied, Early Modern women need to be specifically recovered in the field of drama" insists Williams. Since the whole concept of "closet drama" is retroactively imposed (none of these authors "chose" such a genre because it did not exist, being most probably invented in the late eighteenth or early nineteenth century to describe a quite different set of plays by Romantic poets, and only attached retrospectively to these earlier works[12]) Williams, Findlay, and Hodgson-Wright believe that creating a performance history of women's plays will redress the gender imbalances of both the theatrical drama itself and its critical tradition. They have collaborated with actors and directors to actually produce several plays in a variety of venues: Lumley's *Iphigenia at Aulis* and Cavendish's *Convent of Pleasure* were staged in university theatres, while *The Tragedy of Mariam* was given a studio premiere, and *The Concealed Fancies* debuted in an actual country house, Bretton Hall. These productions and the critical work of all three critics have contributed significantly to revitalizing our sense of the dramatic skills of their authors. In performance, the comical social portrait of excluded men trying to scale the walls to invade a women's retreat like the *Convent of Pleasure*, the potential ludicrousness of the "action" described by Cary's stage direction that Constabarus and Silleus duel with swords (in stark and uncomfortable contrast to the devastating tragedy the women's parts convey) or the sense of temporary pastoral peace and social order within a home besieged by Parliamentary forces all emerge in ways that attest to the dramatists' ability to manipulate stage conventions.[13]

But as many have pointed out, the Women and Dramatic Production project may inadvertently reimpose the same valorization of stage and theatre that has caused the marginalizing and under-appreciation of early modern women playwrights in the past. Another, quite different and extremely provocative approach comes from Marta Straznicky's work on drama and reading. Using such concrete but often-overlooked aspects of early women's plays as their physical layout on the page, or the exact nature of the rooms in which they might have been read, Straznicky investigates the relationship between the private act of consuming drama-for-reading and the printed and public nature of the play-text itself. Arguing that attempts to "position closet drama within political and even theatrical culture, feminist scholarship has not so much redrawn as collapsed the boundaries between public and private," Straznicky instead describes closet drama "as part of a larger cultural matrix in which closed spaces, select interpretive communities and political dissent are aligned."[14] Further, "marking, and also marketing a text for private reading is therefore a way of specifying rather than renouncing its position within the public sphere."[15] Straznicky sees, as I do in my own work on the same groups of women playwrights, closet drama's differences from theatrical drama as too important to erase or ignore.[16]

Finally, the location of early modern women dramatists in dialogue with their male peers has come to mark more and more criticism in recent years. A quick overview of articles published in the last several years includes several points of comparison such as *The Tragedy of Mariam* with *Othello*, as well as discussions involving *Mariam* and Middleton, *Mariam* and Webster, and *Mariam* and Milton.[17] Cavendish's works find similar treatment in articles comparing her *Unnatural Tragedy* to Ford's *'Tis Pity She's a Whore*, or to Shakespeare's *Measure for Measure*.[18] My own book-length study of closet drama puts the works of Sidney, Kyd, and Daniel into dialogue with one another, Cavendish with Thomas Kyd, and her own husband, and Katherine Philips with Milton. It is my sense that this represents an advance on the anxieties about creating "a room of their own" for women writers expressed in essays like Nancy Gutierrez's 1996 contribution to the *Shakespeare Quarterly* issue on "Teaching Judith Shakespeare."[19] Gutierrez worries that teaching women writers "is a pedagogical activity that inevitably puts Judith into competition with William" with the result that "Judith" remains always "other," always lesser since "we cannot change the extent to which they [women writers] were marginalized in the early modern period."[20] Megan

Matchinske warns that "The easy fix of the comparative model encourages academic tokenism at every level of Shakespearean criticism. At the same time, such framing generally leaves Shakespeare all the laurels."[21] Both critics worry about students simply *not liking* women writers as much as Shakespeare—not finding them as complex, as rewarding, as "universal" in their appeal. Clearly, these are the concerns of feminist scholars breaking new ground: as Gutierrez's accounts of her students' responses to Cary indicate, in 1995 or 1996 many students flat out resisted the idea of reading women writers at all, others found ways to trivialize or reject, and many persistently returned to privileging the issues, approaches, and biases of Shakespeare's plays, thwarting Gutierrez's desire to "decenter" Shakespeare.[22] The bevy of comparative articles in the first years of the twenty-first century is reassuring in that they suggest that invidiousness of comparison has been diminished by genuine progress, if not in fully decentring Shakespeare then at least in allowing the centre to be shared. Recent generations of undergraduates take the works of early women writers in their stride—they seem to have little trouble accepting a slightly larger and more diverse canon.

Critical work on renaissance women playwrights continues to grapple with a host of complex problems that have direct consequences for teaching the plays. The domestic/political, private/public boundaries that define the plays are by no means fully charted yet. And authorial gender makes a difference—it's just not always easy to resolve what that difference is. For instance, reading women's drama against the domestic conditions of women's lives is, to some extent, inevitable: women were more likely to derive their sense of the world through the ideologically prescribed domain with which they were primarily identified; nor would we benefit from discounting the domestic, since doing so would reproduce both an antifeminist scholarly bias and an inaccurate division of worlds—women's writing was lost, in part, because male critics did not recognize or value work that did not have a public or political dimension, yet in the early modern world what was (especially for elites) "domestic" and what was "political" as often intersected or overlapped as not. Yet we do not similarly foreground the personal or biographical aspects of male playwrights' work: most critics know, but are less interested in the idea that Hamlet may be based in Shakespeare's personal experience of losing his son, Hamnet, and very few current debates on Ford, Middleton, Webster, Jonson, or other dramatists insist on tying characters and plots narrowly to actual figures and events in these authors' lives. Diane Purkiss points out:

If Erasmus [whose translation of Euripides influenced Jane Lumley] were a woman, we would be hailing his choice of Euripides's texts for translation as signs of his own life story and experience in the text. Since he is not one, we need an alternative explanation, and we might want to ask if it applies to Lumley too. On the other hand, if *Mariam* were by a man, we would see Mariam's death as the punishment of her rebelliousness and interpret the play in the light of pleasure in the disfigurement of the outspoken woman; concomitantly, we ought to canvass the possibility that Cary was just as caught up in these representations (thought perhaps differently caught up in them) as Webster or Shakespeare.[23]

Mary Wroth offers an especially difficult example of the familial-domestic bind: her pastoral drama, *Love's Victory*, is indeed a kind of *roman à clef*, with characters clearly named for her relatives, and Wroth's work generally focuses repeatedly on problems of love and identity, undoubtedly connected to her own marginalization from court and public life during her long affair with her cousin, William Pembroke.[24] It would be foolish and inaccurate to discount these links; yet we do not read comparable tragicomedies and pastorals that clearly influenced *Love's Victory* with the same tunnel vision Wroth's play seems to invite. From Petrarch to Tasso to John Fletcher, male shapers of pastoral form are assumed to be reaching for broader thematic and structural reference. If we do not accomplish the same kind of reading for Wroth, what are the consequences? Do we entrap her in a domestic world that she herself found restrictive and frustrating? Do we remove her from serious contention with her male contemporaries, many of whom she may have intended to debate? In her case, as in that of most of the closet plays women wrote, we must also ask what the relationship is between familial or coterie readership, manuscript circulation, and print culture or "public" discourse? Wroth did, after all, attempt to publish her *Urania*, while her aunt Mary Sidney published and republished her *Tragedy of Antonie*; whether Cary intended it or not, her play too was entered in the Stationers' Register in 1613, and Margaret Cavendish positively pursued a public readership, suggesting that we must either revise our sense of the "domestic" limitations that govern women writers or take Straznicky's cue in redefining "public" vs. "private" where coterie vs. print circulation are concerned.

Where these plays' content is concerned, there is again a temptation (particularly among students, but critics are not immune) to somewhat simplistically align marital and familial themes with authorial gender. Lumley, Sidney, and Cary write eloquent tragedies about marriage and family. But if, for example, Cary's *Mariam* becomes a play mainly about marriage, but *Othello* gets to be about an epistemological crisis that is expressed through the effects of jealousy—that is, in the one case, the personal trumps much else, while in the latter the personal is a vehicle for "larger" themes— then we are imposing choices on women playwrights that are subtly antifeminist, not to mention potentially wholly inaccurate.[25] Clearly, women writers' gender gives them a different perspective on these subjects and a different relationship to the experiences of their female protagonists. But it would be a mistake to build too far on that difference—or to assign women writers *too* great an interest in the personal vs. the political, the domestic vs. the public, the "feminist" vs. the "universalist." Early modern plays by women can—and often should—be seen to interrogate such gender-based alterity. When Cavendish creates a female retreat from marriage and family in her *Convent of Pleasure* she is creating a traditional, almost Shakespearean obstacle to the harmony and survival of the community. As much as critics want to invest the convent with proto-feminist significance, it can (and I think it should) be simultaneously registered as a deliberate appropriation of a theatrical convention by a playwright who admired Shakespeare above all.[26] The marriage that concludes the play would not thus necessarily betray any dearly-held desire to preserve the convent;[27] in fact, we should probably ask ourselves how serious Cavendish is when she denigrates marriage and its woes in her play-within-the-play—she may well be expecting her readership to see this as mistaken, self-deluding withdrawal on a par with Olivia's mourning for her dead brother in *Twelfth Night* or Navarre's "academy" in *Loves Labour's Lost*. Similarly, *Mariam* could arguably have been received by its contemporary readers as a play about the destruction of the rightful monarch's sanity by his over-indulgence in love and desire—that is, Herod is overthrown by his own uxoriousness, destroyed by his own sexual incontinence and jealousy, made mad by his own insurmountable need for his wife's love. While such a reading obviously ignores much of the play's focus on Mariam and her internal tensions, it would nonetheless have been a pretty standard approach for the time: plays from *Othello* to *Anthony and Cleopatra*, from Fulke Greville's two late-Elizabethan closet plays *Mustapha* and *Alaham*, to later works like Middleton's *The Second Maiden's Tragedy* (1611), Rowley's *All's Lost for Lust* (1619) and Massinger's *Duke of Milan* (1623) repeat and adapt the same scenario. Cary's play both affirms and complicates the established pattern of kings and leaders destroyed by their own passions—not to mention radically shifts the audience's sympathies in the process. Yet it can be extremely uncomfortable to both critics and instructors (not to mention students, who will want women writers either to be early strident feminists or cowed, co-opted victims) to even begin to register what we might call women authors' conservative thematics. Describing her own experiments in teaching women's texts, Paula Loscocco observes that her focus on women, gender, and sex had the inevitable consequence of "fixing students' attention on precisely those topics . . . most likely to prohibit thoughtful or complex discussion. The problem was exacerbated by the fact that few of our many female-authored texts . . . responded with the kind of feminist spit and fire that students had glimpsed in . . . their earlier survey courses."[28]

There is a tricky degree of continuity, rather than clear discontinuity between plays by women and plays by their male peers. Isolating those by women, taking the difference of gender *too far* can have the unintended and erroneous effect of making them seem anachronistically disjunct from the dramatic traditions, concerns, subject positions, and approaches of their time. I do not advocate establishing a separate "room" for Judith Shakespeare, as Gutierrez does, or treating women writers' plays as if they constitute a separate tradition. There is no evidence for a "female tradition" in the early modern drama, and, *pace* Hilda Smith, no reason to see any of these writers as proto-feminists.[29] Extracting them from their intercourse with the works of male authors does disservice to both.

Finally, when considering the very notion of a "woman dramatist" it is important to ask what "norms" of authorship we are assuming. Jane Cavendish and Elizabeth Brackley, like their step-mother Margaret Cavendish, collaborated in writing their works—the sisters with each other, their step-mother with her husband. The lone poet struggling in a cold garret to produce great works of genius is not more accurate when transposed to the creativity of women writers than when it is applied to the early modern male theatrical writer. At the same time there are many kinds of "acts" that might make one a "woman dramatist" if not a traditionally-defined author. Does staging oneself at court count, as in the case of Elizabeth I? Does commissioning, performing in, and even dictating the content of masques allow one to be called a "woman dramatist"? If so, Anna of Denmark was one of the Jacobean court's more prolific "authors," while Queen Henrietta Maria, who actually wrote a lost masque for herself and her ladies and who performed frequently in plays at court, should be included in a review of early modern women dramatists.[30] During the civil war and Interregnum, women sectarians preached in the streets, prophesied publicly, even staged what might now be called "performance art" events—Anna Trapnel, for example, prophesied from her bed at a tavern, and Eleanor Davies desecrated Lichfield Cathedral by sitting in the Bishop's throne and pouring tar over the altar. Combining physical gestures, speech acts, and a sense of space, location, and timing, women like these certainly showed theatrical skill when acting in the drama of civil and religious conflict. Then as now, drama was a varied continuum.

Pedagogic strategies

The most commonly anthologized play by an early modern female dramatic author is Cary's *Tragedy of Mariam*, which exists in several editions[31] and is now excerpted in the Norton Anthology; in 2002, a two-play Longman Cultural Edition volume pairing *Othello* and the *Tragedy of Mariam*, edited by Clare Carroll and David Damrosch, appeared in print, and the play is also grouped with Lumley's *Iphigenia* and Sidney's *Tragedy of Antonie* in a 1999 edition from Penguin edited by Diane Purkiss. Equally available is Margaret Cavendish's *Convent of Pleasure*, in Broadview Press's *Paper Bodies: a Margaret Cavendish Reader* and in the paperback edition of Anne Shaver's 1999 *Convent of Pleasure and other Plays* (Johns Hopkins University Press), as well as appearing in *Renaissance Drama by Women*, the useful Routledge collection by Marion Wynne-Davies and S. P. Cerasano. Other dramatic writings by women, especially the vast quantity written by Cavendish, are still only available in their original form, but the wide access provided by university libraries to *Early English Books Online* makes them vastly easier for students to find and download, even if the lack of modernization makes them harder for students to read. Edited volumes of criticism on drama by women are too numerous to list here, but special mention is merited by Longman's *Women and Dramatic Production 1550–1700* (2000) edited by Alison Findlay, and *Readings in Renaissance Women's Drama: Criticism, History, and Performance 1594–1998*, the companion to Cerasano and Wynne-Davies's collection of primary texts. Both are suitable as supplemental texts for undergraduate or graduate courses.

Where once students might have griped about reading "lesser" works by women writers, my current teaching experience leads me to believe that students are either entirely happy with, or at least unconcerned over, efforts to revise the canon. They take women writers in their stride. Indeed, many of my sophomore survey students end up claiming to prefer Cary's *Tragedy of Mariam* to Shakespeare's works, finding the former to have greater clarity, and for many female students the appeal of presenting a female viewpoint. I suspect they also simply find Cary's play *easier*—shorter, less linguistically challenging. When asked to address the "problem" of comparing women playwrights to Shakespeare, my upper-division Renaissance Women Writers class again appear to have very different reactions than they might have had a decade ago: students are quite clear that they see the connections between plays, but do not feel compelled to elevate Shakespeare. They recognize that women writers were working in an entirely different medium in most cases. If students in Mississippi are able to engage in these ways, then I am confident that students elsewhere can do so as well.

We now have other hang-ups: for most of us our current pedagogical problems lie in our attempts to reproduce our own methodologies as critics in the classroom. In particular, for historically-oriented scholars, there is the problem of generating "thick description" quickly and responsibly with students who do not have a deep or comprehensive historical background. As I've already suggested, another problem stems from our (and our students') reluctance to put pressure on the pieties of past criticism and scholarship. And finally, women writers' works also pose the problem of how we make elite, textually dense, allusive plays comprehensible to a generation drenched in spectacle, a readership fond of blogs, an audience that prefers sound-bites to narratives.

Of course, the easiest and most obvious way to teach drama by women writers is still to set up direct comparisons of plays or to connect male-authored and female-authored plays by topical groupings. Far more complex and apparently appealing, however, is the creation of what Matchinske calls a "cultural thematics" that organizes plays by men and women around historical or literary-historical issues. Matchinske gives several examples, including the following for a unit on "tyranny and rebellion," readings for which might include

> Macbeth and Mariam . . . George Buchanan's *History of Scotland* (1582) and James VI's *Basilikon Doron* can offer useful and oppositional interpretations of tyranny in government and of the right to revel; William Gouge's *Of Domesticall Duties* (1622) and the anonymous *Swetnam, the Woman-hater* (1620) can provide insight into parental tyranny. Explorations focusion on the domestic tyrant might include Cary's *The History of the Life, Reign and Death of Edward II* (1627) and John Webster's *The Duchess of Malfi* (1623) as well as later works by Mary Astell, Aphra Behn, Anne Finch, John Milton, and Katharine Philips.[32]

A quite different grouping might be created around the problem of female rule. Mary Sidney's *Tragedy of Antonie* and Shakespeare's *Antony and Cleopatra*, for instance, while strikingly different in their portrait of the Egyptian Queen, make a fascinating contrast, while the *Tragedy of Mariam* and Sidney's *Antonie* also share a great deal thematically with Marlowe's *Dido, Queen of Carthage*—for example, in their examination of how queens must decide between familial or marital roles and the protection of their people. In contrast, Fletcher's *Queen of Corinth* (1618) offers a relatively successful queen whose gender serves her country when she is able to fashion an advantageous marital alliance, rather than inhibiting her ability to rule through intrusions of the domestic and familial into her political decision-making. Non-dramatic documents like Knox's *First blast of the trumpet against this monstrous regiment of women* (1558) and Aylmer's *An harborowe for faithful and true subjects* (1559) would illuminate the position of queens-regnant like Elizabeth I, while Jonson's *Masque of Queens* (1609), commissioned by Anna of Denmark, could qualify the experience of queens-consort, as would diatribes against and defences of Henrietta Maria.[33] Sexuality and homoeroticism, the gendering of war and heroism, self-fashioning, marriage and property, crime and punishment—the possibilities are numerous for thematic organizations that can incorporate an array of dramatic and non-dramatic, literary and non-literary, high and low sources. "Paramount," notes Matchinske, "to a cultural thematics approach is careful attention to historical contexts and generic boundaries, to geographic and social variables within topics, as well as a willingness to forego such correspondences when the need arises."[34] The attractions of this method lie in its flexibility and its approximation of many of our actual scholarly practices; its detractions may come from its extraordinary level of difficulty and its lack of compatibility with the postmodern cultural skills of twenty-first century students.

Straznicky's work and that of the Women and Drama Project suggest the rather different value of focusing directly on genre, even to its material extremes. How do we represent the generic conventions that guide early modern women writers? How do we make sense for our students of things like coterie circulation, readerly drama and unperformed spectacle, the appeal of closet drama to elite readers and authors, and the vexed relationship between closet and theatre? Creative exercises that emphasize coterie circulation and collaborative composition are easy to invent; comparisons between experiencing a play performed and reading one are easy to make. But to ground these historically requires that students not only have a sense of anti-theatricalism in early modern popular culture, but that they follow the more nuanced atheatricalism of the educated elites. Having students evolve scripts out of women writers' play-texts can highlight the advantages (and disadvantages) of performance. Showing the videotape *Women Dramatists 1550–1670: Plays in Performance* from Lancaster University Television (1999) and other video/DVD productions created by Williams, Findlay, and Hodgson-Wright over the years (most, including Williams's *Margaret Cavendish: Plays in Performance* [2004], available online) will give students a sense of what the reality might have looked like, but it is equally important to ask questions about what limitations performance imposes—imaginative limits, qualitative limits. We are so used to assuming that, as Straznicky notes, publication and performance somehow liberate the caged text,[35] but early modern publication and performance also involved unexpected shackles: students need to become informed about early print culture, the lack of intellectual copyright, the primacy of printers. They equally need to understand the class associations of theater's mixed audiences, the financial and other pressures that dominated theatrical production, the vagaries of taste that bedevilled commercial playwrights. In contrast, Straznicky points out that the "association of the closet with privacy and the individual subject is well documented in the history of interior decoration and domestic architecture,"[36] and so students might profitably be introduced to these discourses as well.

I would also appeal for the expansion of the present "canon" of works by women dramatists. Particularly frustrating are the eternal reproduction of Cary's *Tragedy of Mariam* as the choice of the day for all and sundry, and the limited selection of Cavendish's works in usable form.[37] Cary's play seduces with clarity—as I've said, students love its apparent readability. The unfortunate results might be marked by glancing at how it presently appears in the Norton Anthology: it is redacted to its main storyline only, with all subplots erased, and Herod's lengthy rantings after Mariam's execution cut to a minimum. Headnotes attempt to restore a sense of the play's political focus, which is gone from the play itself. All of this leads to the presentation of Cary's work as first, less coherent than Shakespeare's, Jonson's, Marlowe's, or Webster's, all of whose sample plays are conveyed intact; and second, trapped in that domestic/personal dichotomizing of female-authored texts I've already noted. Moreover, Cary's play was not the popular work in its time that, say, Mary Sidney's was. Like *Mucedorus*, performances of which probably outsold every Shakespeare play ever staged, Sidney's work is doomed to puzzle twenty-first century readers seeking reasons for that early popularity. Cavendish's *Convent of Pleasure*, at present the only widely available of her many, many plays, also seduces with clarity, in this case representing her work as more traditional in form, less innovative and less difficult that the broader collection of her works would indicate. *The Convent of Pleasure* looks and feels like "a real play" in the mode of Shakespeare and his ilk; but Cavendish's plays in general are long, often running to two parts and as many as twenty or more scenes; they are much less "play-like" readerly experiences. And many of the topics Cavendish returned to repeatedly—female oratory, warrior women, social mobility (and its failures) through marriage— are missing from *The Convent of Pleasure*. A good scholarly edition of Cavendish's entire collected dramatic production is past due. And one still rarely encounters the closet plays of Katherine Philips or Anne Finch in critical treatments, let alone classroom texts, which guarantees that Aphra Behn will hold the stage alone for the Restoration, despite, again, the popularity among the reading elite of both her non-commercial competitors.[38] Meanwhile, I would strongly advise using Brown University's *Women Writers Online* resources and *Early English Books Online*, if they are accessible through the university library system, to give students a broader selection of women's plays than those currently privileged by university and scholarly presses.

The time for mourning the absence of women from the canon of dramatic texts may be over, but reshaping the canon has not concluded the process of adapting women writers' work to the classroom—quite the opposite. Those of us who teach these texts regularly find ourselves constantly re-evaluating our own reading and spectating practices, our own uses of theory, or own assumptions about our students' biases and abilities. In fact, I would insist that this is precisely the advantage that teaching early modern women dramatists' works gives any literary scholar of the period: incorporating Elizabeth, Mary, Margaret, Jane, and others by necessity transforms the way that we must approach William—not to mention John, Christopher, Ben, and the rest of the male figures discussed in this volume—and vice versa.

Notes

1. Virginia Woolf, *A Room of One's Own* (New York: Harcourt, Brace, Jovanovich 1929, reprint 1981), pp. 46–8.
2. Margaret Ezell, *Writing Women's Literary History* (Baltimore: Johns Hopkins University Press, 1993), pp. 39–65.
3. "The First Female Dramatists," in *Women and Literature in Britain 1500–1700*, ed. Helen Wilcox, pp. 267–90 (Cambridge: Cambridge University Press 1996).
4. For instance, Cary's *Tragedy of Mariam* was published in 1613, but probably written some time in the early years of the century (perhaps 1603–1604, shortly after her

marriage to Henry Cary); it may have circulated in coterie, and may well have been known to playwrights with court affiliations; Shakespeare's *Othello* was first performed at James I's court in 1604, so some cross-fertilization seems likely. Jane Cavendish and Elizabeth Brackley were most certainly familiar with Ben Jonson's plays since their father, William Cavendish, was an important patron of Jonson's and Margaret Cavendish clearly admired Shakespeare's plays, while also benefiting from her husband's patronage of Shirley and Jonson.

5. Publication, writes Wendy Wall, "figured in Renaissance mythography as a transgressive power" for men of status, as much as for women; but "in a world in which privilege was attached to coterie circulation and published words were associated with promiscuity, the female writer could become a 'fallen' woman in double sense: branded as a harlot or a member of the non-elite," *The Imprint of Gender: Authorship and Publication in the English Renaissance* (Ithaca: Cornell University Press, 1993), pp. 14, 281.

6. *Essays on Elizabethan Drama* (New York: Harcourt, Brace and World, 1932, repr. 1960), pp. 39–43.

7. Woolf, *Room*, pp. 61–2.

8. With the exception of Myra Reynolds's 1920 book, *The Learned Lady in England 1650–1700* (Boston: Houghton-Mifflin) which does offer some early positive criticism on women's writing.

9. Nancy Cotton Pearse, "Elizabeth Cary, Renaissance Playwright," *TSLL* 18 (1977): 601–8; Elaine Beilin, *Redeeming Eve: Women Writers of the English Renaissance* (Princeton, NJ: Princeton University Press, 1987); Catherine Belsey, *The Subject of Tragedy: Identity and Difference in Renaissance Drama* (New York: Methuen, 1985); Betty Travitsky, *The Paradise of Women: Writings by Englishwomen of the Renaissance* (Westport, CT: Greenwood, 1981); Margaret Ferguson, "A Room Not Their Own: Renaissance Women as Readers and Writers," in *The Comparative Perspective on Literature: Approaches to Theory and Practice*, ed. Clayton Kolb and Susan Noakes, pp. 93–116 (New York: Cornell University Press, 1988).

10. Examples include: Margaret J. Ezell, " 'To Be Your Daughter in your Pen': the Social Functions of Literature in the Writing of Lady Elizabeth Brackley and Lady Jane Cavendish," *Huntington Library Quarterly* 51 (1988): 63–71; Mary Ellen Lamb, *Gender and Authorship in the Sidney Circle* (Madison: University of Wisconsin Press, 1990); Danielle Clarke, "The Politics of Translation and Gender in the Countess of Pembroke's *Antonie*," *Translation and Literature* 6, 2 (1997): 163–4; Tina Krontiris, *Oppositional Voices: Women as Writers and Translators of Literature in the English Renaissance* (New York: Routledge, 1992); Marta Straznicky, "Profane Stoical Paradoxes: the *Tragedie of Mariam* and Sidneian Closet Drama," *ELR* 24, 1 (1994): 104–34.

11. Some very few examples are: Laurie J. Shannon, "Cary's Critique of the Founding Discourses," *ELR* 22 (1994): 135–53; Sandra K. Fisher, "Elizabeth Cary and Tyranny, Domestic and Religious" in *Silent But for the Word: Tudor Women as Patrons, Translators and Writers of Religious Works*, ed. Margaret Hannay, pp. 225–37 (Ohio: Kent State University Press 1985); Sophie Tomlinson, "My Brain the Stage: Margaret Cavendish and the Fantasy of Female Performance," in *Women, Texts and Histories, 1575–1760*, ed. Claire Brant and Diane Purkiss, pp. 134–63 (New York: Routledge, 1992); Karen Raber, "Warrior Women in the Plays of Cavendish and Killigrew," *SEL* 40, 3 (Summer 2000): 413–33; Julie Crawford, "Convents and Pleasures: Margaret Cavendish and the Drama of Property," *Renaissance Drama* 32 (2003): 177–223; Meredith Skura, "The Reproduction of Mothering in *Mariam*,

Queen of Jewry: a Defense of 'Biographical' Criticism," *Tulsa Studies in Women's Literature* 16, 1 (1997): 27–56.

12. While the term "closet" is in frequent use in the sixteenth and seventeenth centuries, "closet drama" emerges only at the end of the eighteenth century; for more on the term's genesis, see Catherine Burroughs, *Closet Stages: Joanna Baillie and the Theater Theory of British Romantic Writers* (Philadelphia: University of Pennsylvania Press, 1997), pp. 8–12.

13. See Gweno Williams, "Why May Not a Lady Write a Good Play?" in *Readings in Renaissance Women's Drama*, pp. 95–112; Alison Findlay, "'She gave you the civility of the house': Household performance in *The Concealed Fancies*," also in *Readings in Renaissance Women's Drama*, pp. 259–71; and Alison Finday, Gweno Williams, and Stephanie Hodgson-Wright, "'The Play is Ready to be Acted': Women and Dramatic Production, 1570–1670," *Women's Writing*, 6, 1 (1999): 129–48.

14. Marta Straznicky, *Privacy, Playreading and Women's Closet Drama, 1550–1700* (Cambridge: Cambridge University Press, 1004), p. 4.

15. Straznicky, *Privacy*, pp. 52–3.

16. See Raber, *Dramatic Difference: Gender, Class and Genre in the Early Modern Closet Drama* (Newark: University of Delaware Press, 2001).

17. Jennifer Heller, "Space, Violence and Bodies in Middleton and Cary," *SEL* 45, 2 (Spring 2005): 425–41; Elizabeth Bruber, "Insurgent Flesh: Epistemology and Violence in *Othello* and *Mariam*," *Women's Studies* 32, 4 (2003): 393–410; Reina Green, "'Ears Prejudicate' in *Mariam* and *The Duchess of Malfi*," *SEL* 43, 2 (Spring 2003): 459–74; Christina Luckyj, "Historicizing Gender: Mapping Cultural Space in Webster's *The Duchess of Malfi* and Cary's *The Tragedy of Mariam*," in *Approaches to Teaching English Renaissance Drama*, ed. Karen Bamford and Alexander Leggatt, pp. 134–41 (New York: Modern Language Association Press, 2002); Shari Zimmerman, "Disaffection, Dissimulation, and the Uncertain Ground of Silent Dismission: Juxtaposing John Milton and Elizabeth Cary," *ELH* 66, 3 (Fall 1999): 553–89.

18. Lisa Hopkins, "Crime and Context in *The Unnatural Tragedy*," *EMLS* Special Issue 14 (May 2004) <http://www.shu.ac.uk/emls/si-14/hopkunna.html>; Karen Raber, "*The Unnatural Tragedy* and Familial Absolutisms," in *Cavendish and Shakespeare: Interconnections*, ed. James Fitzmaurice and Katherine Romack (Ashgate 2006).

19. Nancy Gutierrez, "Why William and Judith Both Need Their Own Rooms," *Shakespeare Quarterly* 47, 4 (Winter 1996): 424–32.

20. Gutierrez, "Why William and Judith," pp. 431, 427.

21. Megan Matchinske, "Credible Consorts: What Happens When Shakespeare's Sisters Enter the Syllabus?" *Shakespeare Quarterly* 47, 4 (Winter 1996): 433–50; p. 440.

22. Gutierrez, "Why William and Judith," p. 425.

23. "Blood, Sacrifice, Marriage: Why Iphigenia and Mariam Have to Die," *Women's Writing* 6, 1 (1999): 27–45.

24. Marion Wynne-Davies comprehensively accounts for these familial references in "'Here is a sport will well fefit this time and place': allusion and delusion in Mary Wroth's *Love's Victory*," *Women's Writing* 6, 1 (1999): 46–61.

25. Fortunately, there has been a concerted effort to avoid such a pitfall, but what Purkiss calls the "shibboleths" of feminist interpretation do haunt the field (Purkiss 27). The debate focusing upon critical histories of female-authored plays vs. Shakespeare is to blame in part here: Shakespeare scholars have moved away from

universalizing discourses, toward local, material readings; scholars working on women dramatists began with the personal and have moved toward making claims about the embeddedness of these plays in the great debates of their historical moment.

26. About Cavendish's Bardolatry see Katherine Romack, "Margaret Cavendish, Shakespeare Critic" in *A Feminist Companion to Shakespeare*, ed. Dympna Callaghan, pp. 21–41 (Oxford: Blackwell Publishers, 2000).

27. Irene Dash notes her students' complaints and resistance to the "happy ending" that reverses the gender-bending that came before: "The students were indignant . . . They had loved that ideal convent and the refuge from injustice it represented," "Single-Sex Retreats in Two Early Modern Dramas: *Loves Labor's Lost* and *The Convent of Pleasure*," *Shakespeare Quarterly* 47, 4 (Winter 1996): 387–95, quote from p. 393; rarely, of course, does a student complain about Shakespeare's similarly conservative endings.

28. "Theory in the Teaching of Early Modern Women Writers," in *Teaching Tudor and Stuart Women Writers*, ed. Susanne Woods and Margaret P. Hannay, pp. 227–34 (New York: Modern Language Association, 2000), p. 228.

29. Smith's *Reason's Disciples: Seventeenth-Century English Feminists* (Urbana, IL: University of Illinois Press, 1982) certainly should be celebrated as one of the early attempts to recuperate women's writing in the period, but its desire to find authentic feminist debate, and evaluate women writers from the perspective of how liberal their thought on women's roles was, is highly problematic.

30. Happily, they have: see Leeds Barroll, "The Arts at the English Court of Anna of Denmark," in *Readings in Renaissance Women's Drama*, pp. 47–59. That volume also usefully includes essays on women as patrons of, spectators at, and financial investors in the theatre.

31. The gold standard in editions, however, is still Barry Weller and Margaret Ferguson's *Tragedy of Mariam, Fair Queen of Jewry*, which includes a thorough introduction and reproduces Cary's biography by her daughter (Berkeley: University of California Press, 1994).

32. Matchinske, "Credible Consorts," pp. 442–3.

33. A different, but related kind of grouping is found in Elizabeth Patton's "Seven Faces of Cleopatra" in *Teaching Tudor and Stuart Women Writers*, pp. 289–94, which collects images of Cleopatra in works by male and female authors to track changes in the gender and racial components of representation.

34. Matchinske, "Credible Consorts," p. 442.

35. Straznicky, *Privacy*, p. 3.

36. Straznicky, *Privacy*, p. 114.

37. Even in the most recent, and otherwise superbly varied collection *Early Modern English Drama: a Critical Companion*, ed. Garrett Sullivan, Patrick Cheney, and Andrew Hadfield (New York: Oxford University Press, 2006), out of 27 essays only one deals with a woman writer, and that one concerns Cary's play yet again.

38. Scholarship on Philips and Finch tends to privilege their poetry over their dramatic writing. One exception is Straznicky's *Privacy, Playreading*; another is Sophie Tomlinson's "Harking Back to Henrietta: the Sources of Female Greatness in Katherine Philips's Pompey," in *Women Writing 1550–1750*, ed. Jo Wallwork and Paul Salzman, pp. 179–90 (Bundoora, Australia: Meridien, 2001), and Andrew Shifflet's "'How Many Virtues Must I Hate': Katherine Philips and the Politics of Clemency," *Studies in Philology* 94, 1 (Winter 1997): 103–35.

Selective guide to further reading and resources

Cotton, Nancy. *Women Playwrights in England, 1363–1750*. Lewisburg, PA: Bucknell University Press, 1980.

Brown, Pamela Allen, and Parolin, Peter (eds). *Women Players in England, 1500–1660*. Burlington, VT: Ashgate Publishing, 2006.

Hopkins, Lisa. "Judith Shakespeare's Reading: Teaching the Concealed Fancies." *Shakespeare Quarterly* 46, 4 (Winter 1996): 396–406.

Kemp, Theresa D. "The Family is a Little Commonweal: Teaching *Mariam* and *Othello* in a Special Topics Course on Domestic England." *Shakespeare Quarterly* 46, 4 (Winter 1996): 451–60.

Pacheco, Anita (ed.). *A Companion to Early Modern Women's Writing*. Oxford: Blackwell, 2002.

Quilligan, Maureen. "Staging Gender: William Shakespeare and Elizabeth Cary." *Sexuality and Gender in Early Modern Europe: Institutions, Texts, Images*, ed. James Grantham Turner, pp. 208–32. Cambridge: Cambridge University Press, 1993.

Ziegler, Georgianna. "Women Writers Online: an Evaluation and Annotated Bibliography of Web Resources." *EMLS* 6, 3 (January 2000) <http://purl.oclc.org/emls/06-3/ziegbib.htm>.

Index